Public Education

Defending a Cornerstone of American Democracy

EDITED BY

DAVID C. BERLINER
CARL HERMANNS

TEACHERS COLLEGE PRESS

TEACHERS COLLEGE | COLUMBIA UNIVERSITY

Published by Teachers College Press,® 1234 Amsterdam Avenue, New York, NY 10027

Library of Congress Cataloging-in-Publication Data

Names: Berliner, David C., editor. | Hermanns, Carl, editor.
Title: Public education : defending a cornerstone of American democracy / Edited by David C. Berliner, Carl Hermanns.
Description: New York, NY : Teachers College Press, [2021] | Includes bibliographical references and index.
Identifiers: LCCN 2021034661 (print) | LCCN 2021034662 (ebook) | ISBN 9780807766095 (paperback) | ISBN 9780807766101 (hardcover) | ISBN 9780807779941 (epub)
Subjects: LCSH: Public schools—United States. | Education—Political aspects—United States. | Education and state—United States. | Educational change—United States.
Classification: LCC LA217.2 .P835 2021 (print) | LCC LA217.2 (ebook) | DDC 371.010973—dc23
LC record available at https://lccn.loc.gov/2021034661
LC ebook record available at https://lccn.loc.gov/2021034662

ISBN 978-0-8077-6609-5 (paper)
ISBN 978-0-8077-6610-1 (hardcover)
ISBN 978-0-8077-7994-1 (ebook)

Printed on acid-free paper
Manufactured in the United States of America

Contents

Introduction

The belief in the vital importance and central role of public education in the development of our country and the sustenance of our democracy runs deep, starting with colonial concern that the settlers of the New World be able to read the Bible. The support for public education increased during revolutionary times, so that citizens could read, understand, and come to underwrite the amazing Constitution of our new country's fledgling experiment in democratic governance. This focus on the importance of education as foundational to the success of democracy is illustrated in the following quotes from some of our nation's founders:

> I know no safe depository of the ultimate powers of the society, but the people themselves; and if we think them not enlightened enough to exercise their controul with a wholsome discretion, the remedy is, not to take it from them, but to inform their discretion by education. This is the true corrective of abuses of constitutional power.
>
> —Thomas Jefferson, 1820, *Letter to William Charles Jarvis*

> The advancement and diffusion of Knowledge. . . is the only guardian of true liberty.
>
> —James Madison, 1825, *Letter to George Thompson*

> If Virtue and Knowledge are diffused among the People, they will never be enslavd. This will be their great Security.
>
> —Samuel Adams, 1779, *Letter to James Warren*

> Systems of Education should be adopted and pursued which may not only diffuse a knowledge of the sciences, but may implant in the minds of the American youth the principles of virtue and of liberty; and inspire them with just and liberal ideas of government and with an inviolable attachment to their own country.
>
> —Noah Webster, 1787, "On the Education of Youth in America"

Horace Mann, the founder and champion of the universal public education movement in the United States, was born into these times (1796) and grew up influenced by the zeitgeist reflecting the excitement and progressiveness of those times. Although not without critics, then and now, in the mid-19th century Mann not only argued for free, inclusive public education, he helped to start and obtain funding for such schools. And he did so at a time when influential legislators and industrialists saw no need to use public monies to educate women, immigrants, African Americans, or members of the working class.

Mann wrote that "education is best provided in schools embracing children of all religious, social, and ethnic backgrounds." He believed that "education is our only political safety. Outside of this ark, all is deluge." He thought that "jails and state prisons are the complement of schools; so many less as you have of the latter, so many more you must have of the former." And although it is not yet a fully realized truth, he wrote that "education, then, beyond all other devices of human origin, is the great equalizer of the conditions of men, the balance-wheel of the social machinery."

One hundred years ago, the Horace Mann League was founded to support Mann's vision and perpetuate public education. Today, acting on Mann's belief that public education is the cornerstone of our communities and our democracy, the League is working to *save* public education. This volume of essays, by some of the most articulate scholars and practitioners in the nation, contributes to that effort. Collectively, we commemorate the centennial of the Horace Mann League by looking to the foundational principles of Horace Mann and supporting the commitment to preserve, improve, and expand America's public schools.

Contributors to this volume all share a belief that Horace Mann's passion for and support of public schooling made him one of our nation's most influential citizens. Mann did hold some ideas that would be less universally supported today, but much of what he believed is supported and extended by the editors and essayists in this book in a collective effort to uphold, defend, and perfect the critical and transformative role of public education that Mann envisioned, and for which he advocated.

In these contemporary times, we are seeing alternatives to the public schools proliferate, some as old as the Republic itself, some quite new: religious schooling, private schooling, home schooling, and a vast range of in-person and online charter schools. In a heterogenous, pluralistic democratic society of over 300 million citizens—a society that generally prizes and rewards innovation and entrepreneurship—it is not surprising that alternatives to the nation's public schools exist. The individual authors of these essays recognize and can generally support alternative systems of education, if and when the schools in these systems focus on providing equitable and excellent teaching and learning environments for *every* child in their care—environments that support every student to reach their full potential and find success.

However, one primary concern explored in this volume is the redirecting of public funding from genuine public schools to schools that claim the label of "public" but that are not actually open to the entire public. We reject schools that restrict whom they admit on the basis of religion or race, disability, gender identification, or family income. We reject schools that solicit and accept public financing, but operate without concern for curricular standards, without concern for trained and competent teachers, and that pay excessive amounts of the public's money to their owners and administrative staff. Such schools in no way can make a claim to be part of the democratic public-school system envisioned by Mann.

Horace Mann, and the authors of these essays, would argue that schools funded by the public have obligations to serve the public in ways that honor and promote American democracy and truly democratic ideals. It is this system of genuine public schools—the people's schools—that is addressed by these essayists. Together we stand with Horace Mann as he critiqued the politicians of his day who chose to undermine the successful public educational system that was emerging in our nation:

> In our country and in our times no man is worthy the honored name of states-
> man who does not include the highest practicable education of the people in all
> his plans of administration. He may have eloquence, he may have a knowledge
> of all history, diplomacy, jurisprudence; and by these he might claim, in other
> countries, the elevated rank of a statesman: but unless he speaks, plans, labors,
> at all times and in all places, for the culture and edification of the whole people,
> he is not, he cannot be, an American statesman.

The collective voices of our essayists create a vivid and complex portrait of public education in these United States. It is informed by our authors' multiple perspectives on the history, successes, failures, and above all, the aspirational and transformative potential for our public schools.

The essays are divided into six interrelated parts, based loosely on themes each of our authors chose to explore. Our volume opens with two perspectives on public education's history and future possibilities, beginning with a vividly personalized historical narrative counterposed by a briskly detailed historical overview and summary. In Part II, five authors discuss the critical role that public education has played and continues to play in American life, reminding us of its vital importance to the development of the nation and the evolution and preservation of our communities and our democracy. Framed by Mann's vision of public education as the "great equalizer," Part III presents multiple perspectives from eight of our authors on the status, purpose, challenges, failures, aspirations, and possibilities of our public education system. In Part IV, nine essayists provide insightful views on the role of public education in our democracy and the extent to which it does or does not meet its espoused purpose. These essayists propose a variety of arguments for what we can, and must, learn to do better. In Part V, four of our authors examine the threat to public education by alternative forms of schooling that are misleadingly marketed and promoted as providing necessary competition and choice. They find many of these alternatives to public education to be at the least, very wanting, and at their worst, destructive to the ideals and reality of genuine public education. To conclude our volume, three of our authors reflect on the critical intersection of public education with the future of our democracy, and provide compelling arguments that express both great concern and an abundance of optimism and hope.

This volume, much like our pluralistic democracy, is wide-ranging, expansive, and a bit unruly. Our authors present a treasure of ideas, arguments, and deeply held and ably defended perspectives and points of view. We invite our readers to engage with our authors' voices and perspectives. You are invited to debate the merits of their arguments, and, if moved by this multifaceted and challenging vision of and for our public schools, to join in the continuing work of coming together in solidarity to realize Mann's vision of public education as the cornerstone of our communities and our democracy.

—*David C. Berliner and Carl Hermanns*
Phoenix, AZ

PART I

Source: Image provided courtesy of Boston Latin School.

Boston Latin School, founded on April 23, 1635 by the Town of Boston, Massachusetts, was the first public school in what would become the United States of America. Led by schoolmaster Philemon Pormort and modeled on the Free Grammar School of Boston, England, this boys-only public school taught Latin and Greek as part of a curriculum centered on the humanities. From the beginning, Boston Latin School has taught its students dissent with responsibility, and counts among some of its most well-known revolutionary-era pupils Samuel Adams, John Hancock, and Benjamin Franklin. (See https://bls.org/apps/pages/index.jsp?uREC_ID=206116&type=d for more information on the history of the Boston Latin School.)

In Times of Crisis, Why We Need Public Schools

William J. Mathis

PRELUDE

1865

They warily walked into the churchyard. They had just quit trying to kill each other. The soldiers remembered too much—bushwhackers, splattered brains, and the pregnant widow shot and killed while weeding her garden. Whether wearing dark blue or tattered butternut, they all came home to desolation. Chimneys and ashes remained where their houses once stood. Barns, hay, horses, and cattle were gone to the war. What the war didn't destroy, the Home Guard thugs took. Fallow fields gave rise to salt cedars while the river reclaimed the bottomlands, giving new breeding grounds for the yellow sickness.

My great-grandfather fought for the Union, as did most of his brothers. Cousins, neighbors, and in-laws were secessionists. Yet they all came back to this same valley. Many returned disfigured in mind or body. Fewer came back than went out.

They came home to a new and bewildering world.

For as long as anybody could remember, they had always lived on family farms. But no more. Steam power and manufacturing took over the farms. Trains made a trip to the city as easy as a wagon ride to the county seat. Telegraphers sent messages at the speed of light rather than the speed of a horse. Darwinism shook fundamental religious beliefs and countless denominations multiplied across the land. Youth fled to the cities and the factories.

At the Briar Creek Church, the veterans set aside their differences and sat together. How could they rebuild a community when everything around them was destroyed? All that had held them together, given them meaning, was gone or twisted in some way. Some said they should abandon the community for the cities. Others countered and said this was all the more reason to guard the old ways.

Some blamed the dark-looking Melungeons[1] over on Newman's Ridge with their grave houses[2] and impenetrable language. They said those strange people were the cause of the problems. With the sting of defeat and the sorrow of loss, a few demanded to take to the mountains and renew the fight. Others said they must adapt to a changed world, but this new democracy had just survived a great crisis and we shouldn't give up on it just yet. If ignorance, hate, and division were our problems, we must teach knowledge, compassion, and understanding. They concluded that family, community, and government by the people were too important to abandon. They settled on a solution.

They would build a public school.

They took their misery-whip saws to the mountains and skidded the logs to George Washington (known as G. W.) Mathis's mill, lifted the sluice gate, and loaded the fresh boards on wagons. The family gave the land, a promontory jutting over the Clinch River. The graveyard marked the edge of the playground. A long fly ball could bounce off Aunt Sara's tombstone. She died in the 1918 flu pandemic.

And the Seal-Mathis School was raised—to build community, to teach the skills needed for a new age, and to prepare the citizenry to govern themselves wisely.

G. W. Mathis, my great-uncle, was the guiding light of the building. It still stands.[3] The offspring of the veterans, including my grandfather, taught the next generation. Then my father would teach in that school. My grandfather's 1893 teaching certificate hangs in my office.

After the war, thousands of schools were built across the land.[4] Carried by Jeffersonian beliefs that society and democracy can only be advanced by the education of children, the public school movement swept the nation by the end of the 19th century. Even though we have yet to make the guarantees of our founding fathers a reality for all our nation's children, this was, and is, a great and noble compact.

Like our ancestors, we face the uncertainties of a new age.

Our world was transformed by 9/11 and endless wars, economic crises, contagious diseases, global warming, and terrorists.

Our world continues to fundamentally transform. Steam mills are gone, but the cyber world and the pandemic bewilder our lives in ways we have yet to comprehend. Our population shifts from the farms, while gentrification, racism, and economic inequalities divide our commonwealth. The dissolving of the extended multigeneration farm family dismayed our ancestors; the icon of the new society is an isolated adolescent with a cell phone.

Instead of Darwin, a new absolutist political fundamentalism inflames uncompromising views. Adults curse at the unannounced "upgrades" to their computers. Family tensions fray over lost jobs, the fear of disease, and desperation. The industrial barons of the Gilded Age have been replaced by gray corporate stockbrokers exercising a hegemony over the world's wealth.

Set apart by more than a century, two cultures saw their worlds turned upside down.

How differently they reacted.

Today's school critics say the solution is in the nihilistic fragmentation of vouchers, privatization, charter schools, and home schooling. Where our ancestors chose to hold knowledge and democratic values in common, today's weak image is that education is merely a market choice.

Instead of a society endowed by a common tradition, critics see education as a mindless television remote where some are provided with premium channels, while others have only soaps and sitcoms. In this view, as long as all get a remote, our obligation to equality, to democracy, and to education is satisfied. While advanced by some libertarian and conservative voices, it is a liberty without a responsibility, a conservatism that does not conserve. Chanting in the streets and waving "Freedom" posters does little to advance the fundamental core of civilization, nor does it carry any guarantee that our society or our world will be provided the skills and values for a changed world.

How different from our ancestors.

When the destruction of civil war had to be mended, they put down their weapons and built a school. When technological change made their jobs obsolete and they had to learn new skills, they went to their common school. When new sciences changed their knowledge of the universe, they taught them in their school. When the values of democracy required learning about the Constitution, laws, and humanity, they turned to the schools. Today, the message remains clear and constant. If we are to fulfill and preserve the promises of our Constitution and our communities, we must ennoble our public schools. We must cherish them for all of our children, for the welfare of society and for the sustenance of democracy.

PAST AS PROLOGUE

1890, Sitting Bull: Economics, Education, and Culture

Let us put our minds together and see what life we can make for our children.

—Sitting Bull

Into the thin kerf of black hills, desert and bleached alkali, nomadic tribes were pushed from Minnesota to the South Dakota badlands. Facing the extinction of the Hunkpapa Lakota (Sioux) culture, the Holy Man Sitting

Bull realized their last hope was in the life they made for their children—education not as test-based, academic skills, but as the knowledge of the ways of the society, of sustaining cultural mores, of hunting and gathering, beliefs and rituals, language and bartering. Any society demands the evolution and adoption of common beliefs and laws.

Today on the Pine Ridge reservation, 17 people may live in one bare earth room where temperatures swing from below zero to above 100 degrees. Pine Ridge is the poorest county in the United States. Ninety-seven percent of its population lives below the poverty line. Red Cloud, the only tribal leader who defeated the Anglos, is buried there. A few miles east is the mass grave of the 200 Native Americans massacred at Wounded Knee. Overlaying the native culture is the hazy, impenetrable cloud of the white world. The witches' brew of a changing environment, coronavirus devastation, and poverty forms an unsettled clash.

The coronavirus reminded us that "we are all in this together." The truth is that some are more in this together than others. At our best, we cherish civic virtue, and the building and strengthening of society. At our worst, we dictate unequal educational and social compacts that knowingly advantage one group over another.

Just as they did in the 19th century, the Wasichu[5] meet in Washington to discuss having guns in schools to protect against grizzly bears.[6] Others preach fear of other nations to justify greed and theft of the land. Arne Duncan, the former federal Secretary of Education, said we are falling further behind our international competitors. In the United States, we just talk about the steps many other countries are taking. "Falling behind educationally now will hurt our country economically for generations," we forcefully lament.[7]

Meanwhile, UNICEF's Innocenti Center says the true measure of a nation's standing is how well it attends to its children—their health and safety, their material security, their education and socialization, and their sense of being loved, valued, and included in the families and societies into which they are born.[8]

The United States is ranked 20th of 21 rich countries in the well-being of children,[9] one of the very few nations that spend less on needy children than on the affluent. The achievement gap is not primarily a product of low-quality schools; it directly mirrors the clashing disparities in educational opportunities and educational spending, and the economic gaps of the society.[10] Over the last fifty years the achievement gap has widened.[11] The gap was smallest when our policies focused on building the strength of our schools, rather than just testing and criticizing them.

Thomas Piketty tells us that when profits from invested wealth exceed wealth from production (which is our current situation), then democratic society, economic vitality, and social justice are threatened. Not surprisingly, those who profit from such an arrangement work to protect their advantage. Unfortunately, these wealth inequalities contributed to the recession and slowed the recovery as lower and middle incomes stagnated. And no Western or industrialized nation has a greater wealth or achievement gap than the United States. Thus, the strongest predictor of test scores is not school quality; it is the socioeconomic status of the children. [12]

The Wasichu leaders embrace a far lesser vision than Sitting Bull's. They say we should beat other nations; Sitting Bull focused on people acting together. The president focuses on what we should do for the economy; the Chief concentrated on what we should do together for the children.

Sitting Bull, Sioux Chief and Holy Man, was killed in 1890 by Indian police while incarcerated at Standing Rock. [13]

1916, The Federal Government and the Leadership Imperative: Snatching Defeat from the Jaws of Victory

During World War I, soldiers charged across open fields into machine-gun fire. Among many fiascos, the Gallipoli campaign stands out. Stymied on an entrenched and stalemated western front, the *Entente* (Britain, France, Russia) threw hundreds of thousands of troops against the Otttoman empire. It was supposed to be simple. March up the Dardanelles, defeat "the sick man of Europe," and capture Constantinople.

A half-million casualties and ten months later, the Entente withdrew in failure.

How did "a vastly superior military force . . . manage, against all odds, to snatch defeat from all but certain victory?"[14] In actions that could just as easily explain education failures, Scott Anderson answers: arrogance, political interference, and tunnel vision.

- *Arrogance*—In Gallipoli, the vaunted British navy forgot that in a seaborne invasion, they need landing craft. In the educational equivalent, the federal reformers assume schools do not need money (but corporations do). Compounding the ignorance, the leaders declare that all students must leap over a "higher standard" of five feet when they were having trouble with four. In their educational arrogance, federal reformers assert that the economy will be restored and poverty will be eliminated if we score higher on tests. No research supports this notion. In fact, the evidence points to the contrary. [15]
- *Political Interference*—The federal government ceded certain educational powers to a free-wheeling combination of neoliberal groups, right-wing think tanks, and billionaires. This drove education out of the scrutiny of democracy's public eye.[16] Too many initiatives scatter and waste resources rather than concentrate and focus them.

- **_Tunnel Vision_**—Embracing each other, the proponents of testing and market-driven schools are resolute, committed, and unchanging in their convictions.

Thus, we have the recipe for a fiasco: arrogance, political interference, and tunnel vision. We have 11 million children in our nation's urban schools and half these students are in poverty. Urban districts are on fiscal life support as federal funds shrink and money is siphoned off to support private schools.

CURRENT DILEMMAS

2018, Celebrating the Last Rites of the Educational Reform Movement

It was the hottest ticket since the Led Zeppelin tribute. The president was to issue a few introductory remarks. The vice president arranged the senators and governors on the stage in a phalanx behind the speaker.

The master of ceremonies, an ornamented luminary, gaveled the hall to order and managed to extend four minutes of welcoming into 25 minutes of broad generalizations. The main speaker finally got to the point, declaring the United States' educational system was not what it should be and "harsh new reforms are imperative."

Assessing the crowd, the speaker went on to say, "We can take great pride in what we have accomplished in education over these last 50 years, even though we haven't closed the achievement gap." My colleague whispered, "Oh, for heaven's sake! He can't really be saying that! That's political suicide!"

I responded, "Why can't he say the simple truth?"

"Because that would admit that the reforms didn't work. It's like congratulating a general for his speed and agility in retreating."

We grabbed sandwiches and headed toward the Ellipse to continue over lunch.

"So, what makes you think the reform movement has been a fizzle?" I asked.

"How long have the reformers been reforming?" he countered.

"A fair start date for the beginning of the testing and accountability era would be 1965 with the federal Elementary and Secondary Education law. So, we've been reforming for a half-century."

"So how much has the achievement gap closed?" he asked.

"Well," I said, "some experts say it hasn't closed at all. They say it is steady at about one standard deviation—and that's huge.[17] Other scholars say it's widened dramatically—between 30% and 40% over the past 25 years."[18]

"How can that be?" he questioned. "Are you saying that after all that work, we have nothing to show for it? The entire purpose of Johnson's War on Poverty was to reduce inequality! The result is exactly backwards!"

"What we have to show is the debris field of politicians' magic bombs. None of the initiatives were well thought out or supported in time or in money. During these years we have seen computerized instruction, dashboards, early education, teacher testing, flipping, tracking, detracking, reduced class size, business partnerships, punishment, leveled books, middle school reform, extended school year, extended school day, school closings, consolidations, vouchers, charters, portfolio districts, wraparound services, special education, compensatory education, and social services. Everything now has its own set of standards that are welded into law and regulation. Each of these bombs has fanatical proponents, but none of these notions has shown more than a marginal or short-term effect. There has been no continuity or coherence. We might as well have measured the effects with a kaleidoscope."

"The bigger problem is that we are inequitably assessing and assuring equity. We evaluate schools based on test scores that do not predict the college and career readiness they are said to measure. And then, if the purpose of schools is to build and maintain a democracy, we cannot do so by segregating kids according to which side of the interstate they live on.[19] We know that kids integrate socially in smaller schools.[20] We also know that private school parents can afford opportunities not available to the average mom and pop. Money does matter and schools with little money and limited tax bases cannot afford the kind of experiences that more privileged kids are provided as a birthright."

We took a law that was designed to ensure equal opportunities for all, took away their resources, demanded even higher test scores for impoverished schools and punished them for failing.[21]

And that's our dirty little secret.

2020, A Good Man or an International Competitor?
The Purposes of Education

> We have, in effect, been committing an act of unthinking, unilateral educational disarmament.
>
> —*A Nation at Risk,* 1983

Repeated by platform speakers, think-tankers, lobbyists and politicians, this phrase from the 1983 *Nation at Risk* report[22] continues to be broadly accepted. Even with the end of No Child Left Behind, we continue to hear statements such as, "If we are going to be competitive in the international economy, the children have to master higher standards! Our test scores have to be the best in the world!"

Such righteous assertions send an involuntary shiver down my back. I recall an incident when I was giving a community forum presentation with charts, arrows, and graphs. I blurted, "If we are to be economically competitive in the 21st century, we have to have high test scores."

A mother's hand shot up, and, rising to her feet, she exclaimed, "But I don't want my son to be an international competitor in the 21st century global work force! I want him to be a good man!"

The room fell silent.

Her voice quivered as she said, "I want him to hold a good job, carry his own weight in society and get along with others. I want him to give a little more to his community than what he took. I want him to love and be loved. I want him to be a good husband and father. I want him to be happy. I want him to be a good man."

She was right. Certainly, we want our children to find good jobs and be successful, but these are not the important qualities we want for our children. We want them to be thoughtful, caring, loving, and accomplished, not because that will contribute to international competitiveness, but because these are inherently good things.

* * *

During the 19th century, Horace Mann set forth the reasons for all children to attend a common school. He did advocate for efficiency when talking with manufacturers. He also made the Jeffersonian case for universal education as a necessity for democracy and a civilized society. He told working parents the school would be a child-rearing partner, and assured employers they would be provided a stable workforce. He made the case that common schools were the source of wealth; to the religious he promoted the school as the only nonsectarian institution providing moral education and equitable opportunity.

By the 1950s, universal free public education had carried the day. But things began to change. As the manufacturing industry grew, the notion that education's main purpose is economic gradually ascended. Heavily funded today by billionaires and right-wing think tanks, test-based educational reform became the dominant educational philosophy.

Proponents pummeled policymakers about failing schools, obstreperous unions, antiquated regulations, bureaucracies, and poor teaching skills. If these problems could be swept away, then better accountability measures, rigorously applied, would result in the firing of incompetent teachers and principals. If only schools were properly viewed as a corporate producer, school "output" would soar, the economy would rebound, and wealth would trickle down to everyone. [23]

Things did not work out that way.

* * *

Various reforms have been tried with limited success. Educators, activists, and parents point to the underfunding and inferior learning resources provided to our poor and our children of color. They point to our poverty gap, which is the fifth largest among economically developed nations. [24]

As Kohn points out, needy schools have been systematically deprived compared to those with more affluent populations.[25] About 70 state cost studies have examined the cost of providing an adequate education and have documented this truth: get-tough accountability schemes do not cure systematically deprived communities and broken homes.

In the real world, if an idea doesn't work after a bunch of tries, that's a good reason to stop doing it. In the ideological world, failure does little to shake the underlying belief. Instead, the ideologues say the failure is because their solution was not implemented with enough fervor and force. Or maybe they cling to the one outlier study that supports their view while ignoring the larger body of research. Perhaps they rely on think tanks peddling pseudoresearch to advance predetermined ends.

In this climate, it is possible that public education will become controlled by private oligarchs who hold a narrow view of the purposes of education. Yet there are also glimmerings of a rebirth of the democratic ethos and renewed commitment to all our children. The question is in the balance; will a phoenix rise from the ashes, or will we just have ashes?

FUTURE POSSIBILITIES

c.2065

With artificial intelligence we are summoning the demon.

—Elon Musk, 2014 [26]

Forty-seven percent of American jobs are at risk of automation by the mid-2030s, according to Oxford professors Frey and Osbourne.[27] The Utopians believe that technology will generate more new jobs than it eliminates. The Dystopians see the end of work, a bigger Big Brother, and greater division of wealth.

History shows that these soothsayers are mostly wrong. Nevertheless, there is an emerging consensus that artificial intelligence (AI) will have enormous effects. Witness the profound changes from the Civil War to the present—the continuous acceleration of technological advances is likely to produce even more profound change. It is not too far a leap to see some specific changes.[28] Here are the social premises:

- Routine, low-paying jobs will be eliminated first. Self-driving vehicles, drone delivery, deserted shopping malls and elimination of clerks, and tellerless banking by ATMs are already the norm.
- The most educated will hold the advantages.
- Yet the more affluent are also facing large job losses.
- Rural areas will suffer the greatest declines as the plains empty.
- A huge segment of the population will become unemployed or underemployed.
- Job preparation and retraining will shift more toward corporations and away from community colleges and universities.
- By 2065, artificial intelligence will have transformed the remaining non-routine jobs. [29]

This is within the lifetimes of our children. Machines will be able to repair themselves and enhance their capabilities without humans. The push for more STEM courses will diminish as technical advances will be accomplished much more efficiently by autonomous artificial intelligence. This fundamentally transforms employment, as the need for human technology knowledge drops. When robots become as smart, capable, and efficient as human beings, what will be left for people to do? [30]

This threat comes at an unstable time amidst the hollowing-out of the middle class, environmental degradation, and political instability. The top 1% accumulates disproportionate wealth as the middle class slides into poverty. Wealth is increasingly concentrated in the hands of those who own the machines and the privileged who show no concern for the less fortunate.[31]

> Once the pace of these technological advances and automation changes goes from linear to exponential (becoming self-improving, self-replicating and distributed), the old business models, governance models, management and technology models are going to be crushed . . . (I)t also raises difficult questions about the broader impact on industry disruption, the decline in human workforce and jobs, diminishing wages, shrinking purchasing power, broad systems failure and the crumbling of the economic principles itself as we know now. [32]

We may not notice the point at which the machines surpass human capabilities. In fact, considering whether the self-repair and self-advancement capability of a cyber world is compatible with human beings is no longer just the realm of science fiction writers.

Anomie or a New Direction?

In a world with global warming, climate changes, racial unrest, economic uncertainty, a pandemic and political instability, people are apprehensive about the future. The imperatives proposed here are not conventional. They are based on what we need to survive.

Will they be enough?

On School Governance and Operations

- Lifelong learning is accepted by virtually everyone except that all don't define it the same way. Crises require that education goes beyond elementary and secondary education. The world's knowledge is now in the back pocket of your jeans. Thus, education as knowledge storage will give way to thinking skills and accessing information.
- We must restore common schools and public education for the simple reason that choice or private systems separates a dangerously fractured society and works against the common good.
- Schools and society must practice democracy and cooperation. There must be universal, committed concern for all children and for our environment.
- In many geographic areas, schools are too large to provide the individual and small-group activities necessary for social development.
- Schools should be for universal human and ethical needs and values.
- Technical education should be built and operated as a self-sustaining and separate commercial enterprise. If local, state, or national concerns emerge, temporary start-up and operational funds should be provided.

On Community

- Schools should be the community's house and governed directly by the community's citizens. They should be a center for entertainment, civic gathering, collaborative wrap-around services, viable parent organizations, senior centers, etc.
- School must be committed to integration of all students and members of the school community.
- Children should not be segregated into tracks, races, or perceived capabilities.
- Small schools and local boards have shown strong social behavior outcomes and have thus garnered more sustained community

support. These should be restored particularly at the elementary level.

On Curriculum

- Education needs to be experiential, lifelong, and evolving to accommodate the technological and social changes brought by the Fourth Industrial Revolution.[33]
- Skills, not degrees, will be the reality of the future. Education in affective realms will be essential. Hard science will be ever evolving, which means we must continuously rebalance curriculum content in ways that support scientific inquiry and understanding, and emphasize the interactive, environmental, and cooperative skills required to do so.
- Schools cannot control whether artificial intelligence's demon will be summoned, nor can schools control pandemics, terrorist attacks or hurricanes. What education can do is educate old and new generations to implement more responsible practices.
- Contemporary definitions of high standards, standardized tests, and accountability systems do not represent the best evidence for schools of the future. Affective and social skills will remain while hard knowledge will evolve.
- Knowledge of government must be learned by engagement.
- Teaching of soft skills, such as communications, collaboration, creativity, innovation, inquiry, problem solving, and wise use of technology, is required.
- Computers and the pandemic have permanently changed education. However, mastery of searching for *knowledge* will supersede simply acquiring Internet-available *information*.[34]

A society can exist only as long as it holds inclusive, cooperative, and mutually supporting values. As a nation founded on democracy, we must restore those synergistic bonds. We must redefine our culture, reform our government, and transform our schools for the benefit of our children.

"No government is legitimate," said Ron Dworkin, "that does not show equal concern for the fate of all those citizens over whom it claims dominion and from whom it claims allegiance. Equal concern is the sovereign virtue of political community."[35] It is time for political leaders to care about and act on equality to ensure the continuation of civilization.

NOTES

1. *Melungeons* are a mixed-race people historically associated with settlements in central Appalachia.

2. "Folklife: The Vanishing Grave-houses of Appalachia," *Unmasked History Magazine* (September 25, 2019). https://unmaskedhistory.com/2019/09/25/folk-life-the-vanishing-grave-houses-of-appalachia/

3. Generally speaking, the early Tennessee churches sponsored their own small community schools. Many of those that existed earlier closed during the Civil War. The current building is believed to have been built c.1928. Following school consolidation in the late 20th century, it was converted into a preschool center and now operates as a VA facility. (Source: Debra J. Reed, Sneedville, TN)

4. The nation's first public high school was opened in 1821. Over 3,000 schools were established during reconstruction. *https://prezi.com/kglmbfgrncfs/pre-civil-war-education*; and https://www.raceforward.org/research/reports/historical-time-line-public-education-us

5. *Wasichu* is the Lakota and Dakota word for White people of European descent.

6. Helin Jung, "The Most Damning Moments from Betsy DeVos's Confirmation Hearing," *Cosmopolitan*, January 18, 2017. https://www.cosmopolitan.com/politics/a8610516/betsy-devos-education-secretary-confirmation-hearing/

7. Arne Duncan, *Testimony of U.S. Secretary of Education Arne Duncan*, U.S. Department of Education Fiscal Year 2015 Budget Request, House Appropriations Committee (April 8, 2014). https://www.ed.gov/news/speeches/testimony-us-education-secretary-arne-duncan-us-department-education-fiscal-year-2015

8. UNICEF, "Child Poverty in Perspective: An overview of child well-being in rich countries," *Innocenti Report Card 7* (2007), p. 1. https://www.unicef-irc.org/publications/pdf/rc7_eng.pdf

9. Ibid., p. 2.

10. Laura Meckler, "Achievement gaps in schools driven by poverty, study finds," *Washington Post*, September 23, 2019. https://www.washingtonpost.com/local/education/achievement-gaps-in-schools-driven-by-poverty-study-finds/2019/09/22/59491778-dd73-11e9-b199-f638bf2c340f_story.html

11. Sean F. Reardon, "The Widening Academic Achievement Gap Between the Rich and the Poor," in *Whither Opportunity?*, Greg J. Duncan & Richard J. Murnane (Eds.), Russell Sage Foundation, 2011. https://cepa.stanford.edu/sites/default/files/reardon%20whither%20opportunity%20-%20chapter%205.pdf

12. Thomas Piketty, *Capital in the Twenty-First Century* (Arthur Goldhammer, Trans.), Harvard University Press, 2014.

13. "Sitting Bull Killed by Indian Police," *History.com*, December 11, 2019. https://www.history.com/this-day-in-history/sitting-bull-killed-by-indian-police

14. Scott Anderson, *Lawrence in Arabia: War, Deceit, Imperial Folly and the Making of the Modern Middle East*, Atlantic Books, 2014.

15. David Berliner, "Our Impoverished View of Educational Reform," *Teachers College Record*, 108, no. 6 (2006), 949–955; William J. Mathis & Tina M. Trujillo (Eds.), Learning from the Federal Market-Based Reforms, 2016, Information Age Publishing; Sean F. Reardon, "The Widening Academic Achievement Gap Between the Rich and the Poor," in *Whiter Opportunity?* Greg J. Duncan & Richard Murnane (Eds.), Russell Sage Foundation, 2011. Richard Rothstein, Rebecca Jacobsen, & Tamara Wilder, *Grading Education: Getting Accountability Right*, Teachers College Press, 2008; Reardon, "The Widening Academic Achievement Gap."

16. Part D-Waivers Section 9401 (2004). https://www2.ed.gov/nclb/freedom/local/flexibility/waiverletters/index.html

17. Andy Porter, "Rethinking the achievement gap," *Penn GSE News*, 2020. https://www.gse.upenn.edu/news/rethinking-achievement-gap

18. Reardon, "The Widening Academic Achievement Gap."

19. Rothstein et al., *Grading Education*.

20. Craig Howley, Jerry Johnson, & Jennifer Petrie, *Consolidation of Schools and Districts: What the Research Says and What It Means*, National Education Policy Center, February 1, 2011. http://nepc.colorado.edu/publication/consolidation-schools-districts

21. Lily Eskelsen Garcia & Otha Thornton, "'No Child Left Behind' has Failed," *Washington Post*, February 13, 2015. https://www.washingtonpost.com/opinions/no-child-has-failed/2015/02/13/8d619026-b2f8-11e4-827f-93f454140e2b_story.html

22. National Commission on Excellence in Education, *A Nation at Risk*, U. S. Department of Education, 1983. https://www2.ed.gov/pubs/NatAtRisk/risk.html

23. See William J. Mathis and Tina M. Trujillo, *Learning from the Federal Market-Based Reforms*, Information Age Publishing, 2016, Chapters 22–28.

24. Porter, "Rethinking the Achievement Gap"; Organisation for Economic Co-operation and Development, *OECD Social and Welfare Statistics: Income distribution*, n.d. https://data.oecd.org/inequality/poverty-gap.htm

25. Alfie Kohn, "Poor Teaching for Poor Students," *Boston Globe*, March 20, 2000. https://www.alfiekohn.org/article/poor-teaching-poor-students/

26. Elon Musk, *Washington Post*. https://www.washingtonpost.com/news/innovations/wp/2014/10/24/elon-musk-with-artificial-intelligence-we-are-summoning-the-demon/

27. C.B. Frey & M.A. Osborne (2013). The future of employment: How susceptible are jobs to computerization? https://www.oxfordmartin.ox.ac.uk/downloads/academic/The_Future_of_Employment.pdf

28. Gil Press, "Is AI Going to be a Jobs Killer? Reports about the Future of Work," *Forbes*, July 15, 2019. https://www.forbes.com/sites/gilpress/2019/07/15/is-ai-going-to-be-a-jobs-killer-new-reports-about-the-future-of-work/#4d331824afb2

29. Kevin Drum, "You Will Lose Your Job to a Robot—and Sooner Than You Think," *Mother Jones*, Nov.–Dec. 2019. https://www.motherjones.com/politics/2017/10/you-will-lose-your-job-to-a-robot-and-sooner-than-you-think/

30. Drum, "You Will Lose Your Job to a Robot."

31. Piketty, *Capital in the Twenty-First Century*.

32. Jayshree Pandja, "The End of Work: The Consequences of an Economic Singularity," *Forbes*, February 17, 2017. https://www.forbes.com/sites/cognitiveworld/2019/02/17/the-end-of-work-the-consequences-of-an-economic-singularity/#b1fc93a1d32b

33. World Economic Forum (2020), https://www.weforum.org/agenda/2020/01/reskilling-revolution-jobs-future-skills/

34. Albina Welsh, "How internet affected the modern educational process," *Education Beyond Borders* [Blog post]. http://www.educationbeyondborders.org/profiles/blogs/how-internet-affected-the-modern-educational-process

35. Ronald Dworkin, "Justice for Hedgehogs." https://www.carnegiecouncil.org/studio/multimedia/20111206-justice-for-hedgehogs

A Brief History of Public Education

Diane Ravitch

The public schools of the United States have long been recognized as one of the central institutions that sustain a democratic society. Long before there were public schools, in the early days of the Republic, the Founding Fathers agreed that a democratic society requires an educated citizenry. Education was necessary for informed consent and participation in self-government. Furthermore, although public education was a distant dream, when the Founders passed the landmark Northwest Ordinances of 1785 and 1787, they set aside a parcel of land in every new town that was to be specifically devoted to the maintenance of free public schools. This was an explicit acknowledgement of the importance of free public schools, provided by government. Thomas Jefferson, John Adams, and Benjamin Rush were especially outspoken and eloquent on the importance of government-funded public education. Adams wrote that in the provision of education by government, "no expense . . . would be too extravagant." In 1785, Adams wrote,

> The whole people must take upon themselves the education of the whole people and be willing to bear the expenses of it. There should not be a district of one mile square, without a school in it, not founded by a charitable individual, but maintained at the public expense of the people themselves.[1]

As constitutional lawyer Derek Black points out in his recent book *School House Burning*, "All fifty state constitutions include an education clause or other language that requires the state to provide public education." Most of these clauses were enacted after the Civil War; no state was admitted to the Union without an education clause in its constitution. Moreover, Black notes, "Save the original colonies that predated the Constitution, states' public education systems have all been funded and expanded by federal land grants." These grants "can only be used for public education."[2]

In the early decades of the Republic, communities began to establish "common schools," supported by taxes on themselves, to educate the children of the community. Some common schools charged fees, but this practice was eventually eliminated as public education came to be seen as a right, not a privilege. In addition, private schools, supported by tuition, were available in towns and cities, as well as private boarding schools for the children of the wealthy. Before there was widespread agreement on the principle of public schooling, private societies received charters from their state and public funds to educate poor children, girls, and Black children (today, they would be called "charter schools"). Some churches maintained schools for the children of members of their congregations, and some created parish schools for the children of their congregation or the children of the poor. Catholic schools were opened long before the American Revolution (the first was the Ursuline Academy in New Orleans, founded in 1727), but Catholic leaders determined to build a system of Catholic parochial schools in the 1840s in response to anti-Catholic bias in the common schools and in society. In New York City, Bishop John Hughes considered the "public schools" to be "Protestant public schools," but was rebuffed when he sought a share of public funds for "Catholic public schools."[3] Bishop Hughes made clear that he wanted a Catholic education for Catholic children, not a nonsectarian education. Thus, in the early years of the 19th century, American education was awash in choices for children of every station, though few received more than a few years of any education unless their parents were wealthy and could afford private tutors or an elite boarding school.

Despite the profusion of choices available to families, public schools became firmly rooted in the mid-19th century as the center of community life, encompassing students of different socioeconomic backgrounds. Few students advanced beyond eighth grade, and few Black students were enrolled in school until after the Civil War. As the years went by, the number of students who stayed in school increased, the number of Black students increased, and the demand for schooling beyond eighth grade grew. A historical review of education statistics published by the U.S. Department of Education in 1992 found:

> In 1940, more than half of the U.S. population had completed no more than an eighth-grade education. Only 6 percent of males and 4 percent of females had completed 4 years of college. The median years of school attained by the adult population, 25 years old and over, had registered only a scant rise from 8.1 to 8.6 years over a 30-year period from 1910 to 1940.[4]

Every town or city had one or many public schools, and they were broadly seen as a pathway to opportunity. They enjoyed broad bipartisan support across the nation. Republicans and Democrats alike vigorously supported their local public schools. Civic leaders and Chambers of Commerce took pride in their local public schools. Business leaders often ran to serve as school board president, and members of both political parties boasted about the accomplishments of their community's public schools, in academics, in spelling bees, and on the playing fields. Public schools were the point of entry into American life for millions of immigrants from other lands, where they learned English and the skills needed to fit into American society.[5]

Public schools were at the heart of the struggle for civil rights for Black Americans. The landmark *Brown v. Board of Education* decision of 1954, although implemented slowly in the face of racism and resistance in all sections of the nation, was the focal point for the civil rights movement of the 1950s and 1960s. The public schools were expected to provide equal educational opportunity for all, which the United States Supreme Court ruled was impossible so long as the public schools remained racially segregated.

Southern governors and other elected officials vowed to block desegregation of their public schools. Their rallying cry to preserve segregation was "school choice." Southern legislatures passed laws to enact school choice plans, allowing all families to decide where to send their children. They passed voucher laws, tuition tax credit laws, and other mechanisms intended to preserve their system of segregated schools. They assumed that Whites would choose white schools, and Blacks would choose black schools, and no one would choose the nonexistent racially integrated schools, thus maintaining racial segregation. According to Stephen Suitts in his recent book *Overturning Brown*, the Southern segregationists were aware of economist Milton Friedman's 1955 advocacy of freedom of choice and of vouchers and they embraced his solution, which would produce the same result: all-White schools, all-Black schools, and racially integrated schools for those who might choose them.[6]

For many years, the term "school choice" was stigmatized because of its association with advocacy for school segregation. The courts knocked out all the Southern plans for vouchers, tuition tax credits, and other schemes to evade desegregating their schools. The term disappeared for a few decades because it was so closely associated with racism.

The 1960s were a time of turmoil in American society and in American schools. There were ugly confrontations over busing and what was termed "forced integration." There were civil disorders in which angry Black people protested the conditions in which they were compelled to live. Large numbers of White families deserted urban districts, moving to the suburbs in what was called "White flight," intensifying racial segregation in many school districts across the nation. The Kerner Commission Report of 1968 reviewed the causes of these violent protests; the basic cause was a reaction to White racism, which enabled residential segregation, police brutality, inadequate housing, poorly equipped schools, and a host of other discriminatory and harmful actions and policies.[7]

During this tumultuous time, the nation's public schools were called upon by federal authorities in Congress and the Courts to desegregate; to provide appropriate education for students with disabilities, many of whom had been excluded in the past; and to meet the needs of English language learners. With limited public support and funding, the public schools met these challenges, though never to everyone's satisfaction.

As the schools persisted in their efforts to respond to the social crises of the larger society, critics discovered a new crisis that they could pin directly on the schools: falling test scores. *The New York Times* reported in 1975 that scores on the SAT were falling.[8] Critics complained that something was terribly wrong with the schools. Reasonable voices pointed out that the pool of test-takers had been diversified, expanding from students in the college track to include students who were not among the college-bound elite. More Black and Latinx students were taking the SAT, and the economic background of SAT test-takers was expanding. No matter, the critics insisted that the drop in SAT signaled a dangerous decline in the quality of schooling. A prestigious commission chaired by former Secretary of Labor Willard Wirtz warned that the schools were slipping, and the critics felt justified in lambasting the schools.

When Ronald Reagan was elected, he had a strong interest in vouchers, perhaps derived from his friendship with libertarian economist Milton Friedman, who had been advocating for vouchers and a market-based education system since 1955. Reagan had attended public schools, not private or religious schools, in Illinois, but he was swept away by Friedman's arguments. In 1983, Reagan proposed federal tax credits for private schools, but Congress was not interested. Republicans in Congress still had a vestigial appreciation for their community's public schools. Reagan's first Secretary of Education, Terrell Bell, proposed the creation of a national commission to study "excellence" in the schools. Reagan was hoping for a report that would support vouchers and prayer in the schools. Instead, Secretary Bell's National Commission on Excellence in the Schools produced a report called *A Nation at Risk*, which declared that the schools were in a crisis of "mediocrity."[9] The report lambasted the quality of American education, insisted on changes in the curriculum to make it more rigorous, but did not mention vouchers or prayer in the schools.

Reagan's second Secretary of Education, William Bennett, was a fervent advocate of vouchers and of public support for religious schools. In 1984, the Republican Party's education platform, for the first time, endorsed not only prayer in public schools, but billions for vouchers for low-income students to enroll in private schools. The Republican party, once a stalwart supporter of the nation's public schools, endorsed school choice, echoing the views of Southern segregationists of 25 years in the past.[10]

The release of *A Nation at Risk* had a cataclysmic effect on the reputation of public schools in America. Where once they were the pride of communities, now they were seen as failing, falling away from a golden age when all students were successful. That image stuck for decades. NPR journalist Anya Kamenetz blew away that interpretation in her reconsideration of *A Nation at Risk* in 2018. She interviewed original participants on the National Commission on Excellence in Education and learned that the results of the commission's survey were predetermined. The books were cooked. The purpose of the commission was to create a sense of crisis, and it succeeded. Scores had fallen on standardized tests not because the quality of education had weakened, but because the pool of students taking the tests had grown larger and more diverse. A competing report from the Sandia National Laboratories in 1992 received almost no attention and reached opposite conclusions about the quality of American education, finding that trends in education were steadily and slowly improving.[11]

Commissioner of Education Terrell Bell wanted to dodge President Reagan's demands for vouchers and school prayer, and did so by slamming the good reputation of all of American schooling. The damage done to public discourse about the schools was no less toxic than if the report had actually proposed vouchers and school prayers.

After *A Nation at Risk*, governors of both parties declared themselves to be school reformers, and the only idea they had was to demand more testing and higher test scores and to threaten educators who were unable to produce higher test scores. Teachers and principals were not in the vanguard of this new educational revolution; politicians and think tanks were, and they agreed that standards were too low, and everyone needed to try harder to produce higher test scores.

Reagan's legacy shaped the future of the Republican Party's policies about education. Future party platforms endorsed choice, competition, accountability, and home schooling. Public schools were treated as a stumbling enterprise, a big-government bureaucracy hobbled by federal mandates, and unions, even though the Republican Party in power did nothing to reduce mandates or to fund them. Reagan's legacy reshaped the Democrats' views about education. Where once they had put equity and access first in their educational demands, they began to adopt the language of standards, testing, and accountability. President Bill Clinton joined with President George H. W. Bush to set national goals in 1989, such as demanding that America would be first in the world in math and science by the year 2000. As Governor of Arkansas, Clinton had made his educational mark by demanding teacher testing and accountability. George W. Bush promised choice, testing, and the biggest federal mandate of all in 2000, which he called No Child Left Behind. Bush claimed during the 2000 campaign that there had been an "education miracle" in Texas, the result of annual testing of every child every year: Test scores were up, graduation rates were up, the achievement gap between races was closing. (None of these claims was true.) His proposal was passed by overwhelming bipartisan vote in Congress in the fall of 2001 and signed into law by the new President Bush on January 8, 2002.

NCLB, as it was known, dramatically changed the federal role in education. Henceforward, federal law superseded local control. Republicans, once the champions of local control, abandoned it. The new law required every school to test every child in grades 3 through 8 in reading and math, and again once in high school. No high-performing nation in the world required this intensive annual testing. The law stated that by the year 2014, every child would score at the "proficient" level or schools would face dire consequences for not meeting this lofty and impossible goal. NCLB contained a menu of "remedies," none of which were supported by evidence. A school unable to raise test scores every year, it said, should be handed over to a charter operator or to state control, closed, or "reconstituted" (which meant firing the staff and starting over). No state or district ever met the goal of 100% proficiency. Many schools were punished. Many teachers and principals were fired, their reputations in tatters. All of this was done to satisfy the rigorous demands of a law built on a hoax: There never was a Texas education miracle.

Nonetheless, Congress and state leaders remained fixated on raising test scores. NCLB remained in force until 2015, when it was replaced by the Every Student Succeeds Act, which removed the deadline by which all students would be proficient and dropped some of the other draconian punishments. But what did not disappear was the magical belief that a federal mandate based on annual standardized tests would produce better education. What it did produce was cheating scandals, a dramatically diminished curriculum, a teaching profession tied to the unethical demand to teach to the test, and a mindset that enshrined standardized testing as both the means and the end of education.

In the grip of the policymakers' obsession with testing and ranking and rating and sorting, schools that were important to their communities were closed or replaced or taken over by the state because their scores were too low. Forget the fact that standardized test scores are highly correlated with family income and affected by important factors like disabilities and language ability. Once-sensible men and women in public life agreed that with the right tests and enough pressure, every student would one day be proficient and the gaps between high-performing and low-performing groups would disappear. It never happened.

As politicians and think tank denizens looked about for ways to produce higher test scores, there arose a movement for school choice. John Chubb and Terry Moe wrote a book in 1990 claiming that school choice was "a panacea," the one that would free schools from bureaucracy and politics.[12] Both Republicans and Democrats looked for new answers that bypassed the public schools. The Clinton Administration embraced the idea of charter schools as a "third way" solution, believing that privately managed schools might be more accountable and more effective than regular public schools. In 1994, the Clinton Administration authorized a federal Charter Schools Program to help new charter schools get a start. Beginning with only a few million each year, this program in two decades grew into a $400 million annual fund that was dispensed by Secretary of Education

Betsy DeVos, mostly to benefit the growth of large corporate charter chains, not to help mom-and-pop schools or teacher-led startups.

Despite the sordid history of school choice and its origins in the segregationist movement, the term became a rallying cry for critics of public education. Right-wing think tanks, libertarian billionaires, and groups like the American Legislative Exchange Council—an organization that brought together far-right extremists, big corporate money, and others who wanted to reduce government regulation and unleash free enterprise—unleashed an unmodulated campaign of vilification against public schools. Their propaganda against public schools was echoed even in Democratic think tanks like the Center for American Progress and inside the Obama administration's Department of Education, which favored privately managed charter schools over public schools. The Obama-era Race to the Top was funded with $5 billion for "reform," available only to states that agreed to expand the number of their charter schools, adopt national standards (understood to be the Common Core), evaluate teachers by the test scores of their students, use test score data to rank every school, and commit to harsh penalties for schools that ranked in the bottom 5% of their state. Race to the Top could have easily been sponsored by a Republican administration.

Thirty years since the choice mania first burst onto the national scene, there is now solid evidence that neither charter schools nor vouchers produce better results than regular public schools. If charter schools enroll the same students, they get the same results as public schools; those that get superior results use methods to screen their students or practice careful attrition of their weakest students. Students in voucher schools typically get worse results than public schools, although many states take care to avoid subjecting voucher schools to the same tests as public schools. Neither charter school nor voucher school students are "saved" by leaving the public schools, although the public schools end up with less money and larger classes when students are allowed to take public money as they go to private choices.

Despite the constant turmoil and barrage of "reforms" piled on the schools, improvement on the National Assessment of Educational Progress was glacial after the passage of No Child Left Behind, then stopped altogether by about 2010. The nostrums of "reform," which never advocated for adequate funding for the growing numbers of children in poverty or for smaller class sizes, failed. Charter schools diverted money from public schools, as did vouchers. The "reformers'" great success story, New Orleans, where every school was a charter school, is a low-performing school district (below the state average) in one of the nation's lowest-performing states, Louisiana. At last report, nearly half of the charters in the district were rated either D or F by the state education department.

When the nation was brought low by the coronavirus pandemic in the spring of 2020, almost everyone turned to the public schools and recognized that they do far more than babysit. They continue to be the heart of the community where they are located, the place where students and their families turn for food, occasionally for shelter, for counseling, for medical care. Almost everyone, except the EdTech industry, became tired by distance learning. Some children had no access to the necessary technology, and many of those who did simply turned it off. It was boring. Even Trump and his Secretary of Education Betsy DeVos, both hostile to public schooling, demanded that they reopen so the economy could restart.

Public schools are a central element in the American story. They are the beating heart of every community. The Founding Fathers dreamed of them, imagined them, planned for them. For most of the 19th century, they were revered, even as their reach was limited. They provided the ladder of opportunity that was supposedly open to every boy or girl. In the 1980s, a propaganda campaign was launched against them. That propaganda campaign provided a ready-made platform for fake school "reformers." Their ongoing efforts to undermine public schools have been funded by some of the wealthiest plutocrats in the nation—including the Walton family, the DeVos family, the Koch family, the Bill & Melinda Gates Foundation, Eli Broad, Michael Bloomberg, and a long list of others. (I have a chapter in my book *Slaying Goliath* that names those who seek to disrupt public education and privatize it.)[13]

After 30 years of failed reforms, it is time to abandon the status quo of disruption and turmoil. It is time to reimagine our public schools and to bring a fresh vision to planning for them. They should be, as they were supposed to be, centers of learning that welcome all students. They should have the funding they need to meet the needs of their students and to provide, when necessary, services for their families. No child should go hungry; no child should go without medical checkups. Schools should have the funding to attract and retain well-prepared teachers. They should offer a full curriculum that includes the arts, technology, history, civics, the sciences, and literature. They should be places of joy, places of learning, places to play and imagine, places of creativity, and places of self-discipline and study.

If all of this sounds like a beautiful dream, it is, because we are so far removed from making it happen. But if we may have dreams, they should be the right dreams. Let us recognize the soul-constricting testing regime that we have imposed on our children at great expense and with little benefit. Then dream big.

NOTES

1. Letter, John Adams to John Jebb, September 10, 1785. https://founders.archives.gov/documents/Adams/06-17-02-0232

2. Derek Black, *School House Burning: Public Education and the Assault on American Democracy*, Public Affairs, 2020, 53.

3. Diane Ravitch, *The Great School Wars: New York City, 1805–1973*, Basic Books, 1975.

4. National Center for Education Statistics, *120 Years of American Education: A Statistical Portrait*, U.S. Department of Education, Office of Educational Research and Improvement, 1992, 7.

5. My mother was one of the beneficiaries. She arrived in the United States as an 8-year-old immigrant from Bessarabia in 1917. Her parents immediately enrolled her in the Houston public schools, where she learned to speak, read, and write English. Her high school diploma was one of her most prized possessions.

6. Steve Suitts, *Overturning Brown: The Segregationist Legacy of the Modern School Choice Movement*, NewSouth Books, 2020, 54–60; Milton Friedman, "The Role of Government in Education," in *Economics and the Public Interest*," ed. Robert A. Solo, Rutgers University Press, 1955, 123–144.

7. Report of the Kerner Commission (1968). https://www.hud.gov/sites/dfiles/FHEO/documents/kerner_commission_full_report.pdf

8. Maeroff, G.I. Educators study test score drop. *New York Times*, Oct. 29, 1975. https://www.nytimes.com/1975/10/29/archives/educators-study-test-score-drop-college-board-panel-seeks-causes-of.html?smid=em-share

9. A Nation At Risk: The Imperative for Education Reform. National Commission on Excellence in Education. April 1983. https://edreform.com/wp-content/uploads/2013/02/A_Nation_At_Risk_1983.pdf

10. Suitts, pp. 71–72.

11. Anya Kamenetz, "What 'A Nation at Risk' Got Wrong, and Right, about U.S. Schools," *NPR*, April 29, 2018. https://wamu.org/story/18/04/29/what-a-nation-at-risk-got-wrong-and-right-about-u-s-schools/

12. John E. Chubb and Terry M. Moe, *Politics, Markets, and America's Schools*, Brookings, 1990, 217.

13. Diane Ravitch, *Slaying Goliath: The Passionate Resistance to Privatization and the Fight to Save America's Public Schools*, Knopf, 2020, Chapter 3.

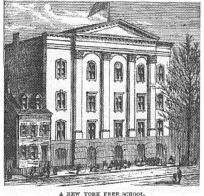

PART II

A NEW YORK FREE SCHOOL.

The whole public school system is free to all the children of the city, whose parents will avail themselves of it. Books, and everything needed, are furnished without charge. The pupil is put to no expense whatever, but is required to maintain habits of order and personal neatness. The cost to the city is gladly borne by the tax payers, for it saves the metropolis from an increase of the great army of ignorant and idle men and women, which are the curse of all great cities. The very poorest men or women can thus give to their children the priceless boon of knowledge, of which their youth was deprived. Profiting by the advantage thus acquired, these little ones, in after years, may rise to fame and fortune. Thus not only the metropolis but the whole country reaps the blessings of this magnificent system of free education. The poor, however, are not the only persons who secure the advantages of the free schools for their children. Many wealthy, or moderately comfortable parents send their children to these schools, because they are the best in the city.

Source: James D. McCabe, *Lights and Shadows of New York Life; or, the Sights and Sensations of the Great City*, National Publishing Co., 1872, text, p. 670; image, p. 667.

Values and Education Policy

Edward B. Fiske and Helen F. Ladd

Good education policymaking is rooted in coherent and enlightened educational values. Judgments about the desirability of any policy should begin with consideration of the valued outcomes that the policy is intended to achieve and with attention to the fair distribution of those outcomes. Which specific outcomes are valued, how tradeoffs might be made among them, and the meaning of a fair distribution will vary across economic, political, and institutional contexts. Moreover, even within any given context they will vary across individuals or groups of individuals because of the differing weights that people may place on specific valued outcomes or because of differing perceptions of their achievability.

Nonetheless, without clear articulation of the valued outcomes of education and how they are to be distributed, policy makers lack the means to argue that one policy is superior to another. One must start with a vision of what one is trying to achieve.

It is in that light that we draw attention in the first part of this essay to the valued outcomes promoted by Horace Mann through his vision of the "common school" in the mid-19th century. We then turn to a modern statement of valued outcomes of education. These are the subject of a recent book called *Educational Goods: Values, Evidence, and Decision Making* (2018), by Harry Brighouse, Helen Ladd, Susanna Loeb, and Adam Swift. Finally, we consider the relevance of these two sets of values to three current education policy issues: test-based accountability, school finance, and charter schools.

HORACE MANN AND THE VALUED OUTCOMES OF EDUCATION

Horace Mann's concept of the valued outcomes of education was rooted in his vision of a system of "common schools" that would be publicly managed and supported, free to students, inclusive in its reach to children of all ethnic and social backgrounds, and profoundly moral, albeit non-sectarian

In these respects, Mann's vision contrasted significantly with most American schooling practice up to that time.

Through the Colonial period and into the early 19th century, it was widely assumed that parents bore the obligation to provide for the education of children. Education was a *private* good, carried out locally and in haphazard fashion by private schoolmasters or sectarian religious groups. By contrast, Mann viewed education as a *public* responsibility that would serve broad collective interests, including political stability and social harmony. In the emerging industrial society of the mid-19th century, where widespread oppression of workers bred social unrest, he argued that education should function not so much as a private luxury but as a public good.

As early as 1635, town officials in Boston identified the need to hire a schoolmaster on a fee-paying basis (Butts & Cremin, 1953, p. 101). Some "charity" or "pauper" schools existed for children of the poor; these bore significant social stigma. The idea of taxing all citizens, including those of the privileged classes who already enjoyed access to private education, in order to finance the education of poor and working-class children was viewed as both wasteful and as an infringement on property rights. Mann argued that free schooling served the collective interests of all citizens, rich and poor alike. "Jails and state prisons are the complement of schools," he wrote. "So many less as you have of the latter, so many more you must have of the former" (Mann, 1867, p. 112).

Puritans viewed schooling as a means of promoting "moral instruction" and teaching children the values essential to maintaining the existing American social order. In practice, the moral values fostered by the early publicly supported schools came to be closely identified with mainline Protestantism, with emphasis on industriousness, frugality, and personal responsibility. Literacy instruction equipped children to read the Bible. Roman Catholics in New York and elsewhere bristled at what they viewed as Protestant bias in public schools and established their own parochial schools. Mann promoted what to his mind was nonsectarian moral instruction.

Education that was deemed to be a parental responsibility required fees, lacked universality, and served to perpetuate existing class, gender, religious, and ethnic differences. Wide gaps existed between the educational opportunities of children from wealthy and poor families, males and females, Whites and Blacks, and schools in urban and rural areas. Challenges to such inequalities appeared soon after the founding of the nation. In Virginia, Thomas Jefferson, who favored universal education as essential to the functioning of democracy, called for the creation of non-tuition elementary schools, which would serve "all the free children, male and female" ("free" being the operative word).

The notion of "common schools" began to take hold in the 1830s in New England under pressure from social reformers, often Whigs, to promote greater government involvement in the schooling of all children. By the time of the Civil War most northern and midwestern states had followed the Massachusetts example and organized systems of schools offering basic literacy and numeracy. Nevertheless, even after Black children had won the right to attend public schools, almost every school they attended was segregated and inferior to those available to their White counterparts. Mann was offended by such inequalities and promoted a system of common schools that would promote shared and unifying experiences. Education, he wrote, is best provided in schools embracing children of all religious, social, and ethnic backgrounds.

In 1837, Mann abandoned his career as a Massachusetts lawyer and legislator to become secretary of the newly established state board of education. Friends and colleagues chastised him for assuming a position with minimal resources, prestige, or power. But he used it to promote the idea of common schools. Mann believed that education is a fundamental human right and that the common school was the most effective vehicle for fulfilling this right. He wrote, "I believe in the existence of a great, immortal, immutable principle of natural law, or natural ethics—the absolute right to an education of every human being that comes into the world" (Mann, 1867, p. 31). He asserted that a free education is as much a child's birthright "as Heaven's bounties of light and air" (Mann, 1846, p. 233). Implicit in Mann's vision of the common school was a coherent set of valued outcomes aimed at reshaping the economic, social, political, religious, and moral nature of society.

Economic and Social Outcomes

Writing at the height of the Industrial Revolution, Mann understood the need for skilled workers. He argued that, by providing such workers, public education would increase economic productivity and overall abundance. "An educated people is always a more industrious and productive people," he wrote (Mann, 1846, p. 110). Significantly, he was not talking about redistributing wealth but rather creating new wealth—making the pie larger. "Beyond the power of diffusing old wealth," he wrote, "it has the prerogative of creating new."

Moreover, Mann lived during a period of intense ferment and agitation. He was a contemporary of Emerson, Thoreau, and other Transcendentalists, as well as reformers advocating for abolitionism, prison reform, temperance, women's rights, and other social causes. He was aware of the extent to which unfettered capitalism had produced huge inequality of wealth in Massachusetts and neighboring states, had led to the domination of owners and the servility of labor, and had created conditions inviting social unrest.

For Mann, using public education to increase economic productivity and abundance was key to reducing economic inequality and promoting the general welfare. He famously declared, "Education, then, beyond all other devices of human origin, is the great equalizer of the conditions of men—the balance-wheel of the social machinery" (Mann, 1848, p. 59). He argued that the common school would empower workers to assert their rights and interests, and would give each man "the independence and the means, by which he can resist the selfishness of other men. It does better than to disarm the poor of their hostility towards the rich; it prevents being poor . . . . It would do more than all things else to obliterate factitious distinctions in society" (Mann, 1848, p. 60).

Political and Democratic Outcomes

Mann understood how the nation was still in the process of creating strong democratic institutions, and agreed with Jefferson that a literate and educated citizenry was essential to the functioning of such institutions. Thus, a major objective for common schools was to foster what he called "democratic competence." Common schools would equip citizens with the tools to function as knowledgeable voters, motivate them for civic engagement, and give them a stake in promoting political stability and social harmony. By ignoring divisions among different groups of people and providing a common educational experience, the common school itself served as a model of democratic institutions.

Religious and Moral Outcomes

Mann believed that building a child's character was as important as the teaching of reading, writing and numeracy. To his mind another important outcome of public schooling was the fostering of religious and moral values. As noted above, this was hardly controversial at the time.

As a Unitarian, Mann was heir to a liberal tradition that accepted the validity of truth coming from multiple sources and encouraged individuals to think for themselves rather than accept the word of ecclesiastical authorities and to show tolerance to differing opinions. Such an approach he argued, was fully consistent with the goals of a public school system. Schools could promote broad religious and moral values without espousing narrow doctrinal choices. Such views were vigorously opposed by leaders of other Protestant churches, who accused him of imposing what seemed like sectarian Unitarian orthodoxy on the public school system.

Nurturing Outcomes

Mann had a strong sense of the value of individual human beings, including children. He opposed harsh disciplinary methods employed by schoolmasters during his day and wrote of the "wonderful provision which the Creator has made for the care of offspring in the affection of their parents"

(Mann, 1846, p. 27). The mission of protecting and nurturing of society's youngest and most vulnerable citizens also extended beyond the immediate family to the common school. Both as individuals and as members of a community, he wrote, "we can cite no attribute or purpose of the divine nature, for giving birth to any human being, and then inflicting upon that being the curse of ignorance, of poverty, and of vice, with all their attendant calamities" (Mann, 1846, p. 31). He spoke with passion about the need to protect orphans or victims of parental abuse. "For these," he wrote, "society is doubly bound to be a parent, and to exercise all that rational care and providence which a wise father would exercise for his own children" (Mann, 1846, p. 27).

21ST-CENTURY VALUED OUTCOMES AND DISTRIBUTIONAL PRINCIPLES

In their 2018 book *Educational Goods: Values, Evidence and Decision Making,* Brighouse, Ladd, Loeb, and Swift introduced the term *educational goods* to describe the valued outcomes of the educational process in the 21st century, defined as "the knowledge, skills, attitudes and dispositions that enable an individual to flourish as an adult and to contribute to the flourishing of others."

To this concept of educational goods, the authors add the concept of *childhood goods,* valued outcomes that may be available only in childhood, such as purposeless play, naïve curiosity, unreserved joy, and carefreeness. Whether or not childhood goods have direct consequences for the quality of adult life, they are valuable in their own right.

Valued Outcomes

It is insufficient, of course, simply to define educational goods generally as those that enable an individual to flourish, and to contribute to the flourishing of others. For this concept to be useful, one must spell out the specific knowledge, skills, attitudes, and dispositions that provide opportunity for flourishing. While educational goods provide an opportunity for an individual to flourish, they do not assure it. Even when equipped with the educational goods to enable them to make good decisions in life, individuals still have the capacity to choose, and not all their choices may be wise. Moreover, luck is likely to be a significant determinant of actual outcomes. Individuals can be lucky or unlucky with respect to their health, unforeseen events, or accidents, and cohorts of students can be lucky or unlucky in terms of the economic conditions they face when they graduate from school or college. Thus educational goods should be interpreted in terms of *opportunity* to flourish and to contribute to the flourishing of others, not as specific outcomes.

To make the concept of educational goods useful, Brighouse et al. (2018) argue that the valued outcomes of the educational process include the following six capacities:

The capacity for economic productivity. Schooling can develop students' knowledge and cognitive skills and help them to develop the attitudes and dispositions that translate into productive work. This capacity is useful both for individuals and for the broader society, provided that the disposition to work is balanced by other dispositions important for individual and societal flourishing.

The capacity for personal autonomy. To flourish, individuals need the capacity to make their own major life decisions, such as what occupation to pursue or what religion to follow, as well as their own everyday decisions, such as what to eat, and what leisure activities to pursue. Although such decisions are influenced by family and friends, individuals need to develop the capacity to make their own choices given their own interests, talents, and experiences.

The capacity for democratic competence. In a democratic society, citizens benefit from the ability to use political institutions both to press their own interests and to give appropriate weight to the legitimate interests of others. The knowledge and skills needed for democratic competence in a complex, multilevel democratic system such as that of the United States include a basic understanding of the history and structures of the society's political institutions, as well as the ability and disposition to bring reason and evidence to bear on the claims and arguments of others. In addition, it requires a disposition to engage in the political process.

The capacity for healthy personal relationships. Although families play a major role in developing the qualities such as kindness and emotional openness that lead to healthy personal relationships, that process can be supplemented and reinforced by other institutions, including schools.

The capacity to treat others as equals. For society to flourish, individuals must be willing to think of all people, whatever their race or ethnicity, for example, as moral equals and to treat them with dignity. Developing and exercising the capacity to treat others with dignity is central to striking the right balance between pursuing one's own flourishing and discharging one's obligation to contribute to the flourishing of others. This capacity is particularly valuable in a society in which some groups have historically been discriminated against or are otherwise disadvantaged relative to other groups.

The capacity for personal fulfillment. Much of paid work is dreary or stressful. School is a place in which children's horizons can be broadened and developed through exposure to music, literature, the arts, games, and sports. The capacity to find joy and fulfillment from experiences and activities is at the heart of a flourishing life.

The authors recognize that different people will disagree about the appropriate balance between families, communities, and schools in the generation of each of these capacities. Nonetheless, there is clearly some role for schools to play in the development of all six of these capacities in the 21st century. Policy makers and others need to think carefully about valued outcomes and to make explicit tradeoffs among them based on reasoned discussion, attention to evidence and their own weights.

Further, tradeoffs must be made not only between one or more of these capacities but also between them and childhood goods. If children are pushed too hard in school to develop the knowledge and skills deemed to be essential for their future productivity in the labor market, they may lose the opportunity to experience the joy and wonder of childhood.

Distributional Principles

Brighouse et al. propose that there are three prioritizing principles for thinking about the distribution of educational goods: equality, adequacy, and benefitting the least advantaged. If the preferred principle is *equality*, then one needs to be clear about what is to be equalized. Ideally, it would be equal access to educational goods, not simply to a prior input measure such as per-pupil funding. Although more equality is generally preferred to less, however, full equalization might be too big a lift if it requires dramatically reducing the educational goods available to advantaged societal groups asserting other values, such as parents' interests in their own children's schooling. Alternatively, one might turn to *adequacy* as the driving distributional principle. The goal in that case would be to make sure everyone has access to a sufficient, or adequate, level of educational goods even if it means that some will have access to more than others. A third distributional principle would assign priority to programs that *benefit the most disadvantaged*. Such a principle might be justified in its own right, while also promoting the goals of equalization or adequacy as well.

BRIEF EVALUATION OF THREE CONTEMPORARY POLICIES

As we emphasized in the introduction to this paper, values are the proper starting point for the formulation and evaluation of education policies. In this section, we discuss how the two sets of valued outcomes for education—those promoted by Mann and those described by Brighouse et al.—can be used to evaluate three contemporary U.S. education policies: test-based accountability, school financing, and charter schools.

Test-Based Accountability

We use the concept of test-based accountability to refer to the policies that have been in place throughout the U.S. for the past 2 decades, starting with the Federal No Child Left Behind Act in 2001 and continuing today, although in slightly broader form, under the 2015 Every Student Succeeds Act. Throughout this period, states have been required to mount extensive standardized testing programs, including assessing all students annually in grades 3 to 8 in math and reading, and to use these test results to hold their schools accountable. Although states can supplement test scores with other measurable outcomes, such as graduation rates or school attendance, test scores remain the principal means of accountability.

This test-based approach to defining the valued outcomes of education is clearly at odds with both the 19th-century values of Mann and the more recent 21st-century concept of educational goods. Were he alive today, Mann would be appalled by the intense focus on test-based accountability. Mann had an expansive view of the goals of education that included, but went far beyond, the limited range of cognitive skills that standardized tests purport to measure. As discussed, Mann looked to the common school to (among other things) train productive workers, foster democratic competence, promote morality, and nurture vulnerable children—none of them outcomes that lend themselves to measurement through the reductionist lens of a standardized test.

As one who thought of education as the "great equalizer of the conditions of man," Mann would also have been troubled by the strong correlations that we observe between test scores and socioeconomic status. As such, he would also most certainly be offended by state-level policies that use the average level of test scores to assign letter grades to entire schools—thereby stigmatizing entire schools and groups of teachers and students.

Brighouse et al. would also find the policy focus on test scores far too narrow (see Chapter 6). As a starter, test scores in math and reading do not even attempt to measure the full range of knowledge, skills, attitudes, and dispositions that individuals need to succeed in the labor market, much less those needed to develop other important capacities such as personal autonomy, democratic competence, healthy interpersonal relationships, and personal fulfillment. When student test scores are used for the purposes of high stakes accountability for individual schools and individual teachers, schools have strong incentives to focus narrowly on the tested material, thereby taking time and attention away from other subjects and activities, such as civics, art, and music, that contribute to the other valued outcomes of the education process. Moreover, an intense focus on testing and test-taking skills is likely to reduce the quality of the school experience for many children, thereby resulting in a tradeoff with childhood goods.

Student test scores are appealing to many policy makers, because they are measurable and therefore subject to relatively inexpensive quantitative

analysis. If they chose to do so, policy makers might focus not only on average levels of student test scores but also on how they change from year to
year (often referred to as value-added measures)—a move that would counter some of the criticism that arises from the fact that student test scores
tend to reflect the backgrounds of the students and not simply the quality
of schools. Such use of more sophisticated quantitative measures, however,
does not make the outcomes measured by test scores any less narrow. An
educational goods perspective would push policy makers to develop approaches to school accountability that take a broader view of the valued
outcomes of education, while at the same time acknowledging that many
of these outcomes are not readily measurable for accountability purposes at
the student level. As part of this broader approach, policy makers will need
to pay attention not only to a narrow range of student *outcomes* that can be
measured but also to the quality of internal school *processes* that promote
the full range of educational goods that schools have the potential to realize.

School Finance

Under the U.S. Constitution, responsibility for elementary and secondary
education lies with states, not with the federal government. In practice,
states carry out this responsibility by delegating much of the authority for
operating schools, and often some or all of their funding, to local districts.
One consequence of this system is that wealthy districts, which have larger
local tax bases from which to raise revenues and may have smaller proportions of expensive-to-educate children, are typically able to provide higher
quality education than their poorer counterparts. Despite a long series of
court cases starting in the 1970s seeking to compel states to equalize school
funding across districts, large disparities in educational spending and quality persist within and across states.

Mann would be troubled by the pervasive disparities in the quality of
education that result from significant reliance on local taxes to fund schools.
As one who looked to common schools to serve as the "great equalizer"
of economic inequalities, he would be offended by a financing system that
allows wealthy communities or states to lavish public resources disproportionately on their own children at the expense of their less affluent neighbors. He would rail against the extent to which the current school funding
system perpetuates rather than mitigates class, racial, and ethnic differences.
We can envision Mann, were he alive today, as a prominent signatory to
court cases challenging state policies that deny access to a "sound basic
education" to all children.

In the absence of experience with a modern system of school finance
and a nuanced view of the distributional principles at stake, Mann would
most likely not be able to provide a thorough evaluation of the tradeoffs
involved in the current United States school finance system. As spelled out
by Brighouse et al. (see Chapter 5), any in-depth judgement must begin

with the distributional goals that one is trying to achieve. Within a state, for example, the question of whether it is fair for some local districts to provide higher quality education than others will depend in part on whether the distributional goal is adequacy or equality and how the two relate to one another. If *adequacy* is the goal, for example, and if there is sufficient state funding to assure that all districts have the resources to provide an adequate education to all children, significant variation in quality across districts might be deemed acceptable. That judgement, however, would also require a careful analysis of what one means by adequate. From an educational goods perspective one would need to interpret adequacy not simply as a minimum level, but rather as a level sufficient for children in each district to have an opportunity to flourish. If the distributional goal is *equality*, then any observed variation in education quality across districts would be deemed unfair. Yet even if the quality were similar across districts, one might still judge the outcome as unfair if the level was deemed too low to be adequate. If the distribution principle is *prioritizing programs that benefit the most disadvantaged*, additional complications arise in evaluating differences in per-pupil spending. Differences in the costs of inputs such as teacher salaries or differences in the proportions of high-need students mean that per-pupil spending in one school, district, or state compared to another may not accurately indicate differences in the quality of education. Some students, such as those from disadvantaged families, English language learners, or those with disabilities, are more expensive to educate than other students. As a result, one way to promote the valued outcome of a fair distribution of spending is for state policy makers to provide more per-pupil funding for districts with large proportions of high-need students, and for districts to do the same across schools within the district.

Charter Schools

Charter schools are public schools authorized by a chartering agency within the state and operated by nongovernmental organizations. Such schools are not subject to many of the regulations that apply to traditional public schools, such as teacher credentialing requirements, and are schools of choice in that no students are assigned to them. They were originally funded to allow educators to establish new schools redesigned for improved student success. Minnesota was the first state to pass legislation to enable charter schools in the early 1990s; now at least 45 states allow them, albeit with specific provisions that differ widely across them; while some charters align with the original model, many are now entrepreneurial and profit-driven. Although about 6 percent of the nation's students attend charter schools, the percentage is as high as 16% in Arizona, exceeds 50% in several large cities (including Washington, D.C., and Detroit), and is close to 100% in New Orleans.

Charter-school proponents justify them on the grounds that they promote experimentation, provide enhanced parental choice, and better educational opportunities for disadvantaged students, and improve education for all students because of the competitive pressure they impose on nearby traditional public schools. The empirical evidence in support of these arguments is mixed at best. An important prerequisite for the use of public funds to support charter schools would seem to be the presence of an appropriate accountability system to assure that individual charter schools are fulfilling not only the private interests of the children who attend them (and their families) but also the broader public interest.

It is probably fair to conclude that Mann would view charter schools as inconsistent with his conception of the valued outcomes of public education. At a time when schools were often in poor condition, teachers underpaid, and teaching methods erratic, Mann used his position as secretary of the state education department in Massachusetts to centralize control of schools, invest in facilities and normal schools to educate teachers, and otherwise build a strong public school *system*. Such a system was to be "universal" in that it was open to children of all backgrounds, and its fundamental building block was the "common school" that offered a shared experience and served as a model of democratic institutions.

To the extent that charter schools lead to a creation of a dual system of public education—two sets of schools operating under different rules—we can thus presume that Mann would have been skeptical. He would most likely view charter schools as undermining notions of universal and common schooling not only because they divert funds from traditional public schools but because they operate outside the discipline of the local political process.

Mann was open to the general concept of "choice" in the sense that, as a Unitarian, he wanted to encourage children to be open to new ideas and to think for themselves. Thus he might have been supportive of charter schools created to experiment with new approaches to pedagogy. However, he would no doubt be critical of the significant proportion of charter schools that, by design or otherwise, take advantage of parental choice to foster racial and other forms of segregation. Mann was highly critical of capital punishment and other harsh disciplinary policies that were common at the time and argued for more humane teaching methods; he most likely would have frowned on the many "no excuses" charter schools that use harsh disciplinary methods to generate high test scores. Kindness and love should guide teacher–student relationships, he said, not authoritarianism (Butts & Cremin, pp. 219–20).

Evaluating charter schools from the perspective of 21st-century values raises a number of thorny issues, but the overall concerns suggested by Brighouse et al. are likely to be quite similar to those that would be raised by Mann.

An initial question is the extent to which charter schools provide a vehicle for increasing school quality and thus the overall quantity of educational goods. Although many research studies have examined that issue, most, but not all, of them focus on the narrow outcome of student achievement as measured by test scores and conclude that, on average across the country, charter schools are no more effective at raising student achievement than are traditional public schools. At the same time, some charter schools, especially those in Boston, appear to generate not only higher levels of student achievement for their many disadvantaged students than the nearby traditional public schools, but also more positive long-run outcomes. But given that charter schools divert funds away from traditional public schools and typically lead to greater concentrations of expensive-to-educate students in the traditional school system, their overall impact on the level of educational goods in the system as a whole is not at all clear.

Two significant concerns about charter schools are similar to those that Mann would have been likely to raise. The first is that they disrupt the coherent operation of local systems of education. Because local school districts are responsible for the collective interests of all children in the community, they must plan ahead to assure sufficient school facilities and teachers for all students who need a seat in a traditional public school. The availability of charters makes that planning process more difficult because in any given year the district does not know how many students will switch to charter schools. Likewise, districts must be prepared to serve any students who return to the public school system when a charter school closes or turns out to be a bad fit for the student. Further, in some areas, such as Detroit, where there are multiple charter school authorizers and where charter and traditional public schools compete with each other for a declining number of students, the resulting excess supply of seats interferes with the efficient operation of the city's school system.

The second concern is the widespread tendency for charter schools to enhance racial and socioeconomic segregation. As schools of choice, charter schools typically cater to or appeal to different groups of students defined often by their racial or economic backgrounds. While there are many reasons to object to racially segregated schools, one worth highlighting here is the fact that they interfere with the educational good of developing the capacity of students to treat others with respect and dignity.

CONCLUDING THOUGHTS

Horace Mann was progressive by the standards of his day and established himself as one of the America's great—perhaps the greatest—educational reformers. His vision of common schools functioning as part of a system of free public schools has become the norm throughout the country and, as he expected, a foundation of the country's economic, social, and political institutions.

This essay has highlighted the numerous parallels between Mann's concept of the "valued outcomes" of schooling and those of a group of four contemporary authors. These parallels extend well beyond the teaching of basic literary and numeracy skills to include the formation of students into engaged citizens, productive workers, and fulfilled individuals. They also include the notion that public education has a mission to narrow socioeconomic and other gaps in society.

Many of the valued outcomes promoted by Mann and Brighouse et al. remain under vigorous attack by politicians and others at both the state and national levels.

For more than 20 years, the United States has struggled under federal education policies rooted in a reductionist view of the goals of education and the notion that successful teaching and learning can be measured by a student's ability to select among predetermined options on a standardized test. The continuing drumbeat of school finance court cases is evidence that the public and its legislative representatives remain reluctant to invest in high-quality schooling and, even more so, to mobilize public schools to function, in Mann's words, as a "great equalizer" in society. Proponents of citizenship education are struggling to find a place in school curricula. Powerful private foundations and individuals, including a recent U.S. Secretary of Education, are raising millions of dollars to undermine the concept of universal education by privatizing public education and, by means of vouchers and charter schools, to break the link between publicly supported schools and democratically elected officials. Racial resegregation of schools is now pervasive, and courts are retreating from the notion that public funds should not be used to further sectarian religious instruction.

In short, Horace Mann's vision of the proper valued outcomes of education remains as powerful and relevant as it was in the mid-19th century. Unfortunately, the battles that he waged to make this vision into a reality continue to be fought.

REFERENCES

Brighouse, H., Ladd, H. F., Loeb, S., & Swift, A. (2018). *Educational goods: Values, evidence, and decision making.* University of Chicago Press.

Butts, R. F., & Cremin, L. A. (1953). *A history of education in American culture.* Holt, Rinehart & Winston.

Mann, H. (1846). *Tenth annual report to the secretary of the Massachusetts state board of education.* Archives.lib.state.ma.us/handle/2452/204729?show=full

Mann, H. (1848). *Twelfth annual report to the secretary of the Massachusetts state board of education.*

Mann, H. (1867). *Thoughts selected from the writings of Horace Mann.* H. B. Fuller & Company.

Public Schooling as Social Welfare

David F. Labaree

In the mid-19th century, Horace Mann made a forceful case for a distinctly *political* vision of public schooling, as a mechanism for creating citizens for the American republic. In the 20th century, policymakers put forth an alternative *economic* vision for this institution, as a mechanism for turning out productive workers to promote growth of the American economy. In this essay, I explore a third view of public schooling, which is less readily recognizable than the other two but no less important. This is a *social* vision, in which public schooling serves as a mechanism for promoting social welfare, by working to ameliorate the inequalities of American society.

All three of these visions construe public schooling as a public good. As a public good, its benefits flow to the entire community, including those who never attended school, by enriching the broad spectrum of political, economic, and social life. But public schooling is also a private good. As such, its benefits accrue only to its graduates, who use their diplomas to gain selective access to jobs at the expense of those who lack these credentials.

Consider the relative costs and benefits of these two types of goods. Investing in public goods is highly inclusive, in that every dollar invested goes to support the common weal. But at the same time this investment is also highly contingent, since individuals will gain the benefits even if they don't contribute, getting a free ride on the contributions of others. The usual way around the free rider problem is to make such investment mandatory for everyone through the mechanism of taxation. By contrast, investment in private goods is self-sustaining, with no state action needed. Individuals have a strong incentive to invest, because only they gain the benefit. In addition, as a private good its effects are highly exclusive, benefiting some people at the expense of others and thus tending to increase social inequality.

Like the political and economic visions of schooling, the welfare vision carries the traits of its condition as a public good. Its scope is inclusive, its impact is egalitarian, and its sustainability depends heavily on state mandate. But it lacks a key advantage shared by the other two, whose benefits clearly flow to the population as a whole. Everyone benefits by being part of a polity in which citizens are capable, law abiding, and informed. Everyone benefits by being part of an economy in which workers contribute productively to the general prosperity.

In contrast, however, it's less obvious that everyone benefits from transferring public resources to disadvantaged citizens in order to improve their quality of life. The word welfare carries a foul odor in American politics, redolent of laziness, bad behavior, and criminality. It's so bad that in 1980 the federal government changed the name of the Department of Health, Education, and Welfare to Health and Human Services just to get rid of the stigmatized term.

So one reason that the welfare function doesn't jump to mind when you think of schools is that we really don't want to associate the two. Don't besmirch schooling by calling it welfare. Michael B. Katz caught this feeling in the opening sentences of his 2010 essay, "Public Education as Welfare" (https://www.dissentmagazine.org/article/public-education-as-welfare), which serves as a reference point for my own essay: "Welfare is the most despised public institution in America. Public education is the most iconic. To associate them with each other will strike most Americans as bizarre, even offensive." But let's give it a try anyway.

My own essay arises from the time when I'm writing it—the summer of 2020 during the early phases of the COVID-19 pandemic. Like everyone else in the United States, I watched in amazement this spring when schools suddenly shut down across the country and students started a new regime of online learning from home. It started me thinking about what schools mean to us, what they do for us.

Often, it's only when an institution goes missing that we come to recognize its value. After the COVID-19 shutdown, parents, children, officials, and citizens discovered just what they lost when the kids came home to stay. You could hear voices around the country and around the globe pleading, "When are schools going to open again?"

I didn't hear people talking much about the other two public goods views of schooling. There wasn't a ground swell of opinion complaining about the absence of citizenship formation or the falloff of human capital production. Instead, there was a growing awareness of the various social welfare functions of schooling that were now suddenly gone. Here are a few, in no particular order.

Schools are the main source of childcare for working parents. When schools close, someone needs to stay home to take care of the younger children. For parents with the kind of white-collar jobs that allow them to work from home, this causes a major inconvenience as they try to juggle work and childcare and online schooling. But for parents who can't phone in their work, having to stay home with the kids is a huge financial sacrifice, and it's even bigger for single parents in this category.

Schools are a key place for children to get healthy meals. In the United States, about 30 million students receive free or discounted lunch (and often breakfast) at school every day. It's so common that researchers use the proportion of "students on free or reduced lunch" as a measure of the poverty rate in individual schools. When schools close, these children go hungry. In response to this problem, a number of closed school systems continued to prepare these meals for parents to pick up and take home with them.

Schools are crucial for the health of children. In the absence of universal health care in the U.S., schools have served as a frail substitute. They require all students to have vaccinations. They provide health education. And they have school nurses who can check for student ailments and make referrals.

Schools are especially important for dealing with the mental health of young people. Teachers and school psychologists can identify mental illness and serve as prompts for getting students treatment. Special education programs identify developmental disabilities in students and devise individualized plans for treating them.

Schools serve as oases for children who are abused at home. Educators are required by law to look out for signs of mental or physical abuse and to report these cases to authorities. When schools close, these children are trapped in abusive settings at home, which gives the lie to the idea of sheltering in place. For many students, the true shelter is the school itself. In the absence of teacher referrals, agencies reported a sharp dropoff in the reports of child abuse.

Schools are domains for relative safety for students who live in dangerous neighborhoods. For many kids, who live in settings with gangs and drugs and crime, getting to and from school is the most treacherous part of the day. Once inside the walls of the school, they are relatively free of physical threats. Closing school doors to students puts them at risk.

Schools are environments that are often healthier than their own homes. Students in wealthy neighborhoods may look on schools in poor neighborhoods as relatively shabby and depressing, but for many children the buildings have a degree of heat, light, cleanliness, and safety that they can't find at home. These schools may not have swimming pools and tennis courts, but they also don't have rats and refuse.

Schools may be the only institutional setting for many kids in which the professional norm is to serve the best interests of the child. We know that students can be harmed by schools. All it takes is a bully or a disparaging judgment. The core of the educator's job is to foster growth, spur interest, increase knowledge, enhance skill, and promote development. Being cut off from such an environment for a long period of time is a major loss for any student, rich or poor.

Schools are one of the few places in American life where young people undergo a shared experience. This is especially true at the elementary level, where most children in a neighborhood attend the same school and undergo a relatively homogeneous curriculum. It's less true in high school, where the tracked curriculum provides more divergent experiences. A key component of the shared experience is that it places you face to face with students who may be different from you. As we have found, when you turn schooling into online learning, you tend to exacerbate social differences, because students are isolated in disparate family contexts where there is a sharp divide in internet access.

Schools are where children socialize with each other. A key reason kids want to go to school is because that's where their friends are. It's where they make friends they otherwise would have never meet, learn to maintain these friendships, and learn how to manage conflicts. Humans are thoroughly social animals, who need interaction with others in order to grow and thrive. So being cooped up at home leaves everyone, but especially children, without a central component of human existence.

Schools are the primary public institution for overseeing the development of young children into healthy and capable adults. Families are the core private institution engaged in this process, but schools serve as the critical intermediary between family and the larger society. They're the way our children learn now to live and engage with other people's children, and they're a key way that society seeks to ameliorate social differences that might impede children's development, serving as what Mann called "a great equalizer of the conditions of men—the balance-wheel of the social machinery."

These are some aspects of schooling that we take for granted but don't think about very much. For policymakers, these may be considered side effects of the school's academic mission, but for many (maybe most) families they are a main effect. And the various social support roles that schools play are particularly critical in a country like the United States, where the absence of a robust social welfare system means that schools stand as the primary alternative. School's absence made the heart grow fonder of it. We all became aware of just how much schools do for us.

Systems of universal public schooling did not arise in order to promote social welfare. During the last 200 years, in countries around the world, the impetus came from the kind of political rationale that Horace Mann so eloquently put forward. Public schools emerged as part of the process of creating nation-states. Their function was to turn subjects of the crown into citizens of the nation, or, as Eugen Weber put it in the title of his wonderful book, to turn *Peasants into Frenchmen*. Schools took localized populations with regional dialects and traditional authority relations and helped affiliate these populations with an imagined community called France or the United States. They created a common language (in case of France, it was Parisian French), a shared sense of national membership, and a shared educational experience.

This is the origin story of public schooling. But once schools became institutionalized and the state's existence grew relatively secure, they began to accumulate other functions, both private (gaining an edge in the competition for social position) and public (promoting economic growth and supporting social welfare). In different countries these functions took different forms, and the load the state placed on schooling varied considerably. The American case, as is so often the case, was extreme.

The United States bet the farm on the public school. It was relatively early in establishing a system of publicly funded and governed schools across the country in the second quarter of the 19th century. But it was way ahead of European countries in its rapid upward expansion of the system. Universal enrollment moved quickly from primary school to grammar school to high school. By 1900, the average American teenager had completed eight years of schooling. This led to a massive surge in high school enrollments, which doubled every decade between 1890 and 1940. By 1951, 75% of 16-year-olds were enrolled in high school compared to only 14% in the United Kingdom. In the three decades after the Second World War, the surge spilled over into colleges, with the rate of enrollment between 1950 and 1980 rising from 9 to 40% of the eligible population.

The U.S. system had an indirect connection to welfare even before it started acting as a kind of social-service agency. The short version of the story is this. In the second part of the 19th century, European countries like Disraeli's United Kingdom and Bismarck's Germany set up the framework for a welfare state, with pensions and other elements of a safety net for the working class. The United States chose not to take this route, which it largely deferred until the 1930s. Instead, it put its money on schooling. The vision was to provide individuals with educational opportunities to get ahead on their own rather than to give them direct aid to improve their current quality of life. The idea was to focus on developing a promising future rather than on meeting current needs. People were supposed to educate their way out of poverty, climbing up the ladder with the help of state schooling. The fear was that providing direct relief for food, clothing, and shelter—the dreaded dole—would only stifle their incentive to get ahead. Better to stimulate the pursuit of future betterment rather than run the risk that people might get used to subsisting comfortably in the present.

By nature, schooling is a forward-looking enterprise. Its focus is on preparing students for their future roles as citizens, workers, and members of society rather than on helping them deal with their current living conditions. By setting up an *educational state* rather than a *welfare state*, the United States in effect chose to write off the parents, seen as lost causes, and concentrate instead on providing opportunities to the children, seen as still salvageable.

In the 20th century, spurred by the New Deal's response to the Great Depression, the United States developed the rudiments of a welfare state, with pensions and then health care for the elderly, temporary cash support and health care for the poor, and unemployment insurance for the worker. At the same time, schools began to deal with the problems arising from poverty that students brought with them to the classroom. This was propelled by a growing understanding that hungry, sick, and abused children are not going to be able to take advantage of educational opportunities in order to attain a better life in the future. Schooling alone couldn't provide the chance for schooling to succeed. Thus the introduction of free meals, the school nurse, de facto day care, and other social-work activities in the school.

The tale of the rise of the social welfare function of the American public school, therefore, is anything but a success story. Rather, it's a story of one failure on top of another. First is the failure to deal directly with social inequality in American life, when instead we chose to defer the intervention to the future by focusing on educating children while ignoring their parents. Second, when poverty kept interfering with the schooling process, we introduced rudimentary welfare programs into the school in order give students a better chance, while still leaving poor parents to their own devices.

As with the American welfare system in general, school welfare is not much, but it's better than nothing. Carrying on the pattern set in the 19th century, we are still shirking responsibility for dealing directly with poverty through the political system by opposing universal health care and a strong safety net. Instead, we continue to put our money on schooling as the answer when the real solution lies elsewhere. Until we decide to implement that solution, however, schooling is all we've got.

In the meantime, schools serve as the wobbly but indispensable balance wheel of American social life. Too bad it took a global pandemic to get us to realize what we lose when schools close down.

Reflections on the Public School and the Social Fabric

*Mike Rose**

This testimony to the importance of the public school opens in the AmVets Club bar in Martin, Kentucky, population 550, circa 1990. I am here as a guest of Bud Reynolds, a celebrated social studies teacher at nearby Wheelwright High School, about whom I would be writing for a book called *Possible Lives* (published by Houghton Mifflin in 1995) documenting good public school classrooms.

It is 9 o'clock on a school night. Bud had earlier introduced me to the bartender, Tad, an ex-coal miner, and two of Bud's high school buddies, Tim Allen and Bobby Sherman Dingas, both of whom work for the one remaining railroad that runs through Martin. While Bud and Tim play a video game, I end up talking with Bobby, a conversation that reveals the place of school in both memory and the practice of day-to-day living.

Bobby is an informed guy with strong opinions, forcefully expressed. When Bud introduced us, he said I was from UCLA and was here to visit Wheelwright High School, so it makes sense that Bobby starts talking to me about his teachers.

He tells me about a high school English teacher who expanded his reading from "sports books" to other nonfiction and fiction, so that today he reads mostly history and politics, continuing to educate himself about the issues and events that matter to him. He also tells me about a chemistry teacher he admired, for he and his classmates "could never stump him," suggesting a respect for intellectual prowess. Bobby still seeks this man's advice, I assume about issues related to coal and the environment—hot topics in this region and for Bobby Sherman. Before the night is over my companion shares with me his frustration and anger about the persistent,

---

* Sadly, during the preparation of this book, Mike passed away. He was a wonderful person, a superb writer, an astute social commentator, and an ardent defender of our public schools. Read more about Mike's life and work here: https://www.newyorker.com/culture/postscript/the-teacher-who-changed-how-we-teach-writing

demeaning stereotypes of Eastern Kentucky, the Appalachian coal country in which Martin, Wheelwright, and a host of other small towns are cradled. "Sometimes I think the rest of the state, the Bluegrass and all, would like to see us disappear, drop off into West Virginia," he grumbles. And coal? While some citizens expressed nostalgic gratitude and support for what limited mining remains—mostly environmentally damaging strip mining—there was also anger over being abandoned and left with closed mines and lung disease.

My evening in the AmVets Club captures many of the issues that defined not only the Kentucky Eastern Coal Field during my visit in the 1990s, but also our national politics today. There is the urban–rural divide, involving economic, cultural, and geographic differences. Deeply imbedded in this conflict is pride of place, an emotional attachment to landscape and people. As well, there is sensitivity to perceptions of intelligence—something the writing of my 2004 book about American workers, *The Mind at Work*, attuned me to. It's about a sensitivity tied to region and economy, the kind of work that defines a place, a factor in our national politics that I think remains under-acknowledged. Finally, there is an important reminder that even in the most easily definable region, the bluest of blue states, the reddest of red, there is complexity—that here in the heart of coal country, there are conflicting political opinions, not infrequently held within the same person. Local schools exist within this regional social and political ecology.

What also stands out to me is the role several of Bobby's high school teachers play in his life. An English teacher changed his reading habits, and in a way, I assume, that contributes to his current political and social views. The expression of those views seem to be important to Bobby Sherman's sense of self and his civic identity. "Politics is real big around here," he tells me. I also can't help but wonder about the degree to which the intellectual challenging of his chemistry teacher—the cognitive give and take, the pleasure in it, his esteem for his teacher's intellectual ability—the degree to which this extended experience with this teacher plays into Sherman's own sense of self as a thinker, and as proof of the presence of "damned intelligent people" in Kentucky's Eastern Coal Field.

* * *

Let us move now from a town of 550 to Chicago, a city with the third largest school district in the nation, and to the story of a school and the community it represents—a quite different illustration of the role a school can play in both memory and in day-to-day life. Like Martin, KY, Chicago was part of my itinerary for *Possible Lives*. I visited six public schools in Chicago, one of which was Dyett Middle School, named after Walter Henri Dyett, a legendary music teacher in the Bronzeville community of Chicago's South Side. From its inception in 1975, Dyett was not only a valuable resource for neighborhood children, but also represented a rich local history of Black artistic and educational achievement. Dyett was a "community school" in more than one sense.

On a sunny and brisk fall morning the students in Kim Day and Dianna Schulla's 6th grade classroom are engaged in silent reading. Their room is orderly and vibrant, stacks of books and newspapers, the walls covered with colorful pictures, student work, inspirational sayings ("Hope, dream, and set goals"), large posters of Martin Luther King, Jr., and Malcolm X, and inviting pillows, rugs, a futon, a stuffed chair, where students are lying with their books.

Kim and Dianna then call the class to "Advisory," a time for students to say anything on their minds. The students return to their desks. They have questions about their books, for they will be giving reports on them. The teachers use each question as an occasion for instruction, having students engage their questions with their peers. When a question comes up about a book's difficulty, Dianna asks for their thoughts, then wonders how they could tell, in turn, if a book is too *easy* for them?

Students raise the issue of school transportation. A new bus schedule is resulting in some students getting home late, and a new driver is missing some stops. The students have a lot to say and the two teachers listen intently. Kim shakes her head, "Boy, it sounds like things are getting really confusing," and, along with Dianna, says they will report this to the school administration. The teachers offer advice about what the students could do to assist the new driver. Several children, still visibly concerned, raise their hands. Dianna steps closer to them, leaning forward, and says, "Talk to me." An inviting gesture. I leave at the break, so have a chance to talk to several students. "Students learn here," one boy tells me. "They teach you how to speak and write," a girl adds. "You feel at home here," says another boy. "They don't make fun of you if you mess up."

Twenty years later, Dyett was one of 54 "failed" schools targeted for closure by Mayor Rahm Emanuel and the CEO of the district. These schools were "underenrolled and underperforming." The story of how Dyett— which had been converted to a high school—ended up in this precarious state is comprehensively and powerfully conveyed in Eve Ewing's *Ghosts in the Schoolyard* (University of Chicago Press, 2018). What I offer here is a brief sketch of complex processes that affected Dyett—and a host of other schools in urban districts across the United States.

By 2000, interwoven with large-scale transformations in the economy, urban revitalization projects, and changing demographics and gentrification, a new wave of school reforms had some urban districts attempting to reorganize their schools into a "portfolio" of choices. Some schools were converted to selective admission schools or to magnet schools with a thematic focus—the performing arts, for example, or STEM, or healthcare— while other schools were defined as general admission schools. Add to this mix the growing number of charter schools, and one result is the diminishment of general admission community schools like Dyett, as their enrollment is drained away. And rather than the portfolio of schools opening up options for the young people in the Dyett community, many faced a host of constraints: transportation, crossing gang turf, and inflexible parental work schedules. Dyett fell prey to this web of forces. Its enrollment had fallen and it was slated for closure once its current students graduated.

But the community around Dyett wouldn't allow it, mounting a protracted, multipronged campaign that led, finally, to a hunger strike that made national news. In *Ghosts in the Schoolyard*, Ewing asks: If schools like Dyett are so terrible, why do people fight for them so adamantly? In essence, people fought so hard to keep Dyett open because it was *their* school in their community, a school for their kids and their neighbors' kids. "I just wanted to drop my children off," said Jeanette Taylor-Ramann, one of the hunger strikers, "and know that they would be educated the way I was." But they were also fighting for all Dyett represented, for a history of Black achievement in this special place, Bronzeville, and against a history of Black disempowerment, against having what is yours ripped away.

The children I saw during my visit to Dyett would have been in their late twenties by the time the order to close the school was issued—their parents in their forties or fifties. We have, then, a sizeable number of people in the community who associate Dyett with, as the 6th grader put it, feeling at home, with being valued and guided, and with learning about themselves, each other, and the world. These are the same qualities and outcomes parents want for their children. It is not hard to imagine all these people saying *no. This is our school. NO.*

* * *

There are over 130,000 public K–12 schools in the United States, Bobby Sherman's high school and Dyett Middle School (now a high school) among them. They have origins in Horace Mann's revolutionary reimagining of schooling. Before Mann, schools in the United States were private, religious, or charity-based institutions of limited reach; Mann's vision was of a universal common school, free to all children, not attached to church, funded by the public, for the public. Under his leadership as the first Secretary of Education for the state of Massachusetts and his subsequent advocacy, lecturing and writing, schools proliferated throughout Massachusetts and other northern states. Mann was a mid-19th century social reformer, so elements of his world view are certainly ripe for criticism—for example, that universal schooling could remedy the damage of economic inequality—but he still achieved something extraordinary: He generated a new idea into public consciousness. The public school became part of the American social fabric and the American identity.

While this connection of school and society is one of our country's democratic achievements, the connection also results in school enacting our society's capital sins: racial segregation, assaults on culture and language, economic inequality, gender, race, and class biases encoded in curriculum. Several of the teachers in *Possible Lives* experienced these violations as students—or knew of them from forebears—and the experience shaped their commitment to teach. These teachers represent the drive within the history of our schools—from educators, parents, and activist groups—to realize the promise of public education in the United States. Some of the tensions in this history emerge in the case of Dyett.

The public school has evolved into a complex, multidimensional institution. To examine this institution as it exists today and to help us further consider Bobby Sherman's high school and Dyett and its community, I'm going to adapt a technique from a classic article by historian David Tyack ("Ways of Seeing: An Essay on the History of Compulsory Schooling," *Harvard Educational Review,* 46[6], 355–389, August 1976). Tyack sets out to explain the development of compulsory school in our country by applying five different conceptual frameworks or "ways of seeing" to the emergence of legislation, from the mid-19th through the early 20th centuries, requiring that children attend school. Each of the frameworks reveals certain political, economic, or sociological-organizational aspects of the rise of compulsory schooling while downplaying or missing others, for as rhetorician Kenneth Burke, whom Tyack quotes, puts it, "A way of seeing is always a way of not seeing." Tyack argues that each of these conceptual frameworks draws on different kinds of evidence and "depicts different levels of social reality" and, therefore, by strategically combining them we gain "a wider and more accurate perception" of how and why compulsory schooling developed as it did. In practice, in its day-to-day functioning, the American public school is an amalgam of all that is revealed by these individual ways of seeing, but for analytic purposes, let us take each in turn.

Public schools are governmental and legal institutions and therefore originate in legislation and foundational documents. Both Bobby Sherman's high school and Dyett Middle School began as site-specific proposals. They, like all schools, exist in bureaucratic systems of administration and managerial authority, and decisions made about one school have the potential to affect other schools in the district. They are supported with public funds which are subject to oversight, and they have codified legal obligations and protections for employees and for students. Though school systems function according to the principles of modernity's organizational rationality, they are also subject to the turbulence of local and national politics, which affects funding, regulations, and the content of curriculum. Because public school funding in the United States is typically dependent on local property taxes, broader patterns of economic inequality get reflected in a particular school's budget. And, finally, in our time, there has been resistance to the structures of school bureaucracy with attempts to create alternative management structures, such as charter or pilot schools, which, whatever their merits, affect the funding and enrollment of other schools in the district.

All *institutions are created for a reason, have a purpose, are goal-driven.* The public school's primary purpose is to educate, so it exists in a policy web of curriculum frameworks and standards, textbooks and instructional materials and technologies, student grades, certificates, and assessments, teachers' contracts and union negotiations, counseling and advising practices, and more. These elements are subject to change for a host of reasons, from budget allocations to emerging societal demands—in our time, for example, there are calls for more math and science, for instruction in computer technology and literacy, for courses on the histories of non-dominant groups, and for compensatory programs to address inequality. The class I visited at Dyett was part of a program to enhance the education of low-income Students of Color.

Equally important as the content of curriculum are the underlying *institutional assumptions about ability, knowledge, and the social order.* The distinction between academic and vocational knowledge, the practice of curricular tracking, gifted and talented programs, honors courses are all based on theories of intelligence, the structure of knowledge, and the role of schooling in the social order. And although the fundamental purpose of the public school is to educate the young, within that meta-goal there are historically shifting goals concerning *why* we educate. For Horace Mann, a preeminent goal was to heal social fractures and level class differences through a common educational experience. There is in our history also a strong civic goal—we educate to create citizens—and an ethical-moral goal, to foster virtue and right action. (Mann also subscribed to these.) We educate, as well, to aid intellectual and social development. And we educate to enable people to participate in the economy—a prevalent goal in the contemporary United States.

Public schools are *physical structures.* Each has an address, sits on a parcel of land with geographical coordinates, is of a certain size, spatial configuration, and architectural design. Within its boundaries are buildings, classrooms, seats, walkways, benches, tables, and possibly landscaped spaces, playgrounds, and athletic fields. These physical features affect the flow of social life in the school, and can reflect levels of funding and of political and/or community support. Other features of the built or natural environment—which can change over time—surround the school and affect both the function and perception of it. The removal of public housing projects close to Dyett significantly reduced its enrollment, and low enrollment would become a factor in the decision to close the school.

By virtue of its location in a community, the school is embedded in the social and economic dynamics of that community. Current employment patterns and job opportunities, demographics, and political decisions affect a school's reputation, enrollment, workplace satisfaction, and a host of student characteristics from security about housing and food to beliefs about opportunity. Bobby Sherman was in high school when coal was in decline. There is a history to this current reality, which has an effect on the present. Earlier economic conditions, demographics, and political and policy decisions live on, affecting current educational and administrative practices as well as narratives and attitudes about the school. The designation of Dyett as a "failing school" and its scheduled closing was rooted in the demolition of public housing, changing demographics, and earlier administrative decisions to convert it from a middle school to a general admission high school.

The school is a multidimensional social system rich in human interaction. The continuous and fluid relationships among students, teachers, aides, counselors, and coaches are central to the school's educational mission. And there are other planes of interaction as well: among custodians and groundskeepers, food-service workers, administrative staff, yard monitors, security, and, one hopes, nurses and librarians. Professionals from outside the school's regular staff—social workers to speech therapists—as well as parents and other caregivers also enter this social system. And because schools are porous, social norms and structures beyond the school involving race, class, gender, sexuality, can be replicated within the school or, with effort, revised or resisted. There is much life lived on any given day, which in small ways and large affects the experience of attending or working at the school.

With the increasing application of technocratic frameworks to social and institutional life, it becomes feasible to view schools as *quantifiable systems*, represented by numbers, tallies, metrics. Some school phenomena lend themselves to counting, though counting alone won't capture their meaning: budgets and expenditures, seating capacity, attendance, truancy, and graduation rates. Other phenomena that are more complex have been converted to numbers, for example using standardized test scores in reading and math to measure learning or teacher quality. Numbers provide precision, an air of certainty when faced with multilayered and often politically messy policy decisions. Declining attendance and low standardized test scores were key metrics used in the decision to close Dyett.

And schools can be thought of as part of the social fabric of a community, serving civic and social needs: providing venues for public meetings and political debate, polls, festivities, and, during crises, shelter, distribution hubs, sites of comfort. But, of course, it is as an educational institution that the school becomes embedded in community and family life. Young people spend critical years of cognitive and social development in school, learning about themselves, others, and the world. To varying degrees, parents participate in their children's schooling; if nothing else, kids bring their school experiences home with them, affecting family dynamics. Because children come of age in school, school lives on in them, sometimes to damaging effect and sometimes positively, as was the case for Bobby Sherman Dingas. And over the years schools become part of community history and memory, at times with vital local meaning, as we can assume with Bobby Sherman's high school in a small coal-mining town, and as we saw with the protest activities surrounding the threatened closure of Dyett in Chicago.

* * *

It might not be possible to consider all of these perspectives when making major policy decisions about a school, but involving multiple perspectives should be the goal. The more ways we have of seeing a school, the more information from more vantage points we have, the richer and more comprehensive our understanding will be. As a rule, public policy decisions in our technocratic age tend to focus on the structural-bureaucratic and quantitative dimensions of the institutions or phenomena in question—that which can be formalized, graphed, measured. The other perspectives we've been considering, those dealing with economic, political, and social history and with the place of the school in a community's social fabric, tend to be given short shrift or are ignored entirely.

When egalitarian goals are involved in policy decisions, they tend to be defined within a technocratic framework, and therefore are understood and implemented narrowly. For example, in major school reform legislation of the early 21st century (No Child Left Behind and Race to the Top), *equity* was operationalized as reducing achievement gaps in standardized test scores. Responding to concerns about equity, implementing an equity agenda, should involve assessments of student learning, but the assessments need to be adequately robust to capture a wide range of cognitive and social learning as well as be sensitive to the cultural and historical context of the learner.

Creating or expanding opportunity for underserved populations is another equity goal given for contemporary school-reform policy. As we saw in the Dyett/Chicago example, opportunity was put into practice by creating choice options—which, paradoxically, involved closing existing options. In technocratic frameworks, *opportunity* easily becomes an abstraction. But opportunity is a lived experience, grounded in a time and place, and, therefore, there can be situation-specific constraints on opportunity. With school choice initiatives, one must ask if there are geographical and physical barriers to taking advantage of options, or transportation limits, or social barriers—barriers such as gang turf, or, as we sadly see in the news, hyper-vigilant, dangerous, racist neighborhoods to traverse? Also, opportunity has a social context and history to it. What past political decisions and economic and social practices—for example, union-busting or red-lining—killed opportunity in one's community and how do these decisions live on in the present, affecting not only the current material conditions of people's lives but also, through communal memory and story, how those going to school think about what is possible for them?

The technocratic orientation is so characteristic of our time that it affects everything from our approach to school and work to fundamental human pursuits such as ethics and happiness—yielding what the editors of a recent collection of essays call "the quantified life" (*The Hedgehog Review*, Summer 2020, 22[2]. Questioning the Quantified Life). It will not be easy for education policymakers to broaden their analyses of schooling, to interpret metrics and formalisms in the context of what one learns from the economic and political history of a place, from its social and cultural practices, from talking to the people who live there. But without this wider view, policy will be made outside of the multidimensional human reality of the institutions policy makers are trying to serve.

* * *

The journey I took across the country visiting schools for the writing of *Possible Lives* enhanced my understanding of the complex position the public school holds in the social fabric. *Journey* functions on several levels in *Possible Lives*. It provides a literary device to sequence my visits to different schools, a narrative throughline, a travelogue of schooling. *Journey* also has psychological significance. A journey is an odyssey of discovery, not only of the world out there—I would learn a huge amount about the United States and the schools in it—but metaphorically of inner worlds as well: from reflection on what it means to be an American to the emotional weight and texture education has for me. And journey becomes method. A journey certainly can be routine and functional, but it also has the potential to open one to experience, to learn, to grasp what architect and urban historian Dolores Hayden calls "the power of place." You talk to a guy in a bar who lives his decades-old education through conversation, an education he received in a school founded three-quarters of a century ago when the region's economy was emerging. That school would become embedded in local civic and social life while opening worlds to generations of students like the fellow standing before you.

If this kind of journey attunes you to the particulars of place and its people, it also provides the longer view. As you visit schools, you see similarities across difference and, eventually, interconnectedness and pattern. There is a grand idea in all this—and you sense it—a vast infrastructure of public schooling. Over its history, the idea has been subverted and violated, but revived by teachers and parents and communities across widely varied landscapes and populations, alive in a classroom in Chicago where two young teachers take their students seriously, inviting them to think and talk together, creating for them the deep sense that school is a good place to be.

Our Schools and Our Towns Belong to Each Other

Peter Greene

After all these years, I'm still a knight.

I don't mean a medieval tin-can clanging knight. When I graduated from high school in 1975, the school's mascot was a knight, and it was still a knight when I taught there for most of my teaching career.

Franklin Area High School is situated in a small town in a small county in Pennsylvania. It is the type of area where the high school you attended is on your list of identifiers, along with your family connections and your job. Tell someone where you went to college and they may well reply, "Yes, but where are you from."

We weren't always knights. The first high school in town ("The Academy") was set up in the late 1800s, providing only 3 years of high school education. By the turn of the century, we had added a fourth year. The first mascot had nothing to do with the school at all. A state politician wanted to make fun of how our little town boasted about some of the important figures who had come from here, and he mocked us as "the nursery of great men." The city simply picked it up and ran with it; consequently, the school's sports teams were dubbed "the fighting nurserymen." Unique, but not likely to strike fear in the hearts of opponents. But it captures how closely the town and school system identified with each other.

In Pennsylvania, every little township had its own local school system until the 1960s, when the state pressured them to merge. Many kept their elementary school, so that younger children were still attending school right in the community where they lived. These schools were part of the community identity. My own children attended an elementary school where the annual art display, talent show, and ice cream social were attended by everyone in the community—not just those who had children in school. Those mergers didn't just combine school districts; they shaped people's ideas of what towns they were connected to.

The school system made numerous changes and adaptations over the decades, adding courses of study and new facilities. While parts of the education world have recently discovered career and technical education, we've been doing it in a special multidistrict co-op school for over 50 years. I've had former students enroll in Ivy League schools to become doctors and others who became welders or musicians. Our students have a multitude of choices, and they don't have to go through the business of withdrawing from one school and enrolling in another to exercise those choices.

Imagine a society in which each child will enter adulthood by building their own home.

Some children will be born into families with ample tools and building supplies to pass on and share. Some children will be born into families with far fewer resources. We know—particularly in a small community—that the whole community benefits from having each child build the best home possible. So let's invent a facility where children are given access to tools and materials and guidance from experts in the many relevant fields.

Each community issues a guarantee—a promise that every child will have at least twelve years at this facility to learn as much as they can, to acquire as much familiarity with as many resources and tools as they can.

That's the promise of public education in the United States: that every single child will be given the chance to get as much help, as much training, as much knowledge as they can to help them build a life. They will be given time, resources, and expert support to figure out how to become more fully themselves, to understand what it means to be fully human in the world.

Have we always fulfilled that promise? Not at all. But the promise has been made, and that means we know what we are supposed to live up to.

Critics of public education like to label public schools a monopoly; I expect many residents of my city would be puzzled by the charge. It would be like complaining about the monopoly on streets or city parks—the school system is seen as belonging to everyone in town, a source of community pride.

A school system closely tied to its community does have its drawbacks. Whatever prejudices and biases live in the community will find their way into the schools as well, including biases about education itself.

And it can be tricky to balance the needs and interests of so many different stakeholders. Our community has always been invested in local employers and corporations, but those are businesses, and people mostly don't believe it is their place to tell business leaders how to conduct their business. But the school is an extension of the community, and everyone has ideas about how the local schools should be run—even if they have no students attending those schools. On some level, most folks in town understand that schools and businesses are two different things.

In recent decades, we've heard much about the notion that private businesses can better serve students. But business and the free market are fundamentally unable to honor the promise of public education.

Every business makes a judgment (sometimes explicitly and sometimes not) about which customers it is *not* going to serve. Whether selling widgets or waffles, a business must conclude that some potential customers are too difficult, too costly, too hard to profit from, to be worth that business's effort. Branding, marketing, and company procedures make it clear that some customers will not be served. There is no business in this country that declares, "We will make sure that our product or service gets to every single citizen of this country no matter how much time, trouble or money it costs us." Only public schools (and the U.S. Postal Service) make any such promise.

Over the past few decades, privatizers have worked to frame education as a service with parents and students as the customers. It's a useful framing if you want to cast education as a commercial transaction with a narrow outcome ("I'm going to buy this thing called Education for my kid so that she'll be useful enough to future employers that they'll pay her.") It's not a very rich or expansive view of education, or even of life. Certainly we want students to grow up to be employable, but surely being molded into useful meat widgets for future corporate bosses can't be all there is to life. This is not building a home for the future; it's helping some businessman build his home and hoping he'll let you live up over the garage. The business approach talks about accountability to the families, but underneath that, it's about accountability to the future employer. As Allan Golston of the Gates Foundation once put it, "Businesses are the primary consumers of the output of our schools" (see http://curmudgucation.blogspot.com/2013/12/the-wrongest-sentence-ever-in-ccss.html). Business demands the accountability of data and standardized tests and spreadsheets.

Accountability looks a little different in a small-town school system. If you work in a school, you meet stakeholders everywhere you go, from church to grocery store to local sporting events. After decades of teaching, there is not a bit of business I can conduct, from getting my car worked on to health care to eating in a restaurant, where I will not encounter a former student or their relatives. Communities like mine underline the argument of political scientist Benjamin Barber: Our public schools don't merely serve the public, but actually create the public.

But our public has varied goals. Some students want the tools to build a home far from here; some want to make a home right here. Some want to devote themselves to a profession, and some want to find an income that will allow them to enjoy their life. Certainly, we want students to grow up to be employable, but again, being molded into widgets for future corporate bosses can't be all there is to building a life, to building a future in which our students can be more fully themselves.

The idea of education as training for future employees is also a narrow view of education because it ignores so many other stakeholders. Families have a stake in education, and so do future employers, neighbors, spouses, fellow voters and taxpayers. Widespread ignorance is not healthy for any culture. No country benefits from an excess of dopes.

Balancing the concerns of all these stakeholders is always a challenge. It would be efficient for society for schools to determine what career path a child will be allowed to follow, but that approach strips a student of their freedom to build the future they desire. Additionally, society is seriously damaged by a school system that lets me look after only my own child's future and tell the rest, "I've got mine, Jack. I'm not paying to help educate Those Peoples' Children." To balance all these concerns, we need a system of resources that are publicly owned, publicly accountable, publicly managed, and so, publicly haggled over.

That haggling occurs in the context of diminished resources. Here in knight territory, we aren't as large as we once were. At its peak, the local system graduated about 200 seniors every year. Now the numbers are more commonly around 110, 120. There are four separate school systems in the county, and by all practical considerations, they should be combined. But though it is often discussed, it still seems unlikely to happen. Each school district is tied to its own town or village, and to give up the school as a separate entity would be to sacrifice part of community identity.

We have already taken several hits. About half of the elementary schools in the county have been closed and consolidated, and each closing has been a gut punch to the village where that elementary school was located. At first taxpayers blamed bad school board management and shrinking tax bases, but they have come to understand that other forces were at work. While brick and mortar charter schools have mostly avoided rural and small-town areas, Pennsylvania is a playground for cyber charters (i.e., charter schools that are completely online), and poor rural districts are among the worst hurt in real and visible ways. In one year, my old district closed two elementary schools hoping to save about $800,000; in that same year, their cyber charter bill was about $800,000.

The emphasis on high stakes testing has also taken its toll. Combining schools is one way to game the system; putting all your tested grades under a single roof means that one or two low scoring students have less effect on your district's ratings.

But those school closings have come as a shock; people expect their public schools to be there forever, and they expect such decisions to factor in the health and well-being of community, because folks see the schools as part of the soul and sinew of the community. We have a lovely park in the center of town; if the city council sold that park to a private company that then fenced it and decided who would and would not be allowed to buy admission tickets, city officials who okayed the deal would not survive the next election. Privatizing the school system would likewise be poorly received. The schools and the town belong to each other.

A system that honors the promise of public education will always have thousands of moving parts, always be out of balance, and always need constant adjustment. It is, as they say, the worst possible system except for every other system.

Every child deserves a chance to grow up with the opportunity to acquire all the skills and knowledge they can carry, everything they could want to build that future home, and as a society, we owe it to them—and ourselves—to give them that chance.

Such a system costs a lot of money, and there are plenty of folks looking at that mountain of money thinking that it should be in their hands. When they complain about "barriers" and "monopolies" and a "lack of freedom," they are talking about the barriers that keep them having a shot at profiting from education in this country.

Business and education don't mix well. Business likes simple, clear metrics, and a good educational system doesn't provide them. So we have seen metrics that are simple, but bad, forced on education. High-stakes test scores are clear and precise; they are also educational junk. Nor is business's other favorite metric—profit—useful in education. Schools don't make money, and the only way to make them make money is to spend less money on the students.

"All you need for your future home is this little, simple shack," say the edu-entrepreneurs. "It will save us money, and it's all you'll need for your life serving your employer's needs."

We have to do better than that. The freedom that students need is the knowledge and skills and resources to build the future home they dream of, plus the encouragement to dream big.

PART III

One of the bravest young students in America, Ruby Bridges, helping the nation to end the shame of segregation in 1960. U.S. Marshals were required to escort this young Black girl to the William Frantz Elementary School, in New Orleans, after a federal court ordered the desegregation of schools in the South. As soon as Bridges entered the school, White parents pulled their own children out; all the teachers except for one refused to teach while a Black child was enrolled. That teacher was Barbara Henry from Boston, Massachusetts, and for over a year Henry taught her alone, as if she were teaching a whole class. Ruby Bridges was initially apprehensive upon meeting Henry for the first time, recalling later that "Even though there were mobs outside that school every day for a whole year, the person that greeted me every morning was [my teacher], a white woman, who actually risked her life as well," and "I had never seen a white teacher before, but Mrs. Henry was the nicest teacher I ever had. She tried very hard to keep my mind off what was going on outside. But I couldn't forget that there were no other kids."

Image source: Wikimedia Commons

The Great Equalizer of the Conditions of Humanity

How Transformative Can Schools Be When Society Itself Remains Inequitable and Quarrelsome?

Peter Smagorinsky

Education then, beyond all other devices of human origin, is a great equalizer of the conditions of men—the balance-wheel of the social machinery.

—Horace Mann, 1848

Horace Mann's proclamation about the potential of public education to provide open, equitable access to the American Dream is still widely quoted. Its optimism about the transformational possibilities of schooling still inspires and confounds the 21st-century educator who is both committed to the prospect of an educated populace and frustrated that society remains divided and inequitable. I remain both moved by Mann's words and deeply disturbed at the number of obstacles to realizing their promise.

In this essay, I first review the prospects for equality in the U.S. at the time of Mann's famous dictum. I then look at what Berliner (2014) calls exogenous factors that affect schooling, that is, those from outside the school, particularly poverty. In my conception, I focus more specifically on factors that emerge from federal policies, and in particular on the top-down imposition of standardized tests as an exogenous factor that deeply affects education. Within schools I find inequities as well, particularly those that are structured to maintain the status quo. Finally, I consider Mann's rationale for universal schooling. He intended it to help assimilate a broad mix of immigrants into a national culture. Recently, however, trends towards multiculturalism among educators are thwarted by policy mandates for homogenization that often use Mann's vision for support. I explore how Mann's emphasis on assimilation is woven throughout the United States's historical effort to provide mass public education.

THE LACK OF EQUAL OPPORTUNITY IN MANN'S DAY AND BEYOND

Mann offered his view of public schooling as a great social equalizer at a critical point in U.S. history. In 1848, the United States was involved in a war with Mexico whose outcome greatly expanded the nation's western and southwestern territories, producing the present-day states of Utah, Nevada, New Mexico, Arizona, California, Texas, and western Colorado. Henry David Thoreau's opposition to the war and seizure of Mexican territory produced *On the Duty of Civil Disobedience* (1849). His treatise on the need for social life to be governed by matters of conscience was written from his jail cell, following his arrest for his refusal to pay the poll tax that supported the war and the expansion of slavery, both of which he found immoral. According to legend, fellow Transcendentalist Ralph Waldo Emerson visited Thoreau at the jail and asked through the cell bars, "Henry, what are you doing in there?" to which Thoreau replied, "Waldo, the question is, what are you doing *out there?*" To Thoreau, "The State never intentionally confronts a man's sense, intellectual or moral, but only his body, his senses. It is not armed with superior wit or honesty, but with superior physical strength. I was not born to be forced. I will breathe after my own fashion. Let us see who is the strongest" (p. 19). Going to jail imprisoned his body, but left his mind and conscience free to oppose the injustice that permeated the growing nation and its expansionist agenda, in spite of its claims to democratic ideals.

Social injustice was rampant during Mann's lifetime, which began in 1796, the year in which John Adams defeated Thomas Jefferson to succeed George Washington—the latter two both slaveholders—as the United States' second president. Mann lived until 1859, two years before the outbreak of the Civil War, a secessionist movement triggered by Abraham Lincoln, he of reluctant abolitionist ambitions (Harris, 2016), and his 1860 election to the presidency. At the time of Mann's famous dictum, the enslavement of people of African descent was legal throughout the South and some of its borderlands. Many of the military leaders of the Mexican War went on to serve as officers on both sides of the Civil War, including Robert E. Lee, Ulysses S. Grant, Stonewall Jackson, and William Tecumseh Sherman.

Although slavery and racial prejudice are attributed to the Confederate states, there was no public education for people of African descent throughout the nation during Mann's lifetime. Northern schools for Black children were a long time coming, and typically were set in dilapidated buildings and provided few educational resources. In the 19th century, it was illegal in many Southern communities for Black children to be taught reading and other educational basics, and the schools remained legally segregated through much of the 1960s under "separate but equal" policies that produced anything but equal educational conditions. This deficit of opportunity remains embedded in societal structures and helps account for the current "achievement gap" between Black and White students, which might more appropriately be termed an *opportunity gap*. This chasm has been deliberately crafted to produce inequity, established intentionally and systemically in both schools and the broader society (Lipsitz, 2006).

Native people were faced with educational inequities as well, during and beyond Mann's lifetime. They were granted citizenship in the lands they had occupied for 12,000 years only in 1924, through the Indian Citizenship Act. In the 19th century, through the Compulsory Indian Education Act (Lawrence, 1977), they were subjected to forced attendance at residential religious schools designed to efface their cultures, suppress their languages, and assimilate them to White ways. These schools persisted in some areas through 1980, in spite of efforts in the early 1900s to address Native poverty through more conventional educational experiences, whose goals nonetheless remained assimilationist at least as much as academic.

Native people had opposed this effort to Anglicize them from the outset of the republic, as evidenced by the Iroquois response to an invitation to "civilize" a set of native youth at Williamsburg College, reported by Benjamin Franklin in his ironically titled *Remarks Concerning the Savages of North-America*:

> We know that you highly esteem the kind of learning taught in those colleges, and that the maintenance of our young men while with you would be very expensive to you. We are convinced, therefore, that you mean to do us good by your proposal, and we thank you heartily. But you who are wise must know that different nations have different conceptions of things, and you will therefore not take it amiss if our ideas of this kind of education happen not to be the same with yours. We have had some experience of it. Several of our young people were formerly brought up at the colleges of the northern provinces, they were instructed in all your science, but when they came back to us they were bad runners, ignorant of every means of living in the woods, unable to bear either cold or hunger, knew neither how to build a cabin, take a deer, or kill an enemy, or speak our language. They were, therefore, neither fit for hunters, warriors, or counselors; they were totally good for nothing. We are not, however, the less obliged by your kind offer, though we decline accepting it, and to show our grateful sense of it, if the gentlemen of Virginia send us a dozen of their sons we will take great care of their education, instruct them in all we know, and make men of them.

As this response shows, not all believed in the civilizing effects of education, at least as defined by people of European descent whose values were inscribed in law and custom. Those who departed from enculturation to such standards were subjected to imperatives to assimilate to the dominant culture. Mann's faith in public institutions was grounded in their socializing potential. These institutions included public schools, which many saw as a vehicle for transforming unruly White boys, often from immigrant and working-class backgrounds, into disciplined members of an emerging national society. This goal was as much oriented to socialization as it was to learning academic subjects. Academic discipline could lead to personal discipline that could help those from "uncultured" backgrounds to fit better with the machinery of commerce and perhaps ascend into higher socioeconomic classes.

This endeavor was focused on the socialization of males, pointing to the great gender inequities of the 19th and 20th centuries, which persist today. The masculine emphasis is evident in the use of Mann's reference to "the conditions of men," the default term for humanity through the 1990s and remaining in currency through the present. In 1848, U.S. women were still over 70 years from being allowed to vote. In 1848, women in New York were granted the nation's greatest property rights with the passage of the Married Women's Property Act, and then the Act Concerning the Rights and Liabilities of Husband and Wife in 1860. These concessions still limited the opportunities for women to assert themselves economically and socially.

Mann promoted women's education, principally to prepare them for work as teachers. Prior to this period, women rarely were educated beyond elementary school, given the assumptions that their role in society was to stay home and raise their families, a value that has persevered in many streams of U.S. society. Teaching, nursing, and social work remained their primary possibilities for working outside the home, and then for the most part only until they married. It was not until President John F. Kennedy enlisted Eleanor Roosevelt to head a Commission on the Status of Women in 1963 that the U.S. government formally sought to create pathways for women to contribute to society outside the domestic realm.

Although the history of the early United States is often told in Red, White, and Black (see Nash, 2014), the nation included many Brown people during its Western expansion, particularly following the annexation of lands in the wake of the Mexican War that roughly doubled the size of the nation, and appropriated Mexicans as well as their territory. Mexican American children in Southwestern and Midwestern states attended "Mexican" schools on the assumption that these students had language deficiencies, even though many children enrolled in them spoke only English. White people of the era supported this segregation on the grounds that they didn't want their children to mingle in schools with what they called "dirty and diseased" Mexicans (San Miguel, 1988), among a host of other racist perspectives that helped to subordinate people of color. These prejudices persist today, not only among White nationalists but also visibly among many rank and file White citizens and those people of color who affiliate with their views (see Stirgus, 2019). Furthermore, children of color were essentially barred from university entrance under the belief that they represented a barbarian and lower social class to whom access to White privilege should be denied. Many states with large Latin[1] populations had a two-tier school system, one for "American" or White students, one for "Mexican" or Brown students.

Mann's famous vision from 1848 was thus an ideal that his society could not support. The nation was entangled in violent conflicts that produced and reified social hierarchies grounded in racism, sexism, and other forms of discrimination. His view that schools could serve as a great equalizer was thwarted by the systemic forces that produced inequities too great for schools to overcome. Those same challenges surround schools today, modified by changing times but tenacious in durable ways. I use my space in this volume to consider the degree to which Mann's faith in the power of public education is justified. The fervent belief in public education as the great equalizer and a cornerstone of our democracy is tenaciously held by many of our fellow citizens, even as privatization has systematically undermined public education, as people passionately disagree about how public education should be conducted, and as the debate continues about which alternatives, if any, should be available with government funding. But can schools produce equal opportunity in a nation that seems hell-bent on denying it, at least to some of its citizens? That question is well worth pondering.

MODERN SCHOOLING IN THE FACE OF EXOGENOUS OBSTACLES

Berliner (2014) has argued that *exogenous factors* account for variations in school performance, particularly as evidenced by test scores. In Berliner's account, exogenous factors refer to the conditions in which students are raised, that surround them in home and community life. They exert powerful influences outside the school's purview. In particular, poverty has demonstrable effects on students' performance in school, including how they do on high-stakes tests, the sole measure of achievement in educational policy. Policymakers, who often have little or no experience as educators, find reductive test scores to fit with their neoliberal accountability approach to measure the effects of complex phenomena such as teaching and learning. Meanwhile, researchers doing community ethnographies find that the same students who do poorly in school and on tests often are involved in sophisticated literacy practices in their lives outside school (Kirkland, 2014). They are not recognized as evidence of achievement because they take place outside school, they adhere to standards not recognized in school or in testing, and they validate the cultural practices of diminished groups in society, particularly those marginalized by race.

A broader conception of exogenous factors would look to systemic societal suppression of opportunity for women and people of color, both legal and in such less visible practices as redlining and discrimination in mortgage lending, housing discrimination, hiring discrimination, and many other discriminatory practices (Lipsitz, 2006). These barriers were in play in Mann's day, and remain factors today. School, Mann felt, could provide the socialization and academic knowledge that would enable people to defy the reproduction of the social division of labor (Williams, 1977) across generations and improve their prospects for prosperity, and the nation's prospects for growth and international standing.

Even with great advances in school enrollment, retention, and graduation, exogenous factors continue to overwhelm the possibilities for schooling to produce an equitable society. School's potential for realizing Mann's vision remains compromised by what goes on beyond education's reach. When a social system is stacked to benefit White people born into privileged circumstances, schooling's possibilities run aground of these systemic obstacles. Late in the 20th century, Kozol (1992, 1995, 2006) described the "savage inequalities" that produced differential resources and opportunities for wealthy communities and impoverished ones. The East St. Louis schools he featured were unsanitary and in such poor shape that the facilities threatened students' and teachers' health and well-being. But just as critical, the communities in which the school stakeholders lived were neglected and dangerous due to health risks that followed from contaminated living conditions. In contrast, the youth attending Winnetka, Illinois's, New Trier High School were supported by magnificent facilities, and returned home to mansions, tutors, and private coaches. The school and the community setting were conducive to the high expectations set by society and the community for achievement and success.

The schools could never solely make up for these differential opportunities. A person's prospects for living a healthy, satisfying life was rooted in the condition of the community. Communities like East St. Louis are pathologized and blamed for their own circumstances and the low character of their people. Yet the inequalities that Kozol termed as savage began outside the schools, making schools' academic task nearly impossible to achieve, and the decrepit conditions of the school facilities made teaching and learning secondary to staying healthy amidst the squalid physical environment. It's hard for schools to serve as equalizers of society when society is structured to reproduce inequity.

Impoverished schools and communities occupied by people of color persist today. Stories of unsanitary conditions continue to shock and dismay those who believe in the transformative potential of schools. In Trenton, New Jersey, "Students, teachers and faculty members have said the high school roof leaks, there is mold throughout the building and paint peels off the walls. They say brown water spews from water fountains and sinks fed by rusty pipes. School officials say they are concerned that the long-standing conditions at the school threaten the health and safety of students" (Pizzi, 2013). The nation's disregard for people born into disadvantage is greater now than ever (Alston, 2018).

MANN'S VISION AND THE CURRENT EDUCATIONAL LANDSCAPE OF EXOGENEITY

Mann's view that public schools can serve as the "great equalizer of the conditions of men" has been invoked by people from varying perspectives. Arne Duncan (2018), following his term as U.S. Secretary of Education during which he imposed the most extensive high-stakes testing in U.S. history, used Mann's idea to justify his neoliberal "reforms." His regime produced a "race to the top" of the test-score competition pitting schools, teachers, and students against one another in the quest for higher scores in order to receive funding. Duncan has relentlessly asserted that these tests provide the gold standard measure for assessing academic learning in ways that promote societal equality. He has claimed that his term as President Obama's Secretary was successful because of what he believes to be his "higher standards" for school achievement:

> the national graduation rate has hit a record high, with some of the greatest gains being made by low-income students, English-language learners, and Black, Native, and Hispanic students.

I don't know where Duncan looked to reach this conclusion, but it wasn't in many of the schools I'm familiar with. In Atlanta, high stakes testing produced a cheating scandal in which the only people punished were the teachers, who did as they were told by administrators held to Duncan's high standards. Many other school districts across the country learned that to play Duncan's game, they needed to cheat (West-Faulcon, 2011). Testing has long been a stimulus for cheating (Beckett, 2013), including that done by wealthy White parents who get their children benefits such as extra time through dubious medical exemptions (Downey, 2019).

High stakes tests have other social consequences. They are tied to dropout rates (Madaus & Clarke, 2001), leading Shriberg and Shriberg (2006) to conclude that

> Students, especially those from lower socioeconomic backgrounds, appear to be dropping out of school earlier and in much greater numbers than previously believed, and high-stakes testing may be a leading cause. Moreover, schools overestimate graduation rates, and NCLB [No Child Left Behind] actually provides incentives for schools to encourage students, particularly students expected to

perform poorly, either to drop out or transfer before taking their proficiency exams. (n. p.)

The imposition of testing regimens on schools is another form of exogenous factors affecting education. Berliner's (2014) conception primarily focused on the conditions of students' lives. My adaptation identifies a force from outside school, federal testing mandates believed to have an equalizing power, that comes from higher authorities rather than the community conditions that affect students' potential for learning. Taken together—cruel conditions and insensitive measures of achievement—they produce devastating circumstances for teachers and students for whom both are beyond their control.

INEQUITY WITHIN SCHOOLS, INCLUDING THE IMPERATIVE TO ASSIMILATE

Schools tend to replicate the social inequities that surround them, undermining their potential for making society more equitable. Racism provides a good example. Schools and society are segregated by race, among other demographic traits (Sikkink & Emerson, 2008). This segregation is manifested both in the enrollment of charter schools at the expense of neighborhood public schools, and in the "ability" tracking of students, which tends to produce segregated classrooms at the top and bottom of the hierarchy (Davis, 2014, and many others).

At the broad social level, according to Rothstein (2013),

> Narrowing the achievement gap will require housing desegregation, which history also teaches cannot be a voluntary matter but is a constitutional necessity— that is, voiding exclusionary zoning laws, placing low- and moderate-income housing in predominantly white suburbs, and ending federal subsidies for communities that fail to reverse policies that led to racial exclusion. Relearning our racial history, however, should be the first step. (n. p.)

Even in schools that enroll multiple racial groups, the classrooms are often not integrated (Fuller et al., 2019; Meckler & Rabinowitz, 2019). Yet integrating classrooms could produce a different sort of inequity. The rationale for desegregating schools and classrooms has often relied on the case that it's advantageous to have integrated schools so that youth of color can be around White youth, and strive toward their code of conduct. This perspective views the assimilation of students of color to White, mainstream conduct and values to be the first step toward creating equality. The same assumption drove the effort to "civilize" Native people. Socialization remains a major factor in the purpose of schooling. This perspective has been challenged by people of color who say that it's access to White resources, not White people, from which they would benefit (Leonardo, 2004).

The commonsense notion of school integration, then, can produce inequity, even as its proponents assert its potential for serving as Mann's "balance wheel of the social machinery." What appears fair to those in power, even those with good intentions, can be interpreted as patronizing and colonizing by those expected to gravitate to another culture's norms. This problem leads me to reconsider Mann's vision of education as an assimilation vehicle for a nation in which people from diverse national heritages were assembled, along with enslaved and conquered people from radically different cultural orientations.

MANN'S VISION REVISITED

Mann's vision of the possibility for schools to serve as equalizers across the spectrum of U.S. people has been met with resistance. His valuing of assimilation has come in conflict with the celebration of cultural diversity, however superficially practiced (Mills, 2008). His noble and admirable ambition provided the basis for mass education, and ultimately the possibilities for women to earn college degrees. I will try to put implementation of his vision into perspective in the 170 or so years that education has expanded following his leadership.

Multiculturalists have resisted the notion that homogenization is the optimal means of developing a greater civilization. They have argued instead that gravitating to the norms of the dominant White culture was not in the best interests of people from outside this historically central society. Consistent with Ogbu's notion of voluntary and involuntary minorities (Ogbu & Simon, 1998), they assert that there are vast differences between those who immigrated to the United States voluntarily to seek a better life, and those who are either subjugated natives or descendants of captured and enslaved people, in their willingness to adapt to White ways.

We are now in an era long removed from the inception of public education and its nation-forging mission. The nation has formed and reformed many times over. There was a hostile response to Outcomes-Based Education, for instance, which its critics believed was designed to produce a particular kind of person, but not the kind that many parents wanted to cultivate at home (O'Neil, 1994). Unless parents elect to enroll their children in a private school with specific contours, there simply will be no agreement on the sort of person a school should socialize students into becoming. The assimilationist intention thus stands on fragile footing in the current era of fractured relationships in a fragmented society.

Mann saw nation and person evolving together through the vehicle of school. Schools could help students view themselves as Americans and learn how to act American. Regardless of origins, they would all salute the same flag every morning, speak the same language, and learn the same norms. In hindsight, critics might find his influence to have had a patronizing, colonizing effect, imposing one notion of proper social conduct on all. This critique might emerge from many perspectives: postmodernism, critical theory, poststructuralism, postcolonialism, and others. Each would identify Mann as the embodiment of White paternalism, privilege, and imperialism, and note his use of power to subordinate people to comply with his social order, one that reflected his own upbringing.

Yet I believe it would be presentist to accuse Mann's assimilationist vision of being oppressive. I am using the conception of *presentism* that involves making moral judgments based on present-day values and knowledge about the thoughts and actions of people from prior eras and contexts (Fisher, 1970; Power, 2003). A presentist view of Mann would find him paternalistic in deciding what is good for outsiders and uncultured residents, who must gravitate to dominant values to improve their lives; or for women, for whom low-wage teaching positions consistent with their historical domestic roles were the only options in the workforce. Yet the needs of his day and those of the present are quite different.

Although presentism is inappropriate in judging his place in history, it is also inappropriate to invoke Mann as though nothing has changed. His phrase has become all things to all people, as evidenced by its summoning by Arne Duncan, whose fervent belief in endless testing has done far more harm than good for U.S. schools (Smagorinsky, 2012). Traditionalists might nostalgically yearn for a day when melting pot conceptions ruled public discourse, a memory likely reliant on mythology more than reality (Smith, 2012). However, the world is a different place from the world faced by Mann, although U.S. society was an unintegrated stew in his day, as it is in ours. Wretched living conditions for many nondominant people in his era, and every era since, suggests that his own times were highly problematic in ways that provide the template for today's inequities. Through education, many of the marginalized social groups of his day have indeed achieved higher social status. The assertion of their right to determine their own notions of appropriate cultural values and conduct, however, has complicated the effort to homogenize all into a national culture.

Paternalism and the imperative to assimilate diverse students into a single culture have long been at work. Head Start, for instance, tries to teach parents in poverty how to raise their children according to the values of financially stable White families. With good intentions of jumpstarting children's school success, it assumes that impoverished people benefit from lessons in a specific sort of childrearing designed to help their children start school on an even footing (see Schanzenbach & Bauer, 2016, for Head Start's account of "positive parenting"). Schools have similarly used both an overt and a hidden curriculum (Jackson, 1968) to structure school to reward those who best fit established norms, and to socialize students from nondominant backgrounds to the values of White professional-class people.

Assimilationist values thus have both been engrained in U.S. schooling, and critiqued by those dedicated to cultural diversity. Broadly speaking, these perspectives are manifested in what have been termed the Culture Wars (Hunter, 1992), pitting those who seek to conserve what they believe to be historical American values against those who find that effort to be oppressive to those from outside the dominant culture. If Haidt (2012) is right in concluding that defenses of each position are largely emotional and that argumentative reasoning is used as a *post hoc* means of justifying an established position, then it's unlikely that the Culture Wars will end any time soon, because no one can win them with logic or facts. The question of schools' mission—to serve as a homogenizing force, or to be fertile ground for cultivating diverse people's potential—will continue to be argued across the ideological spectrum, whose present poles are worlds apart.

DISCUSSION

I've reviewed here the ways in which Horace Mann sought to use education to solve a critical national problem of creating a unified nation out of culturally diverse people, including those either conquered by people of European descent on our continent, or abducted from Africa to do forced labor, or whose lands were taken by force. Schools have since served as the instrument through which other social goals have been promoted: moral training (Smagorinsky & Taxel, 2005), keeping up with foreign technology in military and commerce (Witkin, 1958), closing the gender gap in salary (Bobbitt-Zeher, 2007), and much more.

Exogenous factors have both produced these imperatives and compromised schools' efforts to achieve goals. Some exogenous factors are imposed through authoritative bodies that create assimilationist tools such as standardized tests designed to make curriculum, instruction, teachers, and students as uniform as possible. Some originate in students' home and community lives (Zigler, 1970), themselves subject to manipulation and oppression by those in power, yet often used to pathologize the students and their families and blame them for their own circumstances, and in turn, to blame teachers for not producing transformations that defy what students living in poverty often have available to them.

These factors compromise the possibilities for schools to serve as society's great equalizer and balance wheel. I've identified several factors that remain obstacles to schools' potential to produce a nation of equal opportunity. First, the nation has always structured opportunity inequitably, leaving schools in the challenging position of doing what can't be done elsewhere, and what many people are bound and determined to prevent from being

possible: equalizing advantage so that more people have access to constructing life on their own terms. Second, Mann's vision relied on his faith in homogenization, a process that met the needs of his day but that is contested in
today's pluralistic demographics where people may affiliate with more than
one culture at a time. Third, when schools have taken on a mission to mold
a particular sort of person, they have often been challenged by parents who
don't want other people deciding what kind of adults their children should
become.

There is also no consensus on how to achieve homogenization. Arne
Duncan thinks he's already done it, but I don't think so. Betsy DeVos believes that privatization is the answer, but that effort serves a small, wealthy
segment of the population well, along with edu-entrepreneurs eager to cap-
italize on scholastic markets in which consumers can get the facts that they
prefer to believe. At least DeVos doesn't quote Horace Mann, and indeed
finds him to be the problem: "According to DeVos, those who direct the
prevailing K–12 system are 'trapped in an outdated education model,' beholden to the 'wrong and manipulative' theories of Horace Mann and John
Dewey" (quoted in DeGrow, 2017). DeGrow summarizes a fundamental
divide in how people perceive the role of schools in 21st century U.S. society: "The education secretary sharply criticized the orthodoxy that entitles
government officials to use parents' tax dollars to decide where and what
and how their children learn, even though parents are accustomed to making choices in nearly all other aspects of their children's lives." I'd add to the
list of choices: What sort of person should emerge from a public education?
There's simply too much contention around this issue for it to be resolved, a
problem especially evident when the wealthiest people control public institutions in the interests of people like themselves.

Can the public school system produce an equal society? Not on its own,
I'm afraid; and not in an era when class resentments make it unlikely that
people will set aside their own gains to help others get a leg up. As Grunwald (2018) and many other commentators have noted, the Culture Wars
are fiercer now than ever, with schools more a battleground than equalizer,
a point that has become amplified since Nieto (2005) made it during George
W. Bush's presidency.

And so, I remain torn between hope and discouragement. I believe in education, although don't always agree with how it's conducted. But it seems
increasingly dwarfed in potential by the political cacophony that surrounds
it, the culture wars, the public policies that benefit the wealthy, neoliberal
values that don't look beyond reductive bottom line indicators, and many
other exogenous factors. As long as the public remains at odds, schools will
have difficulty becoming the dog that wags the social tail and will constantly
be at the mercy of those holding the most power.

NOTE

1. I use "Latin" rather than Latino, Latina, Latino/a, Latin@, or Latinx, all of which include suffixes with a gendered identification (Latinx, the au courant term, takes its suffix from the transgender movement).

REFERENCES

Alston, P. (2018, June 4). "Contempt for the poor in US drives cruel policies," says UN expert. *United Nations Office of the High Commissioner on Human Rights.* https://www.ohchr.org/EN/NewsEvents/Pages/DisplayNews. aspx?NewsID=23172&LangID=E

Beckett, L. (2013). America's most outrageous teacher cheating scandals. *ProPublica.* https://www.propublica.org/article/americas-most-outrageous-teacher-cheating-scandals

Berliner, D. C. (2014). Exogenous variables and value-added assessments: A fatal flaw. *Teachers College Record, 116*(1), 1–31.

Bobbitt-Zeher, D. (2007). The gender income gap and the role of education. *Sociology of Education, 80*, 1–22.

Davis, T. M. (2014). School choice and segregation: "Tracking" racial equity in magnet schools. *Education and Urban Society, 46*(4), 399–433.

DeGrow, B. (2017, October 30). DeVos: Fight for students, not over them: Secretary of Education makes powerful case for parental choice. *Mackinac Center for Public Policy.* https://www.mackinac.org/devos-fight-for-students-not-over-them

Downey, M. (2019, October 1). Should clock be ticking during SAT and other high-stakes tests? Affluent parents take advantage of loopholes to earn their kids more time on exams. *Get Schooled Blog of the Atlanta Journal-Constitution.* https://www.ajc.com/blog/get-schooled/should-clock-ticking-during-sat-and-other-high-stakes-tests/p6GaDK8gXGwXoXkGnmPFuI/

Duncan, A. (2018, May 25). Education: The "great equalizer." *Britannica.com.* https://www.britannica.com/topic/Education-The-Great-Equalizer-2119678

Fisher, D. H. (1970). *Historians' fallacies: Toward a logic of historical thought.* Harper & Row.

Fuller, B., Kim, Y., Galindo, C., Bathia, S., Bridges, M., Duncan, G. J., & García Valdivia, I. (2019). Worsening school segregation for Latino children? *Educational Researcher 48*(7), 407–420. https://doi.org/10.3102/0013189X19860814

Grunwald, M. (2018, November/December). How everything became the culture war. *Politico.* https://www.politico.com/magazine/story/2018/11/02/culture-war-liberals-conservatives-trump-2018-222095

Haidt, J. (2012). *The righteous mind: Why good people are divided by politics and religion.* Vintage.

Harris, C. (2016, August 9). *#NEVERLINCOLN: Abolitionists and the 1860 election.* President Lincoln's Cottage. https://www.lincolncottage.org/neverlincoln-abolitionists-and-the-1860-election/

Hunter, J. D. (1992). *Culture wars: The struggle to control the family, art, education, law, and politics in America.* Basic Books.

Jackson, P. W. (1968). *Life in classrooms.* Holt, Rinehart, & Winston.

Kirkland, D. E. (2014, November). *The lies "big data" tell: Rethinking the literate performances of black males through a modified meta-analysis of qualitative "little" data.* Paper presented at the annual convention of the National Council of Teachers of English, National Harbor, MD.

Kozol, J. (1992). *Savage inequalities: Children in America's schools.* Harper Perennial.

Kozol, J. (1995). *Amazing grace: The lives of children and the conscience of a nation.* Harper Perennial.

Kozol, J. (2006). *The shame of the nation: The restoration of apartheid schooling in America.* Three Rivers Press.

Lawrence, R. (1977). Indian Education: Federal Compulsory School Attendance Law Applicable to American Indians: The Treaty-Making Period: 1857–1871, *American Indian Law Review, 5*(2), 393–413

Leonardo, Z. (2004). The color of supremacy: Beyond the discourse of 'white privilege.' *Educational Philosophy and Theory, 36*(2), 137–152.

Lipsitz, G. (2006). *The possessive investment in whiteness: How white people profit from identity politics.* Temple University Press.

Madaus, G. F., & Clarke, M. (2001). The adverse impact of high-stakes testing on minority students: Evidence from 100 years of test data. In G. Orfield & M. Kornhaber (Eds.), *Raising standards or raising barriers? Inequality and high stakes testing in public education* (pp. 85–106). The Century Foundation. https://files.eric.ed.gov/fulltext/ED450183.pdf

Meckler, L., & Rabinowitz, K. (2019, September 12). The changing face of school integration. *The Washington Post.* https://www.washingtonpost.com/education/2019/09/12/more-students-are-going-school-with-children-different-races-schools-big-cities-remain-deeply-segregated/?arc404=true

Mills, C. (2008). Making a difference: Moving beyond the superficial treatment of diversity. *Asia-Pacific Journal of Teacher Education, 36*(4), 261–275.

Nash, G. B. (2014). *Red, white, and black: The peoples of early North America* (7th ed.). Pearson.

Nieto, S. (2005). Public education in the twentieth century and beyond: High hopes, broken promises, and an uncertain future. *Harvard Educational Review, 75*(1), 43–64.

Ogbu, J. U., & Simons, H. D. (1998). Voluntary and involuntary minorities: A cultural-ecological theory of school performance with some implications for education. *Anthropology & Education Quarterly, 29*(2), 155–188.

O'Neil, J. (1994, March). Outcomes-Based Education comes under attack: OBE supporters try to counter recent setbacks. *ASCD Education Update, 36*(3). http://www.ascd.org/publications/newsletters/education_update/mar94/vol36/num03/Outcomes-Based_Education_Comes_Under_Attack.aspx

Pizzi, J. (2013, October 11; updated March 30, 2019). School Development Authority asks court to throw out Trenton school board's lawsuit. *NJ.com.* https://www.nj.com/mercer/2013/10/school_development_authority_asks_court_to_throw_out_trenton_school_boards_lawsuit.html

Power, C. L. (2003). Challenging the pluralism of our past: Presentism and the selective tradition in historical fiction written for young people. *Research in the Teaching of English, 37*, 425–466.

Rothstein, R. (2013). Why our schools are segregated. *Faces of Poverty, 70*(8), 50–55. http://www.ascd.org/publications/educational-leadership/may13/vol70/num08/Why-Our-Schools-Are-Segregated.aspx

San Miguel, G., Jr. (1988). *"Let all of them take heed": Mexican Americans and the campaign for education equality in Texas, 1910–1981.* University of Texas Press.

Schanzenbach, D. W., & Bauer, L. (2016, August 19). The long-term impact of the Head Start program. *The Brookings Institution.* https://www.brookings.edu/research/the-long-term-impact-of-the-head-start-program/

Shriberg, D., & Shriberg, A. B. (2006, Fall). High-stakes testing and dropout rates. *Dissent Magazine.* https://www.dissentmagazine.org/article/high-stakes-testing-and-dropout-rates

Sikkink, D., & Emerson, M. O. (2008). School choice and racial segregation in U.S. schools: The role of parents' education. *Ethnic and Racial Studies, 31*(2), 267–293.

Smagorinsky, P. (2012, March 11). Why the Ed Department should be reconceived—or abolished. *Washington Post, The Answer Sheet.* https://www.washingtonpost.com/blogs/answer-sheet/post/why-the-ed-department-should-be-reconceived--or-abolished/2012/03/09/gIQAHfdB5R_blog.html

Smagorinsky, P., & Taxel, J. (2005). *The discourse of character education: Culture wars in the classroom.* Erlbaum.

Smith, D. M. (2012). The American melting pot: A national myth in public and popular discourse. *National Identities, 14*(4), 387–402.

Stirgus, E. (2019, June 7). Georgia professor's immigration comments cause stir on social media. *Atlanta Journal-Constitution.* https://www.ajc.com/news/local-education/georgia-professor-immigration-comments-cause-stir-social-media/17i7NphdnCroxthP0Sz5hJ/

Thoreau, H. D. (1849). *On the duty of civil disobedience.* https://www.ibiblio.org/ebooks/Thoreau/Civil%20Disobedience.pdf

West-Faulcon, K. (2011, August 22, revd. 2017). The real cheating scandal of standardized tests. *Pacific Standard.* https://psmag.com/education/the-real-cheating-scandal-of-standardized-tests-35282

Williams, R. (1977). *Marxism and literature.* Oxford University Press.

Witkin, R. (Ed.) (1958). *The challenge of the Sputnik.* Doubleday.

Zigler, E. (1970). Social class and the socialization process. *Review of Educational Research, 40*(1), 87–110.

The Mythical Great Equalizer School System

Exploring the Potential to Make It Real

Kevin Welner

In 1848, the same year that Karl Marx published the *Communist Manifesto*, Horace Mann articulated a very different vision for how society should elevate people living in poverty. For the prior 11 years, Mann had served as the first Secretary of the Massachusetts State Board of Education, and he had come to embrace the potential of common schools to bring about non-revolutionary change. In today's parlance, he saw education as a way to *expand the pie* by increasing innovation and productivity, rather than fighting over how to re-divide the existing pie.

This vision is set forth in Mann's best-known work, his 12th Annual Report to the Massachusetts State Board of Education. Consider the following passage, which includes his often-cited "Great Equalizer" language:

> Education, then, beyond all other devices of human origin, is the great equalizer of the conditions of men,—the balance-wheel of the social machinery. I do not here mean that it so elevates the moral nature as to make men disdain and abhor the oppression of their fellow-men. This idea pertains to another of its attributes. But I mean that it gives each man the *independence and the means* by which he can resist the selfishness of other men. *It does better than to disarm the poor of their hostility towards the rich: it prevents being poor.* (Mann, 1848, pp. 59–60, emphasis added)

Notwithstanding the phrasing in Mann's report, "preventing" or "removing" poverty is not the same thing as being a "great equalizer of the conditions of men." Mann is piling hyperbole upon hyperbole when he ramps up from the former to the latter. But he is not alone in rhetorically invoking the ideal of the Great Equalizer. President Obama's Education Secretary Arne Duncan, for instance, asserted at a college graduation in 2011 that, "in America, education is still the great equalizer" (Duncan, 2011).

President Trump's Education Secretary Betsy DeVos agreed: "Education is indeed the great equalizer" (DeVos, 2018). (Tellingly, she also embraced "school choice" as the "great equalizer" [DeVos, 2019].) Secretary Miguel Cardona lost no time joining in. At his Senate confirmation hearing, he said, "If I am fortunate enough to be confirmed, I will work tirelessly to make sure our education system is a door to opportunity. A great equalizer, for every American" (Cardona, 2021).

These are examples of using "great equalizer" as a rhetorical flourish. They are nods in the direction of a comforting myth, unaccompanied by a serious consideration of what the idea might really encompass or what an actual great equalizer would entail. A myth is very different than an outcome standard or a concrete policy goal.

Yet such serious consideration is important, if only to concretize the gap between where we are and where we hope to be. What would it take for schools to play this extraordinary role of the Great Equalizer, if we are to assume its plausibility? Can schools balance out societal inequality? If that inequality is left unaddressed, along with the harm it does to children, can policymakers reasonably expect an outcome of rough equality through focusing instead on building a dazzling public school system that would envelop those children in rich opportunities to learn? Admittedly, this describes an odd (and cruel) policy approach: to first inflict awful harm on children and then pour resources into schools in a desperate attempt to mitigate that harm. Yet the unabated harm is being inflicted whether or not we approve, so it behooves us to consider the second half of the policy equation. What would public schools have to be in order for them to meet the Great Equalizer standard? I define that standard—based on my understanding of the myth—as a public school system that counterbalances societal inequities and gives each new generation a relatively equal chance at success, by providing students from all backgrounds with educational opportunities that prepare them to succeed economically and socially in college, careers, and life.

TWO WAYS TO LIFT UP ALL CHILDREN

In 2016, working with colleagues including Patrick St. John of the Schott Foundation, I helped present some of these ideas in an infographic titled "Lifting All Children Up."[1] In Figure 8.1, which incorporates some of that infographic, Great Equalizer Reforms are represented by attaching balloons to lift up our schools. Alternatively, a second option that we call Systemic Social Safety Net Reforms focuses on addressing the concentrated poverty and racism that drive so many of the opportunity gaps. This option is represented by cutting off the weights that pull down our schools and communities, and it turns to social policies outside of schools (e.g., healthcare, housing, and employment) that can address the weights directly. It shifts the

Figure 8.1. Great Equalizer vs. Systemic Social Safety Net

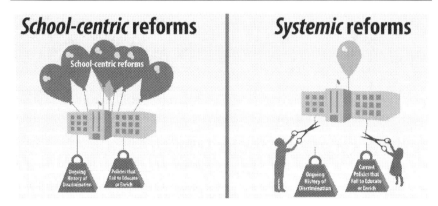

burden from public schools to society as a whole. Good policy would turn to both of these approaches, but current policy in the United States does neither.

A key problem that state legislators, courts, and educators all face is that they are working within the constraints of school-centric reforms, as shaped by the Great Equalizer myth. To understand this problem, consider the "education production function" and "variance decomposition" research that attempts to apportion variance to different predictors (such as teacher quality) of measured student outcomes.

> This body of research provides us with a clear range. At the high end are estimates that apportion test-score variance at about 20 percent school plus another 20 percent classroom/teacher, and at the low end are estimates that apportion about 20 percent combined for school plus classroom/teacher. The remaining 60–80 percent is then assigned to student-level factors, such as race/ethnicity, wealth/income/socioeconomic status, and prior measured achievement—plus unobserved and unexplained (error) factors. "[T]hough precise estimates vary, the preponderance of evidence shows that achievement differences are overwhelmingly attributable to factors outside of schools and classrooms" (Welner & LaCour, 2018).

Imagine a task whereby you are given a heavy vehicle with two engines that work in concert, one of which provides 70% of the horsepower. Your task is to double the power of the vehicle's combined engines, but you are told to leave the larger engine alone and tinker only with the smaller engine—the one accounting for the remaining 30% of the horsepower. To get that 100% increase, you will have to increase that smaller engine's power by 433%. In a nutshell, that is the irrational challenge of "Great

Equalizer" thinking: when we fail to address larger societal inequalities, we place unreasonable demands on our schools. Nonetheless, that is the challenge framed by the nation's long-standing policy approach.

WE ARE FAR SHORT OF THE GREAT EQUALIZER

Meanwhile, the national discussion of school funding is so impoverished that we celebrate small charitable donations to donorschoose.org and pat ourselves on the back for allowing teachers an annual federal tax deduction for up to $250 for their out-of-pocket spending for classroom expenses (Ujifusa, 2017). We hail states like New Jersey and Washington when legislators finally stop dragging their feet in response to decades of court orders in adequacy cases (O'Sullivan, 2018). But the legislators never actually meet or exceed the adequacy standard—and that standard remains far below what is needed if those states' schools are to have a decent shot at becoming the Great Equalizer.

In 2019, I worked with colleagues including Ichigo Takikawa to present, again in the form of an infographic, the steps that some states have taken in meeting schools' resource needs (see Figure 8.2). We graphically represent the difference between stepping up to an adequacy goal and then reaching for a great-equalizer goal. A constitutional floor of adequacy means, for example, that school districts in more impoverished communities receive funding that is roughly the same as wealthier districts (*Abbott v. Burke*, 1994). At best, courts require the legislature to fund specific supplementary programs addressing schools' most dire needs (*Abbott v. Burke*, 1994). With New Jersey serving as a best-case scenario of resource reform, we can consider how far states must still improve before reaching a great-equalizer standard. The state's achievement gaps are around the national average, which is quite large (The Nation's Report Card, 2019).

Imagine school finance reform as a set of stairs, as shown in Figure 8.2. Ground level is the level of inequality that existed in the mid-1960s, before the first wave of school-finance litigation. Currently, a state is on one of the first three steps depending on the level of progress it has made toward addressing those inequalities. The states on the highest of these steps use their funding formulas to target more resources to school districts with the greatest need.

However, no state has yet reached the fourth step—the level of equity that we call "minimal adequacy." This is defined as the additional resources needed to give all students a realistic shot at reaching basic levels set forth by state standards and accountability systems. Even if we were ever to get to that point, vast inequality would remain in place because of opportunity gaps that arise due to societal inequalities. Closing those opportunity gaps via formal schooling will require a great deal more in terms of school resources.

Figure 8.2. Climbing Toward the Great Equalizer

Climbing Toward the Great Equalizer

The **opportunity gaps** children face in schools are greatly expanded by inequalities tied to concentrated poverty and racism that children and their families face outside of school. If schools are to become the **Great Equalizer** and close those cumulative gaps, they need much greater resources.

States must therefore climb these steps, moving beyond low levels of support, toward minimal adequacy and then climb up to the "Great Equalizer" standard. This is the true top of the staircase, where the level of enrichment provided in schools is sufficient to bridge the vast opportunity gaps.

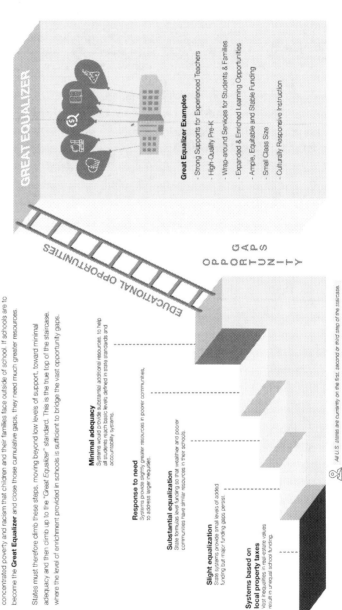

Minimal adequacy
Systems would provide substantial additional resources, to help all students reach basic levels defined in state standards and accountability systems.

Response to need
Systems provide slightly greater resources in poorer communities, to address larger inequities.

Substantial equalization
State formulas level funding so that wealthier and poorer communities have similar resources in their schools.

Slight equalization
State systems provide small levels of added funding but major funding gaps persist.

Systems based on local property taxes
Vast inequalities in real-estate values result in unequal school funding.

Great Equalizer Examples
- Strong Supports for Experienced Teachers
- High-Quality Pre-K
- Wrap-around Services for Students & Families
- Expanded & Enriched Learning Opportunities
- Ample, Equitable and Stable Funding
- Small Class Size
- Culturally Responsive Instruction

All U.S. states are currently on the first, second or third step of the staircase.

DEVISING A TRUE GREAT EQUALIZER

Recall the above-defined Great Equalizer standard:

> a public school system that counterbalances societal inequities
> and gives each new generation a relatively equal chance at success,
> by providing students from all backgrounds with educational
> opportunities that prepare them to succeed economically and socially
> in college, careers, and life.

Setting aside the practical, educational, and political feasibility of creating this system, what might it include? How might it differ from the system that we currently have?

Looking at the high school level, my colleagues[2] and I arrived at ten criteria that true "Schools of Opportunity" address:[3]

Criterion 1: Broaden and enrich learning opportunities, with particular attention to reducing disparities in learning created by tracking and ability grouping;

Criterion 2: Create and maintain a healthy school culture, with attention to diversity and to reassessing student discipline policies;

Criterion 3: Provide more and better learning time during the school year and summer;

Criterion 4: Use a variety of assessments designed to respond to student needs;

Criterion 5: Support teachers as professionals;

Criterion 6: Meet the needs of students with disabilities in an environment that ensures challenge and support;

Criterion 7: Provide students with additional needed services and supports, including mental and physical health services;

Criterion 8: Enact a challenging and supported culturally relevant curriculum;

Criterion 9: Build on the strengths of language minority students and correctly identify their needs; and

Criterion 10: Sustain equitable and meaningful parent and community engagement.

But this is merely a starting point. It does not address opportunity gaps relevant to earlier grades and ages, such as high-quality preschool and intensive early interventions in math and reading. It does not include issues of class size, which are also particularly important during the elementary years. It does not include access to technology and equipment—not just computers, but science labs and the like; and not just the equipment but deep, engaging uses of that equipment. It does not include career and technical education, financial literacy, driver's training, or social–emotional learning. Our initial brainstorms with community members (discussed below) raised additional resource needs, such as clothing, libraries and librarians, removal of fees for AP and SAT tests, safe and reliable transportation, and academic tutoring. Moreover, the list itself does not tackle the level or intensity of a given resource or intervention.

My colleagues and I therefore designed a process for determining what formal schooling must entail if it is to become the great equalizer, and for estimating its price tag.

BREAKING FREE: PURSUING A VISIONING STRATEGY

Knowledge about what children and youth need from their school systems is distributed among those children and youth, as well as their parents and community members, their teachers and school administrators, and others within their school communities (e.g., counselors and social workers). Researchers also develop expertise, often about a particular element of students' needs, such as career and technical education or special education. Accordingly, the process of designing a great-equalizer school system must engage with these sources of knowledge and expertise. Rural teachers and high school students may, for instance, point to different needs than those living in suburban or urban areas. The perspective of community members may yield different insights than those of mental health workers. Given the extraordinarily challenging lift demanded by the great-equalizer standard, all of the needs identified by these different stakeholders should be considered.

My colleagues[4] and I have begun a process of convening stakeholders and asking them to collaboratively think through what resources and opportunities schools would incorporate if they were to have a hope of becoming great equalizers. This process is loosely guided by the "professional-judgment panel" approach used in some so-called adequacy studies (see Augenblick & Myers, 2003); it uses deliberative panel discussions to brainstorm about and craft a comprehensive set of redesign and resource needs.

Professional judgment panels of the past have brought together educational practitioner participants for deliberations. Within the context of litigation, these deliberations are guided by an academic standard (i.e., a target, goal, or expectation) that is usually determined by a state's constitutional duty concerning P–12 education. These deliberations typically involve the identification of the resources and program designs necessary to reach the chosen standard. In addition to being used in litigation, this approach has become a commonly relied upon method for researchers to identify educational resources and estimate their cost.

Our approach, however, is substantially different from past professional judgment panel studies. First, we raised the standard of education to the "Great Equalizer" (rather than a constitutional adequacy standard), to identify the educational resources necessary to ensure that all children are afforded equitable opportunities to learn and succeed in life. Participants deliberate about the resources necessary to approximately equalize a student's opportunities in life, rather than considering only the resources required to attain adequate outcomes on standardized test scores or to yield acceptable graduation rates.

Second, we broadened the drawn-upon expertise. Typically, professional judgment panels have relied upon the expertise of educational practitioners who have experience in the provision of public education—e.g., teachers, principals, district-level support staff, and district administrators. We modified this to reflect our belief that the identification of resources and program designs necessary to meet a "Great Equalizer" standard requires additional types of expertise. In particular, we need participants with knowledge and expertise about out-of-school obstacles that can be addressed by in-school resources. We therefore add several groups as participants: parents, community activists, and youth. Each of these groups presents valuable perspectives on out-of-school needs that build on the perspectives presented by educational practitioners.

We are using that process to generate one set of reforms, which we then will cost out. We also are convening a second set of panelists, this time consisting of educational researchers with expertise in students' general and specific needs and in evidence-based interventions, policies, and practices. This second approach thus offers research-based judgment rather than experience-based judgment. Both perspectives are valuable, and using the pair of approaches will allow us to triangulate our estimates.

To estimate the costs associated with the policies identified in our modified professional judgment panels, we will compile data on student enrollment and demographics and regional differences in personnel and resource costs, to predict a range of costs associated with resource and policy implementation. Because state systems of public education vary in their needs, we will calculate a national estimate of a "great equalizer" system of schools and an estimate for the individual states that we study.

CONCLUSION

President Bush famously said that disadvantaged students were subjected to the "soft bigotry of low expectations." And he was right. High expectations are indeed important. But high expectations become a punitive false promise if combined with low resources, low opportunities, and low supports. Because of vast societal inequalities, children throughout the United States face those challenges every day.

Nevertheless, many policymakers and others are still mired in a type of magical thinking. They have somehow convinced themselves that children's opportunities to learn outside of school are not particularly important—that policy should simply focus on making schools more equal. While school inequality is a serious problem that must be addressed, this sort of school-focused thinking is also a problem. As noted above, relatively little of the variation that we see in average test scores between schools is attributable to differences in what the schools are doing.

These results arise, in part, because families with different resources are able to buy very different opportunities to learn for their children. That purchasing power is much higher for White families than for Black and Latinx families, and it is rooted in a long history of discrimination and racist policies (Rothstein, 2017).

The U.S. has recently, in response to murders by police and others, shown some inclination to acknowledge and address this racism. Moreover, the expanded Child Tax Credit in the American Rescue Plan passed in March 2021 would—if made permanent—represent a serious step toward addressing child poverty. But overall there is little reason to presume a real shift away from the Great Equalizer myth. That is, American policy is still less focused on cutting off the weights pulling down families and communities than on relying on schools to overcome those injustices.

Our common schools—at least as we currently provide them—have not met Horace Mann's expectation. The school system has not prevented being poor. Wealth inequality has been rising each decade, and we (in the U.S. and globally) are now in the midst of another Gilded Age. The world's wealthiest individuals capture, each year, more and more of its wealth; "In the U.S., the richest 0.1% control a bigger share of the pie than at any time since 1929" (Metcalf & Witzig, 2019). And the overall pie size in the United States is growing far too slowly to even keep up with the inequality.

In hindsight we can see that Horace Mann was right to argue for the power and potential of schools. But he oversold the product, and children suffer from the Great Equalizer myth. School systems shouldn't be asked to prevent poverty, let alone to equalize students' opportunities in life.

NOTES

1. https://nepc.colorado.edu/publication/lifting-all-children. Note that all graphics presented in this chapter are reproduced with permission.

2. The research team includes, or has included, Carol Burris, Anna Deese, Michelle Doughty, Matt Garcia, Kathleen Gebhardt, Linda Molner Kelley, Rhianna Kirk, Sarah LaCour, Anna Noble, Kate Somerville, Michelle Renee Valladares and Adam York.

3. Details, as well as the scoring rubric we use in evaluating schools for recognition as a School of Opportunity, can be found at SchoolsOfOpportunity.org.

4. The research team includes, or has included, Frank Adamson, Allison Brown, Anna Deese, Kathleen Gebhardt, René Espinoza Kissell, Sarah LaCour, John Myers, Jeannie Oakes, Chris Saldaña, Cassie Schwerner, Michelle Renee Valladares and Kathryn Wiley.

REFERENCES

Abbott v. Burke (1994). New Jersey Supreme Court. 136 N.J. 444, 643 A.2d 575. https://edlawcenter.org/assets/files/pdfs/abott-v-burke/Abbott%20III.pdf

Augenblick & Myers. (2003, January). *Calculation of the cost of an adequate education in Colorado using the Professional Judgement and the Successful School District approaches.* Colorado School Finance Project. https://cosfp.org/wp-content/uploads/AdeqUpdate/AdequacyWork/Adequacy2003/Adq2003.pdf

Cardona, M. (2021, Feb 3). Cardona vows to tackle problems worsened by virus. *Associated Press.* https://news.yahoo.com/cardona-vows-tackle-problems-worsened-185421871.html

DeVos, B. (2018, June 7). *Prepared remarks from Secretary DeVos to the International Congress on Vocational & Professional Training.* U.S. Department of Education. https://content.govdelivery.com/accounts/USED/bulletins/1f57435

DeVos, B. [@BetsyDeVosED]. (2019, August 16). Walter is such a strong advocate for #EducationFreedom because he knows the difference it has made in his life. Hear [Tweet]. https://twitter.com/betsydevosed/status/1162471030788632578.

Duncan, A. (2011, December 10). *Leading a life of consequence: Remarks of U.S. Secretary of Education Arne Duncan at the Fayetteville State University Winter Commencement.* U.S. Department of Education.

Mann, H. (1848). *Twelfth Annual Report to the Massachusetts State Board of Education.* https://usa.usembassy.de/etexts/democrac/16.htm

Metcalf, T., & Witzig, J. (2019, December 27). World's richest gain $1.2 trillion in 2019 as Jeff Bezos retains crown. *Bloomberg.* https://www.bloomberg.com/news/articles/2019-12-27/world-s-richest-gain-1-2-trillion-as-kylie-baby-sharks-prosper

O'Sullivan, J. (2018, June 7). Washington Supreme Court ends long-running McCleary education case against the state. *Seattle Times.* https://www.seattletimes.com/seattle-news/washington-supreme-court-ends-100000-per-day-sanctions-against-state-in-mccleary-education-case/

Rothstein, R. (2017). *The color of law: A forgotten history of how our government segregated America.* Liveright Publishing.

The Nation's Report Card (2019). *New Jersey student groups and gaps data: Mathematics, Grade 4.* https://www.nationsreportcard.gov/profiles/stateprofile/overview/NJ?cti=PgTab_GapComparisons&chort=1&sub=MAT&sj=NJ&fs=Grade&st=MN&year=2019R3&sg=Race%2FEthnicity%3A+White+vs.+Black&sgv=Difference&ts=Single+Year&tss=-2019R3&sfj=NP

Ujifusa, A. (2017, November 2). Teacher deduction for classroom expenses scrapped in GOP tax bill. *Education Week.* http://blogs.edweek.org/edweek/campaign-k-12/2017/11/taxes_school_choice_trump_GOP_biggest_education_shift.html

Welner, K. G., & LaCour, S. (2019). Education in context: Schools and their connections to societal inequalities. In K. L. Bowman (Ed.), *The Oxford Handbook of U.S. Education Law.* Oxford University Press. doi:10.1093/oxfordhb/9780190697402.001.0001

Democracy's Wobbly Cornerstone

Seeking to Be the "Great Equalizer" in a Deeply Unequal Culture

Jeannie Oakes and Martin Lipton

The history and traditions of the United States reflect deep conflicting national values: for example, equal justice for all and capitalism often don't play well together, and conceptions of individual freedom may push against ideas of the common good. In this essay[1] we explore how tensions such as these, embedded in our national character, are expressed in public schools. In particular, we look at the cultural assumptions of meritocracy and racial superiority that continue to defy Horace Mann's predictions of public schools becoming the nation's "great equalizer." by providing a universal education for generations of democracy-minded citizens. We conclude with an homage to those time-tested cornerstones of the quest for justice: hope, struggle, and participation.

Society's demands on schools have frequently distorted Mann's vision. Educating students to function in and contribute to a democracy, although still a schooling goal, has been complicated by expectations that public schools will also preserve a predominantly Anglo Protestant culture, prepare the nation's workforce, develop the scientific prowess required for national security, ameliorate social inequalities, and develop the human capital required for international competitiveness. Policymakers' and educators' decisions about how schools should meet these demands reflect prevailing ideologies that, over time, shape what people consider to be the best ways to operate schools.[2]

Those ideologies both support and undermine equitable public schooling in the United States. Although they include a commitment to fairness and equality, they also reflect the efforts of powerful groups to make their dominance seem legitimate and essential to social cohesion and prosperity. These ideologies underlie our social structures and clarify why changing those structures is so difficult. Deeply held views of meritocracy and racial superiority characterize our country's culture and our schools' enactment of that culture, and together they constrain society and schools from realizing their democratic possibilities.

THE MYTH OF MERIT

Historically, Western societies distributed wealth and privilege according to how close one was to an elite or ruling class. Prior to the surge of democratic thinking in the 17th century, societies were organized to concentrate wealth among royalty, church leadership, landowners, and wealthy merchants—not artisans, peasants, and slaves. Not everyone thought this was fair, but few with power apologized or felt they had to justify their relative comfort and prosperity. Explaining such disparities in wealth and privilege remains a central dilemma of modern and more egalitarian societies.

Since the colonial period, one source of national pride has been the idea that the United States, unlike its more aristocratic European cousins, forged a fair society. A society in which individual ability and determination, rather than wealth or personal connections, hold the key to success and upward mobility. In practice, this interpretation was at odds with early conceptions of merit, which drew from Calvinist and Puritan religious ideas of predestination and "election." Wealth was a sign of God's favor, and poverty was also God's will. Either way, inequality was within the natural order. These ideas, and their resulting confusion, continue to influence how Americans construct impressions of merit.

The United States has historically considered itself a democratic system in which merit imparts moral legitimacy to what otherwise might appear unfair or undemocratic. Merit presents an easy, if often circular, rationale for why some citizens and their children are well off while others have so little. Merit also asserts that the wealthy and powerful deserve their wealth and power because of their determination, cleverness, or hard work (Stille, 2011). And, of course, God has never left the equation of who gets and deserves blessings. Even so, an increasingly small percentage of the population now controls most of the nation's wealth and sends its children to well-resourced schools. This lopsided distribution of wealth and power cannot be attributed to most people lacking cleverness or ambition. The emphasis on meritocracy—and not equality—is what Swedish economist Gunnar Myrdal, after studying democracy in the 1940s United States, called the "American Creed" (Myrdal, 1944).

We are used to thinking of merit as a universal Good, but we tend to distribute and justify social benefits according to wide and conflicting metrics of that goodness. As told in the song, "them that's got are them that gets" and they *deserve* it, too.

Teacher and social theorist Jay MacLeod advanced what he considered to be the *myth* of merit in his 1987 book (revised in 1995), *Ain't No Makin'*

It. He tells of the hopes and disappointments of young men growing up in a low-income neighborhood. MacLeod describes "the achievement ideology" and explains:

> In this view, success is based on merit, and economic inequality is due to differences in ambition and ability. Individuals do not inherit their social status; they attain it on their own. Since education insures equality of opportunity, the ladder of social mobility is there for all to climb. A favorite Hollywood theme, the rags-to-riches story resonates in the psyche of the American people. Horatio Alger's accounts of the spectacular mobility achieved by men of humble origins through their own unremitting efforts occupy a treasured place in our folklore. The American Dream is held out as a genuine prospect for anyone with the drive to achieve it. (McLeod, 1995, p. 3)

MacLeod notes that "for every Andrew Carnegie" there are uncountable hardworking and able others who fare much less well, and that most people in the United States wind up in positions similar to their parents. In fact, with the exception of the wealthy, there is evidence that those now entering the labor market will do less well than their parents (Fry et al., 2011). MacLeod is one of many to identify schools' complicity in inhibiting social class mobility. Schools tend toward "social reproduction"—or the perpetuation of class status generation by generation. Scholars such as W. E. B. Du Bois, Carter G. Woodson, and a host of others (e.g., indigenous peoples who resisted the schooling that the Europeans forced on them) have long opposed their people being "trained"—what Woodson called "mis-educated" —for their "proper place" in society (Woodson, 1933).

The myth of merit draws its strength from the grain of truth embedded in it. All other things being equal, more ambitious and hardworking people may achieve more success in society than their less ambitious and hardworking peers. Effort and persistence are important to children's school achievement. The problem with the myth of merit is its misguided focus on qualities presumed to be inherent within individuals or some class of persons—mirroring familiar prejudices around race, gender, social class, and so forth. Merit does not presume basic equality of opportunity and resources; it assumes that individual merit represents the *only* variable of real consequence to schools. Conceptions of merit are used not just to *explain* achievements such as wealth or school success, they are used to *predict* (or *prejudge*) the resources and opportunities one deserves in order to attain school success.

How else might we explain or justify the uneven distribution of school resources, personal wealth, and status, or group-based (race, gender, etc.) benefits, if not by looking to individual merit? Society is shaped by social *structures* that constrain what is possible for people to achieve. Social structures are firm and stable arrangements of social roles and relationships—for example, school attendance zones drawn by those with relative power, or a 10-month school year and a 6-hour school day that pose far more challenges for some families than others (e.g., families helmed by single working parents versus economically stable families who can hire caregivers). Such structures are typically rationalized because they make some administrative sense, even if they don't produce good education for all children. When we look closely at social structures in and beyond schooling, including those related to health, housing, transportation and so forth, a consistent pattern emerges: Children from wealthy, White families generally receive the advantages provided by those structures, while children from poor families of color are less likely to benefit from them.

The common characteristics associated with merit (hard work, social awareness, intelligence, etc.) occur with no less frequency in low-income families or families of color. However, inequalities in opportunity and resources limit the degree to which children in such families can parlay qualities like determination and hard work into school success and enhanced life chances. The myth of merit distracts us (or lets us hide) from confronting those social structures that exacerbate inequities (Bourdieu & Passeron, 1990; Bowles & Gintis, 1977; Morrow & Torres, 1995).

Attempts to Address Structural Inequality: The War on Poverty

After World War II, Americans were confident about the goodness of their democracy. Although these years were filled with unsettling discord, including the start of the Cold War, McCarthy-era political repression, and the Korean War, and internally Jim Crow and racial violence and segregation, this was also a time of unprecedented prosperity, growth, and optimism. The nation occupied an undisputed position of political and economic world dominance. The dark days of the Great Depression were over, and many thought that the abject poverty of that period would never be seen again. The G.I. Bill opened college to returning WWII servicemen, and federal housing policies opened the doors to home ownership for enormous numbers of first-time (mostly White) purchasers.

Given the optimism of the 1950s, most people were unsettled in 1962 when Michael Harrington's influential book *The Other America: Poverty in the United States* documented a huge underclass of unemployed and working poor (Harrington, 1962). How could it be that such a large segment of society simply did not "earn" better conditions? Harrington argued that this underclass, contrary to popular view, was not an artifact of temporary economic conditions. Rather, increasing numbers of people were tangled into lifelong and intergenerational webs of poor education, housing, nutrition and health care, and more.

Many who read Harrington's revelations were disposed to social action that would right the obvious wrongs. At this time, civil rights activism was gaining mainstream support. By the mid-1960s, it had become clear that some groups of people could not overcome the inequitable conditions into which they were born. In the eyes of many, unjust social structures needed to be examined and changed.

From the mid-1960s until 1980, the federal government pursued social policies designed to level the structural playing field on the principle that some groups should not have to "overcome adversity," while others had no such obstacles. The War on Poverty legislation, for example, sought to remedy hunger, inadequate housing, and under-resourced schooling. These actions paid off. The War on Poverty slowed the widening gap between rich and poor. Programs fed hungry children and provided important learning experiences. Activism and progressive social policies during this period led to significant political gains for African Americans and strengthened the social safety net for poor people, but the programs were stopped short of eradicating the structural problems if and when they would cause discomfort to the privileged who wanted to hang onto that status.

Furthermore, the country lacked the patience and expertise to formulate and administer antipoverty programs and equity-minded interventions. National politics allowed little room for error. When programs faltered or needed reworking, skeptics eagerly judged them failures. Any sign of "inefficiency" (not uncommon in America's cumbersome bureaucracies, and among humans, generally) was taken as proof that "you just can't help those folks." Unlike a national highway program that produced tangible and relatively quick fixes for travelers and transport, or a moonshot with a televised and pride-inducing victory, Americans were not prepared to accept costly and difficult changes to social and economic structures (Katz, 1989). Thus the groundwork was laid for the systematic dismantling of antipoverty policies, even in the midst of the successes of those programs, beginning in the Reagan administration and continuing today.

Enduring Challenges

Our society supports the convoluted logic that failure to overcome poverty or inferior education proves a lack of merit. Many people believe that their own *relative* privilege stands on a moral platform; the unpalatable alternative being that their accrued benefits require the lesser status of others. Also, like many ideologies, the myth of merit depends on *everyone* believing in the myth almost as strongly as those who benefit from it. Many poor and minoritized people in the United States also believe schooling benefits are equally accessible to all. Even students with dismal schooling experiences often blame their own lack of ability or effort or their failure to take advantage of opportunities. Describing "the Brothers"—the young African Americans he studied—Jay MacLeod put it this way:

They blame themselves for their mediocre academic performances because they are unaware of the discriminatory influences of tracking, the school's partiality toward the cultural capital of the upper classes, the self-fulfilling consequences of teachers' expectations, and other forms of class-based educational selection. Conditioned by the achievement ideology to think that good jobs require high academic attainment, the Brothers may temper their high aspirations, believing not that the institution of school and the job market have failed them, but that they have failed themselves. (MacLeod, 1995, p. 126)

In sum, merit permeates how people make sense of schooling—emphasizing the role of the individual and de-emphasizing the responsibilities of school or society. And yet, as attention turns to the widening wealth gaps between rich and poor and the corollary extreme concentration of wealth among the top 1% of the population, broad-based skepticism is growing about the degree to which such enormous financial success could ever be explained by individuals' efforts alone. Whether that realization takes hold and weakens the myth of merit remains to be seen. We are cautiously encouraged that more people may start to question the degree to which merit could account for such "wealth undreamed of" for so few among us.

CRACKS IN THE IDEOLOGY OF MERIT

The ideology of merit is driven by two understandings of the human condition: Merit is either a matter of inborn, immutable inheritance, or merit is a volitional matter of personal choice or individual will. Either way, merit or the lack of it provides a convenient way—a kind of fate beyond the reach of social influence—to explain social hopelessness: "Gosh, we'd love to do more to help those kids, but there's nothing society can do." However, ever since the illogical and circular reasoning put forth by early America's religious sects, including but not limited to the concept of predestination, the culture has embraced movements and primitive science that try to patch cracks in the myth of merit. Sadly, when the old patches lose favor new ones arise to replace them. Deficit thinking, genetically based racial superiority, White privilege, and other culturally embedded forms of bias comprise an ongoing narrative around a common theme: White and wealthy people are more likely to deserve their advantages over all others; attempts to have it otherwise cause harm and waste.

Deficit Thinking

Powerful societal assumptions support the view that youth who are not White come to school with deficits that make their school success difficult, if not impossible. This system of thought is often referred to as "deficit thinking"—a belief that the source of academic struggle is flawed or undeveloped genetic makeup, cultural background, and/or students' individual experiences. Deficit thinking is particularly corrosive when it is generated by persons with superficially egalitarian intentions. Americans have a powerful commitment to charity; they often seek to be generous in their giving and tolerance of others. Even people who acknowledge social injustice and bias may prefer feeling sorry for "victims" over pursuing a change to underlying causes. For example, caring teachers might excuse poorly performing students by pointing to the hopelessness of their homelife. Students might be tracked into easy classes instead of college prep ones so as not to unduly stress them or risk exposing them to failure.

Historically, people have resorted to all manner of scientific foolishness to support their prejudices. For example, what greater deficit to human achievement or morality can there be than having a brain that is too small? Or so thought a group of modern, mid-18th century natural scientists, the craniologists. These folks offered empirical evidence that White superiority rested on racial differences in skull size, with the larger skulls of Caucasians proving their greater capacities. Continuing this line of thought: Because they were born with significant deficits, we should not *blame* groups of people for their deficiencies, which are not their fault; neither should society waste its efforts to correct the immutable distributions of superiority and inferiority. Such easy to grasp, if unexamined, understandings of complex phenomena are quickly seeded into the culture, especially when they comport with broader social narratives.

As the nation expanded westward, new groups and rearrangements were added to racial and ethnic hierarchies—groups were aligned according to a descending ladder of deficits. Whites migrating to the Southwest judged Mexicans to be "half-civilized" (in comparison to "uncivilized" Indians) but also "White," due to their Spanish language, Catholicism, and the presence of a property-owning elite boasting European as well as Indian heritage. On the other hand, Asian men, imported in the late 19th century to build California's railroads and work its mines and farms, joined the ranks of the Black slave laborers brought from the American South and were disdained for their "strange" customs, "pagan" religions, and "incomprehensible" language. In the mid-19th century a California court classified the Chinese officially as Indians and, therefore, non-White.

Social Darwinism

Darwin's *Origin of Species*, published in 1859 had established that all humans were of a single species; therefore, no humans were more advanced or developed on an evolutionary scale or ladder. However, that work spawned "social Darwinists" who advanced theories that Whites were a more highly evolved, socially and cognitively superior, race. Such theories fit well with slavery and segregation, adding a faux-scientific imperative to racism. Even after the abolition of slavery, most Whites viewed Blacks as inferior and supported racial segregation. Many of those who joined and led in the abolitionist movements championed "freedom" for slaves without giving up their convictions about racial deficits.

Although the U.S. government had declared in 1868 that "compulsory ignorance" laws were illegal and native-born people of color were citizens, the states could—under the principle of states' rights—choose whether to fund schools for children of color. Many opted not to do so, and it was not until 1910 that the majority of Black children attended school, and not until 1920 that the majority of Mexican, Asian, and Native American children attended school.

Applying Darwin's evolutionary theories to cultural as well as racial groups confirmed for many that immigrant students were less socially and morally developed. Consider, for example, the superintendent of Boston schools, who warned in 1889: "Many of these children come from homes of vice and crime. In their blood are generations of iniquity. . . . They hate restraint or obedience to the law" (quoted in Gould, 1996, p. 24). Because immigrants at the turn of the 19th century arrived from different parts of Europe than previous waves of immigrants, racial and religious prejudices were typically at the core of such warnings and worries. Writing about recent immigrants in 1909, for example, prominent educator Ellwood Cubberley explained: "These southern and eastern Europeans are of a very different type from the north Europeans who preceded them. Illiterate, docile, lacking in self-reliance and initiative, and not possessing the Anglo-Teutonic conceptions of law, order, and government, their coming has served to dilute tremendously our national stock, and to corrupt our civic life" (Cubberley, 1909, p. 15).

These sentiments led many to believe that Americanization and assimilation should serve as common schools' principal objectives. Although many considered immigrants' language and culture to be biological, and therefore unchangeable, reformers expressed hopes that schooling could offer immigrant children constructive direction. In Cubberley's words, "Our task is to . . . assimilate and amalgamate these people as a part of our American race and to implant in their children, as far as can be done, the Anglo-Saxon conception of righteousness, law and order" (Cubberley, 1909, p. 15).

Lewis Terman Tries to Make Prejudice OK

As children of color and children from southern and eastern European immigrant families began attending school in larger numbers, a new "science" of intelligence emerged. With it came theories and data with which its proponents argued that mental deficits among these youth would necessarily limit their school achievement. Among the most well-known developers of the science of intelligence was Stanford University professor Lewis Terman, who promoted intelligence tests for U.S. schoolchildren. Although Terman purported that his IQ tests measured innate abilities, items taken from his test make clear that children from educated, culturally mainstream families were more likely to earn high IQs (Bigelow, 1994). Because children of color and those from poor families scored lower than more socially advantaged ones, Terman used IQ test results to confirm his view that heredity determined intelligence. He also used test results to support his advocacy of low-level schooling for those who tested poorly as well as for population control among those he called the "feebleminded." After testing a group of boys who lived in an orphanage, Terman wrote:

> The tests have told the truth. These boys are ineducable beyond the merest rudiments of training. No amount of school instruction will ever make them intelligent voters or capable citizens . . . . Their dullness seems to be racial, or at least inherent in the family stocks from which they came . . . . [O]ne meets this type with such extraordinary frequency among Indians, Mexicans and Negroes . . . . Children of this group should be segregated in special classes and be given instruction which is concrete and practical. . . . There is no possibility at present of convincing society that they should not be allowed to reproduce, although from a eugenic point of view they constitute a grave problem because of their unusually prolific breeding. (Gould, 1996, p. 121)

Although IQ tests were periodically modified after the 1920s, their use (and the scores their use generated) was continually marshalled as "evidence" in support of deficit views and assumptions of racial superiority similar to those held by Terman.

The second half of the 20th century brought significant structural changes that promised to alter deficit thinking. The civil rights movement brought political gains, particularly in voting rights. *Brown v. Board of Education* overturned the *Plessy* decision, ruling that separate is inherently unequal, and ordered schools to desegregate with "all deliberate speed." However, the initial promise *Brown* held for equal opportunity has never been realized. Today, Black students in the United States remain nearly as racially isolated as before *Brown*, and Latinx students' racial isolation increases steadily. There is evidence that segregation has *increased*, and schooling conditions have *worsened* for many students since the *Brown* ruling (Kozol, 2005; Orfield & Lee, 2007).

The 1954 *Brown* decision overturned laws that separated children in school by race, and the *Lau v. Nichols* decision in 1974 set forth the constitutional requirement that equal educational opportunity demanded that schools offer help for students unable to understand English. However, neither these decisions nor considerable ensuing legislation intended to make schools more respectful and inclusive eradicated the prevailing ideologies of deficit thinking and racial superiority. Terman's bias-infused "science" has never left the scene. In 1969, for example, Harvard psychologist Arthur Jensen argued that because national poverty programs did not appreciably raise children's IQs, children of the poor must be genetically intellectually inferior. Around the same time, physicist William Shockley reemerged, years after coinventing the transistor, to contribute his scientific authority to a proposal for reimbursing voluntarily sterilized individuals according to their number of IQ points below 100.

Not all persons succumbed to faux-scientific ideologies that support racism and deficits, but modern-day deficit thinking is alive and well. A case in point is the enthusiastic reception given to *The Bell Curve*.

The Bell Curve

Two months after its publication in 1994, *The Bell Curve: Intelligence and Class Structure in American Life* had 400,000 copies in print. Richard Herrnstein and Charles Murray's best-selling book claimed scientific proof that African Americans inherit lower IQs than Whites and that these IQ differences are virtually impossible to change. Put bluntly, Herrnstein and Murray argued that the average African American was less well educated and less wealthy than the average White person, because he or she was not born with the capacity to be as smart. Therefore, the authors also claimed, social programs that attempted to close opportunity gaps—programs such as Head Start, compensatory education, and affirmative action—were both costly and useless. Following this logic, the authors argued that (1) such programs hurt those they intend to help by steering them away from the lower-level aspirations and occupations that suit their abilities, and (2) such programs harm society because they give less intelligent people access to social positions that require greater aptitude. The authors, well-known academics from prestigious universities, bolstered these claims with impressive-looking charts, graphs, and statistics in their eight-hundred-plus-page book.

The Bell Curve claimed profound implications for schools and teaching. More likely, the book just emboldened people who already subscribed to ideologies of merit and deficits. *The Bell Curve* argued that "in a universal education system, many students will not reach the level of education that most people view as basic" (Herrnstein & Murray, 1996, p. 436). Moreover, according to the authors, efforts to teach groups of children with low IQs—disproportionately, disadvantaged children of color—more than the most modest skills will benefit neither those children nor society. Rather, government and educators should shift most of their teaching resources and efforts from the disadvantaged to the intellectually gifted.

Readers of *The Bell Curve* and of the reviews that followed its publication, as well as listeners of TV shows and radio programs about the book, were frightened and enraged. Those who liked the book were angry, because it confirmed their political views about the futility (or worse) of social programs that aimed to improve life chances among people of color. Many looked back on the short-lived but significant national effort on behalf of African Americans and immigrants as confirmation that the cause of disappointing reform results lies with the underserved themselves and with their misguided helpers.

What is notable is the tendency of such views, once expressed, to quickly gain popularity. In each instance, findings from these reports made front-page headlines and gave readers permission to speak aloud otherwise private convictions about racial superiority, merit, and the deservingness of the poor. Respected scholars instantly refuted the books and reports, but they were consigned to smaller platforms with narrow audiences. Under these conditions, some of the most fair-minded teachers were shocked by the extent to which *The Bell Curve*'s racist perspectives remained in the minds of so many, including among their school colleagues.

The theories of race and intelligence embedded in *The Bell Curve* are not objective scientific discoveries. They reflect the beliefs and values of the cultures—like our own—in which they develop. In turn, the theories that gain acceptance most readily and hold enduring sway over the norms and practices of schooling nearly always serve the interests of those in power. In contemporary schools, such theories are still used to explain a wide range of conditions including, for example, the overrepresentation of students of color and English Learners among students designated as having "special needs," and their underrepresentation among those identified as "gifted" (Artiles, Klingner, et al. 2010; Artiles, Kozleski, et al., 2010). Even today in the 3rd decade of the 21st century, much of the nation's leadership—especially its education leadership—attained prominence under regimes guided by these corrosive assumptions of intelligence and intelligence testing. They have had a lot to unlearn before they could cast off this discriminatory legacy.

These ideologies—and the norms and practices to which they give rise—kept most neighborhoods and schools segregated and have perpetuated discrimination, disadvantage, and disparity. However, they have not gone unchallenged. Those who disagreed with *The Bell Curve*'s argument were furious because they found the book dishonest, unscientific, and morally offensive. Moreover, since the 1980s, critical race scholars like Derrick Bell and Kimberlé Crenshaw have pressed members of academic and legal communities to analyze the complex intersections of race, law, and power. Others, like Gloria Ladson-Billings, have explored how these intersections relate to education in particular. These scholars have argued that by focusing on individual and intentional acts of explicit racism, people have tended to overlook the broader conditions of inequality and racism that permeate social structures, institutions (like schools), and face-to-face relationships in all facets of life in the United States. Thus, their arguments work to unsettle mainstream assumptions about why our society—and its distribution of wealth and opportunity—look as they do. Ladson-Billings, for example, has argued that the term "education debt" offers far more accuracy than the term "achievement gap," because it locates the source of contemporary achievement disparities in this country's long history of having disproportionately denied people of color equal educational opportunity (Ladson-Billings, 2006).

Racial Superiority and White Privilege

Most scientists today agree that race is not a useful scientific category because any discernible genetic differences between races are irrelevant as they pertain to schooling and learning. Most consider race "a social construct without biological meaning" and find racial categories to be "weak proxies for genetic diversity" (Gannon, 2016, n.p.). And yet, Whites in U.S. society continue to experience numerous privileges, which are rooted in long-standing beliefs that associate more or less moral and intellectual capacity to biologically different racial groups. Onto these beliefs are layered powerful social preferences (not held exclusively by Whites)—for example, consistent messages about the relative aesthetic value of lighter versus darker skin.

White privilege is a difficult concept for many White people to understand because its benefits are indirect. In the absence of a strong critical perspective, it may feel unpleasant to acknowledge how one benefits from race-based advantages. In addition, "privilege" doesn't necessarily produce an immediate tangible benefit that registers on a conscious or subconscious level; privilege is often so ingrained that it goes unrecognized—for example, it is hard to identify a palpable *freedom from* a deficit bias that other groups feel, often with pain, on a daily basis.

Increasingly, White people have worked to process, understand, and redress how Whiteness works to their advantage. Some have written at length and in accessible terms about the structural dimensions of their own White privilege. For example, likening White privilege to the male privilege she studied as a professor of women's studies, Peggy McIntosh offered in the late 1980s a still-timely framework for grappling with these issues in one's own life. In her most famous essay, she recounts her realization that being White brings considerable advantages that she had previously taken for granted as simply normal features of her life. McIntosh wrote:

> I think whites are carefully taught not to recognize white privilege . . . . So I have begun in an untutored way to ask what it is like to have white privilege. I have come to see white privilege as an invisible package of unearned assets that I can count on cashing in each day, but about which I was "meant" to remain oblivious. White privilege is like an invisible weightless knapsack of special

provisions, maps, passports, codebooks, visas, clothes, tools, and blank checks. (McIntosh, 1988, n.p.)

McIntosh made a list of fifty everyday privileges she believes came with the color of her skin. She noted that some of the items on the list were "what one would want for everyone in a just society," and that others allowed Whites to be "ignorant, oblivious, arrogant, and destructive." McIntosh explained that her recognition of these racial privileges challenged her understanding of the United States as a meritocratic society.

> For me white privilege has turned out to be an elusive and fugitive subject. The pressure to avoid it is great, for in facing it I must give up the myth of meritocracy. If these things are true, this is not such a free country; one's life is not what one makes it; many doors open for certain people through no virtues of their own. (McIntosh, 1988, n.p.)

Notably, McIntosh realized that these privileges are structural, not simply a matter of individual prejudice. She also understood how hard such structures of privilege are to change.

> In my class and place, I did not see myself as a racist because I was taught to recognize racism only in individual acts of meanness by members of my group, never in invisible systems conferring unsought racial dominance on my group from birth.
>   Disapproving of the systems won't be enough to change them. I was taught to think that racism could end if white individuals changed their attitude. But a "white" skin in the United States opens many doors for whites whether or not we approve of the way dominance has been conferred on us. Individual acts can palliate but cannot end these problems. (McIntosh, 1988, n.p.)

McIntosh's provocative observations have since caught the attention of many educators seeking to explain why and how, decades after the end of legalized segregation and racial discrimination, race still plays such a powerful role in access to education and opportunities. Because race and racism manifest in different ways at different historical moments, it's worth asking how White privilege will tilt how powerful interests address global crises: mass and social media, global migrations and demographic shifts, differential impact of climate change, and so on.

POSTSCRIPT:
TWO STEPS FORWARD, ONE STEP BACK, AND SIX OFF TO THE SIDE

Philosopher and public intellectual Cornel West views democracy as a process rather than a perfect or fixed state. West argues that in diverse cultures like ours, "prophetic pragmatism" would have us place our trust in "the abilities and capacities of ordinary people to participate in decision making procedures of institutions that regulate their lives." For educators, these abilities and capacities are bolstered by experience, critical dialogue, and vocation-specific knowledge that also "keeps track of social misery, solicits and channels moral outrage to alleviate it, and projects a future in which the potentialities of ordinary people flourish and flower" (West, 1990, p. 1747).

Many years ago we (Oakes and Lipton) wondered what teacher preparation might look like if it were freed from the constraints of polite and inoffensive neutrality and allowed for misery, outrage, and hope to inform decisions and careers and institutions. Oakes led the establishment of such a program at UCLA, and, together, we wrote a foundations of education textbook, *Teaching to Change the World,* to support new teachers to develop "prophetic pragmatism" and a critical stance about schooling for Los Angeles' low-income children of color. (Oakes, 1996; Oakes & Lipton, 1999; Oakes et al., 2018). This essay was largely adapted from portions of our book.

First published in 1999, *Teaching to Change the World* was conceived five years earlier as the smoke was clearing from the Los Angeles Rodney King insurrection. In the aftermath of King's beating, we tried to confront how public education helped create and did too little to ameliorate the context in which such abuses become predictable and such protests become necessary. We wanted to provide technical, normative, and political knowledge so that highly skilled teachers, equipped with a social justice perspective, would cope with institutional oppression to limit the damage and change the world. Our goal was to document and organize the history and best practices of teaching in ways that could support a new generation of teachers to be agents for equitable schooling.

We hoped to join like-minded educators across the country to change public education—structurally, systemically, and equitably. Such schooling would require that educators actively counter persistent ideologies of merit and racial superiority with educational practices driven by ideological commitments to justice and equity in a diverse democracy. We believed then and now that teachers, in their classrooms and beyond, can make our national rhetoric of justice and equality real.

And that has gradually happened . . . sort of, in bits and pieces, here and there. The 21st century shows signs of hope and optimism, even in the wake of the terrible killings of Breonna Taylor, George Floyd, Ahmaud Arbery, and so many others. Today's Black Lives Matter, Me Too, and other citizen-led movements, along with the end of the Trump administration, show that the struggle for justice has many achievements. And these achievements are fueled by how teachers and their students think about learning and injustice and what they do about it. We continue to believe that teachers and schools—all of us in our way—can be part of a hopeful solution.

NOTES

1. The material in this essay is adapted from Jeannie Oakes, Martin Lipton, Jamy Stillman, and Lauren Anderson, *Teaching to Change the World*, 5th Edition (Routledge, 2018).

2. It is worth noting that the term *ideological* is often used in debate to describe—and dismiss—opponents' arguments or approaches as being rooted in efforts to legitimize their own claims to, or critiques of, authority and power.

REFERENCES

Artiles, A.J., Klingner, J., Sullivan, A. & Fierros, E. (2010). Shifting landscapes of professional practices: English learner special education placement in English-only states. In P. Gándara & H. Hopkins (Eds.), *Forbidden language: English Learners and restrictive language policies* (pp. 102–117). Teachers College Press.

Artiles, A. J., Kozleski, E., Trent, S., Osher, D., & Ortiz, A. (2010) Justifying and explaining disproportionality, 1968–2008: A critique of underlying views of culture, *Exceptional Children* 76(3), 279–299.

Bigelow, B. (1994). Testing, tracking, and toeing the line. In W. Au, B. Bigelow, & S. Karp (Eds.), *Rethinking our classrooms: Teaching for equity and social justice*, Vol. 1. Rethinking Schools.

Bourdieu, P., & Passeron, J.-C. (1990). *Reproduction in education, society and culture* (2nd ed.) (R. Nice, Trans.). Sage Publications, Inc.

Bowles, S., & Gintis, H. (1976). *Schooling in capitalist America: Educational reform and the contradictions of economic life*. Basic Books.

Cubberley, E. P. (1909). *Changing conceptions of education*. Houghton Mifflin.

Fry, R., Cohn, D., Livingston, G., & Taylor, P. (2011). *The rising age gap in economic well-being: The old prosper relative to the young*. Pew Research Center. http://www.pewsocialtrends.org/2011/11/07/the-rising-age-gap-in-economic-well-being/

Gannon, M. (February 5, 2016). Race is a social construct, scientists argue. *Scientific American*. https://www.scientificamerican.com/article/race-is-a-social-construct-scientists-argue/

Gould, S. J. (1996) *The mismeasure of man* (2nd ed.). Norton.

Harrington, M. (1962/1977). *The other America: Poverty in the United States*. Collier Books.

Herrnstein, R., & Murray, C. (1996). *The bell curve: Intelligence and class structure in American life*. The Free Press.

Katz, M. B. (1989). *The undeserving poor: From the war on poverty to the war on welfare*. Pantheon Books.

Kozol, J. (2005). *The shame of the nation: The restoration of apartheid schooling in America*. Crown Publishing.

Ladson-Billings, G. (2006). From the achievement gap to the education debt: understanding achievement in U.S. schools: 2006 American Educational Research Association presidential address. *Education Researcher* 35(7), 3–12.

MacLeod, J. (1995). *Ain't no makin' it*. Westview Press.

McIntosh, P. (1988). *White privilege and male privilege: A personal account of coming to see correspondences through work in Women's Studies*. Working Paper 189. Center for Research on Women, Wellesley College.

Morrow, R. A., & Torres, C. A. (1995). *Social theory and education: A critique of theories of social and cultural reproduction*. State University of New York Press.

Myrdal, G. (1944). *An American dilemma: The Negro problem and American democracy*. Harper and Brothers.

Oakes, J. (1996). Making the rhetoric real. *Multicultural Education* 4(2), 4–10.

Oakes, J., & Lipton, M. (1999). *Teaching to change the world*. McGraw-Hill.

Oakes, J., Lipton, M., Anderson, L. & Stillman, J. (2019). *Teaching to change the world* (5th ed.). Routledge.

Orfield, G., & Lee, C. (2007). *Historic reversals, accelerating resegregation, and the need for new integration strategies*. UCLA Civil Rights Project/Proyecto Derechos Civiles.

Stille, A. (October 22, 2011) The paradox of the new elite. *New York Times*. https://www.nytimes.com/2011/10/23/opinion/sunday/social-inequality-and-the-new-elite.html

West, C. (1990). The limits of neopragmatism. *Southern California Law Review* 63(6), 1747–1752.

Woodson, C. G. (1933). *The mis-education of the Negro*. Associated Publishers.

Reflections on What Might Have Been

Sonia Nieto

I was a good girl in school. I always did my homework, raised my hand when I wanted to speak, never misbehaved, and always brought back signed parental permission forms on time. Even before I began first grade, my parents made sure I knew what "being good" at school meant: paying attention to what the teacher said and being obedient at all times. At school, being good meant following the rules and learning to parrot back the right answer. I did both because from a young age I learned that being good and doing well in school was the way to a better life than my parents had. I heeded this message throughout my public schooling, grades 1 to 12. My mother saved all the report cards that my sister and I got, keeping them in a safe place as a sacred testament to the importance of education. (This is why it never made sense to me that to this day many educators still assume that Puerto Rican, immigrant, racially marginalized, and other parents with an inadequate education and limited financial resources don't care about education).

Unfortunately, what no one ever told me was that the purpose of schooling was not only to educate and socialize us, but also to act as a sorting machine (see Spring, 1988; Oakes, 2005), to prepare us for either factory jobs, professional careers, or leadership positions. Just like at the Hogwarts School in the Harry Potter books where children were sorted into one of four mythic houses—Gryffindor, Hufflepuff, Ravenclaw, or Slytherin—children in U.S. public schools were, and many still are, also sorted from an early age. In elementary school, we were placed into reading groups depending on our proficiency in reading: the Blue Jays, the "high" group; the Robins, the "middle" group; or the Crows, the "low" group. Although this was never explicitly stated, we were also sorted based on our appearance, the color of our skin, and our ability to speak "standard" English. In New York City's public junior high schools, we were sorted into either the regular or the SP program (the so-called "special progress" program, where students skipped a grade, a precursor to Gifted and Talented programs), and in high school, we were destined for either the general, vocational, or academic track. The sorting worked pretty much as intended: those of us, who like me followed the rules in school, spoke English well, and were light-skinned, or who, unlike me, came from the middle class and had informed or pushy parents, often ended up in prestige programs, while those less fortunate ended up with a less privileged education, often with little hope of advancing any further. Of course, the results were rarely as clear-cut or stark as this; nevertheless, they echoed to a remarkable degree the economic, social, and racial backgrounds from which we had started. This is still the case.

Just as the Declaration of Independence through its lofty promises has been heralded as the savior of democracy, albeit initially intended only for White, propertied males, public education has often been declared "the great equalizer" and the best hope for the chance of a promising future for all young people regardless of station or rank. The truth, of course, has been more complicated. As a product of public schools, and as a public school educator, first in elementary and middle schools and later in higher education, I have thought a great deal about this state of affairs. Thus, I write this essay as a hopeful critique and a fervent expectation for a more just education for all children.

Public education is the institution largely responsible for where I am today as a highly educated, middle-class professional and privileged member of U.S. society. At the same time, many others who started life in similar circumstances to mine find themselves in a very different place, particularly children of the working class, Black and Brown children, immigrants with little formal education, and English language learners. In this essay, I want to highlight what I needed, but never received, from my public school education.

First, a bit more about me.

Born and raised in New York City, I am the daughter of Puerto Rican [im]migrants[1] to the United States in the first third of the 20th century. Like most other newcomers to the nation, they had hard lives on the island and came escaping poverty while also seeking a better life for their families back home and for the children they hoped to have in the future. They met and married in Brooklyn, where my sister Lydia, then me, and finally my brother Freddy were born. With a meager 4th-grade education on the island, for 20 years my father worked in a Jewish delicatessen on Delancey Street in Manhattan, the first job he landed when he got off the boat in New York harbor in 1929, just a month before the stock market crash. He began by sweeping floors and ended up a cook and union member, eventually bringing a sister and two brothers from Puerto Rico to join him at the deli. When the business was demolished to make way for a bank, he took his paltry savings to buy a tiny bodega in the basement of a tenement building a block away from another tenement building where my family lived. In those days, it was still possible for someone who could barely read and who never mastered the English language to make an adequate life for himself and his family as long as he was willing, like my father was, to work up to 18 hours a day.

My mother, who made it through sophomore year of high school in Puerto Rico, briefly worked at a candy factory in the neighborhood but soon settled down to become a full-time mother. We lived in a fifth-floor walkup apartment in a working-class immigrant neighborhood.

My sister, Lydia, being older than me by a year, was the first to start school. Since neither she nor I spoke English, she became the guinea pig for learning the language. This was long before ESL services were widely available. Lydia struggled through that year but was fortunate to have a teacher, Miss Powell, whom today we might call an ESL specialist. She would come to pick Lydia up every day for a brief English lesson. Sadly for me, Miss Powell was gone by the time I started school a year later. Lydia remembers her fondly to this day because she made school life more manageable. I had precious little English when I began school a year later, though I know that Lydia, knowing a bit more of the language, helped me navigate this very scary terrain. But in spite of feeling like a fish out of water, from the very start I was sold on school: I loved the rhythm of it, the weekly spelling tests, the homework, the workbooks, the Dick and Jane readers, even the smell. I decided from the time I was in 4th grade, and perhaps even earlier, that I wanted to be a teacher.

When my mother brought my brother Freddy, 3 years my junior, to enroll him in school, he cried every day for a week. My sister, by then in 4th grade and fluent in English and Spanish, was called to the main office every day to see if she could comfort Freddy. Lydia and I weren't aware that he had a developmental disability. By the end of his first and only week at school, my parents were called to the principal's office and told that they couldn't enroll Freddy because "he's not normal." Freddy spent most of what would have been his schooling years at home, cared for lovingly by my mother. Initially diagnosed as "mentally retarded," a designation no longer in wide use now, years later he was determined to be autistic.

All of this is to set the stage for what I've been thinking about as I prepared to write this essay; that is, *What would I have wanted school to be like? What might have made it a more welcoming, caring, and academically challenging place for me and for my siblings? How might it have been a more respectful place for my parents and others like them? What might have made me feel that I belonged?* These are the questions that motivated me to go to graduate school and that eventually led to the kind of research, writing, and teaching that I've done since I entered the academy. The quest to answer them has been my lifelong odyssey.

What follows are some of my thoughts on what I would have wanted school to be like for me and for many other children who, like me and my siblings, do not receive the schooling they deserve.

First, I wish someone, even just one person, had been able to speak to me in Spanish, the only language I knew. What a difference that would have made!

For at least the first year of my schooling, I often struggled to say the words I knew I needed to say but did not yet have. Of course, I had many words, but they were in the wrong language, a language not deemed adequate for learning. My mother, who would sometimes become exasperated with how much I talked, affectionately told people that I was "*una cotorra*," a parrot, because I never stopped, but in school I was at first mute. It is no surprise, then, that in 1968 I became a teacher at P.S. 25 in the Bronx, the very first public fully bilingual school in the Northeast. There, I gave my 4th graders what I never had from any teacher: a person who could speak to them in their home language, who could read them stories in Spanish, who could comfort them in a language they understood when they fell or were hurt, and who could communicate with their families with respect and understanding. I also gave my students the gift of the English language, a language I had learned to love and that gave me the education I craved, while still cherishing my mother tongue. One of the greatest gifts I have is my bilingualism and, through my languages, the ability to be bicultural. I am grateful for this gift every day (Nieto, 2011).

I wish that I had seen myself, or someone who looked or lived like me, in a book or in the curriculum. When I started school in 1949, neither bilingual education nor multicultural education had made an appearance. Although I liked reading the Dick and Jane books—I was an avid reader and they read like fantasy stories to me, because the life they described was so far removed from my own—the characters in those books didn't look anything like me or my family, and their suburban lifestyle was completely alien to our urban experience. Our families were usually bigger and extended, not nuclear, we lived in different kinds of housing, ate different foods, rarely had pets, didn't have music or dance lessons or play organized sports. Although by then there were already over a million Puerto Ricans living in the United States, mostly in New York, our experiences never made their way into the books we read at school. Interestingly but perhaps not surprisingly, years later when I became an academic, children's literature with diverse protagonists and themes became one of my research interests. I guess it was my way of making visible the lives of children of diverse backgrounds, giving them what I never had.

When I was in school, Columbus "discovered America," George Washington "never told a lie," and Brown and Black people were invisible in any substantive way from the school's staff to the curriculum. I absorbed all the "lies my teacher told me," in the words of James Loewen's groundbreaking book (2018), lies that did a magnificent job of whitewashing United States history by excluding anything even slightly controversial or against the official canon. We were never in the curriculum, at least not in any meaningful way. The only time I heard Puerto Rico mentioned was when I was in an 8th grade history class. Our textbook contained one page about Operation

Bootstrap, an economic development program purportedly created to promote industrialization in Puerto Rico. That was the story the textbook told,
but it took me years to learn the whole story: Through economic incentives
(few or no taxes, for example), Operation Bootstrap mostly helped U.S.
companies to make tremendous profits while diminishing farming and leaving Puerto Ricans more dependent on U.S. goods, including food products.
It also led to wholesale migration to the United States. That was the extent
of Puerto Rico or Puerto Ricans in my curriculum.

**I wish that educators at the schools I attended hadn't made so many assump-
tions about us.** When I say "us," I mean any children who don't fit the profile
of white middle-class English-speaking children. I remember when my sister
Lydia's 5th-grade teacher suggested that Lydia needed a more nutritious
diet, though not in so many words because he was a caring teacher who
probably wanted to be helpful. True, we didn't eat the traditional U.S. diet,
but we had a substantial breakfast every morning, a good lunch at home,
and then a dinner that consisted of rice, beans, some kind of meat, and often a salad. Because she was so thin, he might have assumed Lydia wasn't
getting enough to eat, or enough of the "right" foods. Rather than probing
into his concerns in more detail, he probably made an assumption based on
our social class and immigrant standing. However, his was a concern from a
caring teacher. There were others who were less discreet, more uninformed,
and more bigoted.

When I was 14 years old—by this time, we lived in a more middle-class
Brooklyn neighborhood and I went to one of the best high schools in the
city—another situation stands out. There, I was one of a small number of
Puerto Ricans in our huge high school of over 5,000 students. One morning,
my homeroom teacher loudly asked me if I was in a special English class.
Any 14-year-old would have been embarrassed to be singled out in that
way. There was nothing wrong with the question; in fact, it no doubt meant
that by that time, there were finally services for English learners—but the
way he asked the question showed a lack of tact, to say the least. That's because the assumption was, as it still often is, that speaking a home language
other than English is a deficit rather than the tremendous gift that it is. I
guess I felt a bit smug when I told him that, yes, I was in a special English
class: "I'm in Honors English," I said.

I wish someone could have told teachers, including this one, that they
should approach students individually and with discretion, especially 14-
and 15-year-olds who tend to be embarrassed by *everything*. But more important, I wish someone had taught him about students like me, both those
who were in ESL classes and those who were in Honors English.

**I wish that my teachers had taught me to think critically and to challenge
the way things are.** No child wants to feel invisible in school, so in spite of

the absence of my family in the curriculum, I remember trying desperately to insert us in it. For example, I knew that my father, despite his skimpy education, was a smart man who had made a decent life for us. He was a bodega owner and his miniscule store was often the center of the community. He was widely respected, referred to with the honorific "Don Tito." He let many of his customers take *fiao*—credit—until they received their next check, helping many in the community whose finances couldn't always cover their basic nutritional needs (naturally, even though most of his customers paid him back when they were able, he lost a great deal of money this way). Mostly I remember the dignified way my father carried himself. To me, he was a hero.

When I was in an economics class in high school, we were learning about the difference between low-skilled, semi-skilled, and skilled workers. When the teacher asked us how many of our fathers (mothers weren't even mentioned) were skilled workers, the answers came quickly: "My father is a doctor," one said, and another added, "Mine is a lawyer." I raised my hand to proudly say, "My father owns a bodega." My teacher smiled weakly and said, "Well, maybe *semi-skilled*."

I'm sure my teacher thought she was being kind and helping me save face, but I was crushed. This is not to say that she should've just accepted the response but only to suggest that she might have taken the opportunity to ask us to think about why these classifications existed in the first place. Who decided and why? Why do some professions have more status than others? Who has access to these professions? I think having a conversation about these questions might have led to a conversation in which we could have learned about the arbitrary nature of such designations and the right to question them. I wish my teacher, and all teachers, would engage in what Carmen Martinez-Roldán has termed *daring* pedagogies, that is, equity-oriented and caring pedagogical practices and policies meant to dare young people and their teachers "to co-create a more equitable world" (Martinez-Roldán, 2021).

I wish there had been a place for Freddy. My brother spent nearly the first 30 years of his life at home, mostly with my mother, attending school for only a month at a special school they had found for children like him. But the cost ($150 a month) was prohibitive—remember, this was the early 1950s—so they reluctantly withdrew him. The rest of his life he spent eating, sleeping, staring ahead, and communicating as best he could with us. He learned to say each of our names and a few other words, all of which disappeared years later. By the time my father died, Freddy was in his 30s and my mother was in her 60s. He was a handful, and it became clear to us that she could no longer care for him. With our prodding, she agreed to place him in an institution for the mentally retarded, a place just 3 blocks away from her home. Although it was a beautiful new building, the conditions were horrific. It should have been called a warehouse. She brought him a big hot home-cooked meal every day, but she suffered seeing the conditions in which he lived.

After my family and I moved to Massachusetts, we worked hard at convincing my mother to move near us, but she agreed to do so only if we did everything to somehow bring Freddy too. Fortunately, Massachusetts had recently passed the first law in the nation to deinstitutionalize its hospitals for people diagnosed as mentally retarded, brain injured, autistic, and with Down syndrome. Even more fortunate was the fact that I had recently completed my doctorate and was working at the regional office of the Massachusetts Department of Education. There, I sought out a colleague whose responsibility it was to help the state with the implementation of the new law. He put me in touch with someone who could help us find a place for Freddy and within a month, he and my mother moved to Massachusetts. She spent the remainder of her life living near us and visiting her beloved son with us every week.

This is not a "happily ever after" story, but it certainly turned out far better than it could have been, or than it was for most people like Freddy who never received an adequate and respectful education. After my mother died, I became Freddy's guardian, and his placements improved each time he was moved. When he died a couple of years ago, he was one of 4 men with developmental disabilities living in a beautiful home with excellent care. I gave the eulogy at his service, thanking those who loved and cared for him but bemoaning the fact that he never received the education he deserved. This is part of what I wrote:

> We in the family prefer to keep funny and happy memories of Freddy's life in our hearts, rather than focus on the difficult and sorrowful moments. But I can't help but think about "what might have been" if deinstitutionalization and special education had come three decades earlier when Freddy was a child, than in the 1970s when they began here in Massachusetts. I always wonder what was locked up in that brain of his and what we missed—and he missed—because it stayed locked forever. I feel both a profound sadness, as well as tremendous gratitude that today children and adults with developmental disabilities can finally get the help they need and grow to their full potential. It's probably no surprise that even though there were no teachers in our family, Lydia and I both became educators, me specializing in bilingual education and she in special education.

FINAL THOUGHTS

What might have become of Freddy if all children like him had been offered an excellent and high-quality education despite his disability? What might I have learned in school about my people and others of diverse backgrounds if I had received what we now call *multicultural education* (Nieto & Bode, 2018), *culturally responsive education* (Ladson-Billings, 1995), or *culturally sustaining education* (Paris, 2012)? How much sooner might I have become a critical thinker rather than a "good girl" who followed all the rules if I had received an education that taught me to think more deeply?

Yes, things have changed since I was in school and, yes, there are now more services for children who don't fit the mold of White, middle-class, English speakers. Thankfully, through the hard work of numerous advocates and activists for social justice over many years, children who begin school without knowing English, children with autism and other special needs, and children whose families live in poverty have more protections than was the case when Freddy was supposed to go to kindergarten. But is it enough?

I'm grateful that some of these things are now a reality for some students in our country—though certainly not all—and that, because of this, they can feel visible and included, and have their families honored in our public schools. But that's certainly not the case for all children and, unfortunately, zip codes still matter and relegate children to unequal educational opportunities and outcomes. And although some differences shouldn't matter, being light-skinned still matters, as does speaking "standard" English and living in the "right" neighborhood and being perceived as "normal." Yet all young people deserve to be taught in equitable, humanizing, and caring educational contexts. If we want to work for the day when all young people are given the opportunity to have a consequential life, then we need to begin now, so that in 50 years they don't have to write about "what might have been."

NOTE

1. Puerto Ricans are neither strictly "immigrants" nor "migrants," but occupy some in-between space: we are immigrants in the sense that our people have moved to the continental United States from another place, but we are "migrants" in that we have moved from one place in the nation to another. That is, while Puerto Rico is a territory of the United States, all Puerto Ricans are U.S. citizens, whether born in Brooklyn or San Juan or anywhere else in either the continental U.S. or Puerto Rico. At the same time, Puerto Ricans who reside on the island do not pay federal taxes, nor do they have the right to vote in national elections. It is a strange identity, one that is unknown in other places and that relegates Puerto Ricans to a kind of second-class citizenship (see Nieto, 2000).

REFERENCES

Ladson-Billings, G. (1995). Toward a theory of culturally relevant pedagogy. *American Educational Research Journal, 32* (3), 465–491.

Loewen, J. (2018). *Lies my teacher told me: Everything your American history book got wrong.* New Press. Originally published in 1995.

Martinez-Roldán, C. M. (2021). *Latina agency through narration in education: Speaking up on erasure, identity, and schooling.* Taylor & Francis.

Nieto, S. (Ed.) (2000). *Puerto Rican students in U.S. schools.* Routledge.

Nieto, S. (2011). On learning to tie a bow, and other tales of becoming biliterate. In M. Reyes (Ed.), *Words were all we had: Becoming biliterate against the odds* (pp 15–25). Teachers College Press.

Nieto, S., & Bode, P. (2018). *Affirming diversity: The sociopolitical context of multicultural education* (7th ed.). Pearson.

Oakes, J. (2005). *Keeping track: How schools structure inequality* (2nd ed.). Yale University Press.

Paris, J. (2012). Culturally sustaining pedagogy: A needed change in stance, terminology, and practice. *Educational Researcher, 41*(3), 93–97.

Spring, J. (1988). *The sorting machine revisited: National educational policy since 1945.* Addison-Wesley-Longman.

Necessary But Insufficient

Why Public Schooling Alone Cannot Equalize

Prudence L. Carter

Since a tender young age, I have held the belief that education is the ticket from the bottom to the top of the mobility ladder. My parents, who endured the hardships of cotton picking and extreme poverty as children, demanded a college degree as the minimal educational aspiration for my siblings and me. Like Horace Mann, they believed in education as a great equalizer. I am the product of my parents' socialization and investments—an accomplished scholar, researcher, and now university administrator with a strong educational pedigree. And yet, paradoxically, more schooling and greater knowledge has robbed me of the idealism of education's promise. Twenty years into academic research and teaching in higher education, I no longer espouse the myth that education is the great equalizer. Education—specifically as schooling, an oft-touted panacea for America's various social, health, and economic woes—won't save us. Not in its current formulation, at least.

A NEED FOR SOCIETAL AND EDUCATIONAL TRANSFORMATION

Confronting the existential nature of the COVID-19 crisis has plunged me into deeper philosophical thought. Who and what do we really want to be as a society? How can we reimagine a more effective, visionary 21st-century approach to educating millions? Nearly everyone beats up on U.S. public schooling, especially in central cities and rural communities where the resources are modest, and students tend to perform less well on standardized assessments. Somehow, we expect all of our youth to perform relatively well to exceptionally well on these standardized assessments regardless of sociocultural context and gaping resource disparities. While some students are supported with resources that could fill an ocean tanker, others are expected to attain the same level of performance with resources that could fit in a small freight car. This is flawed thinking at best.

Often, I dream of a United States with equitable education where every level of government works in concert and gives parallel attention to students' critical life needs. In my educational fantasy, policy makers and practitioners rip off the centuries-old façade that *proclaims* equal opportunity, demolish what is in fact an uneven (read unequal) foundation, and rebuild it from the ground up. Knowing and acknowledging that schools alone cannot solve the multifaceted problems of inequity that our society has created and continues to grapple with, federal, state and local departments of education, health and human services, and housing and development would then collectively address the intersecting areas of food, health, and housing security to increase all students' chances for obtaining a high-quality education.

Several years ago, some of the nation's leading thinkers on education argued, in a book edited by University of Colorado–Boulder Professor Kevin Welner and me, that inequality creates opportunity gaps that produce persistent achievement disparities, commonly referred to as "achievement gaps" (*Closing the Opportunity Gap: What America Must do to Give All Children an Even Chance*, 2013). Scores of studies and decades of research had already revealed that to create an even chance of success for most American learners, our leaders would have to address the core needs of children and families: from jobs and income to affordable housing and healthcare to high-quality teaching and learning in culturally rich (and sustaining) school environments. All are necessary: none alone is sufficient to reduce the vast inequalities among the races and social classes today.

Tellingly, the very conditions that denied equal opportunity in schooling for youth from marginalized class, ethnic, and racial backgrounds in the early to mid-20th century are the same conditions that predict enduring patterns of achievement disparities observed nearly a century later. The twin forces of racism and economic inequality that plague our society continue to permeate our schools' walls across the nation's more than 13,000 districts. Racial disproportionality in school discipline, like unbridled, systemic police violence against Black people in wider society, expose what education has been unable to do—and cannot do alone—despite the political mobilization throughout the Civil Rights era of the 1950s and 60s and through the present.

Currently, our nation is in crisis. My research in both the United States and South Africa—two historically racially troubled nations built on the precepts of white supremacy—has taught me that education's importance is fundamentally broader than individual advancement. Rather, there is urgency in this moment for societal transformation that pivots from a narrow and egocentric focus on individualistic attainment and the private good to an inclusive vision of the common good in a richly pluralistic democracy. A just, inclusive, democratic society demands an educational system that not only builds human capital but also fosters students' critical thinking, breeds social cohesion, and cultivates healthy debates in the face of enormous diversity. And yet, many of our children are reared to believe that racial segregation is the natural order of things. Meanwhile, the Southern Poverty Law Center has reported an exponential rise in visible hate crimes in the United States in the aftermath of the election of an unabashed racist for President of the United States. By keeping us separate (and not even close to equal), contemporary school and housing segregation undermine any structural attempts to build an inclusive, democratic nation.

THE NOBLEST PROFESSION AND CULTURAL COMPETENCE

"A teacher who is attempting to teach without inspiring the pupil with a desire to learn is hammering on cold iron," said Horace Mann (1867, p. 225). Two of the most fundamental inputs of schooling are high-quality teaching and curriculum. Teachers have the power to shape minds and shift consciousness. But that often requires a shift in the mindsets and consciousness of teachers themselves. They must understand human development and master engaging pedagogy to be effective. In most schools, teachers expend much effort to impart the basics to their students. Often well-meaning and well intentioned, many teachers desire that their students will master the curricula encapsulating the standards for which teachers are held accountable to convey. Yet to do so effectively and equitably, teachers must possess the cultural competence—the know-how—to understand both their own cultural practices and those of their students, and to firmly grasp that culture is an important part of learning (King, 1994).

Educators are better equipped to teach diverse students if they understand that individual children's development can only be understood in terms of their participation in cultural activities. For example, in his study of high school African American males, Kirkland (2011) found that improving student engagement requires "bridging ideological distances" between students and teachers. Ideology—or beliefs about what people think should be done by others or what is perceived as appropriate—is held within both students' and educators' cultural practices and behaviors. Understanding that learning is a culturally mediated activity enables educators and others to construct a way of seeing how *all people* learn through the prism of their everyday understandings (Howard & Aleman, 2008). Dynamic student engagement is the essence of schooling.

SCHOOLING IN THE WAKE OF A PANDEMIC AND CLIMATE CHANGE

The advent of global pandemics and catastrophic climate changes—producing massive hurricanes and wildfires—has precipitated another cultural change. Millions of schoolchildren and educators in the United States are now forced to learn and teach from home, respectively. To do so effectively, they have to rely heavily on digital learning and curricular tools which, in turn, necessitate reliable Internet access. For some students and their families, this new radical cultural shift to digital technology works; for others, it does not. Fifteen percent of U.S. households with school-age children do not have a high-speed internet connection at home, according to a Pew Research Center analysis of 2015 U.S. Census Bureau data. More than one-third of households with children ages 6 to 17 and whose annual income falls below $30,000 a year do not have a high-speed internet connection at home. Compare this to only 6% of such households earning $75,000 or more a year. This digital divide, which is amplified by the pandemic and climate change events, further compounds the significant academic disparities among ethno-racial and socioeconomic groups. Meeting these challenges for assuring equitable digital access and appropriately evolving curricula and pedagogies is critical for the maintenance of and access to strong, dynamic public education where students of very modest means can avail themselves of the advanced curriculum tools of the moment.

Of course, this assumes that the federal and state governments will provide schools with the additional resources required to attain even a modicum of equity. And the lack of broadband internet access is only a tip of the iceberg in this internet-dependent era. Many teachers have faced a crash course lesson in the provision of online pedagogy, scrambling to learn the ins and outs of Zoom and Google Classroom, in addition to specific programs. The implications for teacher education loom great here: In a digital age, pre-service teachers will require methods courses in digital pedagogy and computer literacy for their respective fields.

ON EDUCATIONAL EQUITY AND ASSESSMENTS

Since the passage and implementation of No Child Left Behind (NCLB) in 2002, and its reincarnation as the Every Student Succeeds Act (ESSA), an intensive focus on high-stakes standardized tests has proven to be a blind spot in the realm of educational reform. Targeted goals for test-score performances for specific student groups were not only unattainable by the mandated year of NCLB (2014), but also not necessarily ameliorative in terms of the wider goals embedded within the original goals of the 1965 Elementary and Secondary Education Act. That is, the intense focus on standardized tests has impeded rather than aided the reduction of inequality in America's schools. Over time, many researchers and practitioners realized that test scores—the outputs of student success—could not be jumpstarted considerably without sufficient attention to inputs—the resource contexts of students' lives inside and outside of schools, including teacher quality, school climate, and broader societal sociocultural conditions (Carter, 2016;

Carter & Welner, 2013; Duncan & Murnane, 2011). That is, some understood that to concentrate too intently on a singular indicator of student success was myopic if we were to understand more holistically what factors could lift the majority of students toward greater educational achievement and mobility in life.

For the 2019–20 school year, K–12 schools did not offer spring testing while in the immediate grip of the COVID-19 pandemic, and colleges and universities suspended the SAT and GRE. Testing students under COVID at any level would surely have reflected more acutely the same cleavages of racialized socioeconomic disadvantage. In a rare instance of unanimity, on May 21, 2020, a few days after the 66th anniversary of the *Brown v. Board of Education* decision, the University of California Regents turned toward the historic direction of progressive change to cast open further the doors of opportunity for more high-potential students rendered invisible by their test scores. They acknowledged that thousands of public school students with strong academic profiles exist in California and around the nation—African American, Latinx, and Indigenous students—disproportionately low(er)-income and underrepresented in the upper echelons of higher education institutions. As the National Center for Education statistics show, these students do not ordinarily attend resource-rich K–12 schools, yet the high achievers exhibit strong effort, enroll in their schools' meager offerings of honors and accelerated classes, achieve As and Bs, serve as leaders in myriad extracurricular activities, and frequently score high on in-class exams.

We have heard repeatedly that the College Board tests correlate strong to family background and resources, and their companion narrative of merit echoes alongside them loudly and convincingly. The Regents' decision will disappoint and create fear in the minds of the tests' proponents, many of whom come from affluent families, schools, and communities that facilitate high scoring. They will also fear a loss of "objectivity" in selective college admissions. But let's be honest: Very little about college admissions and mobility is objective. The stark disparities among our nation's schools and districts, exacerbated and illuminated by the current COVID-19 pandemic, expose that myth. As research studies have shown, not one school district where most students face socioeconomic disadvantage (and generally, by high correlation, are Black and brown youth) has produced median test scores above the national median. Only affluent school districts do (Reardon et al., 2019). This by no means erases the accomplishment of a critical number of students from lower income and/or racially minoritized backgrounds who score very highly. Still, on average, both school and family context explain more about school achievement than do standardized tests. Furthermore, if either private tutor support or preparatory programs can manipulate performance on standardized achievement tests, then inequality stares us in the face even more directly.

A MOMENT OF RECKONING AND TIME FOR CHANGE

The 2020 COVID-19 pandemic is forcing a reckoning with both how we organize school and what we expect children to learn. From the Reagan-era *A Nation at Risk* report to the Bush- and Obama-eras No Child Left Behind and Common Core, education reformists have rallied behind standards, the idea that students need to obtain specific skills and hold particular facts in their heads by a certain age and grade. But at the most, these policy changes have led to only modest improvements in student achievement throughout the nation, especially for historically racially minoritized and low-income youth. Have we really gotten to the bottom of what is driving educators' and policy makers' myopia about teaching and learning, and how schools might do away with their current factory model where teachers are expected to impart information in groups of 25–30 similarly aged kids?

I have no doubt that now is a time to radically reimagine the why, what, and how of American public education. In these strange times, the words of the celebrated Indian writer and activist, Arundhati Roy, have resonated with me. She has written: "Historically, pandemics have forced humans to break with the past and imagine their world anew. This one . . . is a portal, a gateway between one world and the next. We can choose to walk through it, dragging the carcasses of our prejudice and hatred. . . . Or we can walk through lightly, with little luggage, ready to imagine another world" (Roy, 2020). More than a century prior, Horace Mann is believed to have declared: "Let us not be content to wait and see what will happen, but give us the determination to make the right things happen." We can choose to cross to the other side of this historic pandemic and pick up where we left off, mired in current public education's inability to realize its fullest potential, or we can be determined to begin afresh, with determination to "make the right things happen." Will we dare to be bolder and forward-thinking?

In our commitment to public education, like Horace Mann, can we imagine an educational system that gets us closer to our capacity to be an engaged, dynamic society committed to equity, justice, and empathic understanding across multiple lines of social difference? Critically, are educators and policy makers able to implement policy and practice in a manner that cultivates the deepest love for learning and nurtures the greatest potential of all students despite their social backgrounds? Our public schools *alone* cannot transform our society into the more equitable and just democracy our nation's founding documents promise, but neither can society achieve this transformation *without* our schools. Our public schools can rise and transform to meet this moment. Can we summon the necessary will and commitment to ensure they do?

REFERENCES

Carter, P. L. (2016). Educational equality is a multifaceted issue: Why we must understand the school's sociocultural context for student achievement. *Russell Sage Foundation Journal of the Social Sciences, 2*(5), 142–163.

Carter, P. L., & Welner, K. G. (Eds.). (2013). *Closing the opportunity gap: What America must do to give all children an even chance*. Oxford University Press.

Duncan, G. J., & Murnane, R. J. (Eds.). 2011. *Whither opportunity?: Rising inequality, schools, and children's life chances*. Russell Sage Foundation, Spencer Foundation.

Howard, T. C., & Aleman, G. R. (2008). Teacher capacity for diverse learners. In M. Cochran-Smith (Ed.), *Handbook of research on teacher education: Enduring questions in changing contexts* (Vol. 3). Routledge.

King, J. E. (1994). The purpose of schooling for African American children: Including cultural knowledge. In E. R. Hollins, J. E. King & W. C. Hayman (Eds.), *Teaching diverse populations: Formulating a knowledge base* (pp. 25–56). State University of New York Press.

Kirkland, D. (2011). Books like clothes: Engaging young Black men with reading. *Journal of Adolecent and Adult Literacy, 55* (199–208).

Mann, H. (1867). *Thoughts selected frm the writing of Harace Mann*. H. B. Fuller & Co.

Reardon, S. F., Weathers, E. S., Fahle, E. M., Jang, H., & Kalogrides, D. (2019). *Is separate still unequal? New evidence on school segregation and racial academic achievement gaps*. [Working Paper 19-06]. Stanford Center for Education Policy Analysis. https://eric.ed.gov/?id=ED600999 .

Roy, A. (2020). The pandemic is a portal. *Financial Times*. https://www.ft.com/content/10d8f5e8-74eb-11ea-95fe-fcd274e920ca

Public Education for the Public Good

Black Teachers and Teaching

H. Richard Milner IV

In this chapter, I highlight the importance of public education and discuss some of the important practices and contributions of Black teachers over the years. Although the teaching profession receives much criticism, I argue that teachers within the profession support student learning and development in profound ways—despite structurally and systemically challenging contexts.

It is no secret: Teachers play an enormous role in the success and sustainability of traditional public schools across the United States. Although teachers tend to work hard within what can be described as challenging conditions and situations, they are constantly under attack. Teachers seem to be blamed for just about everything. For instance, under the guise of achievement, teachers are blamed for low test scores among their students even though it is clear that student learning far exceeds what a test can measure (Brady, 2015). Teachers are blamed for the lack of motivation and engagement among students, for mandated assessment practices that do not well align with student needs, and for decreased curriculum and instructional time in physical education and the arts. While teachers certainly play some role in what I have described above, many of the challenges extend far beyond the locus of control among teachers.

Blaming and attacking teachers is a consequence, in part, of how the public views and values the profession of teaching. For instance, when I shared with my father that I desired to become an English teacher, he strongly rejected my interest and encouraged me to pursue a different line of work. It can be argued that the teaching profession is too often disrespected and undervalued (Milner, 2013), and such disrespect and disvalue manifest in, for example, compensation models that send a negative message to all about teachers' material worth. Indeed, teachers tend to be poorly compensated for their work (Frolich, 2018), although they tend to work overtime to support student learning and development. The top five states in terms of compensation in 2018 were New York, Connecticut, California, Alaska, and Massachusetts, with median annual salaries ranging from $78,576 in New York to $74,468 in Massachusetts. However, the cost of living in these states tended to be extremely high in comparison to national averages across other states. In Massachusetts, for instance, the cost of living was 6.9% greater than the national average and ranked as the 7th highest cost of living in the U.S. The cost of living in New York is 15.3% greater than the national average and the 2nd highest in the U.S.

Oklahoma, ranked 50th as the state with the lowest median teacher salary at $39,306, was not much lower than states ranked 45th through 49th: In West Virginia the median salary for teachers was $45,437, in North Carolina the median salary for teachers was $45,195, in Mississippi the median salary for teachers was $44,294, in Arizona the median salary for teachers was $44,284, and in South Dakota the median salary for teachers was $41,271 (Frolich, 2018).

Weak compensation scales can result in teachers working part-time jobs after school and on weekends. These part-time positions are sometimes in education (such as work in tutoring or enrichment programs) and at other times outside of the field of education (such as work in restaurants or supermarkets). My point is: if we valued the profession of teaching and consequently teachers, they would be much better compensated for the important work they do in light of costs of living that force them to work multiple jobs just to survive. Teachers make significant contributions to the lives of young people and to advancing the ideas and ideals of democracy.

While the points I will make potentially have implications for all racial and ethnic groups of teachers, in this chapter, I especially highlight the many contributions of Black teachers in the profession of teaching. My focus on Black teachers provides an important context and a case for the essential roles Black teachers have played throughout history to form, shape, and advance the very best of what we call public education. My advancement of this argument—that Black teachers have made truly significant contributions to the very core of the good in public education—is grounded in established and foundational research of Michele Foster, Jackie Irvine, Vanessa Siddle Walker, and Gloria Ladson-Billings. These researchers have well established the many contributions of Black teachers, describing and documenting the practices of these teachers before and after the *Brown* (1954) decision as well as their tenacity and fortitude to educate all students in the midst of racist and sexist social contexts.

Before outlining elements and contributions of Black teachers as exemplars to public education, in the next section, I discuss and situate challenging images and perceptions of teachers and teaching as a profession.

TEACHERS AND THE TEACHING PROFESSION

Indeed, teaching has been seen as a semi-profession, as an occupation unworthy of professional status (Connelly & Rosenberg, 2009). Rotherham (2011) explained that "true professions are structured like medicine and law" (p. 184). Unlike fields such as medicine, engineering, or law, people may believe that one is simply "born to teach" or that teachers rely mostly or solely on their intuition in making pedagogical decisions with their students rather than on their pedagogical knowledge, skill, and ability. Moreover, in a compulsory educational system such as in the United States, people in society tend to have some view of the profession of teaching and what teaching should look like because most have been students themselves in traditional public schools. For example, some may believe that if teachers simply or solely have good intentions, "care about education," and "like children," they should be able to teach. Knowledge in a subject matter area like mathematics or history may be the central requirement for an effective teacher for others. But is it enough to simply have good intentions, or for one to have a deep knowledge, understanding, and expertise in a subject matter domain without the pedagogical knowledge, understanding, expertise, skill, and ability to actually teach effectively in that domain? In other words, is there a professional skill base for teaching a subject, or is building that kind of knowledge and skill to teach an afterthought about which we should not be concerned?

The lack of control by teachers over the development and implementation of what they teach (the curriculum) plays a role in the way teaching is seen. For instance, if teachers are reading from a predetermined pacing guide or script or are teaching to a test they had no input in developing, they are not drawing much from their professional knowledge and judgment, as other professionals are able and expected to do. Teachers not being able to or expected to draw from their professional knowledge and judgement contributes to the de-professionalization and negative perception of teaching as a field.

Moreover, variation in how teachers are prepared as well as the amount of time they spend preparing to learn how to teach also can lead to negative images of teaching as a profession. Fast-track teacher preparation programs that are called non-traditional teacher education programs (Zeichner, 2017) make it difficult for the public to view teaching as a real profession. How can one build the knowledge, insights, and skills necessary to succeed in a profession over a few weekends such as those that fast-track teachers into the profession? But the work of teaching, when considered as a profession, is complex, arduous, multifaceted, and difficult.

What Teachers Know and Do

To be effective in different sociopolitical contexts, teachers must know and understand a deep and wide range of matters, and they must navigate and negotiate policies, expectations and practices emerging inside and outside of a school building. Building on their knowledge, teachers must understand how to best handle discipline problems in the classroom, school, or even district. Teachers must learn about and address online conflicts and bullying among young people as students are actively involved in social media dilemmas with friends and associates. In addition, teachers must well know and understand their subject matter, and they need to understand and be able to respond to the contextual idiosyncrasies and nuances of classroom life that manifest as they work to teach their subject.

Shulman's (1987) work pointed to the necessity of teachers' development of subject matter knowledge as well as pedagogical knowledge. His work stressed the convergence of the two: teachers' pedagogical content knowledge, the knowledge teachers have of their content, and how they teach and convey that content to their students. My point is that subject matter knowledge is necessary but insufficient to the work of teachers and teaching. Teachers must know their content but also be able to teach it to real people in real places addressing and responding to authentic issues.

Haberman (1995), building from 40 years of research of teachers of urban and high poverty students, explained that while it is essential for teachers to know their subject matter, this knowing is insufficient for the kind of work necessary to be successful in urban and high-poverty schools. He maintained that many teachers fail in high-poverty environments because they do not have the ability to connect with students and build relationships with them. In the simplest form, an essential element of teaching is learning about the students with whom teachers are teaching.

Thus, in building and supporting the work of teaching in support of public education, it is essential that people understand that teaching involves teachers' ability to (1) build relationships with students; (2) develop classroom management strategies and skills; (3) understand and build on the historical context of a community, school, and district; (4) understand and negotiate the sociopolitical landscape of an environment; (5) develop partnerships with family members of their students, the community, and other stakeholders; (6) work collaboratively with their students, colleagues and administrators in developing learning opportunities; (7) develop culturally relevant and responsive instructional materials and instructional practices; (8) build appropriate assessment tools; (9) build on and from interests of students and the community; (10) identify and build on assets of all students, the community, their colleagues, and themselves (as teachers); and (11) contextualize and transform standards in ways that are instructionally innovative.

My point is that although teaching is often seen in a negative and simplistic light, effective teaching is deeply complex and involved work that requires teachers to be knowledgeable and innovatively skilled to engage and enact practices potentially transformative for students. Teachers must be highly skilled, confident, engaged, and capable of knowing and teaching their subject matter and also connecting with the humanity of students.

While all teachers engage in the work discussed herein and tend to be devalued when the public does not deeply understand their work, Black teachers have historically had to navigate and negotiate systems of racism, sexism, and other forms of discrimination. These teachers make public education an ideal form of what a democratic society can and should be for all young people. My purpose in highlighting some of the work, contributions, and insights from Black teachers is to provide a case for the complexity and vital importance of teachers' work, and to stress the argument that teachers are at the very center of the good in public education.

Black Teachers in/for Public Education

Black teachers and their multiple roles, identities, and contributions have been the focus of many research articles, commentaries, and conceptual analyses (Foster, 1997; Ladson-Billings, 2009; Milner & Howard, 2004; Tillman, 2004). The literature on Black teachers and their teaching spans the pre-desegregation era to the present and focuses on P–12 schools as well as higher education. Research is clear that having more Black teachers in the teaching force could potentially meet a wide range of needs in education. Current studies show that students from different racial backgrounds report Black teachers as their "preference" (Cherng & Halpin, 2016), and research shows that when Black students have even a single Black teacher, their achievement may increase (Easton-Brooks, 2019; Yarnell & Bohrnstedt, 2018). However, many of these teachers have worked through horrific situations (both pre- and post-desegregation), such as lack of necessary resources to support student learning and development. In spite of their challenging situations, Black teachers—and particularly Black women—have worked for the common good. They have gone above and beyond the call of duty for public good, interests, and benefit.

For Public Education and the Public Good

Siddle Walker (2000), in discussing mindsets, practices, and dedication of Black teachers before the *Brown* decision, explained that these teachers were "consistently remembered for their high expectations for student success, for their dedication, and for their demanding teaching style; these [Black] teachers appear to have worked with the assumption that their job was to be certain that children learned the material presented" (p. 265–66). Black teachers have been cited for demonstrating a deep and committed level of care for their Black students, pre-desegregation. Although these teachers were teaching their students during segregation, they were also preparing their students for a world of integration (Siddle-Walker, 1996) as they understood the potential consequences for undereducated Black students during a time when they were already considered less than human. Moreover, as Tillman (2004) found, "these teachers saw potential in their Black students, considered them to be intelligent, and were committed to their success" (p. 282). These Black teachers' instructional and relational practices were designed inside of school to benefit the public good. These teachers taught even when they themselves were struggling (Milner, in press). These teachers taught because they aspired for a better world.

Black teachers saw their jobs and roles to exceed far beyond the hallways of the school or their classroom. They had a mission to teach their students because they realized the risks and consequences in store for their students if they did not teach them and if the students did not learn. An undereducated and under-prepared Black student, during a time when society did not want or expect these students to succeed, could likely lead to destruction (drug abuse, prison, or even death). Perhaps most importantly, these Black teachers empathized with their Black students because many of them were parents themselves. They often saw and connected with their students as parents and refused to allow them to fail (Tillman, 2004).

In addition, Siddle Walker (2000) concluded that because of the hard work and dedication of Black teachers, "students did not want to let them down" (p. 265). The students put forth effort and achieved academically and socially because

> teachers held extracurricular tutoring sessions, visited homes and churches in the community where they taught, even when they did not live in the community, and provided guidance about "life" responsibilities. They talked with students before and after class, carried a student home if it meant that the child would be able to participate in some extracurricular activity he or she would not otherwise participate in, purchased school supplies for their classroom, and helped to supply clothing for students whose parents had fewer financial resources and scholarship money for those who needed help to go to college. (Siddle Walker, 2000, p. 265)

Indeed, Black teachers have historically exemplified the very best of what it means to teach and be part of the teaching profession. They have tended to see their role and work as benefiting and advancing the public good through public education.

CONCLUSIONS

Although, in this chapter, I have showcased Black teachers as ideal exemplars in defending and advancing public education, it is important to know that systemic and structural supports are essential for the social and psychological health of these (and other) teachers. During segregation, although Black teachers struggled with a range of challenges inside and outside of education, they also tended to be supported by their Black leadership (principals, superintendents, and so forth) in cultivating learning opportunities that enhanced the very humanity of young people. In this way, these teachers were defenders and even trendsetters in demonstrating what could be in public education when individuals were committed to the welfare and well-being of Black students placed on the margins of teaching and learning. Moreover, these Black teachers demonstrated what could be in public education when Black leadership, structures, and systems are in place, and embrace a true commitment to educating Black children.

REFERENCES

Brady, M. (2015). The important things standardized tests don't measure. https://www.washingtonpost.com/news/answer-sheet/wp/2015/03/01/the-important-things-standardized-tests-dont-measure/

Cherng, H., & Halpin, P. (2016). The importance of minority teachers: Student perceptions of minority versus White teachers. *Educational Researcher, 45*(7), 407–420.

Connelly, V. J., & Rosenberg, M. S. (2009). Special education teaching as a profession: Lessons learned from occupations that have achieved full professional standing. *Teacher Education and Special Education, 32*(3), 201–214.

Easton-Brooks, D. (2019). *Ethnic matching: Academic success of students of color.* Rowman & Littlefield.

Foster, M. (1997). *Black teachers on teaching.* The New Press.

Frolich, T. (2018, May 16). Teacher pay: States where educators are paid the most and least. *USA Today.* https://www.usatoday.com/story/money/careers/2018/05/16/states-where-teachers-paid-most-and-least/34964975

Haberman, M. (1995). *Star teachers of children in poverty.* Kappa Delta Pi.

Ladson-Billings, G. (2009). *The dreamkeepers: Successful teachers of African American children.* Jossey-Bass Publishers.

Milner, H. R. (2013). *Policy reforms and de-professionalization of teaching.* National Education Policy Center. http://nepc.colorado.edu/publication/policy-reforms-deprofessionalization

Milner, H. R. (in press). Disrupting punitive practices and policies: Rac(e)ing back to teaching, teacher preparation, and *Brown. Educational Researcher.*

Milner, H. R., & Howard, T. C. (2004). Black teachers, Black students, Black communities and *Brown*: Perspectives and insights from experts. *Journal of Negro Education, 73*(3), 285–297.

Rotherham, A. J. (2011). A profession? In D. Drury and J. Baer (Eds.), *The American public school teacher: Past, present, and future* (pp. 185–189). Harvard Education Press.

Shulman, L. S. (1987). Knowledge and teaching: Foundations of the new reform. *Harvard Educational Review*, 19(2), 4–14.

Siddle Walker, V. (1996). *Their highest potential: An African American school community in the segregated south*. University of North Carolina Press.

Siddle Walker, V. (2000). Valued segregated schools for African American children in the South, 1935–1969: A review of common themes and characteristics. *Review of Educational Research*, 70(3), 253–285.

Tillman, L. C. (2004). (Un)Intended consequences? The impact of Brown v. Board of Education decision on the employment status of Black educators. *Education and Urban Society*, 36(3), 280–303.

Yarnell, L., & Bohrnstedt, G. (2018). Student-teacher racial match and its association with Black student achievement: An exploration using multilevel structural equation modeling. *American Educational Research Journal, 55*(2), 287–324.

Zeichner, K. (2017). *The struggle for the soul of teacher education*. Routledge.

Making the Common School Truly Common

Black Americans' Long and Unfinished Fight for Integrated Schools

Jeanne M. Powers

> Education, then, beyond all other devices of human origin, is the great equalizer of the conditions of men—the balance wheel of the social machinery.
>
> —Horace Mann (1848a)

> Black Americans have also been, and continue to be, foundational to the idea of American freedom. More than any other group in this country's history, we have served, generation after generation, in an overlooked but vital role: It is we who have been the perfecters of this democracy.
>
> —Nikole Hannah-Jones (2019)

In this famous quotation from his *Twelfth Annual Report* to the Massachusetts State Board of Education (1848a), Mann describes his vision for the common school as a way to increase the prosperity of entire communities by expanding access to education beyond an elite to "the people at large— . . . the sons and daughters of farmers, mechanics, tradesmen, operatives and laborers of all kinds" (p. 75). This proposal is also an implicit argument for democratizing public education. While expanding access to public education was a consistent theme in Mann's career, this did not include public advocacy for desegregated public schools during his tenure as the Commissioner of Education, when his political influence over the nascent system of common schools was at its highest. Throughout the long history of the common school, the project of improving public schools by expanding access to education was taken up in large part by Black families in both the North and the South, who also saw education as the great equalizer by challenging segregation, a form of inequality that was built into public schools as they developed (Moss, 2009).

SEGREGATION IN THE COMMON SCHOOL PERIOD

As Moss (2009) has documented, after the American Revolution and during the initial period of the development and expansion of the publicly supported common school in the Northeast (1789–1855), towns in Mann's home state of Massachusetts such as Boston, Nantucket, and Salem maintained separate schools for Black students well into Mann's tenure as secretary of the Board of Education. Black families contested segregation in all three towns—young Black women and their families were at the forefront of these efforts (see also Baumgartner, 2020; Devlin, 2018). Black Bostonians ultimately challenged school segregation in court in one of the earliest known school segregation cases, *Roberts v. City of Boston* (1849). Yet Mann did not publicly support the Black families' efforts, although in his private correspondence he discussed them extensively and indicated that he supported desegregation (Moss, 2009).[1] Mann did not publicly support desegregation even after Wendell Philips, a prominent abolitionist, accused Mann of refusing to support desegregation because it would jeopardize his efforts to establish universal public education.

After leaving his post as Secretary of Education in Massachusetts, Mann was elected to succeed John Quincy Adams in Congress (1848), where he became an ardent and outspoken opponent of slavery (Cassara, 1971). In his speeches to Congress, Mann argued that slavery was a barrier to establishing common schools in the South (Mann, 1848b). Enslaved Black Americans comprised the vast majority of the labor in the South at the time and state laws prevented them from being educated. While the children of the white Southern elite would attend schools outside of the South or be taught by governesses, there were not enough children of white laborers to operate community schools because "Common Schools cannot exist where population is sparse" (Mann, 1848b, p. 15). Mann also argued that it was immoral to restrict Black Americans' access to education in his February 1849 speech to Congress entitled "Slavery and the Slave Trade." Mann noted:

> no child in whose skin there is a shadow of a shade of African complexion is to be found there. The channels are so cut that all the sacred and healing waters of knowledge flow, not to him, but by him. Sir, of all the remorseless and wanton cruelties ever committed in this world of wickedness and wo[e], I hold that to be the most remorseless and wanton which shuts out from all the means of instruction a being whom God has endued with the capacities of knowledge, and inspired with the divine desire to know. (Mann, 1849, p. 21)

Both of Mann's stances—his silence on school desegregation and his full-throated opposition to slavery and the denial of education to Black Americans—suggest that Mann engaged in interest convergence tactics (Bell, 1980), where White elites publicly support civil rights only when it advances their own agendas.

The ways that Black Americans engaged with public education systems as they evolved in the North during the common school era, in the South during Reconstruction, and in the aftermath of the *Brown v. Board of Education* decision reflect both what Mann described as a "divine desire to know" and (to paraphrase Mann), Black Americans' "noble careers" to improve public education. In the sections that follow, I reflect upon these two foci in the context of Hannah-Jones's argument in *The 1619 Project*, in which she centers Black Americans as foundational to the idea of American freedom and as resolute perfecters of our democracy. State-sanctioned segregation is an undemocratic practice based on white supremacist assumptions that people can be divided into discrete racial groups that are hierarchically ordered with Whites on the top of the racial hierarchy. In challenging segregation across time, locales, and generations, Black Americans have done critical work toward advancing democracy and realizing Mann's vision. By fighting for inclusive common schools, they embraced education as the great equalizer in an arc of educational activism that occurred alongside the development and expansion of the common school. While this project remains unfinished, and many of their efforts remain unknown, Black Americans' long history of educational activism on behalf of their and future generations of children is as American as public education.

THE EXPANSION OF THE COMMON SCHOOL AFTER RECONSTRUCTION

As Hannah-Jones observed in her essay framing *The 1619 Project*, during Reconstruction Black voters and lawmakers were instrumental in establishing systems of common schools in the South (Hannah-Jones, 2019). Their efforts were documented by W. E. B. Du Bois (e.g., Du Bois, 1911, 1935a, 1935b) and later by James Anderson (1988) in *The Education of Blacks in the South, 1850–1935*. When White plantation owners in the South regained power after Reconstruction, they "contained the expansion of common schools" until the late 19th century, when White small-scale farmers began to demand public schools (Anderson, 1988, p. 148). When White political elites expanded access to public education, they used public school funds to educate White children. Most Black children in the South did not have access to public schools.

In the early 20th century, when the Great Migration began to draw Black agricultural workers out of rural areas in the South, White elites in the South began to recognize the need to increase access to education for

Black children (Anderson, 1988). During this period, Northern philanthropists who were connected with the Hampton and Tuskegee Institutes worked with Southern school officials to support the expansion of public schools for Black children because they wanted to create a well-trained and stable agricultural workforce in the South (Anderson, 1978). One of the most high-profile of these was the Rosenwald Fund, which supported the construction of over 5,000 Black schools throughout the South. However, Black families contributed a substantial share of the funds for public schools for their children through cash and in-kind donations, in what Anderson (1988) described as the "second crusade for common schools" (p. 179). These contributions were in essence a second tax for Black families because most of their tax dollars were allocated to support segregated public schools for White children.

CHALLENGING SEGREGATION: A LONG TRADITION

School segregation is as old as the common school. Decade after decade, Black families both pursued alternative means to educate their children when they were excluded from common schools and contested segregation in common schools (Bond, 1935; see also Anderson, 2016). These efforts occurred in tandem with the development of the common school. For example, in Boston, Black families established a private school when the town government rejected their appeal to provide a separate school for their children because the nascent system of public schools excluded their children (Moss, 2009). As I described earlier, Black Bostonians also challenged school segregation in *Roberts v. City of Boston*. In both Northern and Southern states, school segregation predated the system of Jim Crow laws in the South that White Southern lawmakers passed after Reconstruction ended in 1877 (Peterson, 1935; Woodward, 1955).

At the end of the 19th century, the Supreme Court consolidated segregation as a policy regime by declaring segregation constitutional in *Plessy v. Ferguson* (1896). However, Black and other families of color continued to contest segregation (Powers, 2008, 2014). As Peterson (1935) documented, between 1865 and 1935, 113 cases challenging segregation were brought in state supreme courts in 29 states. While the majority of these cases (58%) were in Southern states, a substantial proportion (27%) were in Midwestern states. Over half of the cases in the South were decided after *Plessy*. All of these cases predated the cases associated with the NAACP's legal campaign against segregation that culminated in *Brown v. Board of Education* (1954), which began when Charles Hamilton Houston was appointed as chief counsel in 1935 (NAACP, 2021). Because challenging segregation in the courts is often a long and drawn-out process, these cases should be viewed as the culmination of long-term efforts by the families that initiated them. It is likely that many of these families engaged in multiple strategies outside of the legal system in the years before they sought redress in the courts. For example, Black Bostonians submitted multiple petitions for desegregation to the school committee in the four years before they finally resorted to challenging segregation in the courts (Moss, 2009). It is also likely that many other efforts on the part of Black families to force school districts to desegregate were never heard by courts, and thus never became part of the public record and archives.

BROWN AND BEYOND: WHITE RESISTANCE AND BLACK PERSISTENCE IN THE SOUTH AND BEYOND

After the Supreme Court's decision in *Brown v. Board of Education* (1954), Black families continued to fight for desegregation, even in the face of massive, and often violent, White resistance.[2] Most of us are familiar with the *Brown* decision in 1954, the "rights" phase, where the Supreme Court declared racial segregation unconstitutional. In the second, less celebrated "remedy" decision, *Brown II* (1955), the Supreme Court remanded cases challenging segregation to the lower courts that had upheld segregation and ordered them to oversee desegregation "with all deliberate speed" (p. 349). White southerners opposed to desegregation saw *Brown II* as legitimizing efforts to resist segregation (Ogletree, 2004). Moreover, the organized activities of Whites resisting segregation were sanctioned by state, federal, and local officials not only in the South, but throughout much of the country (Minow, 2010; see also Anderson, 2016; McRae, 2018). As a result, long after *Brown*, Black families had to challenge school districts to live up to the promise of *Brown*, limited though it was. As Harris (1993) observed, *Brown* dismantled the formal legal structure of segregation that was institutionalized by *Plessy*, but not the way that segregation "structured material inequalities into all socioeconomic relations and institutions, including publicly funded schools" (p. 1751). As Ruth Batson, an activist who fought to end segregation in Boston in the 1960s and 1970s observed:

> When we would go to white schools, we'd see these lovely classrooms, with a small number of children in each class. The teachers were permanent. We'd see wonderful materials. When we would go to our schools, we would see overcrowded classrooms, children sitting out in the corridors, and so forth. And so we decided that where there were a large number of white students, that's where the care went. That's where the books went. That is where the money went. (Hampton & Fayer, 1990, pp. 588–589)

Two scenes from *Eyes on the Prize*, the classic and groundbreaking documentary on the civil rights movement (Devinney, Bond, & Hampton,

2010), provide vivid and important reminders of the resistance to desegregation that Black families faced and persisted against in the years after *Brown*. The first is Elizabeth Eckford's lonely and harrowing walk to school as one of the Little Rock Nine while she was followed and harassed by a howling White mob. The Little Rock School Board decided to comply with the *Brown* decision five days after the decision was announced, although the superintendent took three years to determine how to proceed (Margolick, 2011). In the summer of 1957, a small group of Black students were selected to desegregate Central High School in Little Rock; after many students dropped out, nine remained.

Famously resisting the desegregation plan, Arkansas Governor Orval Faubus had surrounded the school with members of the Arkansas National Guard and ordered them to bar the Black students until a federal court declared that the district's plan must proceed. Because of a breakdown in communication, Eckford ended up taking the bus to school and walking the remainder of the distance by herself instead of approaching the school with the eight other students. After she was prevented from entering the school by the National Guard, she walked to a bus stop to go home, threatened by an almost all-White crowd calling for her to be lynched (see the account in Margolick, 2011). In a clip from *Eyes on the Prize*, Eckford is surrounded by an angry White mob shouting racial epithets. She sits, waiting for a bus to take her home, her eyes covered by sunglasses; Eckford remains silent while a reporter attempts to interview her. A member of the National Guard stands nearby holding a billy club; he has a rifle slung over his shoulder.[3] The Little Rock Nine students' accounts of their experiences during their year attending Central High document the daily racism and violence they experienced at the hands of White teachers and students (e.g., Beals, 1994; Jacoway & Trickey, 2005; Margolick, 2011).

Mann would likely have been a strong critic of the Southern governors who closed public schools in the late 1950s to prevent desegregation like Faubus did in Little Rock in 1958 after the Little Rock Nine had attended Central High School for one year. In his speech "Slavery and the Slave Trade," in which he critiqued laws that prohibited enslaved Black Americans from being educated, Mann (1849) argued that "[t]he man or the institution, therefore, that withholds knowledge from a child, or from a race of children, exercises the awful power of changing the world in which they are to live, just as much as though he should annihilate all that is most lovely and grand in this planet of ours" (p. 23). White students were able to attend publicly funded private segregation academies when the public schools in Southern states were closed, while multiple cohorts of Black students were effectively denied access to education (Anderson, 2016).

The second scene of *Eyes on the Prize* closes the segment on Little Rock. After describing how governors in Southern states closed public schools rather than desegregate, Julian Bond, the narrator, intones, "In the fall of

1960 in New Orleans, four little Black girls were sent to first grade in White schools." The footage shows a car pulling up in front of a school. Two large White men wearing suits get out of the car and accompany a little Black girl up the stairs and into the school. She is wearing a coat with a pleated skirt, white bobby socks and bows in her hair. Bond continues, "It caused a citywide riot." The scene abruptly shifts to the riots in the downtown area. Someone is waving a Confederate flag amidst the sound of glass breaking and sirens. In this footage the police are arresting rioters, although this wasn't always the case.[4]

The little girl was Ruby Bridges, who integrated William Franz Public School by herself; the other three Black girls were sent to another school. Bridges was the subject of a famous painting by Norman Rockwell, and John Steinbeck described the daily mobs protesting desegregation in *Travels with Charley* (1960). Yet that short video segment is particularly poignant because it highlights the depth of anti-Blackness in this country (ross, 2020), such that four little girls going to school would incite a riot and daily mobs of Whites protesting desegregation. As an adult, Bridges wrote a children's book recounting her experiences (Bridges, 1999). In one of the pictures of the White protestors reproduced in Bridges' book, a woman holds up a Black doll in a coffin. Many of the White protestors are children. One child, a White girl no more than 10 years old, holds a wooden cross like the ones burned by the Ku Klux Klan to terrorize Black families. In a 2010 interview, Bridges described having to leave the school and walk through the crowd of angry protestors picketing the school with the doll in the coffin, which gave her nightmares (Martin, 2010). Yet Bridges continued to attend the Franz School for the rest of the school year, although it was at great cost to her family. Her father lost his job, her parents separated, and her grandparents were forced to move from the farm where their family had sharecropped for 25 years (Judson, 1995). Beyond the costs borne by individual families, as desegregation unfolded, in many Black communities the segregated schools for Black children that provided nurturing spaces for Black youth and employment for Black teachers were dismantled (Bell, 1989; see also Siddle Walker, 1996).

Segregation, and Black families' organized efforts to end segregation were not confined to the South (Theoharis, 2018). For example, in the late 1950s, the Milwaukee Public Schools used "intact bussing" to address overcrowding in inner city schools and avoid desegregation. Students, most of whom were Black, and their teachers were bussed as an entire classroom from their assigned schools to schools that could accommodate them (University of Wisconsin–Milwaukee Libraries, n.d.). They would remain together as a class in the new school, in some cases being bussed back to their assigned schools for lunch and dismissal. In 1964, a community group, the Milwaukee United School Integration Committee (MUSIC) challenged the policy of intact busing by organizing protests, boycotts, and Freedom

Schools for Black students. Ultimately MUSIC's leader, Lloyd Barbee, an attorney and civil rights leader, led a legal campaign that led to a federal court decision. The school district resisted the court's mandate, requiring multiple appeals over a 15-year period, culminating in a consent degree in 1979.

In New York City, Black and Latinx families were limited to neighborhoods where poor families were clustered because of racially discriminatory housing practices and policies (Taylor, 1997; see also Rothstein, 2018, more generally). The schools in these communities were racially segregated, overcrowded, and underfunded. In the 1930s and 1940s, parents in these schools organized through their schools' Parent Teacher Associations (PTAs) to improve their children's schools, although the city's schools remained segregated (Taylor, 1997). A month before the *Brown* decision, psychologist Kenneth Clark gave a speech that challenged the New York City school board to address segregation in the city's schools. The school board formed a committee that documented the segregation in the city's schools but did not address it, so grassroots activists organized, building on the work of previous generations of activists (Burrell, 2019; see also Hannah-Jones, 2016; Theoharis, 2018). They boycotted and challenged the district's practices in the courts to bring attention to segregation in Northern schools. In February 1964, these efforts culminated in the largest civil rights protest of the 1960s, when over 460,000 public school students boycotted New York City schools.

San Francisco was the first major city outside of the South to desegregate under court order in the 1970s (Quinn, 2020). During the common school era almost a century earlier, Black families in San Francisco were unsuccessful in their efforts to desegregate public schools in California.[5] *Ward v. Flood* (1874) challenged the segregation of Black students in San Francisco's public schools on behalf of Mary Frances Ward. At the time, the California Constitution had a provision mandating the segregation of Black, Asian American, and American Indian students. Ward's counsel argued that "'Common schools' does not mean ordinary schools. It means public, common to all in a political sense" (*Ward v. Flood*, 1874, ¶15).

The California legislature removed the segregation clauses from state law in 1883. In the following years, Black students in California were not subject to de jure school segregation, although they experienced extralegal[6] segregation (Powers, 2014) that resulted from the policies and practices of federal, state, and local agencies (Rothstein, 2018). In the late 1950s, the NAACP and other civil rights groups began to pressure the San Francisco Unified School District to address the racial isolation of some of the schools in the district (Kirp, 1982; Quinn, 2020). While the school board came to agree with the civil rights groups that segregation was a problem the district needed to address, the district's efforts to desegregate were either insufficient or became mired in political controversy. Ultimately, the NAACP filed a lawsuit to force the district to desegregate, culminating in the federal court's decision in *Johnson v. San Francisco* (1971). While it is a long and complex history that involved the competing interests of multiple racial/ethnic groups, *Johnson* was the first of many court orders aimed at desegregating San Francisco's public schools. By 2005, the federal court relinquished its oversight role of the city's efforts to desegregate.

As a final example, in the 1950s the Boston NAACP started organizing against patterns of school segregation that were associated with inequalities in access to educational resources and opportunities (Theoharis, 2018). These efforts were led by Ruth Batson, a Black mother of three and the activist quoted earlier. The extralegal segregation in Boston's public schools stemmed from the school district's policies and practices, such as race-based student assignment policies and the gerrymandering of school attendance boundaries. Black children attending Boston Public Schools were concentrated in overcrowded elementary schools, some of which were declared health hazards. The average per pupil spending on Black students was 70% of the amount spent on White students, and Black students were more likely to be taught by substitute or inexperienced teachers than their White peers. Black students were also disproportionately tracked into vocational classes and subject to outdated and racist curricula (see Kozol, 1967a, 1967b). Rather than address segregation or even concede that it was a problem, White public officials repeatedly invoked deficit arguments to explain why Black students were struggling in the city's schools (Theoharis, 2018; see also Hampton & Fayer, 1990).

In 1972, after two decades of organized efforts including rallies, student walkouts, a grassroots busing program, and establishing independent schools that had little traction, the NAACP filed a federal lawsuit challenging the segregation in Boston's public schools (Theoharis, 2018). Two years later the court ordered a comprehensive desegregation plan, which included but was not limited to busing to address racial imbalance. While prior to the court order, many White students had been bussed to predominantly white schools to ameliorate overcrowding, White parents opposed using busing as a means to desegregate schools. With the support of school board members, some White parents organized a boycott, while Black students who tried to attend school under the desegregation plan were met with mobs of white protesters, and in some instances, violence. Phyllis Ellison, one of the Black students who attended South Boston High School under the desegregation plan recalled years later that while her education had suffered because of the constant tension and threats of violence at the school:

If I had to do it all over again, for the civil rights part of it, I would do it over, because I felt like my rights were being violated by the White people of South Boston telling me that I could not go to South Boston High School (Hampton & Fayer, 1990, p. 618).

Many of the gains in the 1970s and 1980s have since been rolled back by both the courts and school officials' actions (e.g., Reardon et al., 2012).

Yet much as Hannah-Jones argues that we should see slavery as central to the American story, we should also understand segregation and Black Americans' long tradition of activism challenging segregation as important and essential parts of the common school story. Carol Anderson (2016) sums up the efforts of Black families in a way that both evokes and extends Mann's vision:

> Since the days of enslavement, African Americans have fought to gain access to quality education. Education can be transformative. It reshapes the health outcomes of a people; it breaks the cycle of poverty; it improves housing conditions; it raises the standard of living. Perhaps, most meaningfully, educational attainment significantly increases voter participation. In short, education strengthens a democracy. (p. 96)

NOTES

1. I use the term "desegregation" throughout to note that schools that open their doors to Black students may not necessarily be integrated. I draw upon the distinction between desegregation and integration made by Minow (2010; see also Bell, 1980). Integrated schools are organized around the principles of equity, social equality, and a commitment to fostering the civic participation and capacity of all community members. That is, integrated schools are schools that support the commons. In such schools, all students and their families should feel welcomed and included in all aspects of school life, including but not limited to curricula, school activities, and school and classroom practices. In schools that desegregated but did not integrate, the common school was not truly common, although desegregation is arguably an important step towards integration.

2. White resistance to segregation was not limited to the South and the period after *Brown*. For example, Moss (2009) documents white resistance to desegregation in Northern cities (Baltimore, New Haven, and Boston) during the first half of the 19th century.

3. In her autobiographical account of her experiences as one of the Little Rock Nine, Beals (1994) described how her mother's job was threatened and her grandmother kept watch over their house with a rifle at night. Similarly, Floyd Armstrong, who was one of the first Black students to integrate Graymont Elementary School in Birmingham in 1963, described how his father organized a neighborhood brigade to protect him and his brothers from violence at the hand of White segregationists (Johnson, 2019).

4. In Bridges' (1999) book recounting her experience, her teacher Barbara Henry described how fearful she was leaving the school every day, noting, "The New Orleans Police were supposed to be there to help us, but they very much disliked being the ones to enforce integration, so you could never be confident of their support and cooperation" (p. 20).

5. While it falls outside the discussion here, I note that Chinese families also challenged the segregation of their children in San Francisco during this period.

6. I use the term *extralegal* instead of *de facto* to draw attention to the ways that schools and housing segregation was facilitated by state actors (e.g., school boards and district administrators) working in their official capacities rather than being the outcome of private choices. California legislators subsequently added provisions permitting districts to segregate "Indian children, and children of Chinese, Japanese, and Mongolian parentage" (Powers & Patton, 2008, pp. 142–143; see also Wollenberg, 1978).

REFERENCES

Anderson, C. (2016). *White rage: The unspoken truth of our racial divide*. Bloomsbury.

Anderson, J. D. (1978). Northern foundations and the shaping of southern Black rural education, 1902–1935. *History of Education Quarterly, 18*(4), 371–396.

Anderson, J. D. (1988). *The education of Blacks in the South: 1860–1935*. University of North Carolina Press.

Baumgartner, K. (2020). Searching for Sarah: Black girlhood, education, and the archive. *History of Education Quarterly, 60*(1), 73–85. doi:10.1017/heq.2019.49

Beals, M. P. (1994). *Warriors don't cry: A searing memoir of the battle to integrate Little Rock's Central High*. New York: Pocket Books.

Bell, D. (1980). Brown v. Board of Education and the interest convergence dilemma. *Harvard Law Review, 93*(3), 518–533.

Bell, D. (1989). *And we are not saved: The elusive quest for racial justice*. Hachette Books.

Bond, H. (1935). The extent and character of separate schools in the United States. *The Journal of Negro Education, 4*(3), 321–327. doi:10.2307/2291870

Bridges, R. (1999). *Through my eyes*. Scholastic Press.

Burrell, K. B. (2019). Black women as activist intellectuals: Ella Baker and Mae Mallory combat Northern Jim Crow in New York city's public schools in the 1950s. In K. Woodard & J. Theoharis (Eds.), *The Strange Careers of the Jim Crow North: Segregation and Struggle outside of the South*. New York University Press.

Cassara, E. (1971). Reformer as politician: Horace Mann and the anti-slavery struggle in Congress, 1848-1853. *Journal of American Studies, 5*(3), 247–263.

DeVinney, J. A., Bond, J., Hampton, H., PBS Home Video., & Blackside, Inc. (2010). *Eyes on the prize: America's civil rights years, 1954-1965*. Alexandria, VA: PBS Home Video.

Devlin, R. (2018). *A girl stands at the door: The generation of young women who desegregated America's schools*. Basic Books.

Du Bois, W. E. B. (1911). The common school and the American Negro: Report of a social study. Atlanta University Press. https://hdl.handle.net/2027/uva.x000712834

Du Bois, W. E. B. (1935a). Does the Negro need separate schools? *The Journal of Negro Education, 4*(3), 328-335. doi:10.2307/2291871

DuBois, W. E. B. (1935b). *Black reconstruction*. Free Press.

Hampton, H., & Fayer, S. (1990). *Voices of freedom: An oral history of the Civil Rights Movement from the 1950s through the 1980s*. Bantam Books.

Hannah-Jones, N. (2016, June 9). Choosing a school for my daughter in a segregated city. *New York Times*, M34. https://www.nytimes.com/2016/06/12/magazine/choosing-a-school-for-my-daughter-in-a-segregated-city.html

Hannah-Jones, N. (2019). Our democracy's founding ideals were false when they were written. Black Americans have fought to make them true. *The 1619 Project, The New York Times Magazine*. https://www.nytimes.com/interactive/2019/08/14/magazine/black-history-american-democracy.html

Harris, C. (1993). Whiteness as property. *Harvard Law Review* 106(8), 1707–1791.

Jacoway, E., & Trickey, M. (2005). Not anger but sorrow: Minnijean Brown Trickey remembers the Little Rock Crisis. *The Arkansas Historical Quarterly*, 64(1), 1–26. doi:10.2307/40018557

Johnson, R. C. (2019). *Children of the dream: Why school integration works*. New York: Basic Books.

Judson, G. (1995, September 1). Child of courage joins her biographer; Pioneer of integration is honored with the author she inspired. *New York Times*, B1.

Kirp, D. (1982). *Just schools: The idea of racial equality in American education*. Berkeley, CA: University of California Press.

Kozol, J. (1967a). Death at an early age. *The Atlantic*. https://www.theatlantic.com/magazine/archive/1967/09/death-at-an-early-age/305261/

Kozol, J. (1967b). Where ghetto schools fail. *The Atlantic*. https://www.theatlantic.com/magazine/archive/1967/10/where-ghetto-schools-fail/306687/

McRae, E. G. (2018). *Mothers of massive resistance. White women and the politics of white supremacy*. Oxford University Press.

Mann, H. (1848a). Twelfth annual report of the Secretary of the Board of Education. Commonwealth of Massachusetts Board of Education. https://archives.lib.state.ma.us/handle/2452/204731

Mann, H. (1848b). Speech of Mr. Horace Mann, of Massachusetts, in the House of Representatives of the United States, June 30, 1848, on the right of Congress to legislate for the territories of the United States, and its duty to exclude slavery therefrom. HathiTrust. https://hdl.handle.net/2027/hvd.32044019341551

Mann, H. (1849). *Speech of Hon. Horace Mann of Massachusetts on slavery and the slave trade in the District of Columbia*. Pennsylvania Anti-Slavery Society.

Margolick, D. (2011). *Elizabeth and Hazel: Two women of Little Rock*. New Haven: Yale University Press.

Martin, M. (2010, December 1). Wisdom from a trailblazer: Ruby Bridges talks racism in education. *NPR*. https://www.npr.org/2010/12/01/131727013/Wisdom-From-A-Trailblazer-Ruby-Bridges-Talks-Racism-In-Education

Minow, M. (2010). *In Brown's wake: Legacies of America's educational landmark*. Oxford University Press.

Moss, H. J. (2009). *Schooling citizens: The struggle for African American education in antebellum America*. University of Chicago Press.

NAACP. (2021, August 28). Our history. https://naacp.org/about/our-history

Ogletree, C. (2004). *All deliberate speed: Reflections on the first half-century of Brown v. Board of Education*. New York: Norton.

Peterson, G. (1935). The present status of the Negro separate school as defined by court decisions. *The Journal of Negro Education*, 4(3), 351–374. doi:10.2307/2291873

Powers, J. M. (2008). Forgotten history: Mexican American school segregation in Arizona from 1900 to 1951. *Equity and Excellence in Education, 41*(4), 467–481. https://doi.org/10.1080/10665680802400253

Powers, J. M. (2014). On separate paths: The Mexican American and African American legal campaigns against school segregation. *American Journal of Education, 121*(1), 29–55. https://doi.org/10.1086/678124

Powers, J. M. & Patton, L. (2008). Between *Mendez* and *Brown*: Gonzales v. Sheely (1951) and the legal campaign against segregation. *Law and Social Inquiry, 33*(1), 127–171. https://doi.org/10.1111/j.1747-4469.2008.00096.x

Quinn, R. (2020). *Class action: Desegregation and diversity in San Francisco schools.* University of Minnesota Press.

Reardon, S. F., Grewal, E. T., Kalogrides, D., & Greenberg, E. (2012). Brown fades: The end of court-ordered school desegregation and the resegregation of American public schools. *Journal of Policy Analysis and Management, 31*(4), 876–904.

ross, k. m. (2020, June 4). Call it what it is: Anti-blackness. *New York Times.* https://www.nytimes.com/2020/06/04/opinion/george-floyd-anti-blackness.html

Rothstein, R. (2018). *The color of law: A forgotten history of how our government segregated America.* New York: Norton.

Siddle Walker, V. (1996). *Their highest potential: An African American School community in the segregated South.* University of North Carolina Press.

Steinbeck, J. (1962). *Travels with Charley: In search of America.* New York: Viking.

Taylor, C. (1997). *Knocking at our own door: Milton A. Galamison and the struggle to integrate New York City Schools.* Perseus Books.

Theoharis, J. (2018). *A more beautiful and terrible history: The uses and misuses of Civil Rights history.* Beacon Press.

University of Wisconsin–Milwaukee Libraries. (n.d). Bussing, intact. *March on Milwaukee Civil Rights History Project.* https://uwm.edu/marchonmilwaukee/keyterms/

Ward v. Flood 48 Cal. 36 (1874). *American Law Times Reports 1*(5), 204 et seq. https://www.blackpast.org/african-american-history/ward-v-flood-1874/

Wollenberg, C. (1978). *All deliberate speed: Segregation and exclusion in California schools, 1855–1975.* University of California Press.

Woodward, C. (1955). *The strange career of Jim Crow.* Oxford University Press.

PART IV

The rural one-room schoolhouse, like the one pictured here, was prevalent in the common school era and has been romanticized in American folklore. It was, indeed, the predecessor to many of today's modern school buildings and the systems of which they are a part. But students, particularly in rural America, rarely went beyond eighth grade, often leaving school for work, as soon as the basics of readin,' 'ritin,' and 'rithmatic were mastered. These schools were often poorly funded by townspeople, and teachers were often not much better educated than their students. The schools typically were only 7 feet high and 22 by 20 feet in area, were frequently unshaded and unprotected, and often isolated and not kept up well. They were exposed to the fierce winds of winter and the scorching heat of summer and the air was described as dank and filled with noxious fumes. Horace Mann knew that such schools, whether rural or urban, had to be redesigned to create more desirable environments for teaching and learning. The Republic would not stand long, he argued, without adequately resourced, publicly funded schools that effectively supported the development of productive and democratic citizens.

We Know Better and Must Do Better

Martin Brooks

Recently, a small group of middle school students spoke with a group of visitors about their school's mathematics program. The first student said, "Hi, I'm Beth. I'm in the 6th grade, and I don't know why I was picked for this group. I'm not good at math. I'm a 2."

Let those sentences sink in. Beth was referring to the score she received on her most recent state math proficiency exam. But, more profoundly, this is an 11-year-old girl describing herself as a learner ("I'm not good at math"), and also a number ("I'm a 2"), and wondering why a "2" would be selected to speak with a group of adults about math. Had Horace Mann been in the room, he would have cringed. Those of us meeting with Beth sure did.

As educators, we all want our students to expand upon their understandings of self and the world in which they live, and to learn—both from success and failure. We want our schools to be the laboratories in which this grand and ongoing experiment called public education will flourish. Most educators entering the field are motivated by the belief that we can help students realize possibilities not yet known by them. As Mann wrote in 1848, public education can be the "great equalizer," the hope-fueled launchpad toward upward social and economic movement.

Mann's optimistic view has inspired educators for over a century, but somewhere along the line those charged with overseeing public education have lost their way. Education policy—and the direction of education practice—has been hijacked by people more interested in political and remunerative outcomes than social justice and student learning. This shift has given outsized value to content knowledge and to tests that purport to assess that knowledge, and has diminished the role of schools as incubators of thought through play, experimentation, innovation, and the development of personal agency.

No one contests that students must be knowledgeable—that they be literate, compute accurately, understand scientific principles, and have familiarity with the foundations of democracy. Mann understood this, and he also knew that education must transcend inculcating assimilating content and address not only what students know but also who they are and wish to become, and what they may contribute to society. In 1847, he wrote that education's purpose is to foster "conscientious jurors, true witnesses, incorruptible voters" (Mann, 1842–1848). This vision of education rings truer now than perhaps any time in our nation's history.

In the early 1900s, John Dewey reinforced Mann's view, arguing that schooling isn't only preparation for adult life but is life itself (Hickman & Alexander, 1998). Dewey contended that schooling is a function of what students do with learned information and the manner in which they choose to do it. Dewey, like Mann, was more concerned with the personal relevance of each student's journey than what, precisely, each knew. He, too, would have winced at "I'm a 2."

Yet, this is where we are in 2021. Our nation's public schools are mired in a decades-old, pernicious cycle driven by politicians, federal policy makers, and reformers that exalts content standards and uses them (really, misuses them through a set of specious tests mandated at the federal level) to promote the narrative that public schools are failing. They buttress this myth by citing the stagnation of NAEP scores and the middle-of-the-pack performance of American students on international assessments, such as PISA, despite a growing body of powerful critiques of the methodology, structure, and intent of these assessments, and the inaccurate and inappropriate interpretations of data generated by them (Koretz, 2017; Loveless, 2019; Zhao, 2018).

America's educational system, despite some undeniable flaws, is not failing. But it has been misdirected by a test-based reform movement that is failing, a movement that is causing harm to individual students, the schools in which they are educated, the communities in which they live, and our national approach to learning. In a 2017 article in *The Atlantic*, Erika Christakis, echoing the beliefs of Mann and Dewey, summed it up this way:

> Our public-education system is about much more than personal achievement; it is about preparing people to work together to advance not just themselves but society. Unfortunately, the current debate's focus on individual rights and choices has distracted many politicians and policy makers from a key stakeholder: our nation as a whole. As a result, a cynicism has taken root that suggests there is no hope for public education. This is demonstrably false. It's also dangerous.

We know better and must do better.

"I'M NOT GOOD AT MATH."

For educators seeking to inspire their students, this sentence reveals some of the flaws plaguing the test-dominated state of schooling in America. To begin, creating and sustaining silos for content runs counter to the structure of the world that students will encounter upon graduation, and the world in which they presently live. That world, the real world, is largely transdisciplinary, requiring people to integrate multiple "content areas" simultaneously in identifying and working through problems. Transdisciplinary thinking—thinking holistically about big ideas—is different from unitary content thinking, yet, with the exception of the occasional performance-based task, students rarely are invited to think or to demonstrate knowledge in this way. Normatively, students work on defined content in preparation for tests created to assess how much content they know.

Beth likely has had reading time, writing time, math time, social studies time, science time, library time, physical education time, music time, art time, and perhaps world language time. Each block of time was discrete and focused solely on the content for which it was created, and each activity in which she engaged was unique to, and completed in, that specific block of time. For some blocks of time, she may have been placed with other students into "high," "middle," and "low" groupings (likely the result of a test score), and possibly moved to different classrooms depending on her teachers' expertise and/or certification. On her report card, she received separate grades for the content covered in each block, and during conferences her parents were told that she is a stronger student in some blocks of time than she is in others. Beth's sense that she is "not good at math" is a result of the purposeful architecture of her school experience, and the messages that architecture has transmitted to her.

Several years ago, a group of middle school principals shadowed students for a morning in a well-regarded middle school that educates mostly wealthy, "high-performing" students. When the principals returned to debrief over lunch, all were disheartened by what they had witnessed: students passing from room to room every 41 minutes, passively receiving content, and engaged with ditto and workbook sheets. Much of the work was aligned with the tests the students would take later that year. The students had very little time to ask questions or work collaboratively.

Although many of the overt signs in this school were positive—the teachers were knowledgeable about their content and clearly liked and connected personally with their students, the students seemed cheerful and scored well on their required assessments, and parents were supportive—the principals used words like "bleak," "boring," and "dull" to describe what they had seen. One likened the experience of the student she shadowed to machinery on an assembly line, while another said that she was physically exhausted and "wanted to cry."

Although Beth attends a different school, these observations mirror her school life, raising two important questions: What, exactly, does "not good at math" mean to Beth, and how did she develop this view of herself? While we cannot understand all the circumstances affecting any one student, what we do know is that this self-assessment already has colored her view of her academic abilities, and likely will continue to do so throughout her academic career, and perhaps her journey through life. Think of the many people we all know who, well into their adulthood, continue to say, "I'm not good at math," instead of understanding that "I was not taught math well."

As educators, our hope is to keep as many doors open for our students for as long as we can—"I'm not good at math" signals a closing door. John Merrow (2019) suggested that educators must stop using tests to ask, "How intelligent is this child?" and instead find more meaningful ways to ask, "How is this child intelligent?" The same five words, two very different questions. One question closes doors and the other keeps doors open. Rather than Beth learning the ways in which she may be an intelligent mathematician, the current testing regimen has convinced her that she is "not good at math," that she is "a 2." This number defines and limits her destiny.

We know better and must do better.

"I'M A 2."

This sentence, equally troubling as "I'm not good at math," is a direct outgrowth of the misguided national reform movement and accompanying state policies aligned with that effort. In both structure and function, schools are complex social systems. When people in social systems are reduced to numbers, something has gone awry.

Let's be clear: The "2" to which Beth is referring is a score attained on one exam administered for 3 hours on one day during a 180-day school year. It does not describe or define her intelligence, her daily in-class performance, her array of skills and abilities, her personal proclivities and dispositions, her persona, or her future prospects for success and happiness. Yet, for Beth, it is a defining label, as clear as the scarlet "A" on Hester Prynne.

The creation of numbered categories enables statisticians and policy makers to rank, sort, and track large cohorts of students. But when these largely political aims are applied to the education of individual students, they can have debilitating consequences. For some students, these numbered categories represent a huge distinction in how they are educated (i.e., whether or not they are required to receive additional support, the academic tracks into which they are placed, and the classes/curriculum to which they will have access as they move through their academic careers) and, even more consequentially, how they come to think of themselves as learners.

All of this is inexcusable, because there is no legitimate research base on which the testing/accountability reform model is built. First, there is no reputable research directly linking the tests to the standards they claim to assess. Furthermore, the numbered categories derived from these tests are artificially constructed and labeled, and the dividing lines between categories are artificially calculated. In New York, raw scores on annual tests are sent to the State Education Department. Then the department decides where the lines between categories are to be drawn. It is possible for the same raw score in one year to be "proficient" and the next year to be "below proficient." At its core, this is a purely political undertaking dressed up to look like an educational endeavor. The public is catching on. In New York in 2019, nearly 20% of the state's students were opted out of the tests by their parents.(Hursh, et al., 2020). Is there any wonder why?

Beth's conception of herself as "a 2" emanates from a political process designed to achieve purposes other than helping her to grow as a learner. We can only speculate about the number of other children who have formed similar views of themselves based on scores on tests.

We know better and must do better.

SO, WHAT MATTERS AND WHAT CAN WE DO?

Virtually all school districts espouse commitment to a set of worthy outcomes, such as becoming a critical thinker, excelling at problem solving, engaging productively with the world, developing a deep understanding of citizenship in a democratic society, tapping into creative abilities, and finding meaning and happiness in life.

The accomplishment of any one of these outcomes would make educators proud of their work and engender strong community support for their schools. But there is a profound disconnection between the outcomes school districts profess to value and what they assess, and therefore between what they profess to value and what they actually do with students. The preponderance of school districts do not intentionally document or assess the outcomes they consider most worthy, and instead allow their efficacy to be defined by test scores.

This disconnection promotes teaching to the tests and communicates to faculties and educational communities a mixed message that casts doubt on the extent to which districts are committed to the outcomes they claim to value. By telling only a partial story, the part that pertains to test scores, districts marginalize the grander outcomes they seek. The full story that links practice to vision and mission remains unassessed, and therefore subordinate to the story told by test scores.

Districts interested in providing a broader, more holistic education for their students—and telling that story—might consider three suggestions, two presented here and one at the end of this chapter.

1. Seek and value student voice. When asked, students happily and openly discuss their educational experiences. Every student has given thought to how their schooling is structured, and how school "feels." Students always appreciate the opportunity to share their thinking and say they wish their schools' administrators and teachers would engage them in similar conversations because they know a lot about their schools. These are important conversations to have.

Discussions with students indicate there is good reason to be optimistic about the future of schooling. Many students speak enthusiastically about a range of newer activities that have resonated with them. These activities have promoted their sense of agency and engaged them as thoughtful and self-regulating learners. For example, students often speak about the impact of authenticity and active learning through activities such as:

- being exposed to "real world" dilemmas on which they can take action (e.g., cleaning pollution from a local river, helping their teacher research and weigh variables in purchasing a safe, fuel-efficient car, preparing a presentation to the local board of education on the potential benefits of installing air conditioning in their schools, running food and toy drives for families in their districts and nearby districts)
- participating in project-based and problem-based curriculum activities (e.g., developing proposals to bring potable water to African communities in which the water is undrinkable, trying to identify common ground between the Democratic and Republican political parties in the United States, making arid land in areas stricken by drought more amenable to farming)
- debating opposite sides of paradoxical issues (e.g., should large donors to education, such as the Gates Foundation, have greater say in national education policy decisions, should crimes committed out of need be treated differently than crimes emanating from greed, should breathalyzers be installed in all newly manufactured cars)
- responding to questions that require meaningful research, deep thought, and often challenge their current suppositions (e.g., why, no matter where we stand on Earth, do we always see the same side of the moon, can GMO food really be considered organic, what might have happened to Lenny if George hadn't killed him at the end of *Of Mice and Men*)

These activities excite and engage students. When describing these experiences, students also discuss the benefits of working collaboratively with and learning from their peers. They describe growing through listening to the ideas of others and incorporating those ideas into their own thinking. They speak with animation about the camaraderie that emerges through working together, the widening of their own perspectives that accompanies the opportunity to offer constructive feedback, and the personal reflection that occurs through receiving critical feedback from others.

These are powerful, generative experiences that reflect the world in which students live and into which they will graduate, and they contrast sharply with the activities these same students describe as more common in school—reading texts, completing repetitive homework assignments, working alone, complying with teacher directions on how and when to complete assigned tasks, and, perhaps most concerning of all, preparing for and taking tests.

Students crave both independence and interdependence, want to spend time on worthy activities, and have a wealth of questions and ideas about which they are curious. Meaningful change is possible if the adults in their schools hear what students think and honor their voices in structuring school experiences.

We know better and must do better.

2. Assess what matters, not just what is required. To reiterate: What districts decide to assess communicates a clear message to staff, and students, too, about what is valued. When districts' visions and actions are at odds, people view the visions as aspirational rhetoric and default to the actions to determine what really matters.

Some districts bring together teams of teachers and administrators to reconfirm their commitment to the outcomes most valued by their districts, examine student work for evidence connected to those outcomes, and create processes to capture that evidence. This is a powerful way to assess both the performance of students and the extent to which the schools in which they are being educated are focusing on the outcomes that are most highly valued. The Looking at Student Work protocol (National School Reform Faculty, 2017a; see also 2017b, n.d.), for example, enables educators, collaboratively, to dig deeply into the sense students make of the assignments they are given, to surface the skills and concepts students demonstrate through their work, and to make desired modifications to curriculum and instruction based on their findings. Recently, a team of five elementary school teachers examined three poster boards created by students for a 5th grade Science Fair. Although the scientific concepts were considered appropriate by the teachers, they perceived that much of the information presented on the poster boards demonstrated more rote copying than critical thinking, and they decided to add an oral student explanation to the process to encourage students to think more deeply about their work.

Critical thinking is a valued outcome. With any valued outcome, three key questions for a district to examine are: Where in the curriculum is it promoted, what instructional practices are most likely to generate it, and how is it reinforced and documented through assessment?

Many curricula emphasize content coverage—the dissemination of facts and information that allows little time for deeper exploration of complex concepts and controversial issues—while other curricula are structured around conceptual understanding in ways that encourage broader investigation and study. It is important for a district to understand whether its curriculum facilitates or militates against the outcomes it seeks.

Similarly, some instructional practices are more amenable to generating valued outcomes than others. A constructivist approach to teaching (Grennon Brooks & Brooks, 1999, 2021), for example, promotes student agency, increased engagement, problem solving, metacognition, critical thought and student choice. It is important for districts to determine the extent to which their faculties' instructional practices support or interfere with the outcomes they seek.

This brings us back to assessment. There is a difference between data, which usually are numerical, and evidence, which can take multiple forms. Most schools focus on analyzing data, but daily in every classroom there is much evidence about the extent to which critical thinking, creativity, problem solving, engagement and a multitude of other desired outcomes are occurring. Classroom walls, school hallways and students' notebooks are brimming with evidence about the work in which students are engaged every day. Ditto for most student utterances—they also constitute evidence. Districts needn't administer tests or wait for the arrival of external data to know the extent to which their students' work is connected to their districts' visions, or what their students are doing and how well they are doing it, when the evidence is in front of them in every classroom every day.

One powerful way to assess what students know and are able to do is through performance-based assessments. Typically, PBAs are long-range, student-driven, research-based, transdisciplinary, and culminate in a performance or exhibition or demonstration that enables the student to explain what was learned, the process by which it was learned, and their thinking about how that process worked.

PBAs stand in contrast to tests. Tests ask the question, "Do you know *this*?" "*This*" is defined by the maker of the test. "Do you know *this*" is a very different question than "*What* do you know?" In response to "Do you know *this*?" the answer is either yes or no; students either pass or fail. In response to "*What* do you know?" all students know something and are able to demonstrate that knowledge through PBAs. When "Do you know *this*?" is the only question asked, it yields an incomplete picture of what students know and are able to do. It must be asked in conjunction with "*What* do you know?" to derive a fuller and more accurate sense of each student's unique knowledge and ability.

There are some students who, for various reasons, simply do not perform well on tests, but who can demonstrate that they know "*this*" in other ways (such as PBAs), and there are yet other students who may not know "*this*," but do know "*that*." Because "*this*" is considered more important than "*that*" by the maker of the test, these students never get recognized for their knowledge or intelligence and, like Beth, come to think of themselves as "not good at math."

We know better and must do better.

WHAT'S REALLY GOING ON?

The periodic release of state, national, and international test scores always results in some public outcry about the quality of education in our nation's public schools. Much of the consternation emanates from federal education officials and the editorial pages of newspapers, claiming these scores are proof that students are not learning to a sufficiently high standard and are not college and career ready. However, recent research (Harvey & McKay, 2019) shows that the percentage of adults 25+ with a high school diploma continues to rise in the United States, and student achievement for every major ethnic group is higher now than in the past. Moreover, data from numerous sources indicate that the literacy rate in the United States is 99% for those over the age of 15, and the nation's dropout rate has declined consistently for the last 40+ years, this in a nation that educates over 50 million students in its public schools, well more than any other nation participating in international assessments. These are impressive data pointing to the success of public schools. Yet, the criticism continues.

For years, public school educators have questioned the motives behind the federally promulgated reform movement, beginning with No Child Left Behind in 2001 and followed by Race to the Top and most recently the Every Student Succeeds Act. Educators wonder if "reform" is really a publicly supportable catchword to describe an effort, promoted ironically by several U.S. secretaries of education, aimed at discrediting public school education and funneling more funds to private, parochial and charter schools, essentially creating a parallel, market driven, for-profit option to public schooling. It is plausible that another agenda was and remains at work, an agenda purposely designed to plant doubt in the public consciousness about the quality of the nation's public schools and to forward a commercial alternative.

In New York in 2013, when new federally mandated tests were initially administered, the percentage of students attaining passing scores in grades 3–8 dropped by about 30% from the previous year, and under 50% of the state's students were deemed "proficient" in meeting the standards. Had the quality of New York's schools declined so precipitously from the previous year, and had students become less knowledgeable? Were more than 50% of the students in New York suddenly unable to reach reasonable standards, and were neither college nor career ready? Of course not. These are absurd numbers, and represent the inevitable and irrational outcome that the testing and accountability compulsion has wrought. Students are being harmed by test-based reform (Koretz, 2017). More children like Beth are coming to think of themselves as "failures" when they are not.

It has become clear to teachers and administrators that the new standards are a large part of the problem, that the tests purporting to measure student attainment of the standards are flawed, that the data being generated by these tests are unreliable indicators of student learning, and that the process was rushed into place to meet a set of political, not educational, outcomes designed to stoke concerns about public schooling and lay the groundwork for monetizing education.

Supporters of the testing and accountability machinery—politicians, federal and state education appointees, large publishers and monied entrepreneurs—claim virtuous intentions and argue that more rigorous standards and tests are necessary to prepare students for success in college and career. Yet there is no research that shows a relationship among scores attained by students on 3rd through 8th grade tests, success in high school, and college/career readiness. None.

Perhaps even more appalling, in the years following the rollout of the new tests, many states have (mis)used students' scores to assail teacher competence and school quality. The testmakers themselves acknowledge that their tests were not designed with these purposes in mind and that these are inappropriate applications of the test data.

The impact of this negative narrative has been dramatic. According to Gallup Poll data, the vast majority of parents give high marks to the public schools their own children attend (schools with which they have direct, firsthand experience) while giving public schools throughout the rest of the nation much lower scores. The message seems to be: "My child's school is excellent, but the rest of America's schools are failing." Logically, and mathematically, that message makes no sense.

Education has undeniable problems. The strongest point reformers make is that there is an achievement gap between White students and students of color. On this, they are right. However, the research here is clear. That gap relates to wealth and opportunity, not race, intelligence, and ability.

Nearly four decades of test-based reform have barely budged the needle on the achievement gap, and we know why. By the time some students appear at the schoolhouse door for kindergarten, they already have endured the debilitating effects of substandard pre- and post-natal health care, food and housing insecurity, restricted opportunities for preschool education, limited access to print materials, transience, and a host of other inequities related to poverty. Rather than working on remedies for these real problems, federal policy makers have found it more convenient to blame public schools.

Until federal and state governments address these matters, the achievement gap the reformers cite as a central basis of their criticism of public schools will persist. Focusing on scores derived from specious tests and misusing those scores as proxies for disappointing student performance, ineffective teaching, and poor school quality diverts attention from the nation's real problems and causes the public to get caught up in a false debate about the effectiveness of our nation's public schools, which may have been the goal of the reformers all along—and subverts real reform.

Thus, here is the third suggestion:

3. Focus on the Opportunity Gap, not the Achievement Gap. Because schools have little control over the societal factors that contribute to the achievement gap, trying to narrow that gap has been an unsuccessful endeavor for decades and promotes the myths that public schools are failing and certain subgroups of students are incapable of high performance. Instead, it is far more productive to focus time, energy, and resources on a matter over which schools do have control—the *opportunity* gap.

Access to thought-provoking and rigorous curriculum affects future options for students, options having to do with the opportunity to attend a post-secondary school, the caliber of the school they attend, the types of careers they pursue, and, ultimately, the amount of money they earn in their lifetimes. Remember Mann's admonition: Education can be the "great equalizer."

Many school districts have erected gates students must pass through in order to participate in honors, Advanced Placement, International Baccalaureate and other upper-level courses. These gates consist of prerequisites students must fulfill in order to be admitted into these classes. Often, these upper level classes are filled with mostly White, wealthier students, while lower tracked classes are populated disproportionately by equally intelligent and capable students from lower socioeconomic households—typically, students of color or students who speak a different language natively. Most schools don't do this intentionally, but whether by design or accident the result is the same. By placing students in classes based on test performance, grades, and adult perceptions of where they are most likely to achieve success, schools actually perpetuate a permanent underclass of students.

It doesn't have to be this way. Opportunities matter. Some schools permit students to self-select into upper-level classes, irrespective of prerequisites, and actively encourage—and recruit—traditionally underserved students to challenge themselves in these classes. Throughout this writer's career, many students have taken advantage of this opportunity, have self-selected into higher level classes, and have performed well. Keeping doors open and providing enriching opportunities for all students is how the real story of the success of America's public schools is told.

We know better and must do better.

REFERENCES

Christakis, E. (2017, October). Americans have given up on public schools. That's a mistake. *The Atlantic.* https://www.theatlantic.com/magazine/archive/2017/10/the-war-on-public-schools/537903/

Grennon Brooks, J., & Brooks, M. (1999). *In search of understanding: The case for constructivist classrooms*. ASCD.

Grennon Brooks, J., & Brooks, M. (2021). *Schools reimagined: unifying the science of learning with the art of teaching*. Teachers College Press.

Harvey, J., & McKay, J. (2019, November 5). Giving schools an honest grade. *Washington Post, The Answer Sheet*. https://www.washingtonpost.com/education/2019/11/05/were-public-schools-better-way-back-when-giving-todays-schools-an-honest-grade/

Hickman, L. & Alexander, T. (1998). *The Essential Dewey: Volumes 1 and 2*. Indian University Press.

Hursh, D., Deutermann, J., Rudley, L., Chen, Z., & McGinnis, S. (2020). *Opting Out*. Meyers Education Press.

Koretz, D. (2017) *The testing charade: pretending to make schools better*. University of Chicago Press.

Loveless, T. (2019, December 8). Be skeptical of China's showing on PISA. *Diane Ravitch's Blog*. https://dianeravitch.net/2019/12/08/tom-loveless-be-skeptical-of-chinas-showing-on-pisa/

Mann, H. (1842-1848). *Life and Works of Horace Mann, Vol IV*. https://books.google.com/books?id=2V8WAAAAIAAJ&printsec=frontcover&source=gbs_book_other_versions_r&cad=4#v=onepage&q&f=false

Merrow, J. (2019, July 29). Did public schools elect Trump? Will they re-elect him? *The Merrow Report*. https://themerrowreport.com/2019/07/29/did-public-schools-elect-trump-will-they-re-elect-him/

National School Reform Faculty (2017a). *Looking at Student Work*. https://www.nsrfharmony.org/wp-content/uploads/2017/10/lasw_equity_0.pdf

National School Reform Faculty (2017b). *Learning from Student Work*. https://www.nsrfharmony.org/wp-content/uploads/2017/10/lasw_overview.pdf

Zhao, Y. (2018). *What works may hurt—side effects in education*. Teachers College Press.

If We Believe That Democracy Is Such a Great Idea, Why Don't Schools Practice It More?

Deborah Meier

If you had 12 years of young people's lives to show them how democracy works and why it is important, would you embed them in authoritarian institutions, segregated by race and class?

Yet that is what we do in our public schools every day.

I would argue that public schools are among the institutions *with the least democratic cultures* in our society. From the way adults relate to children to the way they treat each other, schools teach antidemocratic lessons. They teach that even minor decisions are made by superior authorities that cannot be questioned. They teach that even expert adults aren't free to make decisions about their own work. Sabotage and secrecy are the only recourse for both adults and students when they disagree with authorities. Even the principal, superintendent, and elected local school boards have limited say over school norms, rules, curriculum, and staffing.

What's worse, schools reinforce social inequalities that work against robust democratic life. In many societies, schools reinforce the habits and mindset that differentiate the ruling class from others. Although it is less explicit in our society than in others, our public schools do a pretty good job of reproducing class and other inequalities, generation by generation. As Ted Sizer, the founder of the Coalition of Essential Schools and one of the 20th century's leading educational visionaries often noted, you can tell who the school serves very quickly upon entering it. And even where a mixture of social classes and racial and ethnic groups exists within a building, the tracking system based on "ability" breeds resentment as it does the job of hierarchical sorting. Only in some after-school functions, like sports, do students often mix fully as equals. And only in the top tracks, or gifted classes and specialized schools, does one find at least some of the features of a democracy. In those settings, there may be a tone of mutual respect, the absence of rigid and silent lines in the hallways.

The generally undemocratic structures and cultures found in most of our K–12 schools also affect the way that teachers and other adults in our schools relate to each other. In one of my first encounters with low-income public schools as a substitute teacher, I was shocked to hear adult teachers scolded by the principal, in the presence of their class. It also surprised me to have younger but experienced teachers in the school I later worked at ask me to bring up certain subjects at the next staff meeting.

"Why not you?" I asked.

"Because she doesn't seem to get angry when you make suggestions."

Unlike me, these teachers usually went directly from one subordinate role to another, carrying with them the habits learned earlier in school. They were keenly aware that being a teacher might intimidate youngsters, but that otherwise they were in almost the same position as their students in relationship to the principal. The existence of unions surely helped, but most teachers were not accustomed to fight for their rights, and rarely called in the union. And of course, there were subtle ways principals could retaliate: room assignments, daily schedules, evaluations, and so on. Students were well aware that their teachers were as afraid of the principal as they were.

I noticed that teachers who had already been a part of the adult working world before they became teachers were treated somewhat differently when they entered the teaching profession. They had been away from school long enough to have lost some of their deferential habits. This influenced me in gathering colleagues when we were starting a new democratic school. We hired older men and women who had both teaching and nonteaching experiences as adults. Maybe this should be a requirement for all teachers.

And even ordinary citizens—parents and nonparents alike—usually act as if this antidemocratic school culture is natural and correct. When I was on the school board in New York City, we were presented with a petition from 99% of the staff of my children's junior high declaring that they needed a new principal. We were already aware from other sources that the principal was having difficulty, but the petition almost consolidated the board's support for her. "So, she's a tough principal. That's perhaps what the school needs." Equally, the board (made up of very liberal community activists) was reluctant to choose a successor whom the staff avidly supported.

Teachers, in turn, tended to be very suspicious of parents, and easily intimidated by them, believing that the voices of parents had more power than their own. Conversely, parents often perceived that they had little, if any power. Principals and administrators hardly saw themselves as powerful authorities either. No one did.

At best, students saw democracy as a system where ordinary people had a voice only over trivial matters such as the decorations for the classroom walls, which is often celebrated as a civics lesson. But rarely is anything substantial at stake in the vote, and so what's learned is often the opposite of what was intended.

If we believe that democracy is really such a great idea, one we claim to be willing to go to war to save, how come our public schools are anything but democratic? Could we structure them differently? What kind of system or nonsystem of schooling might better serve democracy?

Here are four principles to consider.

Principle One—Governance. Let's begin with a system of *self-governing schools* with responsibility to the larger public where every school has its own school board. The board should equally represent the students, families, staff, and the larger community. In addition, some overarching governing body should have limited administrative oversight in serving a network of locally controlled schools. This could include lean, "essentialist" collectively bargained oversight and employee contracts, with each individual school negotiating the details as appropriate for its context. And there need to be some state and national rules decided by legislators regarding equal treatment, integration by class and race, safety, union representation and other basic civil rights afforded to educators, students, and parents.

To support this type of structure, decisions affecting the school should be made by those as close as possible to those most directly affected by those decisions. Some system of consensus rather than majority voting might be developed. The process of intentionally working towards consensus has an amazingly positive effect on the tone of arguments and the breadth of the audience one must take into account. In the 30-year history of Mission Hill school, the use of consensus decision-making has been an important reason it has survived so many sticky disagreements.

Principle Two—Leadership. School leaders shall be chosen by the people they serve, not vice versa. It is vital to say, over and over: The school's leadership must be accountable to all the constituents of the school. And perhaps, can we rethink the concept of a principal altogether? The alternative to that could be teacher-directors. In East Harlem in the 1970s and 1980s, Tony Alvarado started more than 20 small schools and almost all were led by teams of teacher leaders. In keeping with this kind of administrative structure, collective bargaining contracts should be lean enough so that the school representative body can determine the composition of the majority of these leadership teams. Mission Hill now has two elected teachers as leaders.

Principle Three—Transparency. Schools must provide open access to all relevant and appropriate data for assessing a school's progress (with appropriate provisions for privacy) to all parties. Truly democratic public schools will hold themselves transparently responsible for fulfilling their promise to their parents, students, and communities. Democracy presumes shared information and time available for taking it in and for hearing alternate arguments. This has implications in thinking about work schedules—and about the role of leisure. It even has implications for school size!

Principle Four—School Size. While smaller school size does not automatically guarantee democracy, smaller size minimizes the pitfalls and inefficiencies inherent to democracy. Mission Hill, a K–8 school, had 350 students and suggests what I mean by small, where the entire staff can sit together in a circle and meaningfully interact together. It makes it easier to avoid the suspicions that go with insiders and outsiders, the hiding of important information and much more. Small size makes it easier to respond to the unexpected, and mistakes are hard to hide. Revisions and exceptions can be made and unmade quickly.

In short, these four principles together don't dictate a particular model of schooling, but they share tenets of good government for schools that are committed to preparing adult citizens, not just employees. What none can guarantee is the kind of mutual respect that democracy rests on. But these four principles improve the odds.

I recommend giving all schools more or less the kind of authority that charter schools have in many states, but not the type of charter boards that too often represent everyone but those most impacted by its decisions. We can learn a lot from charters about autonomy, but not much about democracy. It could also be interesting to explore possibilities for existing independent charter schools to become members of the collective geographic public networks.

Of course, as I've learned over time, "it depends" is the answer to many situations in education. "It depends" is the appropriate response much more than I would have imagined. And certainly, it's quite possible that there could be better solutions than those I've outlined here. But the crucial criteria undergirding any solution must be that schools *serve* democracy by *being* democracies: designed and operated of, for, and by the people.

Maybe the starting point for the schools we wish to have would be bringing together "the people" to decide on some basic principles of what it means to them to live in a democracy of, for and by "the people." This may entail exploring, studying, and perfecting over time how that might be operationalized in the everyday lives of our schools. Perhaps then our schools will go from functioning like an oligarchy with a few hard-won democratic features, to functioning like a real democracy—an idea that has rarely been tried but is surely worth trying. Maybe it will affect our democratic state and national practices.

Twenty-five years ago, in a book about my experiences at Central Park East called *The Power of Their Ideas,* I wrote that "the idea of democracy is once again (is it ever otherwise?) in perilous danger." And later in the book I noted that "there's presently more racism and meanness in my hometown, and the nation, than I ever recall witnessing before." That was 1995, and yet I could have written it yesterday. Back then I wrote about my passion for democracy and my fears for its future; how intolerance and dogmatism, narrow and often murderous national and religious loyalties, and the casual acceptance of the most grotesque inequities, had made democracy's promise seem at times improbable rather than inevitable.

But I also argued that we cannot afford to give up. Democracy is based on our power to influence by our public statements and actions what we want the future to look like. And so it matters a lot whether the schools in which our youth spend 18 years foster democratic or undemocratic values, and in turn nurture the habits of mind and skills to truly make this country a "more perfect union."

The changes I propose here are about creating a more powerful citizenry and a more caring one. Even then we'll still have lots to argue about, but it's about our kids and our shared future with them. Worth arguing about.

REFERENCE

Meier, D. (1995). *The power of their ideas: Lessons for America from a small school in Harlem*. Beacon Press.

The Role of Public Schools in the Preparation of Young People to Engage in Civic Reasoning and Discourse

Carol D. Lee

Horace Mann's admonitions and proactive work around the critical role of public education in a democracy connect both with Thomas Jefferson's beliefs in the democratizing possibilities of public education and with arguments by Amy Gutmann (1999) in *Democratic Education*. Gutmann argues that public schooling is the only institution in our democracy that can prepare young people to engage in civic deliberation. The evolution of the common school is rife with persistent challenges that were in the forefront during the times of Jefferson and Mann and continue today. Public schooling evolved in the North as institutions funded by local tax bases. Prior to public funding, again primarily in the North, children's access to basic schooling was a result of ad hoc local efforts to recruit teachers, who often traveled from one village or small town to another. With the example of Mann's work in Massachusetts, public schools as government-based local institutions evolved. Even with these developments, schooling access was still highly influenced by class, with children from wealthy families receiving a very different education than children of the poor, and the opportunities for White boys differed from those for White girls. Education in the South was a very different story. Up until the mid-1800s, public education was not available to poor White children. African Americans in the South were subject to enslavement where learning to read and write was illegal. In his autobiography, abolitionist Frederick Douglass (1845) documents the complicated pathway through which as an enslaved person he learned to read and write. Horace Mann, too, was an abolitionist, an indicator that he understood one of the most fundamental conundrums of the idea of a public school system, namely how can schooling wrestle with the persistent inequities in this democratic experiment. The early work of Mann and others

(Mann & Fowle, 1839) conceptualized the common school as a site not only of basic literacies but also a site for moral development. And even then there were debates over what such moral development entailed and what pedagogical strategies were best to instill evidence of a strong moral foundation.

This volume will be published during a period in our history where the United States faces a triple quandary: a worldwide pandemic; economic instability; and a massive social protest movement addressing racial inequalities, particularly around police violence against Black and brown peoples. It is a period of deep political divisions with little evidence of a willingness of politicians, for sure, and others with different ideological positions to communicate and collaborate. It is a period in which extremist organizations publicly spout racist and antisemitic claims and infiltrate social protest movements instigating violence. And while this historical moment feels important because we are living through it right now, its challenges are not new. We faced the flu pandemic of 1918, the depression of the 1930s, and public wrestlings with racism throughout our history (the holocaust of enslavement, Jim Crow, race riots, responses to social protests during the civil rights movement of the 1960s). The question before us is: What role can public education play in preparing young people, each new generation, to interrogate these persistent conundrums and to engage in civic reasoning and civic discourse, informed by a commitment to democratic values. The Civic Reasoning and Discourse project of the National Academy of Education is taking on this question.

The issues that come before us in the public arena are complex and multidimensional. How do we understand climate change and what are the implications of such understandings for policies in multiple areas? How do we navigate containing COVID-19 while managing the economic and social impacts on how schools and businesses operate involving face-to-face interactions? How do we manage the tensions between individual rights and the needs of the larger population? How do we navigate between minority and majority rights? The knowledge required to interrogate these real problems in the public domain is complicated and wide ranging. We have argued in the report *Educating for Civic Reasoning and Discourse* (Lee et al., 2021) that socialization and preparation for such civic engagement cannot be reduced to civics courses at 8th grade and the end of high school. Such socialization and preparation must be longitudinal across the K–12 sector and must be embedded across the spectrum of the curriculum. Such socialization and preparation involves knowledge, epistemology, dispositions, and ethics. There is also a complementary challenge for practitioners and others of understanding how the sciences of learning and human development can inform what must be considered to optimize such learning (Nasir et al., 2020). And finally, there are the policy and systems level challenges of how to build systems of schooling that can indeed carry out this work (Darling-Hammond, 2010), challenges of particular complexity in the federal system of United States where education is constitutionally the purview of the states. I will briefly address each of these issues, but note a further explication is available in the report *Education for Civic Reasoning and Discourse* of the National Academy of Education (Lee et al., 2021).

THE MULTIDIMENSIONALITY OF CIVIC REASONING

I am defining *civic reasoning* as the recruitment of logical processes to interrogate warrantable evidence available around issues in the public sphere in ways rooted in consideration of democratic values. Such reasoning can be particularly difficult when there is competing evidence available and when we already hold entrenched beliefs that may be in tension with available evidence, and when there are tensions between what we perceive to be our self-interests (as individuals or members of groups) and those of others. From work in cognitive science, these tensions are captured around issues of *conceptual change*. Conceptual change (Disessa & Sherin, 1998) involves learning that requires fundamental restructuring of existing knowledge or beliefs in order to accommodate the demands of new learning targets. This requires safe opportunities to examine our own sources of knowledge and beliefs and the potential tensions between existing knowledge and the targets of new knowledge. There is so much knowledge of the world—both the physical and social world—that we intuit from observations (Lee et al., 2020). For example, very young children intuit that there is a force that appears to pull objects that are dropped to the ground. This intuitive understanding of gravity is deeply entrenched. Studies (DiSessa, 1982) have shown that even college engineering students hold on to this intuitive understanding of gravity as the force impacting falling objects even when they have studied formal physics where they learn there are multiple forces acting on falling objects. So if we identify any given problem in the public sphere which the actions of individual persons in our society can impact (e.g., by voting, by advocacy, by individual practices such as wearing a mask in the middle of a pandemic or using paper products instead of plastic, or buying hybrid cars, etc.), that problem will entail some kind of content knowledge that is more likely to be learned in the contexts of schooling than everyday life.

In our democratic society, so much of our wrestlings in the public sphere involve our relationships with others and especially our attitudes toward those not in our perceived social circles (e.g., differences with regard to class, gender and sexual orientation, conceptions of race and ethnicity, language, perceptions of ability, etc.). Interrogating our perceptions of the other often involves recognizing and acknowledging implicit bias. Just as is the case with the research on conceptual change, there is also substantive research around implicit bias (Kelly & Roedder, 2008), including its nature but also conditions which optimize opportunities to self-interrogate.

Civic reasoning also has an ethical dimension, largely because it involves thinking not only about oneself, but also about others. It involves issues that impact the quality of life for oneself and for others. The foundations of U.S. democracy, as articulated in the Declaration of Independence and the U.S. Constitution and its amendments are largely about rights, about human rights, the inalienable right to life, liberty and the pursuit of happiness. These same broad ethical goals are articulated in the United Nations Declaration of Human Rights. We know that children from a very young age intuitively and from observation develop basic conceptions of fairness (Cowell & Decety, 2015). Social cognition—learning to read the internal states of others—is a lifelong developmental task (Flavell & Miller, 1998). How children come to consider the needs and perceptions of others is a foundational shift from decision-making that is purely based on the ego. Moral development is part of the work of human development across the life course and certainly comes into play in the work of schooling.

Finally, we know that robust learning requires supports that increase a sense of self-efficacy, beliefs that effort matters rather than perceptions of ability, and a sense of safety (Dweck, 1999, 2002; Maslow, 1943). These perceptions of the self, tasks, settings, and others with whom we interact are threaded through the emotional salience we attribute to our experiences, in this case in the context of schooling. Perceptions that we can do the work and that the work is relevant to some goals are strong predictors of robust learning.

These issues of prior knowledge, implicit bias, ethics and moral reasoning and perceptions of self, others, tasks, settings, and relevance become particularly salient in a society in which longstanding structural configurations have constrained opportunity to learn among populations that vary by race, class, and gender. These structural configurations are informed by deeply and long held metanarratives around difference: proclamations about IQ, poverty, and race; about the limitations of particular languages and language varieties; about gender and learning in mathematics and science; about presumptions of assumed class-based practices in families. These beliefs become institutionalized, particularly in schooling, in terms of pedagogical practices, the training of teachers, the content of curriculum, the nature of financial and other resources made available to different groups, and systems of accountability.

I begin then by framing the problem space of learning to engage in civic reasoning in broader foundational terms, seeking to conceptualize what this problem space requires beyond requirements for singular civics classes.

RELEVANCE OF THE ACADEMIC DISCIPLINES TO CIVIC REASONING

There are important movements in development around the importance of civics in the K–12 curriculum. Projects such as iCivics and standards developed by the National Association for the Social Studies are important. The U.S. assesses what is presumed as knowledge in civics in the Civics Assessment of the National Assessment of Educational Progress (NAEP). NAEP civics identifies targets of knowledge to be assessed in various categories, two of which follow:

Civic Knowledge

- What are civic life, politics, and government?
- What are the foundations of the American political system?
- How does the government established by the Constitution embody the purpose, values, and principles of American democracy?
- What is the relationship of the United States to other nations and to world affairs?
- What are the roles of citizens in American democracy?

Civic Dispositions

- becoming an independent member of society;
- assuming the personal, political, and economic responsibilities of a citizen;
- respecting individual worth and human dignity;
- participating in civic affairs in an informed, thoughtful, and effective manner; and
- promoting the healthy functioning of American constitutional democracy. (NAEP, 2020; https://nces.ed.gov/nationsreportcard/ civics/whatmeasure.aspx)

This knowledge is typically addressed in social studies classes in middle schools and history and civics classes in high school. Knowledge of political decisionmaking in the United States is particularly important and complex. Our complicated governmental system, including relationships among executive, legislative, and judicial branches of government at both federal and state levels, must be understood so we can navigate our political interests as citizens. However, there are at least two additional dimensions to such learning that are crucial. One involves the development of dispositions to be active in civic life, in terms of voting in local, state and federal elections; in terms of local governmental institutions from local school boards to city councils; in terms of community service that addresses community needs— but also dispositions to empathize with others, to listen to alternative points of view, to weigh competing evidence. These dispositions can and should be socialized across the curriculum. These dispositions can be socialized in the study of history, but this requires a willingness on the part of schooling to wrestle with the contradictions of our history. As an abolitionist, Horace Mann was deeply aware of these contradictions, yet still believed that the common school, the public school, was a necessary democratic institution.

The United States is without question one of the major experiments in democratic governance in human history. At the same time, it was born on the back of two holocausts: our country's enslavement of human beings, and its treatment of its indigenous peoples.

I define holocaust as violent actions taken against human communities at such as a scale and with such destruction as to defy the bounds of human morality. The slaughter of 6 million Jewish people by Germany during World War II is viewed as the classic example of a human holocaust. Our ability to see this terror—through direct experience, through the stories captured by those who lived through it, through collected archives—assures our understanding of its evil and hopefully inspires us as civic actors, both within our country and as citizens of the world, to say "Never Again." And yet there are fringe communities and organizations, within the U.S. and elsewhere, who either argue that the Holocaust perpetuated by the Nazis in World War II never really happened or who spout antisemitic charges and still engage in acts of terror against synagogues, for example. One of the ethical questions around teaching civic reasoning in our schools is the role of public education in transmitting democratic values, even if these values are not taught in children's homes. This is one reason that many states require public schools to teach about the Jewish Holocaust.

Similarly, how do we help children wrestle with the following historical facts about the two holocausts perpetuated in the birth of our own country pertaining to the treatment of enslaved and indigenous peoples:

- While the Declaration of Independence asserts that all men have the right to life, liberty and the pursuit of happiness, this assertion in law and fact did not apply to poor White men, to women, to people of African descent, to indigenous populations.
- A number of the so-called Founding Fathers were slaveholders, believing they owned other human beings.
- The process of wars, broken treaties, and infestation of diseases in stealing land owned and occupied by indigenous nations is how the United States came into being and expanded beyond the original 13 colonies.
- There is a history of restrictive immigration policies that have demonized particular populations at different points across our history as not worthy and as not "White."
- The history of Jim Crow was one of widespread violence against peoples of African descent; legal apartheid has a longer history in the United States than in South Africa.

In September 2020, the President of the United States hosted a conference at the White House with a politically conservative group of historians. The conference resulted in arguments that projects like the 1619 Project and publications by historians like Howard Zinn should not be used in public schools because they teach young people to hate the United States (https://www.historians.org/news-and-advocacy/aha-advocacy/aha-statement-on-the-recent-white-house-conference-on-american-history-(september-2020). The President said he wants schools to teach patriotism. These efforts presume that confronting these contradictions of our history will have negative consequences. Rather, I and others argue that confronting these contradictions is absolutely necessary to build patriotism, to help our young people understand the power of our democratic structures to wrestle with contradictions, to understand the power of what the late Congressman John Lewis called "good trouble" (Lewis, 2020). Only public schools can provide a system-wide set of opportunities for young people to engage with these political and moral complexities. To not take up this challenge is to foster division and a sense of hopelessness, and ultimately to undermine the nation-state.

And while the study of history is essential to civic reasoning, the other academic disciplines that are the stuff of public schooling also play important roles. In the midst of this pandemic, the public is faced with data based on mathematical modeling, with public discussions about the nature of the SARS-CoV-2 virus and how it spreads that are rooted in foundational understandings of the microbiotic world. Projections about rates of infection entail not only mathematical modeling but also understanding the probabilistic nature of scientific modeling, including its uncertainties. Politicians make proclamations predicated on statistical data, but often based on incorrect mathematical modeling.

If all citizens are to have access to civic decision-making, negotiations over policy ultimately require some level of collaboration and compromise. Citizens' inputs come at many levels—person to person, organization to organization, people's and organizations' access to official policymakers at all levels of the government. Civic decisionmaking inevitably will include contested points of view. I argue then that civic reasoning does require the ability to empathize with others, to seek to understand something about the experiences of others different from ourselves. Literature offers unique opportunities to enter worlds different from our own. Great literature wrestles with persistent conundrums of the human experience. Teaching literature from cultural and national traditions across the world, including the diversity of cultural communities within the United States, across the K–12 sector can play an important role in socializing empathy, in wrestling with moral and ethical complexities, and of developing more empathetic understandings of those we think of as the other.

Across these disciplines, it is important that the focus go beyond content to be rooted in developing rich conceptual understanding and epistemological dispositions valuing complexity. It is important that exemplars studied invite ethical reasoning in terms of applications of knowledge in the world. It is important that the problems examined in each discipline both draw on students' everyday repertoires (an underlying proposition undergirding conceptual change), and equally invite students to examine such repertoires critically in terms of their affordances and constraints. I fundamentally argue that the scope of this work must be distributed across the content areas and the K–12 spectrum.

THE SIGNIFICANCE OF ATTENTION TO DISCOURSE

Our National Academy of Education Project focuses on both civic reasoning and discourse. Discourse involves how we talk to one another in pursuit of wrestling with complex problems in the public domain, particularly problems that address issues of the right to pursue life, liberty, and happiness. This involves how we talk to one another and, equally important, how we understand the modes of communication by others, especially how persons in positions of power communicate with us. That we should seek to speak to one another with respect and to be willing to listen honestly to others who disagree with us are given expectations of civil civic discourse. But I want to point to another important skill that schools are certainly able to address, that of understanding the rhetorical moves deployed in public discourse—by politicians, by public advocates, by the media including digital media—to make claims and to deflect from questions asked of them. Beginning before the 2020 national election and continuing to the present day, the public has been bombarded with divisive claims that are not based in empirical data, with outright lies, with evasive and inciting language. A critical public needs to have both the skill set and the disposition to decompose how language is used in structures of power to convey and to hide points of view. Attention to critical examination of rhetoric needs to be a target of instruction in English Language Arts, Social Studies, History, the Arts and even in Mathematics and Science classrooms, again across the K–12 sector.

CONCLUSION

Horace Mann argued for the power of public education for the sustenance of a democracy in the mid-1800s, at a time when contestations over race, class, and gender were boiling over in the cauldron of civic wrestlings. In 1904, another educator who understood and argued for the possibilities of the common school to prepare those who had been denied citizenship—African Americans—was born: Horace Mann Bond, a Black man, named after the abolitionist educator. Horace Mann Bond examined the possibilities and challenges of public education in his essay "Origins of the Tax Supported Schools During the Reconstruction Period" in his 1934 publication *The Education of the Negro in the American Social Order* (Bond, 1934; see also Bond, 1976). Horace Mann Bond was the father of Julian Bond, one of the founders of the Student Non-Violent Coordinating Committee, president of the NAACP, and civil rights leader. This interesting historical thread embodies the persistent challenges with which we have wrestled in understanding and influencing the ways public education can contribute to our working and evolving democracy.

I argue here that civic reasoning and discourse are essential skills for the maintenance of the democracy and that public schools play an essential role in preparing young people to become civically engaged. Public education, as Amy Gutmann argues in *Democratic Education*, is the only public institution that can ubiquitously seek to socialize democratic values. This does not mean an uncritical patriotism, but a belief that despite our historical challenges around equity and opportunity, the needle moves slowly forward because of our collective efforts and beliefs in our common humanity. While our efforts in public education cannot preclude people holding racist, homophobic, and sexist beliefs, public education can provide emotionally safe opportunities to at least interrogate such beliefs, and the enactments of our Constitution should be able to preclude people from acting on those beliefs in the public sphere in ways that constrain the opportunities of others.

REFERENCES

Bond, H. M. (1934). *The education of the Negro in the American social order.* Prentice-Hall.

Bond, H. M. (1976) *Education for freedom: A history of Lincoln University.* Lincoln University, Pennsylvania: Lincoln University.

Cowell, J. M., & Decety, J. (2015). The neuroscience of implicit moral evaluation and its relation to generosity in early childhood. *Current Biology, 25*(1), 93–97.

Darling-Hammond, L. (2010). *The flat world and education: How America's commitment to equity will determine our future.* Teachers College Press.

DiSessa, A. (1982). Unlearning Aristotelian physics: A study of knowledge-base learning. *Cognitive Science, 6*, 37–75.

DiSessa, A. A., & Sherin, B. L. (1998). What changes in conceptual change? *International Journal of Science Education 20*(10), 1155–1191.

Douglass, F. (1845). *Narrative of the life of Frederick Douglass.* Anti-Slavery Office.

Dweck, C. S. (1999). *Self-theories: Their role in motivation, personality and development.* The Psychology Press.

Dweck, C. S. (2002). Beliefs that make smart people dumb. In R. Sternberg (Ed.), *Why smart people can be so stupid.* Yale University Press.

Flavell, J. H., & Miller, P. H. (1998). Social cognition. In D. Kuhn & R. Siegler (Eds.), *Handbook of child psychology* (Vol. 2., pp. 851–898).

Gutmann, A. (1999). *Democratic education.* Princeton University Press.

Kelly, D., & Roedder, E. (2008). Racial cognition and the ethics of implicit bias. *Philosophy Compass, 3*(3), 522–540.

Lee, C. D., Meltzoff, A., & Kuhl, P. (2020). The braid of human learning and development: Neuro-physiological processes and participation in cultural practices. In N. Nasir, C. D. Lee, R. Pea & M. McKinney deRoyston (Eds.), *Handbook of Cultural Foundations of Learning* (pp. 24–43). Routledge.

Lee, C. D., White, G. & Dong, D. (Eds). (2021). *Educating for civic reasoning and discourse*. National Academy of Education. https://naeducation.org/educating-for-civic-reasoning-and-discourse/

Lewis, J. (2020, July 30). Together, you can redeem the soul of our nation. *New York Times*. https://www.nytimes.com/2020/07/30/opinion/john-lewis-civil-rights-america.html

Mann, H., & Fowle, W. B. (1839). *Common school journal (Vol. 1)*. Marsh, Capen, Lyon, and Webb.

Maslow, A. H. (1943). A theory of human motivation. *Psychological Review, 50*(4), 370.

Nasir, N., Lee, C. D., Pea, R., & McKinney de Royston, M. (2020). *The Handbook of cultural foundations of Learning*. Routledge.

Shulman, L. (1987). Knowledge and teaching: Foundations of the new reform. *Harvard Educational Review, 57*, 1–22.

Tensions Between Teacher Professionalism and Authentic Community Voice in Public Schools Serving Nondominant Communities

Ken Zeichner

Public education is a precious element of our democratic society with the potential to benefit both the individuals who experience it and our nation as a whole. Tensions in schools in our nondominant communities[1] between the professional educators who run our public schools and the families and communities they are supposed to serve have hindered public education from reaching its full potential. This essay's central question is whether it is possible for public schools in nondominant communities both to honor and respect the professional expertise that teachers need to successfully educate all students in ways that support their academic, social–emotional, physical, aesthetic, and civic development, and also to give nondominant families an authentic voice in the education of their children in ways that draw upon their expertise and the cultural wealth in their communities to enrich the cultural responsiveness of teachers' practices (Yosso, 2005). These are the communities in which the attacks on teacher professionalism have been the fiercest and where pressures on schools to narrow the curriculum and teach to the test have been the greatest at the expense of deeper learning for students (Anderson & Cohen, 2018). These are also the communities where deficit views of families and communities have often led to well-intentioned but misguided missionary attempts to try and save students from their allegedly "broken" communities (Ishimaru, 2019). And finally, these are the communities that typically receive fewer resources for their public schools than wealthier communities (Darling-Hammond, 2013). Also, as a result of macroeconomic policies that have continued to widen the gap between the wealthy and everyone else (Anyon, 2014), the majority of public school children come from materially impoverished families (Darling-Hammond & Oakes, 2019). I will begin by reflecting on my own experience in becoming a public school teacher and a teacher educator.

MY UPBRINGING AS A PUBLIC SCHOOL TEACHER
AND TEACHER EDUCATOR

In July 1969, after graduating from Temple University in Philadelphia, I began a one-year master's in teaching program at Syracuse University (the Urban Teacher Preparation Program) to earn my teaching certification in grades 1–6. This teacher education program focused on preparing teachers for Title 1 schools whose mission it was to serve nondominant local communities within the city. I had attended Philadelphia public schools and wanted to teach in urban schools to contribute to broad social transformation. The unpopular war in Vietnam, and Jim Crow and voter suppression laws in the South, were being protested on a large scale. The Civil Rights and Voting Rights Acts had become law just a few years before, and in cities nationwide, nondominant communities were seeking to gain more influence in their local public schools. The Ocean Hill–Brownsville teacher strike in New York City in 1968 was one of the most visible of these struggles between schools and communities (Isaacs, 2014). Frequently, teacher professionalism was pitted against community voice and influence.

In late summer, after completing a few courses and a practicum, I was assigned to Merrick elementary school for my year-long internship, one of two schools in the district that had recently made major changes in an attempt to be more responsive to the predominately African American families they served. On my first day, I learned that the families and local community were at the center of the work of our school. The new African American principal implemented a governance model that established a school cabinet composed of a few teachers, parents and community members, and the principal. This cabinet deliberated on the use of the resources of the school, participated in hiring and evaluating staff, and generally worked to make the school a more helpful resource for the whole community rather than a fortress within the community (Anyon, 1997). A community–school liaison was hired, and courses chosen by the community were offered at night and on weekends at the school. In addition to community members in the cabinet, several local community members, including parents, worked in the school as teacher assistants and lunchroom aides. A big sign in the front entrance to the school said something like "This is a Community School and all are welcome." In fact, our school had received a grant from the Mott Foundation to support its conversion to a public community school (Oakes, Maier, & Daniel, 2017).

I learned that my role as teacher was not just with the welfare of my students, but also with that of the broader community. This contradicted the dominant message of "cultural deprivation" at that time in teacher education, which prepared teachers to save their students from their "broken" communities. Teachers in our school were required to visit the families of all their students before the school year began to establish trusting relationships with them, and we were encouraged to spend time in the community, learning how to utilize community resources and cultural wealth in our teaching. I taught grades 4 through 6 there for 7 years. My life as a public school teacher included a natural extension of my work into the surrounding community. At times, there were conflicts both among the staff, and between the staff and community participants in the school. The work of school–community collaboration was not always easy, but the relationships and trust that emerged over time between school and community made the effort to achieve authentic community engagement in our school worth it for our students and their community.

After a few years, I began my first job as a teacher educator with the Teacher Corps (TC), while I remained in the Merrick school. TC was a federal program that existed in over 100 urban and rural communities highly impacted by poverty, and was designed to prepare teachers to be successful in their Title 1 schools and stay there over time (Edelfelt et al., 1974). The TC was founded on the idea that nondominant communities should be central contributors to the education of the teachers of their children. Each TC project was governed by a local board that had a majority of community members, and TC interns in this 2-year program were encouraged to live in the communities in which they were learning to teach and were required to spend at least 25% of their time working collaboratively with community members on projects. I was the mentor and supervisor for a team of five TC interns over their 2-year internship, supporting their work in the classroom and the community. I learned the value and importance of community voice and expertise in supporting the success of public schooling in nondominant communities.

THE REALITY OF COMMUNITY VOICE IN PUBLIC SCHOOLS IN NONDOMINANT COMMUNITIES

Public schooling in the United States remains extremely segregated and inequitable (Martin et al., 2018), possibly more segregated today than it was in the 1960s (Meatto, 2019). Students of color now represent a majority of students in U.S. public schools, and they disproportionally attend schools that represent higher levels of poverty than White students. For example, in 2017, the proportion of Black and Hispanic students attending "high poverty" public schools as determined by the level of students who qualify for the federal free or reduced lunch program was 45%, compared to only 8% for White students (National Center for Education Statistics, 2020). In many middle and upper middle-class communities, families have either abandoned the public schools or exert much influence on what goes on in their children's public schools. However, in most nondominant communities, families and community members are often excluded from genuine and equal participation in school affairs. This is the case even in situations where schools claim to have shifted from family and community involvement to family and community engagement (Ishimaru, 2019). Both federal legislation (Baquedano-Lopez et al., 2013) and school practices (Hong, 2019; Ishimaru, 2019) have encouraged school-centric as opposed to community-centric family and community engagement, creating mutual distrust between families and schools.

For example, Bryk & Schneider (2002) characterized the relationships between schools and nondominant families and communities in Chicago following the implementation of site-based school management:

> Distrust now characterizes many of the social interactions that poor families have with local schools and other public institutions. Teachers often see parents' goals and values as impediments to students' academic accomplishments. Parents, in turn, believe that teachers are antagonistic toward them and fail to appreciate the actual conditions that shape their children's lives. This lack of trust between teachers and parents—often exacerbated by race and class differences—makes it difficult for these groups to maintain a genuine dialogue about shared concerns. The resultant miscommunications tend to reinforce existing prejudices and undermine constructive efforts by teachers and parents to build relational ties around the interests of children. Instead of working together to support the academic and social development of students, teachers and parents find themselves working in isolation, or, in worst cases, in opposition to one another. . . . Unless substantial attention focuses on strengthening the social relationships among school professionals and parents, efforts at instructional improvement are unlikely to succeed. (pp. 6, 8)

Decades of research on school improvement and policy efforts show that the authentic engagement of families and communities from the very beginning in school improvement work, and mutual trust between families and communities and schools, are important features of improvement efforts that result in positive outcomes for students (Bryk & Schneider, 2002; Hong, 2019; Ishimaru, 2019). When the state pushes reforms through on their own with families and communities playing passive roles, the result has often been failure (see Russakoff, 2015).

CAN TEACHER PROFESSIONALISM AND AUTHENTIC COMMUNITY VOICE AND INFLUENCE COEXIST IN SCHOOLS SERVING NONDOMINANT COMMUNITIES?

In the same year that I began teaching in a public school, Larry Cuban, a prominent professor of the history of education and former teacher and school superintendent published an important article (Cuban, 1969) arguing for a broader role for teachers that includes participation in the surrounding community. Cuban based this argument on his experience working with the Cardozo Project in Urban Teaching, an innovative and successful teacher preparation program that was implemented in the Washington, D.C., public schools and became the basis for the Teacher Corps. Cuban concluded that "Voicelessness and a general lack of participation sum up the inner-city community's traditional role in the affairs of the school" (p. 254). He critiqued what he called "the myth of professionalism" as both the cause and effect of the distance that exists between home and school in nondominant communities.

Cuban (1969) defined the myth of professionalism as:

> The belief that schoolmen know precisely how kids must be taught, how they should learn, and what their "true" nature is . . . that to expect intelligent questions and helpful suggestions from parents would be as unprofessional as for a doctor to ask a cancer patient for his opinion on whether chemotherapy or cobalt treatment should be used. . . . Thus "professionalism" has been a code word for keeping parents at arm's length, for resisting the development of any meaningful face-to-face contact between school and parent, between teacher and community. (pp. 254–255)

There is a long history of tension between teacher professionalism and meaningful and influential participation by families and communities in their public schools, particularly in nondominant communities (Crowson, 1998; Driscoll, 1998). A key question is whether the democratic potential of public education as a public good benefitting both individuals and society can be realized without undermining the dignity and professionalism of the work of teachers.

VARIETIES OF TEACHER PROFESSIONALISM

One way to begin to address this issue is to unpack the nature of teacher professionalism. Teacher professionalism does not have a single meaning agreed upon by all. Several different conceptions of teacher professionalism have emerged, not all of which are hostile to authentic community engagement in schools in nondominant communities.

A large portion of the work on teacher professionalism has operated on the basis of a traditional view of professionalism, a view that Dzur (2008) has referred to as the *social trustee* model. Here it is argued that individuals are entitled to professional status because they possess elements that warrant public trust, such as commitment to client needs, a specialized knowledge base, shared standards of practice, monopoly over service, a high degree of autonomy, long periods of training, and a service ethic (Hargreaves, 2000). Teaching is a semi-profession rather than a full profession because it lacks a number of these elements (Howsam et al., 1976). Much of the professionalization agenda in teaching and teacher education over the last 50 years has revolved around efforts to move teaching closer toward a social trustee model of professionalism or professionalism from within (Evetts, 2009). The social trustee view of professionalism has historically received much criticism in the literature for allegedly serving the self-interest of the professionals rather than the needs of their clients (Dzur, 2008).

A second view of professionalism in teaching, *managerial* or *organizational* professionalism, emerged with the growth of new public management practices in public education that brought practices and structures common in the business world into public schools. This process has brought market models and business management models which have often been funded by venture philanthropy, corporations, and the federal government (Scott, 2011) and have emphasized deregulation and market competition, the growth of corporate-run charter schools, mayoral and state control of school districts, vouchers, high-stakes testing, and the narrowing of the curriculum to tested subjects and content included in the tests under the argument that this is what is needed for the nation to be economically competitive (Anderson & Cohen, 2018; Hargreaves, 2000).

These market-oriented practices have been highly racialized; although they have affected all public schools, they have been primarily focused on schools in nondominant communities serving nonwhite families and families living in poverty. It is in these communities where corporate-run charter schools are most commonly found, where teachers have the least voice and influence in the schooling of their children, and where teachers have the least preparation and experience (Zeichner, 2018).

The growth of managerial professionalism in public schools, rather than empowering teachers, has led to greater intensification and deskilling of teachers' work (e.g., an increase in scripted instruction and reduction in teacher agency) (Hargreaves, 1994) and the transformation of teachers' identities in ways that further discourage their agency (Ball, 2010), particularly in schools serving nondominant communities that have been the most affected by new public management practices.

Finally, a third form of teacher professionalism, *democratic* professionalism, has been advocated for the last two decades as an alternative to the social trustee and managerial conceptions (e.g., Anderson & Cohen, 2018;

Apple, 2012; Dzur, 2008; Sachs, 2001). Dzur (2008) defines democratic professionalism as:

> Sharing previously professional tasks and encouraging lay participation in ways that enhance and enable broader public engagement and deliberation about major social issues inside and outside the professional domains . . . This does not mean that professional authority, status, privilege and responsibility disappear as well, only that they are tightly connected to the empowerment of lay people. (p. 130)

More specific to teaching, Sachs (2001) has argued that democratic professionalism

> seeks to demystify professional work and build alliances between teachers and excluded constituencies of students, parents, and members of the community on whose behalf decisions have traditionally been made wither by professions or by the state. . . . The core of democratic professionalism is an emphasis on collaborative, cooperative action between teachers and other education stakeholders. (p. 153)

The idea of democratic professionalism centers students, families, and communities in teachers' work and helps to productively manage tensions between educators and the nondominant communities they serve. Anderson & Cohen (2018) argue that although current efforts to deprofessionalize teaching have degraded the work of teachers under the guise of professionalism, "the response to deprofessionalization should not be to harken back to some previous era in which teachers were more respected and had more autonomy" (p. 42). Democratic professionalism and supporting more authentic engagement of nondominant families and communities also does not mean letting families and communities or teachers impose their own views on schools without a deliberative process that is guided by democratic principles (Zeichner, 1991).

WAYS IN WHICH DEMOCRATIC PROFESSIONALISM CAN HELP REALIZE THE DEMOCRATIC POTENTIAL OF PUBLIC EDUCATION

There are several ways in which teachers as democratic professionals can enhance authentic family and community engagement in their public schools and maintain the dignity of teachers' work: (1) community teaching and community schools; (2) social movement and social justice teacher unionism; and (3) social movements for educational, social, economic, and political justice. Teachers, and the teacher education programs that prepare them, can begin to create community-centered family and community engagement by prioritizing the development of schools where collaborating with families and communities in respectful ways and where learning from the communities is a priority for all staff.

Currently, there is very little attention to family and community engagement in either teacher preparation programs or district and school professional development opportunities for school staff. (Zeichner, 2018). One of the central elements of effective preparation of school staff for authentic family and community engagement must be the fundamental role of family and community members in codesigning and co-providing that preparation (Zeichner, 2018). The preparation of school staff must focus on what Murrell (2001) has called community teaching that builds on the cultural resources that students bring to school with them and benefits from the expertise and cultural wealth in students' communities. As mentioned earlier, there is substantial evidence that community public schools that engage families and communities in authentic ways, including in decisionmaking, are connected to positive outcomes for students in nondominant communities (Oakes, Maier, & Daniel, 2017).

However, training for teachers and other educational staff is clearly not enough to bring a community-centered approach to teaching and schooling into being and to sustain it over time. Resources need to be made available to make community-centered teaching and school a part of the work of school staff, and community members who participate in these efforts should be compensated for their contributions. School staff should do this work as a part of their workload and not in addition to it.

When this community-centered approach is taken to the school level, there is substantial evidence from a variety of specific community school approaches that include authentic family and community engagement that students benefit academically and progress is made toward narrowing existing racial and economic achievement gaps (Oakes, Maier, & Daniel, 2017; Dyrness, 2011).

A second approach to developing democratic professionalism among teachers that is inclusive of community expertise and responsive to community needs is through teacher unions. While for many years teacher unions focused on strengthening elements of the social trustee view of professionalism, such as salary, benefits, and working conditions, and in fighting against the intensification and devaluing of teachers' work brought about under managerial professionalism, in recent years the work of teacher unions in some parts of the country (such as Chicago, Los Angeles, and Seattle) has taken a new turn toward strengthening democratic professionalism and the responsiveness of teacher unions to local communities. Social movement (Weiner, 2012) or social justice teacher unionism (Peterson, 1999) is a continually emerging form of unionism that seeks to work with and for local communities, rather than struggle with them over power. According to Peterson (1999), a former president of the Milwaukee teacher union, the central elements of social justice teacher unionism include:

- Defend the rights of its members while fighting for the rights of and needs of the broader community and students.
- Recognize that parents and neighbors of our students are key allies, and build strategic alliances with parents, labor unions, and community groups
- View parents and community groups as essential partners in reform . . . committed to a bottom-up grassroots mobilization of teachers, parents, community, and rank-and-file union members. (p. 16)

A key priority of social justice teacher unionism according to Peterson (1999) is "building coalitions and alliances with parent and community advocacy groups that speak to both school reform and ensuring equity in the society as a whole" (p. 19). In recent years teacher strikes in cities like Los Angeles, Chicago, and Seattle have reflected a social justice approach to unionism that went beyond the trade and professional union approaches of focusing on salaries, benefits and working conditions. For example, in the 2015 teacher strike in Seattle, teachers won several things that were also desired by parents, such as 30 minutes of recess daily for all elementary students, a 1-year ban on the suspension of elementary students for nonviolent offenses, and the creation of task forces in 30 schools to examine equity issues including disciplinary ones that disproportionally affect students of color (Strauss, 2015).

A third way in which democratic professionalism can help realize the democratic potential of public education is an extension of the work of social justice teacher unionism. Here, educators have joined or formed alliances with existing social movements for education, racial, economic, and political justice that exist in nondominant communities throughout the nation, and have worked alongside community organizers, parents, and community leaders to address the broad range of inequities that affect nondominant communities, including in education. Inequities in schools are a reflection of inequities in the larger society. There have been many examples in the last decade of local community-initiated efforts to address the systemic racial, economic, and educational inequities that impact the lives of students and their families in nondominant communities. Some of these efforts have involved collaborations between teachers, teacher unions, and community organizers, parents, families, and students and have linked educational reform to community revitalization (Anyon, 2014; Orr & Rogers, 2011; Warren & Goodman, 2018; Warren & Mapp, 2011).

A key element that distinguishes successful justice-based collaborations between educators and families and communities from typical family and community engagement efforts by schools is that in community-initiated collaborations, the expertise that families and communities bring about how to advance educational justice and community well-being is recognized, valued, and utilized (Ishimaru et al., 2019). In many, if not most, school-initiated efforts, families and communities are usually asked to react to plans that have already been conceptualized by school staff.

CONCLUSION

Inequity in public education is a reflection of problems in the broader society such as the lack of access to housing, nutritious food, affordable and high-quality childcare and healthcare, transportation, jobs that pay a living wage, and safety. These societal problems are a reflection of systemic problems of racism and classism and the policies that have created and strengthened these inequities. Problems in schooling cannot be fixed through school improvement efforts alone (Berliner, 2013), and school improvement must be linked with community revitalization. There is substantial evidence that equitable and authentic family and community engagement and collaboration with educators, where the expertise of families and communities is recognized, valued, and utilized, help to shape and implement effective improvement efforts. Such collaboration has addressed some of the inequities in schooling that school improvement efforts alone, or those with school-centric, top-down approaches to family and community engagement alone cannot ameliorate.

My experience as a teacher and teacher educator over the last 45 years and the academic scholarship on these issues indicates that the kind of justice-based collaborative work that is needed is complicated (Ishimaru, 2019; Philip et al., 2013), but working through these complications, tensions, and messiness is necessary for the democratic potential of public education in nondominant communities to be realized. I have argued in this essay that achieving authentic community voice and influence in public schools in nondominant communities does not have to come at the expense of teacher professionalism. A new form of teacher professionalism is growing in our nation, democratic professionalism, where teachers work in solidarity with families and communities to address the broad range of inequities both inside and outside of education. Only through this unified approach will the potential of public education and our nation be realized for all of our people.

NOTE

1. Nondominant communities refers to "historically marginalized communities including indigenous, Black, Latinx, Asian, Pacific Islander, immigrant, refugee, and other intersecting communities systematically excluded or oppressed by formal systems. While recognizing that these groups have distinct histories, experiences, and dynamics in education and society, the term highlights the power asymmetries

inherent in the relationship of these groups to the dominant culture" (Guitierrez, 2006, cited in Ishimaru, 2019, p. 169).

REFERENCES

Anderson, G., & Cohen, M. (2018). *The new democratic professional in education: Confronting markets, metrics, and managerialism*. Teachers College Press.

Anyon, J. (1997). *Ghetto schooling: A political economy of urban educational reform*. Teachers College Press.

Anyon, J. (2014). *Radical possibilities: Public policy, urban education, and a new social movement* (2nd ed.). Routledge.

Apple, M. W. (2012). *Knowledge, power, and education: The selected works of Michael W. Apple*. Routledge.

Ball, S. (2010). The teacher's soul and the terrors of performativity. *Journal of Education Policy 18*(2), 215–228.

Baquedano-Lopez, P., Alexander, R. A., & Hernandez, S. J. (2013). Equity issues in parental and community involvement: What teacher educators need to know. *Review of Research in Education, 37*, 149–182.

Berliner, D. (2013). Effects of inequality and poverty vs teachers and schooling on American Youth. *Teachers College Record, 115*(12).

Bryk, A., & Schneider, B. (2002). *Trust in schools: A core resource for improvement*. Russell Sage.

Crowson, R. (1998). Community empowerment and the public schools: Can educational professionalism survive? *Peabody Journal of Education, 73*(1), 56–68.

Cuban, L. (1969). Teacher and community. *Harvard Educational Review, 39*(2), 253–272.

Darling-Hammond, L. (2013). Inequality and school resources: What it will take to close the opportunity gap. In P. L. Carter & K. G. Welner (Eds.), *Closing the opportunity gap: What America must do to give every child an even chance* (pp. 77–97). Oxford University Press.

Darling-Hammond, L. & Oakes, J. (2019). *Preparing teachers for deeper learning*. Harvard Education Press.

Driscoll, M. (1998). Professionalism vs. community. *Peabody Journal of Education, 73*(1), 89–127.

Dyrness, A. (2011). *Mothers united: An immigrant struggle for socially just education*. Minneapolis: University of Minnesota Press.

Dzur, A.W. (2008). *Democratic professionalism: Citizen participation and the reconstruction of professional ethics, identity, and practice*. Penn State University Press. https://www.jstor.org/stable/10.5325/j.ctt7v51b

Edelfelt, R. A., Corwin, R., & Hanna, E. (1974). *Lessons from the Teacher Corps*. National Education Association.

Evetts, J. (2009). New professionalism and new public management: Changes, continuities, and consequences. *Comparative Sociology, 8*(2), 247–266.

Gutierrez, K. (2006). White innocence: A framework and methodology for rethinking educational discourse and inquiry. *International Journal of Learning, 12*(10), 223–230.

Hargreaves, A. (1994). *Changing teachers, changing times: Teachers' work and culture in the postmodern age.* Teachers College Press.

Hargreaves, A. (2000). Four ages of professionalism and professional learning. *Teachers and Teaching, 6*(2), 151–182.

Hong, S. (2019). *Natural allies: Hope and possibility in teacher-family partnerships.* Harvard Education Press.

Howsam, R. B., Corrigan, D. C., Denemark, G. W., & Nash, R. J. (1976). *Educating a profession: Report of the Bicentennial Commission for the profession of teaching.* American Association of Colleges for Teacher Education.

Isaacs, C. S. (2014). *Inside Ocean Hill–Brownsville: A teacher's education.* State University of New York Press.

Ishimaru, A. (2019). *Just schools: Building equitable collaborations with families and communities.* Teachers College Press.

Ishimaru, A., Bang, M., Valladares, M., Nolan, C., Tavares, H., Rajendran, A., & Chang, K. (2019, July). *Recasting families and communities as co-designers of education in tumultuous times.* National Education Policy Center.

Martin, C., Boser, U., Benner, M., & Baffour, P. (2018, November). *A quality approach to school funding: Lessons learned from school finance litigation.* Center for American Progress.

Meatto, K. (2019, May 2). Still separate and still unequal: Teaching about school segregation and educational inequality. *New York Times.* https://www.nytimes.com/2019/05/02/learning/lesson-plans/still-separate-still-unequal-teaching-about-school-segregation-and-educational-inequality.html

Murrell, P. C. Jr. (2001). *The commiunity teacher: A new framework for effective urban teaching.* Teachers College Press.

National Center for Educational Statistics (2020, May). The condition of education. U.S. Department of Education. https://nces.ed.gov/pubs2020/2020144.pdf

Oakes, J., Maier, A., & Daniel, J. (2017, June). *Community schools: An evidence-based strategy for equitable school improvement.* National Education Policy Center.

Orr, M., & Rogers, J. (2011) (Eds). *Public engagement for public education: Joining forces to revitalize democracy and equalize schools.* Stanford University Press.

Peterson, R. (1999). Survival and justice: Rethinking teacher union strategy. In R. Peterson & M. Charney (Eds.), *Transforming teacher unions: Fighting for better schools and social justice* (pp. 11–19). Rethinking Schools.

Philip, T., Way, W., Garcia, A., Schuler-Brown, S., & Navarro, O. (2013). When educators attempt to make "community" a part of classroom learning: The dangers of (mis)appropriating students' communities into schools. *Teaching and Teacher Education, 34,* 174–183.

Russakoff, D. (2015). *The prize: Who's in charge of America's schools?* Houghton Mifflin.

Sachs, J. (2001). Teacher professional identity: Competing discourses, competing outcomes. *Journal of Educational Policy, 16*(2), 149–161.

Scott, J. (2011). Market-driven educational reform and the racial politics of advocacy. *Peabody Journal of Education, 86*(5), 580–599.

Strauss, V. (2015, September 25). The surprising things Seattle teachers won for students by striking. *Washington Post.* https://www.washingtonpost.com/news/

answer-sheet/wp/2015/09/25/the-surprising-things-seattle-teachers-won-for-students-by-striking/

Warren, M., & Goodman, D. (2018). *Lift us up, don't push us out: Voices from the frontline of the educational justice movement*. Beacon Press.

Warren, M., & Mapp, K. (2011). *A match on dry grass: Community organizing as a catalyst for school reform*. Oxford University Press.

Weiner, L. (2012). *The future of our schools: Teachers unions and social justice*. Haymarket Books.

Yosso, T. J. (2005). Whose culture has capital? A critical race theory discussion of community cultural wealth. *Race, Ethnicity and Education, 8*(1), 69–91.

Zeichner, K. (1991). Contradictions and tensions in the professionalization of teaching and the democratization of schools. *Teachers College Record, 92*(3), 363–379.

Zeichner, K. (2018). *The struggle for the soul of teacher education*. Routledge.

Horace Mann and a New Common Good

Joshua P. Starr

The problem we're trying to solve in public education today is to prepare every child to graduate with the knowledge, skills, and capacities to embrace an increasingly complex world on their own terms. Our economy and our society need critical thinkers, entrepreneurs, and innovators to solve the pressing problems of today, and schools must play a role in developing those competencies. That is the new common good, and schools should be organized so that adults are exercising and constantly improving on the skills they need to enable every child to achieve that goal.

The challenge we face is that our society, and thus our public schools, do not promote the equitable access to resources necessary to solve this problem. In fact, for some Americans, schools are doing exactly what they're designed to do, which is to rank and sort young people in order to slot them into different paths that will determine their futures. Other Americans, however, see the deep injustices of society reflected in how we organize public schools and know the system is designed to oppress many and privilege the few, despite rhetoric to the contrary. Americans aren't likely to agree on a definition of the common good, just as they disagree on the purpose of school. This essay explores how Mann's concept of common schools serving the common good also calcifies the social stratification endemic to American society and suggests how leadership can redesign school systems towards a new common good.

In Mann's time, public school served a narrow purpose. It was only for White young people, mostly boys, and there was a distinct religious undertone to its civic goals. Public schools must, of course, be understood within a temporal context. At the most basic level, the demographics, politics and economy of the mid-1840s was starkly different in every way to ours. The American dream was *de jure* available only to certain people, and the common good served to systematize and entrench that. Public schools, where they existed, were meant to help White boys master the basics in order to be productive and moral citizens who could participate in democracy.

While some would go on to higher education and pursue medicine or law or academia, most needed just enough schooling to participate in their local economy and culture. Schools then, as they do now, serve to perpetuate a chosen social and economic order. In the mid-19th century, when Mann's ideas rose to prominence in New England and beyond, that order was more explicitly stratified than it is now. The myth of rugged individualism that permeates the American psyche was not intended to apply to anyone other than White, Christian men.

Today, in our religiously and demographically pluralistic society, we make great claims that all have equal access to the American dream, and that personal choices, not societal institutions, will lead to one's destiny. Laws and public sentiment may have changed, but the de facto structures and systems in place that bind our public schools are not dissimilar from Mann's time. The difference is that we don't admit it and even articulate the opposite. An example of how schools haven't changed is the role of women as educators. To perpetuate the religious foundation of America, Mann argued that women should be teachers, as it is "one of the clearest ordinances of nature, that woman is the appointed guide and guardian of children of a tender age" (Mann, 1848). This would never be explicitly stated today as a design principle of school systems. Yet, 77% of teachers are women and it's still a grossly underpaid profession. No policy maker, elected official, superintendent, or school board member would ever argue that women make the best teachers, but the intentional design of the structure of public schools perpetuates a female-dominated teaching force. From the pay to the hours, schools have been organized to support Mann's original design, whether we choose to admit it or not (see https://pdkpoll.org/assets/downloads/2016p-dkpoll48.pdf).

Public school, however, is more than the structures and systems of who teaches and who gets to learn. At the core, school is about what students are learning every day. What we teach reflects what we believe students should know and be able to do when they graduate and go on to the next step in their lives. Additionally, what we decide to teach depends on our definition of the common good, and on our expectations of the degree to which everyone should have access to the same kind of learning. What we teach to whom reflects how society thinks about and enacts stratification by race, perceived ability, native language, and socioeconomic status. One way we've seen this play out, as schools became more accessible to more people after Mann's time, is through the question of the extent to which schools should prepare students for work. Whether it was the Hampton model in the reconstructed South that relegated recently enslaved people to an education that prepared them for little more than menial labor to perpetuate the southern agricultural economy, or the efforts to absorb waves of immigrants in Northern cities by preparing them for the factory, public schools have always been used to perpetuate a particular economic model.

Mann didn't believe that school was solely about preparing students for work. In fact, he said, "The man is the trunk, occupations and professions are only different qualities of the fruit it should yield" (Mann, 1891). Contrast that with today's calls for students to find their passions as early as middle school and leave high school prepared to embark on a chosen career path in a 21st-century world in which the kinds of careers that will be required to grow a robust and sustainable economy are not entirely predictable. Yet students are in schools with stilted curricula and a near-obsessive orientation towards standardized test scores in literacy and mathematics. The rhetoric of a new potential common good being one of personalized learning where students are set free to discover their inner selves and activate them upon being released from the strictures of public education flies in the face of how most schools are actually designed.

Beyond preparing students to contribute to the economy, Mann certainly believed a general education that prepared future citizens was the crux of the matter, yet what would that look like today? What does it mean to be prepared for citizenship and what should—and can—schools do to further that end? Again, at the core, this question is about what we teach to whom, and whether all students are given opportunities to develop the knowledge and skills they need to engage constructively in a complex and pluralistic society on their own terms. Do we want young people to learn how to change the world in school, or in spite of school? Schools have not been designed to promote this kind of critical democratic thinking, and in fact, have worked to become depoliticized at all levels while ensuring that curriculum is both neutral and focused on literacy, mathematics, and now STEM. Upper-level courses in high school, such as Advanced Placement and International Baccalaureate, allow for student learning and inquiry into more complex subject matter that may let them understand the world around them at a deeper level. But access to those classes is often limited to students deemed high achieving by standard measures, thereby limiting opportunity for the broader population of students. In fact, one could argue that the design of our current school system is doing exactly what it's intended to do today, by stratifying and limiting many students, particularly students of color, English language learners, students with disabilities, and poor students. That stratification serves the foundation of elitism that our country is built on and that sustains our chosen social and economic order. The rugged individualism of our collective lore fades fast in the reality of the structure of our current society. Public schools reinforce those structures, despite claims to the contrary. The common good, as defined by the elites and the powerful, is, in fact, being served.

As we talk about public education today, we deny and decry our history amidst claims of equity and access. We set high standards for all children to achieve and blame their parents and our schools for not helping all children reach those standards. We constantly measure academic progress and compare different groups of children and provide interventions and supports where necessary. We rarely, however, question or challenge the foundation upon which these systems are built. Schools are still funded through property taxes, more vulnerable students still sit in the most decrepit buildings, food and housing insecurity are still pervasive in poor communities, health care is a privilege, not a right. And the list goes on. These structural underpinnings of our society are reflected in how—and what—we teach our children. We hide behind slogans and hashtags promoting equity and excellence while organizing to the contrary.

How, then, should schools be organized to envision a common good for a truly democratic and pluralistic society, even if that means they're doing so in opposition to the society that students will be graduating into? How can we realize the most American of ideals—that young people should be prepared to embrace an increasingly complex world on their own terms—within the deeply entrenched bureaucracy that is public education? And perhaps a more important question is one of leadership. What actions should a leader take to bend the arc of history more quickly?

First, we need to know what effective schools do. There are certain universal elements of effective schools that serve all students well, regardless of demographics. Typically, these schools have visionary and collaborative leaders who engage others in decision-making, communicate well and create positive school cultures and climates. Teachers in such schools hold each other to a high standard, support each other's learning, and are constantly engaged in improving their practice. Students are given a rich curriculum with opportunities for acceleration and support and their social emotional needs are attended to by caring adults. Parents and families are welcomed and feel part of the school community, regardless of their demographics. I can go on, but the core elements of effective schools are not much of a mystery.

The black box of school improvement lies within the systemic approach to ensuring all schools are effective, not just some. This is where governance, funding, policy, and resource allocation all come into play. Districts that have successfully enabled all schools to serve children well strategically allocate resources so that those who need the most get the most. They put the right talent in the right places and create both supports and accountability for improvement. Elected officials provide enough resources—which is rarely the case—and school boards focus on equity and access rather than getting immersed in political infighting. Communities are deeply engaged and have opportunities to be part of decisionmaking in authentic and meaningful ways. Educators receive comprehensive and intentional professional learning, have a rich curriculum to work from, and have meaningful data upon which to make decisions.

All of these elements of effective schools and districts can be enacted by leaders, albeit not easily and over a long period of time. Regardless of how successful such leaders may be, if their actions serve a current construction of the common good that leans more heavily toward private benefit than public good, our schools and the society they serve will look mostly the same. What, then, might an alternative approach to school and system improvement look like that embraces the core elements of effective schools and systems, but does so towards a different end—that seeks to create a new common good that actually serves all students at high levels?

To my mind, to begin influencing the common good towards a more equitable society, schools must change what they teach and how they do so. While basic literacy and numeracy are essential, they are the floor of the house, not the ceiling. According to Mann, the effect of a good education on a young person is profound:

> Indeed so pervading and enduring the effect of education upon the youthful soul, that it may well be compared to a certain species of writing-ink, whose color, at first, is scarcely perceptible, but which penetrates deeper and grows blacker by age, until, if you consume the scroll over a coal-fire, the character will still be legible in the cinders. (Mann, 1855, p. 17)

If education is so important and enduring for not only the individual but for our society, as Mann suggests, we must ensure it is of high enough quality to help young people embrace an increasingly complex world on their own terms. There are enough examples today of how schools can reorient themselves so that an ever more diverse group of students leave ready to take on the challenges of today's world. Efforts like Freedom Schools, the EdLeader 21 network, High Tech High and the Big Picture Company are proven models. Superintendent David Schuler in D214 in Illinois has implemented powerful career pathway programs, and Michael Hynes in Port Washington, NY, has embraced play as a powerful part of the school day. Susan Enfield in Highline, WA, ensures that every child is known by "name, strength and need," while Sonja Santelises in Baltimore City has revamped their curriculum to both reflect higher standards and be more culturally responsive. Lately we've seen more schools adopting and embedding Nikole Hannah-Jones's *1619 Project* into classrooms, out of the recognition that we need to change how we tell our collective national story.

Such efforts are promising and admirable, but the question remains whether they're scalable without the powerful leadership of a visionary superintendent or school leader. What can a superintendent do to prepare students to graduate ready to create a new common good? The crux of the strategy centers around *content*—what students learn every day and how they are engaged in that learning with adults and peers with whom they have an emotional connection. To anchor content and expertise, standards are necessary to ensure that educators have appropriate outcomes to organize curriculum and assess student progress. These standards can be grounded in understanding how our society is structured, how that came about, and what can be done to improve the human condition. Integrated, problem and project-based curricula that tackle the real conditions within a community can be designed by teachers, community partners, and students. Educators will have to learn how to design, implement, and assess such units of study, but by doing so, students will develop a sense of agency that they can improve their local communities while also gaining a deeper understanding of how our societies are structured.

The superintendent must operate on two levels to achieve the goals stated above. One is to organize their educators to work with students every day so that they learn about how our society is structured and what they can do to change it. This is no easy undertaking, as our educators will have to embrace learning about how their role serves a larger social and economic order. The other is to influence the larger community that doing so is the right thing, while removing institutional barriers of oppression. Convincing a school board, a funding authority, the media, community leaders, and families that tackling local problems and facing the truth about America is to the benefit of children, the community, and our society is no easy task. System leaders must find both allies to support them and common ground with dissenters. Decision-making processes must be open, transparent, and collaborative, and a multiyear plan needs to support these efforts. You can't change everything at once. There's always a group of willing educators and parents within a system who are interested in taking on these issues. Start with them. Leaders must also use aspirational and hopeful rhetoric when arguing for why they're making these changes, rather than oppositional or accusatory language. It certainly won't be easy, but starting small, with clear goals based on shared values, should get things moving.

Along with influencing the community at large so that they understand that the system must prepare students in new ways to take on new challenges, the superintendent must also take a hard look at how the system is designed to oppress many and privilege the few. Whether it's services for special populations like students with disabilities or English learners, access to advanced classes, or the distribution of the most effective teachers, school systems have a myriad of formal and informal policies and practices that perpetuate the status quo. Some of these are baked into policies, while others are past practice. Most perniciously, many of the institutional barriers result from politics, biases, and White privilege. Some school and system leaders are afraid of the very real political and personal consequences of not giving powerful people what they ask for, often at the expense of the most vulnerable. Whatever the genesis of these barriers, superintendents have a responsibility to remove them so that all of our children are able to access an education that truly prepares them for the future.

Transforming school systems to prepare students to create a new common good in our nation is not for everyone. Some leaders may feel that they are in communities and political environments where it's just not possible. All leaders, however, must be mindful of James Baldwin's entreaty to teachers back in 1963:

> The paradox of education is precisely this—that as one begins to become conscious one begins to examine the society in which he is being educated. The purpose of education, finally, is to create in a person the ability to look at the world for himself, to make his own decisions, to say to himself this is black or this is white, to decide for himself whether there is a God in heaven or not. To ask questions of the universe, and then learn to live with those questions, is the way he achieves his own identity. But no society is really anxious to have that kind of person around. What societies really, ideally, want is a citizenry which will simply obey the rules of society. If a society succeeds in this, that society is about to perish. The obligation of anyone who thinks of himself as responsible is to examine society and try to change it and to fight it—at no matter what risk. This is the only hope society has. This is the only way societies change. (Baldwin, 1963/1985)

Horace Mann articulated a vision and structure for public schools to organize around a common good that served mid-19th century America. That common good no longer serves our nation, regardless of whether we want to acknowledge it. System leaders have a responsibility to take a hard look at how they're perpetuating the status quo, even as they claim the mantle of equity. Or, at the very least, they can ask the right questions and start preparing our young people to make a very different nation that truly serves our collective common good.

REFERENCES

Baldwin, J. (1985). A talk to teachers. In *The price of the ticket* (pp. 325–332). St. Martin's Press. (Original published in 1963.)

Mann, H. (1848). *Twelfth annual report to the secretary of the Massachusetts state board of education.*

Mann, H. (1891). *Life and works of Horace Mann, volume III.* Lae and Shepard Publishers.

Mann, H. (1855). *Lectures on education.* IDE & BUTTON, Publishers. https://archive.org/stream/lecturesoneduca01manngoog/lecturesoneduca01manngoog_djvu.txt

Horace and George and Zitkala-Sa
Reimagining Experimentation

Jacqueline Grennon Brooks

Horace Mann is credited with the birth of the United States' public school system. He is famous for saying, "The public school is the greatest discovery made by man." But no one *discovered* public schools. People *invented* them. And it is time for all people, not only men, to reimagine them.

COMMON SCHOOLS

Horace Mann's common schools were envisioned to serve children from all social classes and religions, and to be led by educated, competent teachers. Today, public schools serve as launching points for citizens who design and grow evolving societies, economies, and cultures. In many ways for many people, public schools have become the great equalizer that Mann envisioned—but not for everyone. In Mann's time, schools were segregated, and nonsectarian meant not affiliated with a particular sect of Christianity. Although we've come a long way in actualizing and broadening Mann's vision of inclusivity, the journey is far from complete. To continue his extraordinary legacy of optimism for a more just America, there is more work to be done in weaving a web that connects and strengthens us.

Schools cannot alone battle the negative effects of poverty or the economic and societal barriers that encumber many students of color, non-native English-speaking students, students with special needs, or students seeking freedom of expression around issues of sexuality, identity, and gender. Schools cannot alone surmount the damaging educational impacts of housing and food insecurity, lack of health care, and lower participation in preschool. Schools cannot alone overcome the insidious effects of racism on children's development or community life. These issues require societal transformations.

However, today's common schools, our public schools, can offer welcoming, imaginative, safe, judgment-free spaces with enriching opportunities in which all learners are met and challenged at the leading edge of their current thinking. We know a lot more about learning than we did in Horace Mann's time and that knowledge requires us to be as forward-thinking now about the concept of school as Mann was over 150 years ago.

Today's world is global and interdependent. Within this broadened context, we can restructure schools to promote a more robust version of learning than was understood in days gone by. We can support children's learning by situating practice within the science of learning. An important first step is using what research tells us about the role of self-regulation in healthy development and academic achievement. To carry forward Mann's vision and accomplishment of creating a public school system for all of America's children, it is essential that we base today's schools on what we know about how students construct knowledge—and self-regulation is at the center of this shift in direction. It is time that we restructure schools around the fundamental human quests to manage one's own behaviors and construct meaning.

The global challenges that threaten the planet's sustainability require solutions from imaginative and innovative thinkers, people able to identify concerns and address them proactively. Young people desperately need schools that recognize them as citizens who are and will be contributing ideas and ideals toward the betterment of their lives and the lives of others. This transformation will require normative and structural shifts in schools specifically targeted at fostering students' inherent motivation to make sense of their many worlds. In order for a chess player to set up a board to win in three moves forward or a riverboat captain to navigate the third bend of a river, they both need to line up present actions with where they want to go. In order for teachers to prepare students for the world into which they will graduate, they need to focus on the present, viewing children as young thinkers, and teaching them at the front edges of the understandings and perspectives that they hold in the moment.

THE SEARCH FOR UNDERSTANDING

Mann thought that words should not be taught before ideas and that the social value of schools could only be realized with heterogeneous groupings of students, which would develop students' self-discipline. Mann's conceptions of *pedagogy* were highly influenced by educational thinking in Europe. He respected the Swiss educator Johann Heinrich Pestalozzi, who believed in teaching the whole child by addressing children's physical, intellectual and moral development, often in nature, and always in an emotionally safe space with objects before books.

Mann's conceptions of *school structure* were influenced by the Prussian education model in which public schools were compulsory, tax-funded, and age-graded with a new teacher every year. They stressed conformity and efficiency over meaning-making and individuality. The essential components of Mann's vision—the expansive imagining and creation of public schools, and the limiting factors of paying for and overseeing them—resulted in the uneasy intersection of pedagogy and politics, a dilemma with which we continue to struggle today.

Conceptually, Mann's vision of the learner, more than its enactment in schools, connects with understandings of child development that the Swiss epistemologist Jean Piaget proffered nearly a century later. Piaget produced careful studies of children's thinking that cast a spotlight on children's cognitive development. He offered a learning theory based on the notion that learners generate knowledge through iterative mental formulation and reformulation of ideas that satisfy the search for meaning. This is constructivism. Over the years, understandings of constructivist pedagogy have evolved with new research on human development, the role of cultural contexts in learning, and the transdisciplinary science of learning. Bolstered more recently by neuroscientific research, constructivism is further understood in terms of neuronal wiring and firing: the activation of brain networks and the brain's capacity to reconstitute itself through development and mediation.

Constructivism and the science of learning research that supports it require us to rethink teaching practice, as well as conceptions of success and failure in schools. If a search for understanding is the goal, teaching becomes the practice of negotiating curricula with students, seeking and valuing student voice, and scaffolding student error. These teaching practices promote student self-regulation. Teachers honor each student's educational journey by negotiating curriculum, not delivering it. With learners as builders of knowledge, not consumers of it, error is recognized as a necessary component of learning, not something to be avoided. Teachers create discrepancies and bring ambiguity into classrooms so that students can learn how to handle uncertainty and confusion as conditions of learning, not obstacles to be circumvented. They understand that learning requires disequilibrium, and that as teachers they play powerful roles by mediating students' present ideas with the ideas embedded in the curriculum.

LOOKING CLOSELY AT INCLUSIVITY

Constructivist schools strive to be democratic, equitable, and inclusive, offering all students equal opportunities to learn and shine. Teachers within them anticipate a wide and complex range of learner needs and create learning spaces and curriculum tasks that are flexible by design and accessible for diverse populations. Mann envisioned schools staffed with smart, competent faculties who appreciate students as thinkers, understand the development of reasoning, and have deep knowledge of the concepts embedded in the content they teach. Without these skills and dispositions, teachers sometimes impede learning rather than enhance it by inadvertently privileging certain students, which leads to the creation of marginalized individuals and groups, which inevitably leads to unequal education.

Here's an example. An elementary class is learning some basic elements of electric circuitry by designing and constructing working lighthouses with switches. There is an ample and wide selection of materials for experimentation and meaning-making. The stage is set, but how the lesson unfolds can either support or impede learning.

The teacher opens the lesson with: "Who thinks the Statue of Liberty is a lighthouse?" Half of the students raise their hands for no, half for yes. The teacher acknowledges that the yes voters are correct. He then asks if the students have seen a lighthouse. About half of the students raise their hands. He calls on a few students to share and responds to their answers with "good," "yes," and "excellent"—all directed at the students who have seen a lighthouse. He then reads the beloved classic, *The Little Red Lighthouse and the Great Grey Bridge*, by Hildegarde H. Swift and Lynd Ward. After reading the book, he shows the class the circuit that he has made with an incandescent bulb, two D-cell batteries, and wires. When the bulb lights, the class oohs. (Everyone at any age enjoys seeing a bulb light!) He then invites the students to make their own lighthouses, but with supplies that are different than the ones he used to make his. He hands out coin cell batteries and LED bulbs, and tells the students that the long end of the LED bulb is positive and should be matched to the side of the coin battery that was labeled with a plus sign. The students go to work, and almost all of them successfully complete the same circuit—*almost* all of them.

As the lesson continues, most of the children follow the teacher's directions in lighting their light bulbs. Three who are unable to follow along become increasingly frustrated. One cries and two walk away. The teacher responds empathetically and kindly, and in a comforting manner shows them how to attach their circuit pieces to produce a lit bulb. In the end, the lesson worked out. But, truly, did it?

Using a lighthouse as a contextual focus to study circuitry, including an engaging storybook to extend the context, and providing supplies different than the teacher's model set the stage for experimentation that can be unique to each student through individual decision-making. However, the manner in which the teacher engages with the three students without a lit bulb who are lamenting their lack of success needs examination. She limits, rather than expands, their opportunity to develop self-regulation. The teacher demonstrates the "right answer" to the students who cry or walk away, furthering their reliance on external loci of control, rather than helping them developing internal ones. The manner in which she conducts the lesson for all of the children requires examination as well. What might have been a lesson in experimenting, solving problems, persevering, and searching for patterns turns into a lesson on following directions. Opportunities to self-correct are missing. Opportunities to use self-selected materials are missing. Opportunities to create hypotheses are missing. Opportunities to reflect on findings are missing. Bulbs were lit, but imaginations were not.

An analytical look at this lesson reveals that, at its onset, half the students find out that their guess about the Statue of Liberty is wrong. There is no opportunity to reveal their current definition of a lighthouse or change their definition after listening to others or change their thinking with more information. If there were, the question might be a launch for important discourse, research, and debate. With only the opportunity to respond yes or no, and with the teacher offering the right answer immediately after the question, there is simply no way for students to meaningfully learn from the question. What they learned is that they were right or wrong.

Similarly, the learning value of asking who has seen a lighthouse privileges the more traveled students. It gives them a chance to share, garners the attention of the teacher and classmates, and provides practice in narrating their prior life experiences, all without forwarding learning about circuits or the integrity of structures for either the students who had seen a lighthouse or those who had not. This common lesson opening, designed to engage students by creating a shared context, ironically creates a context of inequality that establishes an unnecessary hierarchy before the big idea of the lesson unfolds. When lessons begin by making it clear that some students are the "haves" and the others are the "have nots," even if the privileging and marginalizing may seem minor or inconsequential, as in the case of being right or wrong about the Statue of Liberty, equity and access for some students are impeded. The students who guessed incorrectly on the first question and answered "no" to the second question were immediately disadvantaged, before the content of the lesson was even introduced. Minor affronts experienced continually over time leave a mark.

The critique of this lesson may seem harsh, but reimagining schools requires critical examination of the longstanding deliverer–receiver model of instruction that continually widens learning opportunity gaps. Teachers who view students as producers of their own knowledge begin lessons in the present, not the past. They narrow opportunity gaps created by uneven life experiences and they widen the prospects of equal access to learning.

ANOTHER LOOK AT INCLUSIVITY

Imagine, instead, students' "playing" with batteries, bulbs, and wires at the onset of the lesson, discovering for themselves that the bulb only lights when the two leads of the bulb and the two sides of the battery connect up in a specific way. Students in this lesson have the opportunity to search for patterns and construct the notion that direction matters with LED bulbs and batteries. Imagine students innovating on their own pathways, making errors, finding out what doesn't work, and working with classmates to experiment with their own ideas. Imagine students working alone or in groups stumbling upon parallel and series circuits and sharing their surprising findings with each other and the teacher. Imagine researching different lighthouses when trying to design one's own, *after* having learned enough about wiring to have a plan for how to illuminate it. Imagine if the teacher had placed all the material on the table, greeted students with the task, gave them the minimum information necessary to begin, and invited them to get to work without his modeling. Imagine what the students might have learned about the conductive nature of materials, the system order that lights a bulb, and the adaptations necessary to install the circuit system into a structure. Imagine what the teacher might have learned about the students through observing and listening to them. Constructivist classrooms strive to offer all students chances to grow from the beginning by focusing on the present.

When students produce something that takes perseverance—a lighthouse, a persuasive essay, an accurate calculation, a watercolor, debate notes—the learning usually heads down wrong paths before right ones. Error is an essential step, and, upon the project's completion, the learning is enduring and the sense of personal industry is strong.

Like America itself, constructivist schools are evolving experiments with enduring complexity. They can't guarantee specific outcomes, but they can guarantee specific inputs, one of which is that each citizen's rights to a free public education will be provided by teachers' seeking and hearing students' voice and fostering students' self-regulation.

BATTLES AND EXPERIMENTS

In 1790, George Washington wrote about America's by-the-people government as a great experiment:

> , The establishment of our new government seemed to be the last great experiment for promoting human happiness by a reasonable compact in civil society. It was to be in the first instance, in a considerable degree, a government of accommodation as well as a government of laws. Much was to be done by *prudence*, much by *conciliation*, much by *firmness*. Few, who are not philosophical spectators, can realize the difficult and delicate part, which a man in my situation had to act.

Constructivist schools are, as Washington said of democracy, places of accommodation and laws. Similar to Washington's leadership, leading a class or a school is a difficult and delicate endeavor requiring prudence, conciliation and firmness. Teachers *prudently* base their practice in learning theory, *conciliate* through organizing fluid, flexible, equitable opportunities for each and every student to learn, and display *firmness* of principle as they negotiate curricula in which students build their own concepts and skills.

Some 50 years later, Horace Mann (1840) recognized that our vulnerable democracy needed schools that honor students as thinkers.

> Never will wisdom preside in the halls of legislation and its profound utterances be recorded on the pages of the statute book, until common schools . . . shall create a more far-seeing intelligence and a purer morality than has ever existed among communities of men. (Cremin, 1957, p. 7)

In a college commencement address soon before his death, Mann said: "Be ashamed to die until you have won some victory for humanity" (Mann, 1859). Lawrence Cremin, in 1957, referring to that quote, wrote:

> Mann had won his victory and it only presaged other great victories to come. . . . As with the battle for freedom itself, victories are never final. And somehow today's educators find themselves fighting the very same battle. (p. 27)

And now, some 60 years after Cremin's comment, we are still, indeed, fighting the battle.

The through line is visible. George Washington fought a victorious battle for political independence in the late 1700s. Educators have been fighting the ongoing battle for democratic and inclusive public schools since the early 1800s. And, of often underacknowledged significance, Native Americans have been fighting the ongoing battle for dignity and freedom on all fronts for centuries. Zitkala-Sa, daughter of a Sioux mother and a White father, and author of *School Days of an Indian Girl*, writes of the long shadow of her painful days in a boarding school for Native Americans that did not honor her culture, did not negotiate curriculum, did not see or care who she was, did not seek or hear her voice.

> These sad memories rise above those of smoothly grinding school days. Perhaps my Indian nature is the moaning wind which stirs them now for their present record. But, however tempestuous this is within me, it comes out as the low voice of a curiously colored seashell, which is only for those ears that are bent with compassion to hear it. (Zitkala-Sa, 1921, Part V, para 8)

Public schools that bend their ears with compassion to honor the disparate histories of students create cultures that foster equality and self-agency. These are the public schools that Zitkala-Sa and all children need. These are the reimagined experiments that lead us forward on the journey.

REFERENCES

Cremin, L. A. (Ed). (1957). *The republic and the school: Horace Mann on the education of free men.* Teachers College Press.

Mann. H. (1840). Fourth annual report: The qualification of public school teachers. In L. A. Cremin (Ed.) (1957), *The republic and the school: Horace Mann on the education of free men* (p. 7). Teachers College Press.

Washington, G. (1790, January 9). "From George Washington to Catharine Sawbridge Macaulay Graham." *Founders Online.* National Archives. https://founders.archives.gov/documents/Washington/05-04-02-0363

Zitkala-Sa. (1921). The school days of an Indian girl. In *American Indian Stories*, pp. 47–80. Hayworth Publishing House.

Public School Funding and the "Reform" Distraction

Mark Weber

It seems bizarre to argue about whether money matters for schools.

How could more money not improve a school? More money means more staff, which helps expand programming, provide remediation, and reduce class sizes. More money means better salaries, providing an incentive for well-educated and talented workers to consider entering the teaching profession (Baker, 2017). More money means better facilities, which are safer, healthier environments for learning (Filardo, 2016).

Certainly, money can be wasted. But it's impossible for schools to spend efficiently if they don't have adequate funds to spend in the first place. Education is like any other endeavor in the public sphere: While inefficiency may be a concern, so is underfunding. There may be waste in the military, for example, but that doesn't preclude the need for money to pay soldiers and buy bullets. Even the harshest critic of profligate military spending would concede that if we want a military, we have to pay for it—and if we want that military to do more, it will cost us more.

This logic seems self-evident, but, sadly, it has been sorely lacking for years in the ongoing debates about school funding. Rather than accept the logical connection between student success and adequate funding, a few economists, think tank fellows, and pundits continue to assert that the United States already spends more than enough to meet its educational goals; the problem, they say, is that we just don't spend wisely. What they offer instead is a series of "reforms" that are supposedly revenue-neutral: competition in the form of charter schools and private school vouchers, pay schemes for teachers based on the test score outcomes of their students, and increased testing and "accountability." The evidence in favor of these policies is mixed; in contrast, the evidence in favor of school funding increases is sizable and growing. But that seems to matter little to those who continue to cast doubt on the need for adequate and equitable school funding; all we need to do, they say, is inject a bit of market-based magic into the system, and our schools will be fine, at no extra cost to the taxpayer.

And so "reform" has become the core of the resistance to meaning-ful and sustained investment in schools. Education reformers are providing cover for those who fear that the United States might take its obligation to fund schools more seriously—starting with raising taxes on the wealthiest of its citizens to collect the necessary revenues. Many of the think tanks pro-moting education "reforms" are funded by some of the nation's wealthiest individuals and their foundations (Reckhow, 2013). If these institutions can keep selling the idea that increased funding is unnecessary so long as their preferred reforms are implemented, it increases the likelihood that their pa-trons will not be subject to greater taxation.

It's difficult to pinpoint a specific start to the modern era of school fund-ing denial; however, the decision in the landmark case *San Antonio v. Ro-driguez* is as good a place to begin as any (*San Antonio Indep. Sch. Dist. v. Rodriguez*, 1973). The plaintiffs argued that the Texas system of school funding, which led to wide disparities in revenues, was unconstitutional under the Fourteenth Amendment's equal protection clause. The Supreme Court's 5–4 majority ruled, however, that there is no specific right to educa-tion enumerated in the U.S. Constitution; consequently, inequitable funding is permissible. The result was that school funding cases moved from the fed-eral to state courts, as most state constitutions require the states to provide a free system of education to their children (Springer et al., 2015). But before leaving the dispute to the states, the Court made sure to convey its doubts about the relationship between school funding and educational quality:

> Apart from the unsettled and disputed question whether the quality of education may be determined by the amount of money expended for it, a sufficient answer to appellees' argument is that, at least where wealth is involved, the Equal Protec-tion Clause does not require absolute equality or precisely equal advantages. Nor, indeed, in view of the infinite variables affecting the educational process, can any system assure equal quality of education except in the most relative sense.

The wave of state court lawsuits and rulings that followed varied widely in their outcomes and levels of judicial restraint; consequently, a variety of school funding systems rose up across the 50 states (*50-State Comparison*, 2019; *SchoolFunding.Info*, n.d.). Underlying many of these decisions was the idea, argued by the majority in *Rodriguez*, that there is a state interest in keeping control of education funding with local school districts. This meant that school funding would vary widely, as communities had different levels of property wealth to tax and raise revenues. Plaintiffs in these cases argued that this was fundamentally unfair: If a town had a strong tax base, it could more easily raise additional revenues and provide a more comprehensive and effective education for its children.

But why worry about such things when the relationship between fund-ing and school quality hadn't been proven anyway? The federal Supreme

Court had cast doubt on the relationship—and the issue would now have to be litigated in the various state courts where school funding lawsuits were playing out. Thus, concurrent with the rush of state-level court cases came a new body of research into the relationship between school funding and outcomes (Springer et al., 2015). At the time when the first cases were being filed, data on school resources was more scarce than today, and analytical methods had not yet been fully developed. This allowed for what appeared to be a balanced debate: Evidence that supported a correlation between funding and outcomes was weighed against what appeared to be equal evidence that the correlation didn't exist (Baker, 2016).

Economists were called as expert witnesses in these trials, charged with the task of casting doubt on the idea that increasing funding to schools might help student achievement (see, e.g., *Legal Testimony | Eric A. Hanushek*, n.d.). Their argument was that the problem wasn't the amount of money being spent; it was that too much money was being spent inefficiently. What was needed, they argued, was innovation, a series of "reforms" that would bring market forces and new levels of accountability into public schools. These reforms would be revenue-neutral, so no additional taxes— particularly on the wealthiest, who were taking increasingly larger shares of the nation's economic gains—would be necessary (Horowitz et al., 2020).

It is no coincidence, then, that the education reforms that rose up over the last few decades gained traction at the same time funding systems for schools were being challenged in the state courts. Foremost among these was an expanded regime of high-stakes testing, with accountability measures attached to student outcomes. The bipartisan No Child Left Behind Act (NCLB, 2002) required mandatory testing in math and English language arts between Grades 3 and 8 and again in high school. Schools failing to make Adequate Yearly Progress (AYP) would be subject to sanctions, including closure or reconstitution.

Studies showed modest gains from these measures, largely confined to outcomes in mathematics, with little to no effects on English outcomes (S. Dee et al., 2010; T. S. Dee & Jacob, 2011). In addition, high-stakes testing has had unintended and pernicious effects on schools: cheating scandals, the narrowing of the curriculum, less focus on struggling students, less instruction in the arts, "teaching to the test," and the shuffling of "good" teaching staff into the older, tested grades and "bad" teachers into younger, untested grades (Au, 2007; Elpus, 2014; Fuller & Ladd, 2013; Grissom et al., 2014; Jacob & Levitt, 2003; Jennings & Bearak, 2014; Neal & Schanzenbach, 2010). Most importantly, NCLB and its subsequent revisions did nothing to break the connection between funding and student achievement. In fact, one reason the results of NCLB were somewhat anemic may be that the act was never fully funded—and its costs were underestimated to begin with (Imazeki & Reschovsky, 2004; Mathis, 2005). Still, NCLB did, in some cases, increase spending per pupil, paid for by increased revenues to schools from state and local sources (Dee et al., 2010). If NCLB was an unfunded federal mandate, at least it drove more revenue toward schools.

Another innovation that became popular within "reform" circles was differentiated pay for teachers based on performance. Commonly referred to as "merit pay," the premise sounded intriguing to many: If teachers were paid based on the results of their students, the best teachers would make more and have an incentive to stay in the profession. Likewise, the worst teachers wouldn't earn as much and would be more likely to leave teaching. Those espousing the idea suggested merit pay would make teaching more like jobs in the "real world." Of course, pay for performance is relatively scarce in other professions, and pay for others' performance is even more rare (Adams et al., 2009). Further, experiments in merit pay kept running up against practical problems: which students, for example, would be assigned the "best" teachers? More importantly, who would be assigned the "worst"? How would teachers in non-tested subjects and grades—the majority of teachers in American schools—be assessed (Croft & Buddin, 2015)? How could factors that influence student outcomes outside of teachers be accounted for? Many experimental merit pay systems used "growth models"—complex statistical models that attempted to account for these factors—and then attributed any differences in outcomes to the teacher. How, though, was a teacher supposed to react to a growth score derived from a complex equation that no lay person could be expected to understand (Sireci et al., 2016)?

A 2017 meta-analysis of merit pay experiments found "a modest, statistically significant, positive effect on student test scores (0.053 standard deviations)." This is the equivalent of moving a student at the 50th percentile in test scores to the 52nd percentile. The effect, however, was even smaller when only including studies from the United States: 0.043 SD (Pham et al., 2020). For comparison, the difference between students in the 90th and 10th percentile for income is on the order of 1.25 SDs (Reardon, 2013). If one of the goals of education is to equalize opportunities for students no matter their family background, merit pay falls far short of that goal.

Perhaps the most controversial reform proposed over the last few decades has been "school choice." Rather than automatically attend their neighborhood public school, families could now choose a school that ostensibly better met their needs. Chief among the options were charter schools, which receive direct public funding but are often not authorized nor operated by school districts. In theory, charters are free from the restrictions placed on school districts and the stipulations found in collective bargaining agreements; they would, therefore, become laboratories of innovation, developing practices that allowed them to become more efficient and effective

(Bulkley & Fisler, 2003). Families could also receive subsidies for private school tuition in the form of taxpayer-supported vouchers. The majority of these schools would be run by religious institutions; First Amendment concerns were brushed aside when the Supreme Court ruled that giving public monies to schools engaged in religious instruction served the public interest (Fiddiman & Yin, 2019; *Zelman v. Simmons-Harris*, 2002).

But did it in fact serve the public interest? Even the most ardent school voucher proponents admit that the evidence shows voucher schools do no better than public schools in educating their students; in fact, many times the results are worse (Carnoy, 2017; Epple et al., 2017). And so these advocates instead point to surveys that show parent satisfaction tends to run high for voucher programs (Dynarski & Nichols, 2017). That shouldn't surprise anyone: no parent wants to believe they've made a poor choice for their child's schooling. But if some parents are happy to send their children to schools that teach dinosaurs and man lived at the same time, that doesn't mean the taxpayers are well served (Postal et al., 2018).

As for charter schools: surveys of the research show that, on average, charters do not get better results than public schools when accounting for differences in student populations (Cohodes, 2018; Epple et al., 2015). The exception appears to be in a subset of urban charters, often identified as "no excuses" schools. These schools are often part of national or regional chains, operating under charter management organizations (CMOs) like KIPP, Uncommon Schools, or Success Academies. A limited set of studies on some of these schools has found that they get better results than their neighboring public schools, even accounting for measured and unmeasured student differences (Abdulkadiroglu et al., 2011; Angrist et al., 2010, 2013). However, these schools tend to have longer school days and years, increasing the time students spend in school (Baker & Weber, 2017; Weber, 2019). The students who apply to these schools tend to differ from students in the general population: they have fewer special needs and are more likely to be native English speakers (Murray, 2016; Rhim et al., 2019; Weber, 2019). School leaders at these schools readily admit they focus on test preparation in their curriculum, even to the exclusion of focus on untested subjects (Koretz, 2017).

And, perhaps most importantly: many of these "successful" charters keep their costs low while simultaneously bringing in more revenues through philanthropic contributions (Baker et al., 2012). Charters operated by the CMOs tend to churn their staffs, keeping their average years of experience far below those of neighboring public schools. This allows them to offer more competitive wages; in turn, their teachers work more hours (Weber, 2019). Enrolling fewer special education students—especially those with the most profound needs—also helps keep costs low. Charter operators often object to this critique, noting that the law forbids them from rejecting applicants based on their special education or English language learner (ELL) status. But such objections ignore that parents rely heavily on their social networks when choosing charter schools; parents of special needs children are undoubtedly well aware that long school days and a test-based pedagogy will not necessarily be a good fit for their child (Altenhofen et al., 2016).

Many CMOs have become adept at fundraising: some hold galas raising millions of dollars on top of what charters receive from the taxpayers (Freeman, 2017; Smith, 2016). If anything, charters that rely on philanthropy have shown that resources can and do matter a great deal in determining student outcomes. "No excuses" charters aren't getting their outcome gains because they have especially innovative instructional practices; curricular narrowing, unique staffing models, enhanced revenues, and self-selected students are far more likely the reasons for their "success" (Lubienski, 2003). But this raises a question: if resources matter, why must a parent enroll their child in a charter school to gain access to those resources for their child? Affluent school districts in the suburbs raise the revenues needed for their students to have a broad, rich curriculum with strong student outcomes; why can't less-affluent communities—which need more resources to give their children equal educational opportunity—have the same? (Baker, 2017).

It turns out that resources do matter—a lot. In the time since *Rodriguez* and the early school funding studies, methods and data have improved substantially. A new crop of school funding research has emerged, and the consensus is clear: school funding reforms lead to better outcomes for students, particularly students who live in disadvantaged communities (Baker et al., 2018; Baker & Weber, 2016; Jackson, 2018; Jackson et al., 2016; Lafortune et al., 2016).

Unfortunately, this realization is happening too late; America's schools have been sidetracked by "reforms" that have shown tepid results. Certainly, there is value in a system of student assessments—although it would be far cheaper and less intrusive to reduce the quantity, using appropriate sampling methodologies. Yes, teacher pay systems might be revised for the better—although competitive pay across the board is the necessary prerequisite for any profession that wants to attract and retain highly qualified workers. There may be a place for school choice—although far better oversight is needed to rein in the self-serving behaviors of too many in the charter sector (Network for Public Education, 2020).

None of these reforms, however, will make substantial improvements in the education of American's children unless and until we make the commitment to adequately and equitably fund our schools. Schools can't be expected, on their own, to overcome the ravages of poverty and systemic racism that keep far too many children locked into lives of despair. But any program of meaningful uplift for the lives of children must begin with a strong education system, and that system must have the revenues it needs to provide all children with access to well-resourced schools. The facile promises of "reform" have never been, and will not be, an adequate substitute for a sustained and substantial increase in the investment in our schools. It is far past time to stop being distracted by them, and to start doing what we know must be done.

REFERENCES

50-State Comparison: K-12 Funding. (2019, August 5). Education Commission of the States. https://www.ecs.org/50-state-comparison-k-12-funding/

Abdulkadiroglu, A., Angrist, J. D., Dynarski, S. M., Kane, T. J., & Pathak, P. A. (2011). Accountability and flexibility in public schools: Evidence from Boston's charters and pilots. *The Quarterly Journal of Economics*, *126*(2), 699–748. https://doi.org/10.1093/qje/qjr017

Adams, S. J., Heywood, J. S., & Rothstein, R. (2009). *Teachers, performance pay, and accountability: What education should learn from other sectors.* Economic Policy Institute. https://files.epi.org/page/-/pdf/teachers_performance_pay_and_accountability-full_text.pdf

Altenhofen, S., Berends, M., & White, T. G. (2016). School choice decision making among suburban, high-income parents. *AERA Open*, *2*(1), 1–14. https://doi.org/10.1177/2332858415624098

Angrist, J. D., Cohodes, S. R., Dynarski, S. M., Pathak, P. A., & Walters, C. R. (2013). *Stand and deliver: Effects of Boston's charter high schools on college preparation, entry, and choice.* National Bureau of Economic Research. http://www.nber.org/papers/w19275

Angrist, J. D., Dynarski, S. M., Kane, T. J., Pathak, P. A., & Walters, C. R. (2010). Inputs and impacts in charter schools: KIPP Lynn. *American Economic Review*, *100*(2), 239–243. https://doi.org/10.1257/aer.100.2.239

Au, W. (2007). High-stakes testing and curricular control: A qualitative meta-synthesis. *Educational Researcher*, *36*(5), 258–267. https://doi.org/10.3102/0013189X07306523

Baker, B. D. (2016). *Does money matter in education?* (2nd ed.). Albert Shanker Institute. http://www.shankerinstitute.org/resource/does-money-matter-second-edition

Baker, B. D. (2017). *How money matters for schools.* Learning Policy Institute. https://learningpolicyinstitute.org/product/how-money-matters-report

Baker, B. D., Libby, K., & Wiley, K. (2012). *Spending by the major charter management organizations: Comparing charter school and local public district financial resources.* National Education Policy Center. http://nepc.colorado.edu/publication/spending-major-charter

Baker, B. D., & Weber, M. A. (2016). Beyond the echo-chamber: State investments and student outcomes in US elementary and secondary education. *Journal of Education Finance*, *42*(1), 1–27.

Baker, B. D., & Weber, M. A. (2017). *Newark's schools: The facts.* New Jersey

Education Policy Forum. https://njedpolicy.wordpress.com/2017/12/13/new-arks-schools-the-facts/

Baker, B. D., Weber, M. A., Srikanth, A., Kim, R., & Atzbi, M. (2018). *The real shame of the nation: The causes and consequences of interstate inequity in public school investments.* Rutgers Graduate School of Education & Education Law Center. http://www.schoolfundingfairness.org

Bulkley, K. E., & Fisler, J. (2003). A decade of charter schools: From theory to practice. *Educational Policy, 17*(3), 317–342. https://doi.org/10.1177/0895904803017003002

Carnoy, M. (2017). *School vouchers are not a proven strategy for improving student achievement.* Economic Policy Institute. http://www.epi.org/publication/school-vouchers-are-not-a-proven-strategy-for-improving-student-achievement/

Cohodes, S. (2018). Charter schools and the achievement gap. *The Future of Children.* https://futureofchildren.princeton.edu/sites/futureofchildren/files/resource-links/charter_schools_compiled.pdf

Croft, M., & Buddin, R. (2015). Applying value-added methods to teachers in un-tested grades and subjects. *Journal of Law and Education, 44*, 1–23.

Dee, T. S., Jacob, B. A., Hoxby, C. M., Ladd, H. F., Dee, T. S., & Jacob, B. A. (2010). *The Impact of No Child Left Behind on Students, Teachers, and Schools.* Brookings Papers on Economic Activity, 149–207.

Dee, T. S., & Jacob, B. (2011). The impact of No Child Left Behind on student achievement. *Journal of Policy Analysis and Management, 30*(3), 418–446. https://doi.org/10.1002/pam.20586

Dynarski, M., & Nichols, A. (2017). *More findings about school vouchers and test scores, and they are still negative* (Vol 2, #18; Evidence Speaks Reports). Brookings Institution. https://www.brookings.edu/wp-content/uploads/2017/07/ccf_20170713_mdynarski_evidence_speaks1.pdf

Elpus, K. (2014). Evaluating the effect of No Child Left Behind on U.S. music course enrollments. *Journal of Research in Music Education, 62*(3), 215–233. https://doi.org/10.1177/0022429414530759

Epple, D., Romano, R. E., & Urquiola, M. (2017). School vouchers: A survey of the economics literature. *Journal of Economic Literature, 55*(2), 441–492. https://doi.org/10.1257/jel.20150679

Epple, D., Romano, R., & Zimmer, R. (2015). *Charter schools: A survey of research on their characteristics and effectiveness.* National Bureau of Economic Research. http://www.nber.org/papers/w21256

Fiddiman, B., & Yin, J. (2019, May 13). *The danger private school voucher programs pose to civil rights.* Center for American Progress. https://www.americanprogress.org/issues/education-k-12/reports/2019/05/13/469610/danger-private-school-voucher-programs-pose-civil-rights/

Filardo, M. (2016). *State of our schools: America's K-12 facilities.* 21st Century School Fund. https://centerforgreenschools.org/state-our-schools

Freeman, N. (2017, October 12). Basquiat's 'Red Skull,' sold at Christie's in London for $21.5 M, will fund new charter schools in New Jersey and Miami. *ARTnews.* https://www.artnews.com/art-news/news/basquiats-red-skull-sold-at-christies-in-london-for-21-5-m-will-fund-new-charter-schools-in-new-jersey-and-miami-9147/

Fuller, S. C., & Ladd, H. F. (2013). School-based accountability and the distribution of teacher quality across grades in elementary school. *Education Finance and Policy, 8*(4), 528–559. https://doi.org/10.1162/EDFP_a_00112

Grissom, J., Kalogrides, D., & Loeb, S. (2014). Strategic staffing: How accountability pressures affect the distribution of teachers within schools and resulting student achievement. *Paper Presented at the Annual Meeting of the Association for Public Policy Analysis and Management, Albuquerque, NM.* http://www.uaedreform.org/downloads/2014/11/strategic-staffing-how-accountability-pressures-affect-the-distribution-of-teachers-within-schools-and-resulting-student-achievement.pdf

Horowitz, J. M., Igielnik, R., & Kochhar, R. (2020, January 20). *Trends in U.S. income and wealth inequality.* Pew Research Center. https://www.pewsocialtrends.org/2020/01/09/trends-in-income-and-wealth-inequality/

Imazeki, J., & Reschovsky, A. (2004). Is No Child Left Behind an un (or under) funded federal mandate? Evidence from Texas. *National Tax Journal, 57*(3), 571–588.

Jackson, C. K. (2018). *Does school spending matter? The new literature on an old question* [Working Paper 24368]. National Bureau of Economic Research. https://www.nber.org/papers/w25368.pdf

Jackson, C. K., Johnson, R. C., & Persico, C. (2016). The effects of school spending on educational and economic outcomes: Evidence from school finance reforms. *The Quarterly Journal of Economics, 131*(1), 157–218. https://doi.org/10.1093/qje/qjv036

Jacob, B. A., & Levitt, S. D. (2003). Rotten apples: An investigation of the prevalence and predictors of teacher cheating. *The Quarterly Journal of Economics, 118*(3), 843–877.

Jennings, J. L., & Bearak, J. M. (2014). "Teaching to the test" in the NCLB era: How test predictability affects our understanding of student performance. *Educational Researcher, 43*(8), 381–389. https://doi.org/10.3102/0013189X14554449

Koretz, D. (2017). *The testing charade: Pretending to make schools better.* University of Chicago Press.

Lafortune, J., Schanzenbach, D. W., & Rothstein, J. (2016). *Can school finance reforms improve student achievement?* Washington Center for Equitable Growth. http://equitablegrowth.org/research-analysis/can-school-finance-reforms-improve-student-achievement/

Legal Testimony | Eric A. Hanushek. (n.d.). Retrieved September 17, 2020, from http://hanushek.stanford.edu/experience/legal-testimony

Lubienski, C. (2003). Innovation in education markets: Theory and evidence on the impact of competition and choice in charter schools. *American Educational Research Journal,* 395–443.

Mathis, W. J. (2005). The cost of implementing the federal No Child Left Behind Act: Different assumptions, different answers. *Peabody Journal of Education, 80*(2), 90–119.

Murray, J. (2016, November 4). District and charter school enrollments are not equal—But Boston could become a national model for education equity and access. *Brookings.* https://www.brookings.edu/blog/brown-center-chalkboard/2016/11/04/district-and-charter-school-enrollments-are-not-equal-but-boston-could-become-a-national-model-for-education-equity-and-access/

Neal, D., & Schanzenbach, D. W. (2010). Left behind by design: Proficiency counts and test-based accountability. *The Review of Economics and Statistics*, 92(2), 263–283.

Network for Public Education. (2020). *Still asleep at the wheel: How the federal charter schools program results in a pileup of fraud and waste.* https://networkforpubliceducation.org/wp-content/uploads/2020/02/Still-Asleep-at-the-Wheel.pdf

No Child Left Behind. (2002). https://www2.ed.gov/nclb/landing.jhtml

Pham, L. D., Nguyen, T. D., & Springer, M. G. (2020). Teacher merit pay: A meta-analysis. *American Educational Research Journal*, 58(3), 527–566. https://doi.org/10.3102/0002831220905580

Postal, L., Kassab, B., & Martin, A. (2018, June 1). Private schools' curriculum downplays slavery, says humans and dinosaurs lived together. *Orlando Sentinel*. https://www.orlandosentinel.com/news/education/os-voucher-school-curriculum-20180503-story.html

Reardon, S. F. (2013). The widening income achievement gap. *Educational Leadership*, 70(8), 10–16.

Reckhow, S. (2013). *Follow the money: How foundation dollars change public school politics.* Oxford University Press.

Rhim, L. M., Kothari, S., & Lancet, S. (2019). *Key trends in special education in charter schools in 2015–2016: Secondary analysis of the Civil Rights Data Collection.* National Center for Special Education in Charter Schools. https://www.ncsecs.org/wp-content/uploads/NCSECS-15-16-CRDC-Report.pdf

San Antonio Indep. Sch. Dist. v. Rodriguez, 411 U.S. 1 (1973).

SchoolFunding.Info. (n.d.). Center for Education Equity at Teachers College. https://www.schoolfunding.info/

Sireci, S. G., Wells, C. S., & Keller, L. A. (2016). *Why we should abandon student growth percentiles* (Research Brief No. 16–1). Center for Educational Assessment, University of Massachusetts, Amherst. https://www.umass.edu/remp/pdf/CEAResearchBrief-16-1_WhyWeShouldAbandonSGPs.pdf

Smith, E. (2016, April 12). Success Academy gala raises over $35M. *Page Six*. https://pagesix.com/2016/04/12/success-academy-gala-raises-over-35m/

Springer, M. G., Houck, E. A., & Guthrie, J. W. (2015). History and scholarship regarding U.S. education finance and policy. In *Handbook of Research in Education Finance and Policy* (2nd Ed., pp. 3–20). Routledge and Association for Education Finance and Policy.

Weber, M. (2019). *Ten important facts about New Jersey charter schools . . . and five ways to improve the New Jersey charter sector.* New Jersey Education Policy Forum. https://njedpolicy.wordpress.com/2019/04/26/ten-important-facts-about-new-jersey-charter-schools-and-five-ways-to-improve-the-new-jersey-charter-sector/

Zelman v. Simmons-Harris 536 U.S. 639 (2002). https://www.law.cornell.edu/supct/html/00-1751.ZS.html

Education Is Our Only Political Safety

James Harvey

It's unfortunate that it took a pandemic to educate the American public about the central role of schools in their communities. As this book went to press, over 660,000 Americans had died of COVID-19, according to Johns Hopkins University researchers (Johns Hopkins, 2021). The number of coronavirus deaths represents a monstrous failure of leadership at the national level.

While many national and state leaders temporized and hoped the problem would solve itself, American schools turned on a dime and addressed the issue. They shut down to protect their students, while arranging for the delivery of tens of millions of meals, online instruction, and hundreds of thousands of tablets, telephones, and hotspots for families unable to access the internet. It was not perfectly carried out, but worked reasonably well in face of a crisis. Meanwhile, the United States, long a byword for productivity and efficiency, found itself short of nasal swabs and protective equipment for frontline workers. It was a national embarrassment.

One positive outcome of this pandemic was that the American people learned that public schools had been providing millions of meals to needy students, who make up the majority of enrollment, along with health care services, counseling, and before- and after-school programs. Meanwhile, parents, including upper-income parents, were reminded of the importance of the school in their lives, because this institutional support was yanked from under their feet. A phrase from Horace Mann could not have been more profoundly demonstrated: "Education is our only political safety. Outside of this ark, all is deluge" (Mann, 1867).

We have arrived at an inflection point in public perceptions of public education. The commendable speed with which educators responded, combined with the new awareness of the importance of schools locally on the part of ordinary citizens, offer school leaders an opportunity to educate key stakeholders on the strengths and contributions of public schools.

But to do that effectively, it is essential that educational leaders understand how we got here. They need to understand that schools (and social services) have been a foil in a long-term con game in which budget assets, including well-funded public schools that could benefit poor and middle-income Americans, have been purloined from the majority of Americans and transferred into the pockets of the wealthy.

Many of our citizens have been persuaded that the United States, the wealthiest nation in the history of the world, is broke. Nothing could be further from the truth. We have enormous wealth. But, genuflecting before the altars of markets and privatization while crying crocodile tears about deficits, American leaders have succeeded in fooling large numbers of American citizens. In the process, they have wrecked public finances and generated levels of income inequality not seen since the days of the robber barons.

So, let's examine how our society adopted a hypercritical attitude toward public schools. What led to these criticisms of their performance? Why have governmental leaders held back on the funds schools so badly need?

It's always difficult to put problems in context. This is particularly true around tricky public policy challenges, such as growing income inequality, community blight in urban and rural areas, transportation policy, or family dysfunction. All of us want easy answers to complex problems.

It's true around schools too. The tendency is to look inside the school to identify problems; if the root of the problem is outside the school, the root is ignored. Indeed, the refusal to consider the root is part of the mindset that insists, despite available data, that public schools are failures.

Social conditions under which some American children live so stunt their development and life prospects that schools face near-insurmountable obstacles in responding to their educational needs. Many students are too traumatized to learn. Confronted with a large body of evidence documenting enormous out-of-school challenges facing many students, the school "reform" movement of recent years has closed its eyes. It's a condition that Nobel Laureate Daniel Kahneman refers to as theory blindness: "[W]e can be blind to the obvious, and we are also blind to our blindness." Kahneman's insight was earlier identified by one of the founders of modern rationalism, scientist and philosopher Sir Francis Bacon, who observed in 1690 that:

> The human understanding when it is has once adopted an opinion . . . draws all things else to support and agree with it. And though there be greater number and weight of instances to be found on the other side, yet these it either neglects or despises, or else by some distinction sets aside and rejects.

But rather than confront the multifaceted challenges described above, school reformers, guided by theories favoring markets and privatization developed by the Chicago school of economics, have agreed that what is measurable is what is important. So, the essential functions of the public school—instruction, meeting standards, providing work-ready job skills, and developing citizens for a democracy—are reduced to cheap metrics of student achievement, the results of which are employed to gauge whether schools merit the support of taxpayers. The tendency is to lay the responsibility for financial challenges on poor spending decisions, ineffective boards, and grasping teachers' unions, not on the fact that schools, as well as other essential government services and functions in the United States, are severely underfunded after decades-long attacks on the competence of public agencies. And the tendency is to put forth standards and assessments as cheap solutions to the problems of learning, in the process ignoring decades of research and experience demonstrating that what goes on outside the school is a much more important predictor of student achievement than what goes on inside it.

Large segments of the American people have been persuaded that government is their enemy. This can be documented most clearly at the national level, where politicians like to pretend the national treasury is empty, but the same patterns prevail at the state and local level, which provide 90% of schools' funding.

GOVERNMENT IS THE PROBLEM

The real roots of the assault on public education lie in President Ronald Reagan's 1980 inaugural address when he said: "Government is not the solution to our problem; government is the problem."

"The Speech"

In the 1950s, while representing General Electric on the chicken-dinner banquet circuit, the future president developed what became known among his allies as "The Speech." In it, he attacked federal programs such as public assistance, aid to farmers, assistance for disadvantaged youth, and urban renewal. He even lambasted the progressive income tax and Social Security. Big government, he charged, wasted taxpayers' money, while Democrats and intellectual elites, marching "under the banners of Marx, Lenin, and Stalin," undermined citizens' freedom.

This was an outrageous and dishonest argument. At the time Reagan was making this case, the argument was a fringe outlook. Unfortunately, it has since become policy orthodoxy in the right wing of American politics.

Americans for Tax Reform

President Reagan's claim during his inauguration that government is the central problem in the United States became a dominant driver of domestic policy for the following forty years. And, because the statement appealed so much to wealthy interests opposed to taxation, it became a rallying cry for anti-government and anti-tax crusaders.

Among these crusaders, Grover Norquist stands out. Norquist, who had worked on Reagan's 1980 election campaign, founded Americans for Tax Reform in 1985, apparently at the request of President Reagan. ATR (Americans for Tax Reform) created a "Taxpayer Protection Pledge," and candidates and elected officials began taking this pledge in 1986, agreeing to oppose tax increases. This pledge is the reason GOP presidential nominee George H. W. Bush accepted the 1988 presidential nomination with the statement: "Congress will push me to raise taxes and I'll say no. And they'll push, and I'll say no, and they'll push again, and I'll say, to them, 'Read my lips: no new taxes.'"

Drowning the Government in a Bathtub

While that promise later became an albatross around Bush's neck, the fact that he felt the need to make it is evidence of the success of Norquist's crusade. ATR claims on its website that some 1,400 elected officials have signed the pledge (ATR, 2021). By 2012, Norquist's pledge had been signed by 95% of all Republican members of Congress and most candidates running in the 2012 Republican presidential primaries (Wikipedia, n.d.). With the support of business groups such as the U.S. Chamber of Commerce, just about every candidate for Congress is asked to sign the pledge and sitting members of the House and Senate are asked to renew their commitment every year.

The goal was avowedly to reduce the size of government. Norquist has been widely quoted for his cynical quip: "I'm not in favor of abolishing the government. I just want to shrink it down to the size where we can drown it in the bathtub."

But while shrinking the government down to size, anti-tax presidents and national legislators have also dramatically shifted the tax burden on Americans to favor the wealthy. In *Triumph of Injustice* (2019), economists Emmanuel Saez and Gabriel Zucman document a startling new reality: While progressive tax policy had traditionally required the wealthy to pay higher rates of taxation than the poor, that balance had been reversed by 2018. Following half a dozen tax reduction and reform measures over the intervening years, the average effective tax rate paid by the richest 400 families in the country was 23% in 2018, a full percentage point lower than the 24.2% rate paid by the bottom half of American households. Tax reform has been a smokescreen behind which national policymakers have helped the wealthy loot the Treasury.

What we find after this sustained 40-year assault on budgets, and on the at-risk populations dependent on the safety net, is growing inequality as a feature of American life. Wealthy Americans now enjoy a much greater share of national income than they did years ago. According to a January 2020 report from the Pew Research Center (Horowitz et al., 2020), most Americans

Figure 21.1. Share of U.S. Aggregate Income, 1970 to 2018

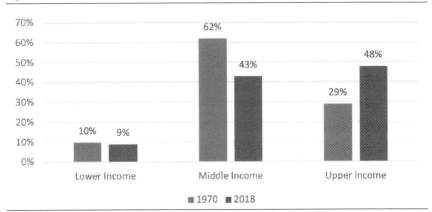

Source: Horowitz et al. (2020)

agree that there is too much economic inequality in the United States. The Pew report documents the growing share of American income enjoyed by upper-income households, at the expense of middle-income households.

Figure 21.1 outlines the Pew findings. The share of national income owned by lower-income households has decreased slightly from ten to nine percent. But the shares owned by middle-income and upper-income households have changed dramatically, and in different directions. Middle-income households, which could claim 62% of national income in 1970, saw this share drop precipitously over the decades to 43%. Their loss was captured by upper-income households, which jumped from 29% of national income in 1970 to nearly half of all income (48%) by 2018 (p. 16).

Forgotten and embittered middle Americans, not understanding the real causes of their economic distress, responded to the populist appeal of candidate Donald J. Trump by elevating him to the Oval Office.

The full effects of this cynicism made their appearance with COVID-19. A government hollowed out by half a dozen tax cuts since 1980 was poorly organized to respond to the pandemic. An in-depth AP examination of public health financing found local "health workers . . . paid so little, they qualify for public aid." A public health system that had been a model for the world in the 1970s had deteriorated by 2019 into a skeletal workforce, according to the AP—with state per-capita spending dropping 16 percent and local per-capita spending dropping 18% (Weber et al., 2020).

Public health funding is far from the only victim of anti-tax zealots. As the 2020 COVID-19 crisis hit, education spending had not recovered from the cuts imposed on schools following the 2008 Great Recession. Widespread teacher protests in 2019 about inadequate salaries generated a great deal of public sympathy.

Meanwhile, safety in the air and of the food we eat, once largely taken for granted, were compromised as understaffed federal agencies transferred responsibility for inspection and certification of airplanes and meat quality to the companies building the planes and operating slaughterhouses. Equally problematic but perhaps less noticeable were the crisis in infrastructure in the United States, threats to clean air and clean water, and unconscionable increases in the prices of life-saving prescription medications. While Mr. Norquist has helped anti-government candidates gain office, in doing so he has done great damage to the institutions on which every citizen depends in this great nation.

A BRIEF PRIMER ON THE FEDERAL BUDGET

One of the effects of the anti-government onslaught since Mr. Reagan took office is that within budgets constrained by repeated tax reductions, programs essential to the public welfare compete with each other for limited resources.

In a large institution such as the federal government, it is easy to find examples of misplaced spending. In the 1980s, an investigation of military spending turned up expenditures of $435 for a hammer, $600 for a toilet seat, and $7,000 for an aircraft coffee maker. Such findings fuel calls for an end to "government fraud, waste, and abuse."

When the example comes tinged with racism, public outrage against the programs (and the recipients) is likely to increase. During his 1980 campaign, for example, Mr. Reagan railed against "welfare queens," implicitly calling up an image of unworthy Black recipients of public assistance—although the large majority of recipients of public assistance have always been rural Whites. Examples such as Reagan's racist assault on welfare focuses attention on a relatively small portion of the federal budget while ignoring the lion's share of federal expenditures.

Mandatory Spending

Figure 21.2 outlines the major expenditures in the federal budget by function. Over 60 percent of the total budget is made up of "mandatory" spending that is required by federal law. This portion of the budget incorporates Social Security, Medicare, Supplemental Security Income, Unemployment Insurance, Temporary Assistance for Needy Families (public assistance), Supplemental Nutrition Assistance Program (food stamps) and the Earned Income Tax Credit. Much of this spending consists of safety net programs that help keep the elderly, the sick, and families fed, clothed, and housed.

Figure 21.2. Distribution of Federal Budget, FY 2018

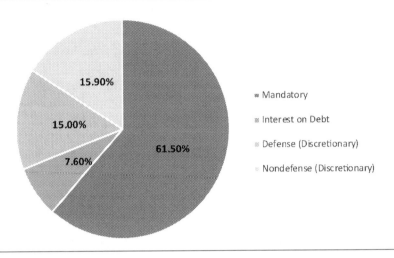

Source: Congressional Budget Office, 2020

Federal Debt

Another nearly 8% of the federal budget is devoted to interest on the federal debt. While not labeled "mandatory," there is no doubt that the good faith and credit of the American government depends on paying this interest annually. In combination, therefore, about 70% of federal spending—mandatory programs plus interest on the debt—is untouchable.

Discretionary Spending

With mandatory spending and interest on the national debt taking huge chunks out of the federal budget pie, we are left with some 30% of total spending in the discretionary category. This is money that Congress has to appropriate and around which it makes judgments about the level of spending. The discretionary budget pot is about evenly split between defense and domestic (discretionary non-defense) spending.

It is in the discretionary non-defense spending category that we find K–12 schools competing for funds with other desirable and highly important programs in the federal budget. So, every dollar allocated to public school finding must be justified in competition with needs for preschool programs, higher education, scientific research, training and employment programs, veterans' benefits, social services, mental health programs, meals for the homebound elderly, rehabilitation services for adults with disabilities, transportation, health, the administration of justice and dozens of other highly valuable national efforts, including support for the arts and humanities.

Figure 21.3. Annual Surpluses and Deficits in Federal Budget, 1980-2020

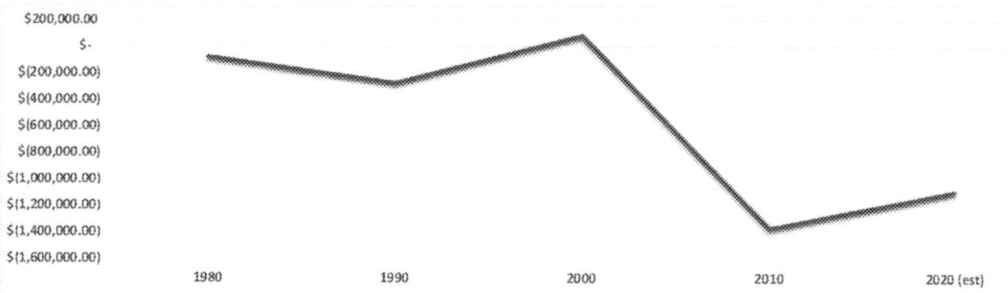

Source: Congressional Budget Office, 2020

THE TRIUMPH OF INJUSTICE

When President Reagan spoke to a joint session of Congress in February 1981 shortly after his inauguration, he argued that the American ship of state was out of control, with national debt approaching $1 trillion.

By 2018, the $1 trillion national debt that so preoccupied President Reagan seemed trivial. It turned out that most Republicans seeking the presidency while bewailing the national debt were only too happy to increase that debt once in office by running excessive annual deficits (see Figure 21.3). Arguing on the basis of the infamous "Laffer Curve" that tax cuts would pay for themselves by stimulating economic growth, tax-cutting zealots have wrecked American finances and undermined the nation's economy.

Once in office, President Reagan happily ran annual deficits of around $200 billion annually. President George H. W. Bush agreed to some tax increases to rein in the national debt only to see his party turn against him. President Clinton succeeded in ramming through some modest tax increases without a single GOP vote in either the U.S. Senate or the House of Representatives leading to modest surpluses of $125 billion in 1999 and $236 billion in 2000. The surpluses were immediately squandered in the administration of his successor, George W. Bush, who pushed through two major tax cuts over 8 years, each heavily favoring upper-income Americans.

The Great Recession of 2008 was generated by irresponsible profit-taking on Wall Street, not by excessive safety net expenditures supporting the most vulnerable Americans. Nevertheless, it forced massive deficit spending by President Obama over 8 years to prop up the banking system, save the American automobile industry, and restore the American economy. However, Obama's progress in restoring the economy was destroyed with another major tax revision in 2018 by President Trump. Once again, this tax revision overwhelmingly benefitted wealthy Americans. A new gusher of red ink flooded the federal ledger book, even before Congress and the Trump administration agreed on trillions of dollars in emergency spending to support the economy amidst the 2020–2021 COVID-19 catastrophe.

The upshot of all this? While the annual deficit in 1980 stood at $73.8 billion, by 2020 the deficit for just a single year topped $3 trillion. Meanwhile, the Federal debt (the accumulation of all these annual deficits), which in 1980 stood at $712 billion, had ballooned by 2019 to nearly $17 trillion. The interest costs on this debt in 2019 totaled $404 billion (Congressional Budget Office, 2020, pp. 3, 5). And most of this debt was piled up by political leaders who campaigned as fiscal conservatives committed to reining in federal deficits and the amount of federal debt.

State and Local Dynamics

Similar dynamics can be documented at the state and local levels, with hostility to taxes encouraged both by policy and anti-tax activists. So we find many states requiring 60% majorities to approve bonds for long-term debt and school construction. At the same time, anti-tax zealots in many states run tax limitation ballot propositions in states, such as Washington and California, which offer such options. Indeed, the grandfather of all ballot initiatives, Proposition 13, enacted in the Golden State in 1978 to control property taxes, has served since as encouragement for similar efforts around the country.

The upshot of 40 years of pretending that taxes benefit other people but not me and that "government is the problem" is that public services generally, and schools in particular, struggle for adequate funding.

WHAT CAN EDUCATORS DO?

In the face of these considerations, it is tempting to throw up one's hands. After all, what can educators do to change the great national dynamics? Actually, they can do quite a lot. Here's a five-part agenda for action.

1. Refuse to Accept the Conventional Wisdom. It is surprising that K–12 educators have sat silent in the face of 40 years of criticism of their performance. The conventional wisdom has been allowed to spread unchecked. 50 years of polling by PDK International shows that the closer people are to a real public school, the higher the grade they give to public education. That is to say, members of the public are likely to think K–12 schools do not deserve good grades, but their own schools are better. And parents with school-age kids give their children's schools the highest grades (see for example, https://pdkpoll.org).

Every time educators hear criticisms of schools, they should make the PDK poll findings the foundation of a rebuttal.

2. Make Your Case. In two research reports from the Horace Mann League & National Superintendents Roundtable (2015) and the National Superintendents Roundtable & Horace Mann League (2018), supplemented by an informative infographic (National Superintendents Roundtable & Horace Mann League, 2019), seven findings stand out:

- In terms of system outcomes (i.e., years of education completed, possession of high school diplomas and bachelor's degrees, and global share of high performing students), the United States is without peer.
- The "proficiency" benchmark of the National Assessment of Educational Progress, frequently used to criticize American school performance, is a misleading standard. Not even Singapore or Finland, normally world leaders in school achievement rankings, can demonstrate that even 40% of their students can clear the "proficiency" hurdle in 4th-grade reading.
- American school performance today is far superior to its performance at any prior time. About 90% of young American adults now hold at least a high school diploma, compared to just 34% in 1950.
- For every major racial and ethnic group in the United States, student achievement is higher today than it was in the 1970s.
- Enrollment of students with disabilities has doubled since Public Law 94-142 was enacted in 1975. Originally known as the Education for All Handicapped Children Act, this law committed the Federal government to covering 40% of the "excess costs" associated with educating children with disabilities. The law is now known as the Individuals with Disabilities Education Act (IDEA). When first passed, just about 3.6 million children with disabilities were enrolled; today that number exceeds 6.6 million.
- Getting to the next level will require policymakers to address out-of-school factors influencing student achievement. The United States is almost off the scale in international comparisons of levels of student poverty and meager support for young families.
- More than one million American students are homeless at some point in the school year—living with relatives, couch surfing, in homeless motels, or living in cars or under bridges with their parents.

3. Enlist Allies to Deal with Out-of-School Challenges. Schools lack the resources, staff, or expertise to deal with the multitude and complexity of out-of-school challenges. School leaders need to collaborate with local agencies and nonprofit groups specializing in housing, transportation, nutrition, and mental health services to provide comprehensive services for children and families in need.

4. Note That You Lead a Large and Complex Enterprise. For school super-intendents, don't be afraid to introduce your community to the complexity of the enterprise you lead as a superintendent and the difficult challenges facing many of your students. These are stories that need to be told. Alonzo Crim, a legendary superintendent in Atlanta in the 1980s, used to tell audiences that Atlanta Public Schools was the largest employer in the city with a budget approaching $1 billion. On a daily basis, he said, the district served more meals than all the restaurants in the city and it transported more people than the city bus service. It also offered more classes to more students than all the universities in the state.

Simply as a management exercise, overseeing a district of any size requires leaders to put on many different hats—as educators, community leaders, politicians, and managers. Nearly half of all school districts in the United States enroll 999 or fewer students. But even in these communities, it is likely that the school system is among the largest employers, if not the largest, in the area.

5. Preach a Crusade Against Ignorance. On August 13, 1796, Thomas Jefferson responded to a letter from George Wythe, a minister who had requested Jefferson's advice on his next sermon. Jefferson responded with a memorable line: "Preach, my dear sir, a crusade against ignorance." Jefferson promoted legislation to create free public education in Virginia as well as a national university. One of his proudest achievements was the establishment of the University of Virginia.

In his letter to Wythe, Jefferson insisted that "the most important bill in our whole code is that for the diffusion of knowledge among the people . . . for no other sure foundation can be devised for the preservation of freedom and happiness." Failing to provide public education would "leave the people in ignorance."

Preaching such a crusade is a principal obligation of today's educators also. Note that Jefferson's object was not the passage of tests or preparation for work but the "preservation of freedom and happiness."

When local citizens and business leaders insist on the utilitarian purposes of schools—meeting performance benchmarks or preparing young people for work—educators obviously should concede the importance of these goals. But they must also insist on the larger obligations of public schools in a democracy. Jefferson understood those obligations. So too did Horace Mann. To repeat, Mann said: "Education is our only political safety. Outside of this ark, all is deluge." He also put it this way:

> Education must be universal, since our theory of government requires that all shall become fit to be a voter.

NOTE

1. Lower-income households are defined as those with less than 67% of median household income; middle-income households are defined as those with annual income that is between two-thirds and twice as much as the national median; upper-income households are those with annual income that is more than double the median.

REFERENCES

ATR (2021). Americans for Tax Reform. *About the Taxpayer Protection Pledge.* https://www.atr.org/about-the-pledge

Congressional Budget Office (2020). Federal Debt: A Primer. Washington, D.C. https://www.cbo.gov/system/files/2020-03/56165-CBO-debt-primer.pdf

Horace Mann League and National Superintendents Roundtable (2015). *School performance in context: Indicators of school inputs and outputs in nine similar nations.* http://www.hmleague.org/wp-content/uploads/2015/01/School-Performance-in-Context-full.pdf

Horowitz, J. M., Igielnik, R., & Kochhar, R. (2020, January 9). *Trends in U.S. income and wealth inequality.* Pew Research Center. https://www.pewresearch.org/social-trends/wp-content/uploads/sites/3/2020/01/PSDT_01.09.20_economic-inequailty_FULL.pdf

Johns Hopkins (2021). Johns Hopkins University of Medicine, Corona Virus Resource Center. https://coronavirus.jhu.edu/region/united-states

Mann, H. (1867). Thoughts Selected From The Writings of Horace Mann. H.B. Fuller & Co.

National Superintendents Roundtable and Horace Mann League. (2018). *How high the bar?* https://www.superintendentsforum.org/archives/2019-2/how-high-the-bar-report

National Superintendents Roundtable and Horace Mann League. (2019). *Giving schools an honest grade.* https://www.superintendentsforum.org/wp-content/uploads/2019/10/Giving-Schools-an-Honest-Grade.jpg

Saez, E., & Zucman, G. (2019). *The triumph of inequality.* Norton.

Weber, L., Ungar, L, Smith, M.R., Recht, H., & Barry-Jester, A.M. (2020). Hollowed out public health system faces more cuts amid virus. https://apnews.com/article/e28724a125a127f650a9b6f48f7bb938

Wikipedia (n.d.). https://en.wikipedia.org/wiki/Grover_Norquist

Is There Still a Public for Public Education?

Gloria Ladson-Billings

My running joke about the University of Wisconsin–Madison is that it was once regarded as a great state university. Later I referred to it as a "state-assisted" university. Today, as an institution that receives less than 17% of its support from the state, I refer to UW–Madison as a "state-located" university. For me, what is happening at the University of Wisconsin–Madison and state universities across the nation is emblematic of the evacuation of the public space we are seeing everywhere in the nation.

Some years ago, when the school choice movement began to gain attention, I argued that we were looking at the beginnings of a plan to destroy public education. There are those who declared I was being "alarmist." But I made this pronouncement after looking at the ways other aspects of public services have faced severe erosion. I grew up in 1950s and '60s Philadelphia. As a child of working-class parents, I used public transportation to navigate the city. I visited the public museums, the public library, and of course shopping districts, via public transportation. It was safe, dependable, reliable, and inexpensive. Today, everyone feels compelled to have and drive their own private vehicles everywhere. When we were alerted to the importance of getting polio vaccines my mother took me to the public health clinic. The clinic was safe, dependable, reliable, and inexpensive. Today, we all want to go to our own doctors. And for many years the road to home ownership for poor to working-class people ran through public housing. Public housing was safe, dependable, reliable, and inexpensive. Today, in cities like Chicago and New Orleans, we are imploding public housing units. Finally, as a child growing up in a large city, public school was the surest way to economic success and social mobility. Our schools were seen as safe, dependable, reliable, and inexpensive. My contention was and remains that public education is the final domino of our public institutions, and it is teetering.

The question of why public education is in this vulnerable position is a complex one that I will certainly not be able to answer within this essay. But I do want to suggest that one of the contributing factors is the loss of a public consensus and will to provide the necessary support. What flows from that assertion is a question about why the public has seemingly retreated from public education. I would like to suggest that this apparent retreat has resulted, in large part, from a long-term campaign by an array of powerful interest groups to portray public education as a failing system. It is important, then, to make a distinction concerning what we mean when we talk about the failure of public education. Almost every pronouncement about the impending destruction of public education references the largest 25 urban school districts. Additionally, this portrayal of destruction most likely also includes desperately poor, rural school districts. There are several factors these types of districts hold in common, which I explore below in the context of my argument that the United States has never fulfilled two promises regarding our public schools. The first unfulfilled promise is the failure to fully desegregate our public schools (see *Brown v. Board of Education*, 1954). The second unfulfilled promise is the failure to equitably fund our public schools (*Serrano v. Priest*, 1971, 1976, 1977).

THE CONTINUED PROBLEM OF THE COLOR LINE

Almost every American knows of the 1954 Supreme Court decision known as *Brown v. Board of Education*. The case is heralded as the nation's finest hour, where it transcends race and racial discrimination in the establishment of its public schools. As lofty as *Brown* seems to most Americans, its promise was never realized. In some extreme cases, states like Arkansas and Virginia closed all of their public schools for an entire year to avoid desegregating their schools. Currently, most major cities do not have enough White students attending their public schools to adequately desegregate them. Hence, we see the prevalence of hypersegregation in major city schools.

Those of us who work in the tradition known as Critical Race Theory do not think of *Brown* as an education strategy. Legal scholars like Mary Dudziak (1995) and Derrick Bell (1980) describe *Brown* as a foreign policy strategy of the Cold War. Consider *Brown's* context. The United States was attempting to stop the spread of communism among emerging third-world peoples and it had to confront its own credibility issues concerning Black people and their civil liberties here at home. The amicus brief filed in *Brown* by the Justice Department argued that desegregation was in the national interest in part because of foreign policy issues. The Justice Department said, "The United States is trying to prove to the people of the world, of every nationality, race and color, that a free democracy is the most civilized and secure form of government yet devised by man." The brief also quoted Secretary of State Dean Acheson's letter to the Attorney General, in which Acheson wrote:

During the past six years, the damage to our foreign relations attributable to [race discrimination] has become progressively greater. The United States is under constant attack in the foreign press, over foreign radio, and in such international bodies as the United Nations because of various practices of discrimination against minority groups in this country . . . . Soviet spokesmen regularly exploit this situation in propaganda against the United States . . . . Some of these attacks against us are based on falsehoods or distortion; but the undeniable existence of racial discrimination gives unfriendly governments the most effective kind of ammunition for their propaganda warfare. (Cited by Layton, 2000, p. 116)

Dudziak points out that the continued legal segregation and racism that pervaded the U.S. society created an embarrassing reality for U.S. foreign policy. "Newspapers throughout the world carried stories about discrimination against non-white visiting foreign dignitaries, as well as against American Blacks. At a time when the U.S. hoped to reshape the postwar world in its own image, the international attention given to racial segregation was troublesome and embarrassing" (Dudziak, 1995, p. 110).

What we have in the *Brown* decision is a prime example of what Derrick Bell calls "interest convergence." In addition to the international embarrassment, Bell suggests that *Brown* provided "much needed assurance to American Blacks that the precepts of equality and freedom so heralded during World War II might yet be given meaning at home" (Bell, 1980, p. 96).

Despite this purported assurance, poor Black and Latinx children are today becoming increasingly isolated from their White, affluent peers in the nation's public schools, according to federal data showing that the number of high-poverty schools serving primarily Black and Brown students more than doubled between 2001 and 2014. These data were released by the Government Accountability Office in 2016, 62 years to the day after the Supreme Court decided that segregated schools are "inherently unequal" and therefore unconstitutional. According to more recent data from the National Center for Education Statistics (NCES, 2020), between fall 2017 and fall 2029 the percentage of public elementary and secondary students who are White is projected to continue decreasing (from 48 to 44%). In contrast, the percentage of students who are Asian/Pacific Islander is projected to continue increasing (from 6 to 7%), as is the percentage of students who are of two or more races (from 4 to 6%). Additionally, the percentage of students who are Latinx is projected to be higher in fall 2029 than in fall 2017 (28 vs. 27%). The percentage of students who are Black is projected to remain at 15 percent in fall 2029. Similar to fall 2017, American Indian/Alaska Native students are projected to account for 1 percent of public elementary and secondary enrollment in fall 2029.

The proportion of schools segregated by race and class—where more than 75 percent of children receive free or reduced-price lunch and more than 75 percent are Black or Latinx—climbed from 9% to 16% of schools between 2001 and 2014. The number of the most intensively segregated schools—with more than 90% of low-income students and students of color—more than doubled over that period.

The problem is not just that students are more isolated, according to the Government Accountability Office, but that minority students who are concentrated in high-poverty schools don't have the same access to opportunities as students in other schools. High-poverty, majority-black and Latinx schools were less likely to offer a full range of math and science courses than other schools, for example, and more likely to use expulsion and suspension as disciplinary tools, according to the GAO.

Rep. Bobby Scott of Virginia announced legislation that would make it easier for parents to sue school districts for civil rights violations, saying the GAO report provided evidence of an "overwhelming failure to fulfill the promise of *Brown*. Segregation in public K–12 schools isn't getting better; it's getting worse, and getting worse quickly, with more than 20 million students of color now attending racially and socioeconomically isolated public schools," he said in a statement, calling on GOP leaders in the House to hold hearings on tackling segregation (Brown, 2016).

THE FALLACY IN THE FUNDING

The second unfulfilled promise is that of equal funding. In three decisions (*Serrano v. Priest* 1971, 1976, and 1977), the California Supreme Court ruled that public schools should receive equal funding. Public schools in the United States, unlike in most modern democracies, receive their funding based on local property taxes. Thus, the schools located in wealthy, property rich communities are well-funded while those in inner cities and poor rural communities are poorly funded, indeed underfunded. Social critic Jonathan Kozol decries something he calls "educational apartheid," in which high-poverty districts spend 15.6% less per student than low-poverty districts do, according to the U.S. Department of Education (Kozol, 2005). Lower spending can irreparably damage a child's future, especially for students from poor families. A 20% *increase* in per-pupil spending a year for poor children can lead to an additional year of completed education, 25% higher earnings, and a 20-percentage point reduction in the incidence of poverty in adulthood, according to a paper from the National Bureau of Economic Research (Jackson et al., 2015).

One of the challenges we face as we look at school funding is that we continue to use what I would argue is a poor proxy for determining equitable funding. Most schools describe their funding based on "per pupil expenditure." They take the amount of money allotted to a school and divide it by the number of students based on something called "average daily attendance." In places like Chicago versus Highland Park, Philadelphia versus Lower Merion, or New York City versus Manhasset, we see a per pupil funding disparity of between eight and ten thousand dollars. But even if we were to agree on a dollar amount to be equally distributed across school districts, we are missing the fact that some schools require more resources than others. A school community with a brand new, high tech, state-of-the-art building requires less in the way of maintenance and can spend much of its resources on enriched curriculum like robotics, aviation, or a new physics lab. Poor schools are sometimes fighting to patch up the roofs and keep their buildings heated.

Beyond the crudeness of the per pupil expenditure measure is also the way "average daily attendance" is derived. In Wisconsin, ADA is calculated on ONE day a year—September 15. Schools with an influx of students beyond that date do not receive additional funding. For those who were fans of the HBO series *The Wire*, you may remember an episode where the Baltimore school is busy rounding up students who are chronically truant because that system requires students to be in school at least 5 days in the month to be considered on the roll. In that scene, the truant officer grabs a student to take him back to school and the student yells, "Hey, I did my 5 days. You're looking for my brother." At that moment, the truant officer releases the student. In California, average daily attendance is calculated each month. Thus, poor schools in California have a better chance than those in Wisconsin to have their state funding reflect the number of students they are actually serving.

But there are other aspects of school funding that are hidden. In 1975 when California experienced its "taxpayers' revolt" and passed Proposition 13, public schools were severely hit. It was the first time the electorate had so roundly rejected school funding. It was a clear indication that the public schools were losing their public. Proposition 13 meant that many schools were forced to cut co-curricular programs like art, music, and afterschool sports. In wealthy communities like Palo Alto or Beverly Hills, the parents formed public school foundations that raised millions of dollars to supplement the reduced funds. Schools in poor districts like Oakland, Inglewood, and Richmond had to make do under severe budget cuts.

WHY WON'T WE KEEP THE PROMISES?

Since *Brown* and the various funding cases, there have been a series of countervailing court cases designed to roll back both school desegregation and equal funding plans. Why won't we keep our promises to truly desegregate and equitably fund our public schools? My naïve theory suggests that when the number of White middle class students decreases, so does public support. To exacerbate this trend, the rhetoric has changed to a concerted discourse of "choice." Thus, voucher programs and charter schools begin to spring up in mostly poor communities. I want to be clear: I am not anti-charter schools. No, I am against the distortion of the original idea proposed by New York Teachers' Union President Albert Shanker. Shanker saw charter schools as a way to free teachers from onerous state regulations and allow them to experiment and try innovative curricular and pedagogical strategies. However, today charter schools have become part of a neoliberal strategy (along with voucher plans) to funnel the public's money into private hands. Teacher or community groups do not run the majority of charter schools in the country. Instead, Education Management Organizations (EMOs) run these schools. In a city like New Orleans where the entire district is a charter district, small community groups are virtually frozen out of the charter authorization process (Henry, 2016).

The dangerous cocktail of race and money seem to set up Black and Brown children for sale to the highest bidder without regard for their educational outcomes. The language that suggests that public schools are "government schools" that have a "monopoly" plays well to White middle-class America, particularly in the context of a continuing neoliberal emphasis on education as a private good rather than a public good, where the school voucher programs create subsidies that allow them to send their children to private schools at reduced prices.

When I talked with Stanford philosopher Eammon Callan about my concerns for the future of public education, he shared an interesting perspective. Instead of public schools, he said, the U.K. developed the "Common School" whose purpose it was to create a U.K. citizen with access to a common culture, echoing Horace Mann's originating vision for public education in the U.S. Perversely, public education in the United States seems to have become a place where students are stratified into elite versus non-elite citizens, and those elite citizens will determine who benefits from the nation's social and economic resources. If this is true, given the rapid demographic shifts in our school populations, there may indeed not be much of a public for our public schools.

REFERENCES

Bell, D. (1980). Brown and the interest convergence dilemma. In D. Bell (Ed.), *Shades of Brown: New perspectives on school desegregation.* Teachers College Press.

Brown, E. (2016). On the anniversary of Brown v. Board, new evidence that U.S. schools are resegregating. Washington Post, May 17. https://www.washingtonpost.com/news/education/wp/2016/05/17/on-the-anniversary-of-brown-v-board-new-evidence-that-u-s-schools-are-resegregating/

Brown v. Board of Education (1954). National Archives. https://www.archives.gov/education/lessons/brown-v-board#background

Dudziak, M. (1995). Desegregation as a cold war imperative. In R. Delgado (Ed.), *Critical race theory: The cutting edge* (pp. 110–121). Temple University Press.

Henry, K. L. (2016), Discursive Violence and Economic Retrenchment: Chartering the Sacrifice of Black Educators in Post-Katrina New Orleans. In T. L. Affolter & J. K. Donner (Eds). *The Charter School Solution*. Routledge. (pp. 80–98).

Jackson, C. K., Johnson, R. C., & Persico, C. (2015, January). *The effects of school spending on educational and economic outcomes: Evidence from school finance reforms* [Working Paper 20847]. National Bureau of Economic Research. https://www.nber.org/system/files/working_papers/w20847/w20847.pdf

Kozol, J. (2005). *The shame of the nation: The restoration of apartheid schooling*. Crown Publishers.

Layton, A. S. (2000). *International politics and civil rights policy in the United States, 1941–1960*. Cambridge University Press.

National Center for Education Statistics (2021, May). *Racial/ethnic enrollment in public schools*. https://nces.ed.gov/programs/coe/pdf/2021/cge_508c.pdf

Serrano v. Priest (1971, 1976, 1977). Public Advocates. https://www.publicadvocates. org/our-work/education/access-quality-education/serrano-v-priest/

PART V

Before America had child labor laws and school attendance requirements: Oyster shuckers and baby tenders at Pass Packing Co. All worked from before daybreak until 5 P.M. for extremely low wages. Location: Pass Christian, Mississippi.

Source: Photo by Lewis Hine, 1911. Library of Congress,
Prints & Photographs Division,
National Child Labor Committee Collection

Public Education at a Crossroads

Will Horace Mann's Common School Survive the Era of Choice?

Carol Corbett Burris

In 2019, the National Center for Education Statistics published *School Choice in the United States* (Wang et al., 2019). Its purpose was to inform the public of the status and popularity of the array of American education options, from neighborhood public schools to private schools to home-schooling.

The report documents the inroads, as measured by attendance, that the school choice movement has made in whittling away the number of children who attend a neighborhood school. In 1999, the percentage of students who attended the public school to which they were assigned based on their neighborhood was 74%. By 2016, the proportion dropped five points to 69%. It is likely that if we had figures for 2020, that number would be smaller still.

Part of the reason for that decline is a surge in enrollment in charter schools. Charter student enrollment grew from one million in 2000 to three million by 2016. Simultaneously, private school enrollment decreased slightly, despite the growth of voucher programs; however, the number of homeschooled children has nearly doubled. In addition, 47 states and the District of Columbia have some program, albeit limited, of intra-district or inter-district choice. These include magnet schools and test-in schools, which are popular in many urban districts.

Has choice increased parental satisfaction? Apparently not. The 2020 PDK poll of the public attitude toward public education asked, "If you could send your oldest child to any school and cost was not a factor, would you send them to the school they now attend or to a different school?" A majority (60%) reported that they would stay with the school their child attends now (*Public School Priorities in a Political Year,* 2020.) That is, according to PDK, about the same proportion of parents who had no desire to leave their present school when asked in both 1996 and again in 2010.

In 1996, Wisconsin was the only state that had a voucher program. National enrollment in charter schools was less than 1,000 students. However, in 2020, a year in which 3.3 million students are enrolled in charter schools (National Alliance for Public Charter Schools, n.d.) and 31 states plus the District of Columbia have some taxpayer-supported voucher and/or neo-voucher programs,[1] satisfaction with schooling has not increased (nor decreased) at all.

MANIPULATING THE DEFINITION OF
WHAT IT MEANS TO BE A PUBLIC SCHOOL

If you ask a friend or neighbor, "How would you define a public school?" they rarely hesitate. The porter in my New York City apartment building told me, "A school like PS 75, where I send my son. You know, the schools the mayor runs." Others I asked said, "Schools run by school boards, not churches," or "A public school is the opposite of a private school." Whether those I questioned liked their public school or not, they all certainly knew what a public school was.

The term public school is generally not viewed as a pejorative, which is why those who oppose public schools are so anxious to either exclude the term from the discourse, blur the definition, or hijack it for privatized systems. Those efforts are deliberate and organized by libertarians and those on the Right.

Recent rebranding efforts focus on calling public schools "government schools" while referring to public education as "government education." The term *government school* was coined by Milton Friedman in the 1950s, although it has recently gained traction in the public square. Most notably, Donald Trump incorporated this rhetoric in his 2020 State of the Union Address when he referred to students being "trapped in failing government schools" as the rationale for his Freedom Scholarship, a neo-voucher tax credit program.

Trump is hardly the first. No organization has been more active in the attempt to undermine our public schools than Michigan's Mackinac Center for Public Policy, supported by right-wing philanthropy including the family of the former U.S. Secretary of Education, Betsy DeVos.

The Center's website features a history of public education entitled "The Origins of Government Education in the United States," the first section of a longer report, *School Choice in Michigan: A Primer for Freedom in Education* (Brouillette, 1999). Authored by Matthew J. Brouillette, presently the president of Commonwealth Partners Chamber of Entrepreneurs, "Origins" begins by presenting a romanticized vision of American schooling before Horace Mann. Brouillette describes early American education as a successful "de-centralized network of schools." That description, of course, is false.

According to education historian Diane Ravitch (Strauss, 2017), before the mid-1800s, there were elite private schools for the rich, church schools for congregants, and some charity schools for the poor. Other children were either homeschooled or not schooled at all. It was not a network. It was an uncoordinated free-for-all that left most children undereducated.

A close reading reveals that Brouillette's account is little more than propaganda, complete with a section that identifies the proponents and opponents of school choice. Although it is no surprise that unions are on the top of the enemies list, so are "Government School Associations," which includes local school boards and PTAs.

In short, wherever the word *public* might logically appear, the word *government* was deliberately put in its place. Any group that supports public education becomes an agent not of the public but of the government.

Joseph P. Overton, an electrical engineer, was senior vice president of the Mackinac Center for Public Policy in the 1990s until he died in 2003. He is most known for the Overton Window—a means by which to analyze and rebrand extreme policies to make them more acceptable to the public (Russell, 2006). According to Overton, only those policies identified as "in the window" are politically possible. Therefore, if one wishes to make the unacceptable or unthinkable acceptable, the solution is to shift the window.

According to Mackinac, the example Overton often used to illustrate the movement of the window is the changed public perception of school choice. In the 1980s, advocating for charter schools was politically dangerous. As charters became more acceptable, so did school choice, which in turn allowed conservative politicians to advocate for homeschooling, private school tax credits, and charter expansion.

CHARTER SCHOOLS AND THE PRIVATIZATION MOVEMENT

There are sincere advocates of charter schools who believe charters provide alternative publicly funded opportunities for children whose families reject their local public schools. Many such schools exist today, some with the support of the local school district that believes the charter provides a needed, alternative service.

However, it is equally true that the charter school movement has been used by those who view charter schools as a stepping-stone on the path to destroy Mann's vision of the Common School. As Overton noted, advocating for unregulated charter schools is a means to shift the Overton Window to make the pre-public school era that existed before the mid-1800s palatable to the public at large.

In the spring of 2017, *Mother Jones*'s Kristina Rizga analyzed the DeVos family's campaign to replace public education with a market-based system in which parents were the deciders of what, when, and where their children learned (Rizga, 2017). According to Rizga, the DeVos family viewed charter schools as a "Trojan horse" to hide vouchers and destroy the public schools.

In 1996, *Metro Times* (Detroit) reporter Curt Guyette first referred to charters as a "Trojan horse" in his expose entitled "Born Again Schools: The Right's Vision for Public Education in Michigan" (Guyette, 1996). The article explains that four foundations (the Richard & Helen DeVos Foundation, the Prince Foundation, the Orville and Ruth Merillat Foundation, and the Cook Charitable Foundation) mounted what Guyette described as a "relentless attack on the state's education system" while using charters to "blur the lines between public and private education." Two of those foundations (the Richard & Helen DeVos Foundation and the Prince Foundation) are funded by Betsy DeVos's family.

Disappointingly, even those charter advocates who oppose vouchers have been eager to play along, using the narrative of failing public schools to expand the charter sector. Over time, they have successfully embedded the adjective "public" before "charter schools," although no charters, even those entirely under the control of for-profit corporations, are ever referred to as "private." For example, Connections Academy, a wholly-owned subsidiary of the multinational for-profit Pearson Education, describes itself (Connections Academy by Pearson, n.d.) as a "tuition-free online public school" that students can attend at home.

Simultaneously, it has become common to use the less attractive adjective "traditional" to distinguish public schools from charters. Using language to shift the Overton Window has not ended there.

THE ENDGAME

During her 2019 appearance at the Education Writers Association, DeVos attempted to remake the very definition of what public education is (Jesse, 2019).

> "Let's stop and rethink the definition of public education," she said. "Today, it's often defined as one type of school, funded by taxpayers, controlled by government. But if every student is part of 'the public,' then every way and every place a student learns is ultimately of benefit to 'the public.' That should be the new definition of public education."

According to DeVos's definition, public education as we know it is government education, while the term public education is used as a substitute for the word "learning." Take your child to a museum—by DeVos's reasoning, that is "public education." Teach them how to ride a horse, how to shoot a gun, or even whom to fear or hate—according to this definition, that would be "public education" as well.

This is not just rhetoric—it is at the heart of the philosophy that believes that parents should be fully in charge of where and what children learn. Given the romanticized musings on American education before compulsory education, it is uncertain if choice advocates believe that the education of children should even be mandated at all.

However, getting Americans to buy into such a radical concept takes a gradual but deliberate shift of the window. At the same EWA event, De-Vos advocated for a new federal neo-voucher program, Education Freedom Scholarships. That program would provide dollar for dollar tax credits for donations to a Scholarship Granting Organization (SGO), entities that presently exist in nineteen states—thus adding federal funding to the state funding already contributed via the state's tax credit program.

Once the funding is received, SGOs distribute the money to qualifying families to use in accordance with state regulations, usually for private school tuition and expenses. Like many of the other voucher and neo-voucher programs, tax credit programs generally expand not only in amount but in who can receive the funds. They are, at their essence, voucher programs since the funding is money that would be otherwise available to the state to support its services to taxpayers. The SGO is merely a middleman that gets to take a cut for administration.

Florida's Family Empowerment Program (Florida Department of Education, n.d.), for which 50% of all families in the state are income-eligible, provides grants that fund up to 95% of what would be spent on the child in the local district, up to the full tuition amount of a private school. That program is one of three that Florida offers. Arizona now has four different tax credit programs—with the introduction of each new program, both the pool of those eligible and the funding expand.

There is little doubt that if such a program were to receive Congressional approval, states without SGOs would likely establish them. Current SGO programs would lessen eligibility restrictions, thereby increasing the percentage of student participation. DeVos, who advocated for "backpack funding," with each school-age child's parents receiving tax dollars to shop for education services, undoubtedly views this tax credit program as one more Trojan horse to reach her ultimate goal.

Given the anti-tax, anti-government proclivities of those who espouse this type of funding scheme, it is likely that fewer and fewer tax dollars would be placed in the backpack over time. Parents once again would assume the sole responsibility for educating their children, buying what services they could afford, with the poor relying on charity.

CAN THE COMMON SCHOOL SURVIVE?

The ideal of the Common School, as proposed by Horace Mann, is most closely realized in our democratically governed public schools. While imperfect, our neighborhood public schools create a common educational experience that allows all children, regardless of race, political beliefs, gender, and wealth, to learn together and learn from each other. The ability to elect those who govern those schools—be they the local school board or a city's mayor—ensures that both parents and the public have a voice in a community's schools. This is very different than the governance provided by the private boards of charter schools and private schools.

The importance of saving our public schools goes well beyond issues of governance. At a time of deep division in our nation, working to support and perfect Horace Mann's vision is vital to restore civility to our national discourse. At a time of instability, public schools are anchors that unite communities across the nation. And in a profoundly inequitable economy, allowing the market to determine schooling will dramatically exacerbate the large gaps in spending between children from low-SES homes and their wealthier peers that already exist. Never have we needed public education more.

It is up to those who still believe that public education is a pillar of our democracy to stop those who would turn it into a consumer good. That means being willing to challenge and expose the agenda behind the word "choice." For some, choice is a cover for keeping taxes low, serving as a distraction from parents insisting on excellent, well-financed schools in every neighborhood. For others on the far right, as this essay shows, it is a means by which to destroy the institution of public education while diminishing the obligation of government at all levels for educating our nation's children. Social Security would not survive if citizens were allowed to opt out of their funding and create private investment accounts. Inevitably, a "backpack"-funded system would cause public education to collapse.

The fight to shift back the window will not be easy, but it can be done. We need to mind our words, being cognizant of how language has been used to shift the perception of privatized choice. Terms like *privately run charter schools* and *neighborhood public schools* should replace *public charter* and *traditional*. Freedom scholarships and other tax credit financing schemes are not scholarships, grants based on achievement, but rather tax dollars diverted to private schools. Backpack funding would force parents to shop for their child's education with a tax subsidy that could be reduced based on a political whim.

We need to use all the good arguments made in this book in support of the vision of the Common School. We must acknowledge the imperfections and inequities that exist in the system and fight to address them. As many have said, every parent's first choice is an excellent neighborhood school. Our job is to do all we can to make that happen.

If Horace Mann were among us today, he would not stand in silent watch as the Common School was dismantled. We best honor his work, ideas, and memory when we expose that the real "choice" we now face is whether public education will survive or not.

NOTE

1. The term *neo-voucher* refers to schemes in which money is funneled to parents and private schools indirectly through parent donations to "charities" or other types of private nonprofit corporations. The charity or nonprofit then issues vouchers to the parents, who subsequently use them to pay for private school tuition.

REFERENCES

Brouillette, M. J. (1999, September). *School choice in Michigan: A primer for freedom in education.* Mackinac Center for Public Policy. https://www.mackinac.org/2031

Connections Academy by Pearson. (n.d.). *Tuition-free online public school.* Connections Academy. https://www.connectionsacademy.com/

Florida Department of Education. (n.d.). *Family empowerment scholarship: frequently asked questions.* http://www.fldoe.org/schools/school-choice/k-12-scholarship-programs/fes/faq.stml

Guyette, C. (1996, June). Onward Christian scholars: How Gov. John Engler and the radical right are campaigning to fund religious schools. *Metro Times.* https://www.scribd.com/doc/315186500/Curt-Guyette-Engler-DeVos-1996

Jesse, D. (2019, May 6). Betsy DeVos: It's not about me, it's about students. *Detroit Free Press.* https://www.freep.com/story/news/education/2019/05/06/betsy-devos-education-secretary-schools/1118730001/

National Alliance for Public Charter Schools. (n.d.). *Research and data.* https://www.publiccharters.org/our-work/research-and-data

Public School Priorities in a Political Year. (2020, September). Phi Delta Kappan. https://pdkpoll.org/wp-content/uploads/2020/08/Poll52-2020_PollSupplement.pdf

Rizga, K. (2017, March). Betsy De Vos wants to use America's schools to build "God's Kingdom." *Mother Jones.* https://www.motherjones.com/politics/2017/01/betsy-devos-christian-schools-vouchers-charter-education-secretary/

Russell, N. J. (2006, January 4). *An introduction to the Overton Window of political possibilities.* Mackinac Center for Public Policy. https://www.mackinac.org/7504

Strauss, V. (2017, July 17). A detailed critique of a PBS-run education documentary. *Washington Post.* https://www.washingtonpost.com/news/answer-sheet/wp/2017/07/17/a-detailed-critique-of-a-pbs-run-education-documentary/

Wang, K., Rathbun, A., & Musu, L. (2019, September). *School choice in the United States* (NCES 2019106). National Center for Education Statistics. https://nces.ed.gov/pubsearch/pubsinfo.asp?pubid=2019106

What's Not to Like About Private Schools?

Jack Jennings

School day mornings are chaotic in the Armstrong household, especially in late August. The family is adjusting to a school routine after two months of summer vacation.

Sam has the airs of a "senior" in middle school. He is making a scene because his mother forgot to buy his favorite breakfast cereal.

His sister, Trudy, is very shy. A 3rd grader, she was the first out of bed and is now ready to go to school. She sits with her coat on and her backpack ready.

Phil Armstrong, the father, is brushing his teeth. Jan Armstrong, the mother, is finishing her yogurt.

In a short while, Phil will drive to work and drop Trudy off at her new school, a private academy several miles away. Sam will walk a couple of hundred feet to the school bus stop for students attending the area's regular public school. Jan is a 5th grade teacher in the neighboring school district. When she leaves work, she picks Trudy up at her school.

It is a complicated life, especially when Phil has to travel for work, or Jan has a meeting after school. But the Armstrongs have chosen this lifestyle.

They like the local public schools, and moved to the neighborhood partially because of the school district's reputation. They have supported tax levies to improve those schools.

Trudy's shyness worried them, though. They came to believe that the local public elementary school with several hundred students was too big for Trudy. They thought a small school would be better so that she would not be overlooked. After visiting several private schools, they chose Huntington Academy. Fortunately, Jan's father had created a trust fund to pay for the children's education, because the tuition is $10,000 a year.

The Huntington teachers there are all young and some lacked even a bachelor's degree. The headmaster explained that the teachers may not have as much experience as those in the public schools, but the teacher–student ratio was better there, which helped the kids more and allowed for individualized attention. The headmaster also cited the graduation rate and the high SAT and ACT scores of the students. He was proud that so many Huntington graduates went on to prestigious colleges.

Sam, on the other hand, is doing fine in public school. His teachers have told his parents that he could take Advanced Placement (AP) classes in high school if he would try harder. Phil and Jan have urged him to study more seriously.

It's not easy today with so many distractions for children and so many burdens on parents.

THE RIGHT SCHOOL FOR EACH CHILD

The Armstrong family is fictional, but their experiences are real for many families. Parents like them support the public schools, but believe that each of their children should have the appropriate setting to do well. In choosing that setting, they may go to a public charter school, or even to a private school. And they may see no inconsistency between their stated support for public education and their choice of a private school. Since many parents go through that decision-making process every year, it would be good to discuss private schools.

A further reason for such a discussion is that the average citizen may not be aware that there has been a considerable increase in government-provided assistance to private schools in the last 20 years. According to the National Conference of State Legislators, "24 states and the District of Columbia have enacted school choice programs that provide support and incentives for parents to choose private schools in place of public schools."[1] School vouchers, scholarship tax credits, and personal tax credits and deductions are options for parents who want to send their children to private schools.

Despite that boost, private schools do not have the dominant role in American elementary and secondary education. In fact, all the media coverage of private schools differs markedly from the reality of enrollments. Public schools educate about 90% of American students in elementary and secondary schools, including about 7% of public school students who attend charter schools. That is why the country's attention has mostly focused on supporting and improving public schools.[2]

This enrollment pattern could change. Proponents of private schools cite polls showing that American parents would place their children in those schools if it were financially possible to do. They also cite polling data showing the support of millennials for private education.[3]

Will the traditional reliance on public schools to educate the great majority of students continue into the future, or will private schools surge in enrollments? Only time will tell.

LAWS, COURT RULINGS, AND POLITICS

Parents have a constitutional right to send their children to private schools. No state can require all students to attend public schools.

In *Pierce v. Society of Sisters,* the United States Supreme Court in 1925 overturned a statute from the state of Oregon which required attendance at public schools.[4] The Court said:

> The fundamental theory of liberty upon which all governments of this Union rest excludes any general power of the State to standardize its children by forcing them to accept instruction from public teachers only. . . . The Oregon Compulsory Education Act which requires . . . every parent . . . having control of a child . . . to send him to the public school in the district where he resides is an unreasonable interference with the liberty of the parents and guardians to direct the upbringing of the children, and in that respect violates the Fourteenth Amendment.

Pierce was a major victory for the proponents of private schools, especially for Catholics. In the 1800s, millions of European immigrants came to the United States, including many Irish Catholics. When their children went to the public schools, they had to join other students in reading from the King James translation of the Bible and singing Protestant hymns. In response, the American Catholic bishops in 1852 established elementary and secondary schools.[5] Catholic schools grew with the increasing numbers of immigrants.

In 1875, Senator James G. Blaine, Republican from Maine, authored an amendment to the Constitution which would forbid any public funds from being "under the control of any religious sect." Catholic schools were targets of this proposed prohibition. As a result, the increasing population of Irish Catholics voted against Blaine when he ran for president in 1884 as the Republican candidate. Blaine's amendment did not make its way into the federal Constitution, but it was adopted by almost 40 states. Currently, Blaine amendments or some version of it are still in force in 35 states.[6] Therefore, when Republican state governors and legislators in those states propose aid to private schools, they must find some way around their states' Blaine amendments. Those strict prohibitions were enshrined in state law by their Republican predecessors a century ago when Republicans were strong supporters of public schools.

Coming back to the story, a while after their victory in *Pierce,* eager proponents of private schools adopted the goal of securing public financial support for those schools. It was a long struggle between those advocates and the opponents of this idea; but, in the 1990s, political winds finally blew favorably for private schools. The key factor was that the Republicans moved to dominance over the Democrats, most dramatically at the state level but also at the federal level of government. By 2019, as a result of a multi-decade trend, 30 states had Republican majorities in both houses of the state legislatures. In Washington, D.C., after 1995, the Republicans have been the majority in both the House and the Senate more often than the Democrats.

Since the 1990s, Republican officeholders have tended to support legislation promoting an expansion of private elementary and secondary schools. In tandem with the growth of Republican dominance of state legislatures within the last 20 years, 24 states and the District of Columbia placed in their laws tax credits and deductions to encourage attendance at private schools. Voucher programs, a more direct support, were also established in that period.

As part of this conflict, in 2002 a case was decided by the U.S. Supreme Court. In *Zelman v. Simmons-Harris*, the justices ruled that public funds could be used to support private schools if certain conditions were met.[7] This was quite a victory for private school advocates. In 77 years, private schools went from challenging a state law requiring all students to attend public schools to being supported through state and federal subsidies.

In *Zelman*, the high court used a complicated five-step test to reach its decision. The key feature was that there had to be an intermediary, generally parents, between the government and the private school when public funds were to be used to support private education.

The following is the idealized process to keep this distance between them, using a state voucher program to make the point. Parents apply to the state government for funding for their child to go to a private school. If they are approved, the parents will receive public funds in a voucher or check for the tuition or other private school costs. The parents then turn over the public funds they receive to the private school. In effect, private schools in those instances are receiving public funding—just indirectly.

BACK TO THE FUTURE?

Private schools are now in a stronger position than they have been for decades to receive increased amounts of government tax revenue, and what would have been tax revenue, for the maintenance and expansion of private education. That is the effect of *Zelman*.

Private school advocates, some state governors and legislators, former President Trump, and others have sought an ever-larger role for private schools. Republican state governors and legislators are far more likely to support aid to private schools than are Democrats. This means that the chances of that expansion occurring depends on which party wins the elections at the state and federal levels during the next decade.

In the election year of 2020, the U.S. Supreme Court ruled that if a state established a program to aid private schools, it could not exclude religious schools. The Court deemed such exclusion by Montana to be a violation of the right to a free exercise of religion. That case further solidified judicial support for aid to private schools.

In considering whether to further expand aid buttressing private schools, American history should be recalled. The United States has been there before, in terms of a large role for private schools. In the 18th century when the new country was being formed, private schools, private tutoring, and other such arrangements dominated. The resulting inequities inspired support for public schools.[8]

As the Center on Education Policy found in its research:

> Before a system of public schools took hold in the mid-19th century, American children were educated through a hodgepodge of mostly private institutions and arrangements. These included church-supported schools, local schools organized by towns or groups of parents, tuition schools set up by traveling schoolmasters, charity schools for poor children run by churches or benevolent societies, boarding schools for children of the well-to-do, "dame schools" run by women in their homes, and private tutoring.

The conclusion from CEP: "This disjointed approach to schooling resulted in many inequities."[9] Among the victims were the obvious ones: African Americans and Native Americans. Others who lost out were girls and White boys whose parents were poor and did not belong to a church with a school. Children in rural areas lagged behind those in towns and cities, and children in the South were far behind children in New England states which would soon have systems of common schools to educate children in every part of those states.

Eighteenth-century America had this "hit and miss" situation among the states and within the states. As a result, many children were not educated at all or were poorly educated. Quality varied according to family income and status as well as geographic area.

Will the efforts being made today to provide aid supporting children in private schools lead the country back to that inequitable chaos? As states and Congress consider legislation to expand the position of private schools in American elementary and secondary education, will they take into account the inequities that may result?

If legislators and other elected officials ignore those effects, then the saying will ring true: "Those who ignore the past are bound to repeat it."

IMPORTANT FEATURES OF PRIVATE SCHOOLS

It is appropriate to talk about some key characteristics of today's private schools. Several features are highlighted, but first a caveat is in order.

Statements about schools in the two sectors of public and private education are generalizations about each kind of school. An individual public or private school may not reflect all the general conclusions about public or private schools. The same is true about differences between subgroups of schools, such as Catholic parish schools and nonsectarian independent schools, and Christian academies and Catholic schools operated by religious orders. On the public school side, there are also differences among schools, such as between large city school systems and suburban schools, and various types of charter schools and neighborhood schools.

That limitation is one factor to remember as the public debate continues. Knowing the main differences, though, helps to understand these schools, their reasons for being, and their activities.

Right to Exclude

The ability to deny a child entry, and the authority to refuse a student further attendance at the school, are commonly assumed to be within the rights of private schools. The right to exclude means that the private school can select whom the owners/administrators want to educate and can exclude students for whom they no longer want to be responsible.

Public schools are in the opposite position. They must educate any child who appears at the school door. That is the essence of public education.

No matter how poor the child's family may be, no matter that the child does not speak English, and no matter that the child has a serious disability, public schools will educate those children. All children have the right to attend public schools in their school district. Districts may vary greatly in the resources available for education, but their school doors are open.

The federal courts and Congress have spoken clearly on the role of public education. The U.S. Supreme Court ruled that public schools cannot deny entrance to a child whose immigration status is not known because their parents may be in the country illegally. The court also decided that public schools must teach English to those who don't speak the dominant language of the country.[10]

In addition to complying with Supreme Court decisions, states have assumed obligations under federal laws. The most prominent such law is the Individuals with Disabilities Education Act (IDEA), successor to the Education for All Handicapped Children Act (1975).[11] IDEA obliges states that accept federal funding to educate children with disabilities, including the provision of related services that are required to assist a child with a disability to benefit from special education. These related services may include transportation, speech language pathology, audiological services, interpretive services, psychological services, and others.[12] Every state has opted to participate in IDEA, and therefore local public schools help children with disabilities to realize their potential.

The principles underlying public education include that every child counts and that educating all citizens is important to maintaining a democracy. Authorities at private schools may assert that they too support those principles, but they cannot be held to account if their actions violate those principles through such behavior as excluding certain types of children. Public schools may not always fulfill their obligations to carry out those principles, but they can be sued for that negligence. In fact, they have been.

Different Obligations

The duty to educate all children, and the right not to do that, are major differences in public and private schools.

An example of this difference took place in the 1970s in many Southern states. The federal courts began finally to enforce the 1954 decision in *Brown v. Board of Education*[13] that barred government-created racial segregation in the public schools.

Many White Southerners did not agree with that U.S. Supreme Court decision or, later, with the remedies prescribed by the lower federal courts to bring about racially mixed schools. The response in many local communities across the South was to create "Christian Academies." Those private schools were the refuge for White youngsters fleeing from the newly racially balanced public schools. Occasionally, a few African Americans might be admitted as students, but usually the enrollment was all White. After all, that was the purpose. Those communities could create such exclusionary schools as long as they did not use public funds.

Another approach was taken by many Catholic schools, especially in large cities. During the 1970s and 1980s local congregations, called parishes, in the inner city lost White parishioners who moved to the suburbs, due to the influx of African Americans into their neighborhoods. Adopting a different attitude than the creators of the new Christian Academies, these parishes generally kept their schools open and welcomed children of the new residents even though most were not Catholic. Over time, though, many of these parochial schools could not be sustained due to reduced revenues in those parishes.

The Student Bodies

These social changes help to explain the differences between public and private school enrollments. Private schools have a larger percentage of White children as students than public schools, and a smaller percentage of students from low-income households.

- Sixty-nine percent of private school enrollments were White students compared to 50% in traditional public schools in 2015.

- Eight percent of private school students lived in poor households, while more than twice that percentage attended public schools in 2016.

These statistics were cited in an article in *The Washington Post* on March 29, 2016, with the headline "The overwhelming whiteness of U.S. private schools."[14] The occasion was the release of a report from the Southern Education Foundation, which found that students in the nation's private schools were disproportionately, and in some states overwhelmingly, White.[15] Another major difference is that three-fourths of private schools are religious schools. Only about 22% of all private schools are nonsectarian.

The distribution of these private schools among various faiths in 2018 was the following.

- 40% are Catholic schools,
- 12% are conservative Christian schools,
- 26% are other religions' schools, and
- 22% are nonsectarian schools.[16]

Religiously affiliated schools vary with regard to which religious practices they require of students whose parents do not belong to the religious group operating the school. Some schools are tightly bound to their founding religion, others less so.

At this point, key features of private schools have been identified. They have a more limited purpose than public schools. They can be exclusive and choose not to educate a person or groups of students. As a result, private schools often have more White students and fewer minority students than public schools. They are also more likely to have religious influence. Additionally, private schools lack interest in being accountable to the public authorities for the financial assistance provided by these new programs.

ACCOUNTABILITY—OR NOT

In February 2020, *Education Week* issued a report on the ways that states were relating to private schools. Since Montana was then before the U.S. Supreme Court on the issue of aid to private schools, that state was used as an example. The report's conclusion was this:

> Montana, like many states, helps some students pay for tuition at private schools. But the rules for the schools that participate in its tax credit scholarship program are scant: They do not have to hire teachers with college degrees or conduct criminal background checks on all their employees. Schools do not

have to publicly report graduation rates or demonstrate that they are on sound financial footing. And, no entity—be it the state, the organization that awards the scholarships or the private schools—is required to track and report basic demographic data on the students who use the program.

Montana is hardly an outlier.

Nearly 30 states have private school choice programs that either directly pay students' tuition at private schools or provide generous tax credits to incentivize businesses and individuals to do so. But, few require private schools to follow standard policies used to ensure transparency and accountability in the nation's public schools. [17]

One would think that parents would want some assurance that their children were safe from predators at school and were being taught by qualified teachers. Shouldn't state legislators who were creating these programs aiding private schools likewise have wanted some conditions on this aid to protect and properly educate children? In the United States, during the past 20 years, a different view dominated. The state laws benefitting private schools embodied the attitude that there was little need for public accountability from private schools.

In contrast to this light-handed way of dealing with private schools, elected officials—during the same period of the past 20 years—used an iron-fisted approach to public schools. No limit was evident on demands for performance, imposition of additional duties, and mandatory testing of students. Federal and state leaders also were easily attracted to unsound measures, such as the federal No Child Left Behind Act, because they were labeled as accountability measures for public schools.

SUCCESS OF PRIVATE SCHOOLS?

Instead of talking about those issues, private school proponents cite data to show educational success. These are some key results that private schools publicize. In a debate on private schools, proponents will argue for little or no regulation, saying that the results speak for themselves.

- Students in private schools score higher, compared to public school students, on a variety of tests, including the National Assessment of Educational Progress, the ACTs, and the SATs. The first is the valued national test, and the other two are the examinations used for college entrance.
- Students in private schools graduate from high school at higher rates than students in public schools.
- Students educated in private schools enter college at higher rates than do students from public schools.

- Students educated at private schools prior to entering college are more likely to finish college with a degree than students from public schools.

Those indeed are impressive results, but a key factor must be brought into the discussion. The missing element has been an acknowledgement of the role that students' family backgrounds play in students' school careers. In 1966, Dr. James Coleman found that the family backgrounds of students were the most important factor in indicating success in school. After 50 years, his findings have not been refuted.[18] The success of private schools must be viewed using the lens of family background. Since parents of private school students are more highly educated and have higher incomes than the parents of public school students, Coleman's work showed that these students as a group would have higher test scores and college-going rates than public school students.

More recently, research has found that when socioeconomic status is controlled, public school students may even out-perform private school students. Because this finding is contrary to the popular view of public and private education, these studies need further discussion

The first round of new research on this issue reached the surprising conclusion that public school students' test scores were as good as those of comparable private school students, and possibly better. Comparability meant students having the same social and economic family backgrounds.

The Lubienski team conducted this research, first releasing their analyses in 2005.[19] This conclusion was shocking to proponents of private education.

As Christopher Lubienski said at the time: "These results are significant because all the most prominent reforms right now assume that private schools do better, and that if you take a disadvantaged kid and give that kid an option to go to a private school, that will boost their achievement." He asserted that their research raised grounds to question that assumption.[20] The critics of this conclusion raised questions about the test used, the methods of analysis, etc. In response, Christopher and Sarah Lubienski continued their research.

In 2013, they reported on the results of their study which was the largest and most comprehensive ever conducted in this area. Their conclusion, now on firmer ground than before, was that no private school advantage for students existed, as commonly believed. Instead, test scores proved that public schools have an advantage.[21] Christopher Lubienski concluded that public schools are "actually providing a more effective education service relative to schools in the independent sector."

A confirmation that comparable results come from comparable students was provided by a more recent study. In 2018, the researchers Robert C. Pianta and Arya Ansari of the University of Virginia reported on the results of their study: While private school students may be outperforming public school students, the difference was eliminated completely when you controlled for family income and the parents' level of educational achievement.[22]

In an interview, Pianta noted: "Kids who come from homes with higher incomes and parental education achievement offer young children—from birth through age 5—educational resources and stimulation that other children don't get. These conditions presumably carry on through the school years."[23]

COSTS

How much does it cost parents to send their children to private schools to get comparable results to those of public schools?

The average yearly cost of a student attending a private school is $10,940. There is a wide range in costs, depending on the type of school. Catholic schools are the most affordable, averaging $7,020 a year, and nonsectarian schools are the most expensive, averaging $21,910.[24] Private schools may thus be out of the question for many families, especially if more than one child is involved. Parents should be aware of other costs such as transportation, since many private schools do not have bus service. Lastly, parents may be called on during the school year to participate in money-raising activities for the school.

Public schools are basically free, with only some small fees each year. That is quite a contrast when there is high-quality research informing us that private schools only get results that are comparable to those of public schools.

WHAT'S NOT TO LIKE ABOUT PRIVATE SCHOOLS

After reviewing the legal, political, demographic, and academic records of private education, what are the most important conclusions?

Private schools give parents an option in considering the best place to learn for each of their children. This seems to be especially important to religious parents.

What is not to like is private schools getting undue credit for the achievements of their students. A fair comparison would show no academic advantage for attending a private school.

To be able to make that assertion is remarkable. Public schools are educating students to do at least as well as private school students while carrying out a much broader mission than private schools. What an accomplishment by public school educators.

NOTES

1. Josh Cunningham, Comprehensive School Choice Policy: A Guide for Legislators, National Conference of State Legislators, March 15, 2018, https://www.ncsl.org/documents/educ/ComprehensiveSchoolChoicePolicy.pdf.

2. U.S. Department of Education, National Center for Education Statistics, "Condition of Education: Public Charter School Enrollment" updated May 2021, https://nces.ed.gov/programs/coe/indicator_cgb.asp

3. CAPE Facts and Studies, Council for American Private Education, 2019, http://www.capenet.org/facts.html

4. Pierce vs. Society of Sisters, 1925, 268 U.S. 510 (1925).

5. Catholic Schools in the USA, International Student, n.d., https://www.internationalstudent.com/study_usa/religious-schools/us-catholic-schools/

6. Lyle Denniston, "Constitution Check: Are the states' "Blaine Amendments" on shaky ground?" Constitution Daily [Blog], National Constitution Center, January 19, 2016, constitutioncenter.org/blog/constitution-check-are-the-states-blaine-amendments-on-shaky-ground; "WhatIsaBlaineAmendment?" FindLaw, June 20, 2016, https://www.findlaw.com/education/curriculum-standards-school-funding/what-is-a-blaine-amendment.html

7. Zelman v. Simmons-Harris, 536 U.S 639, 2002.

8. Nancy Kober, Why We Still Need Public Schools (Center on Education Policy, 2007), 3-4.

9. In 1995, I founded the Center on Education Policy, and was its president and CEO until 2012. The quote is from page 3 of our report, Why We Still Need Public Schools: Public Education for the Common Good. https://files.eric.ed.gov/fulltext/ED503799.pdf

10. Plyler v. Doe, 457 U.S. 202 (1982); Lau v. Nichols, 414 U.S. 563 (1974). Plyler deals with a child's immigration status, and Lau deals with teaching English.

11. Individuals with Disabilities Education Act, 1990.

12. The "related services" provision of IDEA has been controversial over the years because it leads to the question of the responsibility of a school district to fund social and health services that are the responsibility of state and local governments. For an explanation of these services and of the provisions of the law, see Center for Parent Information and Resources, Related Services, 2017, https://www.parentcenterhub.org/iep-relatedservices/

13. Brown v. Board of Education of Topeka, 347 U.S. 483 (1954); Stephen P. Broughman, Brian Kincel, Jennifer Peterson, Characteristics of Private Schools in the United States: Results From the 2017-18 Private School Universe Survey (National Center for Education Statistics, February 2019), https://nces.ed.gov/pubsearch/pubsinfo.asp?pubid=2019071

14. Emma Brown, "The overwhelming whiteness of U.S. private schools," Washington Post, March 29, 2016, https://www.washingtonpost.com/news/education/wp/2016/03/29/the-overwhelming-whiteness-of-u-s-private-schools-in-six-maps-and-charts/

15. Stephen P. Broughman, Brian Kincel, & Jennifer Peterson. Characteristics of Private Schools in the United States: Results From the 2017-18 Private School Universe Survey, June 2019. https://nces.ed.gov/pubs2019/2019071.pdf

16. Arianna Prothero & Alex Harwin. "Private School Choice Programs Fall Short on Transparency, Accountability." Education Week, February 28, 2020. https://www.edweek.org/policy-politics/private-school-choice-programs-fall-short-on-transparency-accountability/2020/02

17. James Coleman et al., Equality of Educational Opportunity (U.S. Department of Education, 1966).

18. Sarah Theule Lubienski and Christopher Lubienski, "A new look at public and private schools: Student background and mathematics achievement," Phi Delta Kappan, 86, no. 9 (May, 2005).

19. University of Illinois at Urbana–Champaign, Research questions belief that private schools are better than publics [press release], April 11, 2005.

20. Christopher Lubienski and Sarah Theule Lubienski, The Public School Advantage: Why Public Schools Outperform Private Schools (University of Chicago Press, 2013).

21. Sharita Forrest, "Book: private schools not as effective as some advocates suggest," News Bureau/Illinois, November 11, 2013.

22. Robert C. Pianta and Arya Ansari, "Does Attendance in Private Schools Predict Outcomes at Age 15: Evidence from a Longitudinal Study," Educational Researcher, Vol. XX, American Educational Research Association, 2018.

23. Valerie Strauss, "No, private schools aren't better at educating kids than public schools; Why this new study matters," Washington Post, March 27, 2018.

24. Table 205.50, "Private elementary and secondary enrollment. . . tuition," Digest of Education Statistics 2013, National Center on Education Statistics, U.S. Department of Education, 2013, https://nces.ed.gov/programs/digest/d13/tables/dt13_205.50.asp.

Scrutinizing the School Choice Equity Ethos for Black Parents

Julian Vasquez Heilig

A narrative purporting the benefits of student and parental choices within a market-based approach to education is the foundation of the charter school discourse (Vasquez Heilig, Brewer, & White, 2018). During the last decade, the number of charter schools in the United States has doubled and the number of students in charter schools has nearly tripled, with approximately 3.1 million enrolled in 2016–17 at a cost of almost $38 billion in taxpayer funding (3.1 million students multiplied by national average per pupil spending of $12,201) (NAACP, 2017). Additionally the Center for Media and Democracy (2016) found that the federal government alone has spent more than $3.3 billion in grant funding over the past two decades to further fuel the charter school industry.

This rapid expansion of charter schools in the United States has been targeted in part at Black communities. One in eight Black students in the United States now attends a charter school (NAACP, 2017). Location and funding are among the reasons for the rapid growth of charter schools in Black communities. That is, charters and private schools have often opened in urban areas where Black families are concentrated and can "choose" them. However, there are now about 7,000 charter schools across the U.S. that regularly enroll millions of children—they are no longer a small-scale, boutique public policy response within Black communities. As a result, Black communities and the general public should carefully consider proponents' framing and opponents' critiques amid a rising tide of market-based, privately managed charter schools.

Do charter schools provide equitable access to educational opportunities for Black communities? Charter school proponents posit an ethos of equity—a claim that school choice will increase student opportunity by creating a competitive marketplace for students, especially those who are most disadvantaged. To test the ethos of equity and advance the policy discussion, this essay offers a critical review of media, reports, data, and research on the U.S. implementation of charter schools to inform Black parents of real-world consequences and implications for families. This essay will address arguments raised in the public discourse and connect those concerns to the central issue of access to opportunity. I will also present a synthesis of media, reports, and research and a concise summary of my own research, law reviews and contributions to *The Progressive Magazine*, to examine the charter school equity ethos in a way that brings access to the fore, with the specific audience of Black parents and communities in mind. The goal is to provide an overview of information about charter schools and equitable educational access and opportunity.

The current political framing espoused by former President Donald Trump, former U.S. Secretary of Education Betsy DeVos, and other school choice supporters is that an educational market is empowering to parents and is a necessary attack on a public education "monopoly" and teachers' unions. Milton Friedman, a libertarian academic, economist, and proponent of market-based school choice, initiated this argument over 50 years ago. Friedman wrote in the 1950s, followed by others such as John Chubb and Terry Moe in the 1990s. They argued for an education system where resources are controlled by private entities rather than by democratically elected governments. They recommended a system of public education built around parent/student choices, school competition, and school autonomy as a solution to what they saw as the problem of direct democratic control of public schools.

The departure from the direct democratic control of schools is now being influenced and supported by elites who seek to privately manage and privatize education (Vasquez Heilig et al., 2019). During the last decade, charter school advocates, supportive policy patron foundations (e.g., Gates, Walton, Broad, and Arnold), think tanks (e.g., EdChoice), and policymakers (e.g., Arne Duncan and Betsy DeVos) have framed an equity discourse around school choice touting the benefits of private management within a market-based system (Blume, 2015). Using the mantra of civil rights, monied interests have aligned with local astroturf organizations such as Parent Revolution and other national organizations such as Black Alliance for Educational Options (BAEO). Astroturf advocacy organizations have appeared (and often quickly disappeared), utilizing resources from billionaires and other neoliberal supporters of school choice to press for privately managed, market-based school choices in the U.S. Astroturf supporters are funded by neoliberal organizations that are allies in pressing for private-management and/or profit-based market approaches to education. Thus, school reform advocates in the U.S. are often a motley alliance between those whose stated primary focus is a greater opportunity for historically underserved students of color and neoliberals who desire to reduce the role of the state in public education and shift the U.S. education system towards a privately managed enterprise (Vasquez Heilig, 2013).

Charter skeptics, including the nation's two major teachers' unions, grassroots organizations, and civil rights organizations—such as the NAACP—have critiqued these equity contentions, focusing on concerns about access, accountability, and segregation, as well as the threat posed by privatization to public schools as a democratic institution (Scott, 2011). The premise that school choice has created a competitive marketplace for students and parents is questionable once market dynamics are considered (Portales & Vasquez Heilig, 2014; 2015). A market is a place of winners and losers. Vasquez Heilig, Nelson, and Kronzer (2018) argued that market-based school choice is problematic for communities as schools are empowered to do the choosing via internal and external policies. The academics who were the progenitors of school choice neglected to mention that external market-based mechanisms are the very system that created the inequities in American public schools today. Along with other public policies, including redlining, market forces linked to the accumulation of capital created racial and economic segregation. Instead of making this situation better, school choice has intensified historical problems such as segregation—a point that will be discussed later in the essay.

Probably the most prominent argument from market-based education proponents is that families can choose their schools. However, the internal mechanisms in place empowering charter schools to control their demographic population are many. The fundamental factor is that they are privately managed. Kevin Welner has identified practices known as "creaming" and "cropping" as primary concerns. Creaming is a mechanism through which schools choose to enroll the best and least costly students. Cropping occurs when charter schools deny services and enrollment to diverse learners based on disability, socioeconomic status, language learner status, and/or other learning related factors. These students prove to be costly to educate, thus charter schools have extensively turned them away. The national data has demonstrated that charters are less likely to enroll these types of diverse learners. Often these students are "steered away" or "counseled out" of the school, which produces access and opportunity issues that are a cause for concern especially because equity, equality, and demographic representation are essential to the goals of public education (Vasquez Heilig et al., 2011). In effect, school choice via charters schools means schools can choose.

Despite these documented practices, proponents of market-based school choice have argued that charter schools were designed to have both more freedom and more accountability. Critics of privately managed schools point out that charters are afforded less accountability. As discussed by Vasquez Heilig et al. (2016), when private entities run schools with public dollars, they are able to choose their students utilizing internal policies without any direct democratic accountability. While public schools must admit all students, privately managed schools have discriminated based on student behavior, academic achievement, personal interviews, income, and costly special needs. Charter schools can remove students if they are deemed disruptive to the learning environment, passing the "problem" down the road to public schools. Proponents of more accountability for charter schools want parents to be able to choose from high-quality public schools. Instead, charter schools have the power to cream and crop students whom they deem will perform well and at a lower cost. Charter school supporters blame a few bad apples for expelling too many students and for selective enrollment that avoids diverse learners. Charter school supporters and their lobbyists ignore the orchard of bad apples and consistently support laws that promote lax regulation and oversight. For example, the California Charter School Association has often actively lobbied against data collection and accountability.

Considering the role of charters in selecting their students in well-documented ways, do they then equal civil rights? NAACP cofounder W. E. B. Du Bois, in his essay "Negroes and the Crisis of Capitalism in the U.S.," extolled the virtues of collaborative social and governmental action. He railed against the role of businesses and capitalistic control that "usurp government" and made the "throttling of democracy and distortion of education and failure of justice widespread." (DuBois, 1953). Malcolm X characterized market-based public policy as "vulturistic" and "bloodsucking." He advocated for collaborative social systems to solve problems. Martin Luther King Jr. argued that we often have socialism in public policy for the rich and rugged free market capitalism for the poor. Du Bois, King, and Malcolm X would have pushed back against the political framing of charters as promoting civil rights and recognized the opportunistic pattern seen in the purposeful and unrelenting location of charters in Black communities. Proponents of market-based school choice ignore this history of Black civil rights leaders' advocating for collaborative, community-based systems of social support and their distrust of market-driven policies.

At separate conventions in 2016, the NAACP and the Black Lives Matter Movement—the nation's largest and oldest civil rights organization and one of the newest—passed resolutions critical of charter schools and the privatization of education, resulting in a barrage of criticism from market-based school choice proponents and charter operators. While the Black Lives Matters Movement was new to charter school criticism, the NAACP has for years been consistent in its critique. At the 2010 convention, the NAACP supported an anticharter resolution saying that charter schools create "separate and unequal conditions." In 2014, the NAACP critiqued the connection of charters with the private management and private control of public education. At the 2016 NAACP national convention, more than 2,000 NAACP delegates from across the nation voted for a charter school moratorium based on a variety of civil rights-based critiques such as a lack of accountability, enhanced segregation, and disparate punitive and exclusionary discipline for Blacks.

Supporters of privately managed schools also argue that the teachers' unions are the primary opponents of market-based school choice. But union leadership has historically shied away from strong opposition to charters because of an apparent strategy to organize them. However, the leadership of teachers' unions, representing millions of educators nationwide, have adopted a more critical role in public discourse concomitant with the burgeoning growth of charter schools and their increasingly widespread opposition to unions, problems with teacher attrition, and hiring of underqualified teachers. Ironically, Albert Shanker, former president of the American Federation of Teachers, brought the charter school idea to prominence in 1988. However, he later saw his interpretation of charters schools as misappropriated, used instead to create antidemocratic, privately managed public schools. He realized that charters were going to a group of people who were "eager for public funds but could care less about public education" (Ravitch, 2013).

It could be argued that this discussion about civil rights, access, and opportunity would be moot if charter schools performed better than neighborhood public schools in a significant way. Charter proponents often cite studies produced by The Center for Research on Education Outcomes (CREDO) at Stanford University. CREDO studies are not peer-reviewed; nevertheless, charter school supporters and the media point to CREDO's 2015 urban charter study to say that Black and Latino students have more success in charter schools (CREDO, 2015). Leaving aside the methodological decisions in the study, what charter proponents don't mention is that the statistical effect is .008 and .05 for Latinos and Blacks in charter schools, respectively. These numbers are larger than zero, but you need a magnifying glass or perhaps a telescope to see the impact. Contrast charter schools' minimal outcomes with policies such as Pre-K and class size reduction, which have far more unequivocal measures of success than charter schools. Meta-analysis studies have identified the impact of Pre-K and class size to be 400% or more effective than charter schools. Also, CREDO doesn't usually compare schools in their studies. Instead, researchers use statistics to compare a real charter school student to a virtual (imaginary) student based on many students attending neighborhood public schools. Despite the fatal criticism of CREDO's methods and lack of impact, charter proponents and the media often cite these studies as important evidence demonstrating charter school success.

Peer-reviewed literature on charter schools and academic achievement across the past decade suggests that statistically significant achievement gains for charter school students in a variety of states are limited and inconsistent across student groups (Vasquez Heilig, Nelson, & Kronzer, 2018). In sum, it is difficult to find rigorous and independently funded scientific studies conclusively demonstrating that charter schools have a positive, empirically measurable impact on student achievement. The predominance of the research conducted on charter schools' effects on student academic achievement offers no widespread or compelling evidence to justify initiating and expanding their use.

Furthermore, Vasquez Heilig (2015) examined the case of Louisiana and New Orleans Recovery School District (RSD), where Teach For America and a cabal of neoliberals transformed the city into a predominately charter school system of education. Research using the NAEP shows that Louisiana charter schools perform worse than *any other state* when compared to the traditional public schools in those states. Also, the RSD dropout and graduation rates are of concern—placing last and nearly last in the state. At 5%, Advanced Placement results have been a disappointment after more than a decade of charter-driven "education reform." The review of data also demonstrates that neither the Louisiana ACT nor RSD ACT scores are positive evidence of success. The national comparative data suggest that there is a dearth of evidence supporting more than a decade of universal charter-conversion as implemented in New Orleans. Widespread implementation of charter schools is not likely to generate substantial gains in student achievement or appreciably improved educational outcomes. Educational policy should be based on data and research rather than ideology.

One of the biggest challenges that charters schools have presented is that they have taken advantage of issues identified as problematic in public schools—i.e., school finance, segregation, graft, teacher quality, and school discipline. For example, some proponents frame charter schools as a productive and useful alternative to increased state education spending. Although cost reduction is put forth as a potential positive, the financial benefit often accrues at the statehouse and not the local level. Dependent upon district level funding, a state may derive large cost savings from charter schools. For example, per pupil funding might average $9,000 in a state that funds charter schools based on average per pupil spending (like Texas); a "savings" of approximately $4,000 would be achieved if a district's per pupil funding is $13,000– ideal for state policymakers, but not for local communities. Why? In this case, financial inefficiency is created in public schools from a funding drain of students no longer attending. Districts that lose students to charter and private schools will see a decrease in state revenue that may not be accompanied by a decrease in district costs. For districts to realize cost savings, students who exit the district should come from the same schools and grade levels so the district can reduce personnel costs, by far the largest portion of a district's budget. Otherwise, districts would have to employ the same number of teachers, counselors, librarians, and support staff to serve fewer students. In rural schools, this would increase the already problematic diseconomies of scale. Thus, not only do charters often fail to decrease costs, they may cause an increase in per pupil costs in a district's schools. In essence, the state and local taxpayers now have to fund two separate systems of education. In states where there are school vouchers, taxpayers are then funding three separate systems of education—public, charter, and private.

While charters make up only approximately 7% of U.S. schools, prior research using national data has found that they are the most segregated of the nation's schools, especially for Black and Latinx students (Frankenberg et al., 2010). Many of the nation's charters can even be classified as "apartheid schools," a term coined by UCLA Professor Gary Orfield for schools with a White student enrollment of 1% or less (Orfield, Ee, & Coughlan, 2017). School choice supporters point out that neighborhood segregation is out of their control—although in some states charter schools can use neighborhood borders to fix enrollment. Most charter schools have not prioritized or experienced desegregation as a desired outcome (Scott, 2018). Vasquez Heilig, Brewer, and Williams (2019) conducted descriptive and inferential analyses of publicly available federal data to examine segregation at the local, state, and national levels and found that higher percentages of charter students of every race attended intensely segregated schools, controlling for neighborhood demographics, and found that double segregation by race and class is higher in charter schools. So while geography and residential segregation patterns contribute to the segregation in charter schools, Vasquez Heilig and Clark (2018) argued that in reality the schools with the most flexibility to achieve significant diversity have instead chosen not to address the problem.

In addition, there is growing evidence that charter school managers are wasting hundreds of millions of taxpayer dollars on grants awarded to charter schools that never open or quickly close their doors. The U.S. Department of Education (DOEd) is also funding charter schools that blatantly discriminate in their discipline, curricular, and enrollment practices. In the policy report by the Network for Public Education entitled *Asleep at the Wheel: How the Federal Charter Schools Program Recklessly Takes Taxpayers and Students for a Ride,* it is estimated that the federal Charter Schools Program (CSP), over its history, has awarded over $4 billion in seed money to charter schools (Burris, 2019). In California, the state with the most charter schools, the failure rate for federal grant-awarded charters was 39%. The report also argued that hundreds of millions of federal taxpayer dollars were awarded to charter schools that never opened or opened and then shut down. In some cases, schools received federal funding even before securing their charter—nearly one in four either never opened or shut its doors, according to the report. The report also relayed the DOEd's analysis from 2006–2014 of its direct and state pass-through funded programs, which found that nearly one out of three charter schools that were awarded funds eventually closed. Burris (2019) also found that the DOEd did not demonstrate oversight when state education agencies passed funding along to individual charters or charter organizations as subgrants and that the Office of the Inspector General's 2016 audit of CSP funded Charter Management Organizations (CMO) and their related schools showed that of the 33 schools they reviewed, 22 had one or more of the following: conflicts of interest between the CMO or the charter, related-party transactions and insufficient segregation of duties. The Network for Public Education has extended its research on financial malfeasance in charter schools to daily public posts on Twitter about charters' financial scandals under the hashtag #AnotherDayAnotherCharterScandal.

Disproportionate and excessive discipline for students of different kinds—especially students of color—has been historically problematic in neighborhood public schools (Cole & Vasquez Heilig, 2011) and it is another issue that charter schools have made worse. The NAACP High Quality Task Force toured the country holding townhalls after the 2016 call for a charter school moratorium. Community members who testified in the townhalls from several cities cited research that showed charter schools exhibit disproportionate and excessive discipline in their communities relative to neighborhood public schools. NAACP (2017) relayed that

> The claim that charter schools provide greater options for families was often countered by accounts of exclusionary enrollment and pushout practices that are viewed as common to many charter schools. Bob Wilson, a member of Journey for Justice from Chicago, Illinois, testified about a local study that found that Chicago charter school expulsion rates were more than 1,000% higher than those of Chicago Public Schools on a per-pupil basis. Wilson noted that one charter school in Chicago claims a 100% graduation rate, "yet only 40% of their incoming freshmen graduate. So, between freshman year and senior year, 60% are pushed out due to suspensions, expulsions . . . [and] counseling-out students as well." Other studies mentioned by witnesses described similar patterns. For example, a review of three years of expulsion data found that Washington, D.C. charter schools expelled 676 students, while the traditional public schools expelled only 24. During the Los Angeles hearing, a panelist mentioned a recent study that found "charter schools suspended higher percentages of Black students and students with disabilities than traditional public schools." (p. 16)

The last study that the NAACP townhall panelists referenced found that Black males are over three times more likely to be suspended or expelled from charter schools than their White peers (Losen et al., 2016).

CONCLUSION

Students living in poverty-stricken areas within the United States have fewer opportunities for a high-quality education than students living in wealthy areas. Financial resources in the United States are unequally allocated between majority Black and majority White school districts by about $23 billion (EdBuild, 2019). Thus, it is understandable that Black parents are searching for alternatives to the status quo, as the U.S. has a history of underserving students of color. Black parents and communities often turn to charter schools in hopes that they offer a better educational opportunity, comparable to what White and wealthy students receive. As a result, during the past two decades we have seen billions of dollars redirected to charters from neighborhood public schools and charters being peddled by policymakers and others as an alternative to adequate funding for public education.

Notably, the same legislators that have used politics to force inadequate funding of U.S. public schools are also arguing that public schools are inadequate. Colin Powell once said, "If you break it, you own it." That's the endgame for neoliberals. First, they seek to transfer public education from direct democratic control and the state budget to private management and privatization of public funds (Brewer et al., 2018). Second, civil rights and equity are not their true priorities. Neoliberals do not have the best interests of Black students at heart; they are supporting school choice because they are seeking to shift the U.S. education system to derive and maximize control of financial resources while limiting democratic control of public schools. Neoliberals have co-opted the equity discourse by offering a carrot (sometimes millions of dollars as in the case of BAEO) to factions of people of color and astroturfing community organizations while cloaking the inequity that private management and profit-based approaches present.

School choice proponents often utilize fairly simplistic arguments about markets, competition, and educational opportunity as justification for charter schools. A common strategy of proponents is to trumpet waiting lists and showcase convincing student stories—especially those of Black children. However, neoliberal proponents of school choice support the policies because they are seeking a fundamental shift in the funding of education that market-based school choice presents and empowers. The implementation of charter schools is a slow-moving takeover of public education by privately managed organizations that drains state funding and will eventually starve and close public schools. Clearly, scaling up charters across the nation to the nearly complete level (as implemented in New Orleans) is the direction the U.S. is headed; it would introduce a permanent private management and privatization paradigm for the funding and control of U.S. education.

To conclude, it is important to underscore the predominance of media, reports, and research on charter schools that have indicated that market-based school choice is not the most effective solution to remedy longstanding achievement gaps or improve student success. The data and peer review research do not support charter school proponents' grandiose assertions. In summary, some of the most important critiques associated with charter school implementation in the U.S include the following:

- Although a reduction in educational costs due to private management is put forth as a potential benefit, that benefit often accrues at the statehouse and not the community level and is tainted by intensified graft and malfeasance.
- Widespread implementation of school choice is not in alignment with civil rights and won't generate substantial gains in student achievement or in the success of the U.S. PreK–12 public education system.
- Charter schools have not increased opportunity, have used mechanisms to exclude students, and have exacerbated longstanding issues (i.e., school finance, school discipline) that were already problematic for Black students in neighborhood public schools.

Charters are not a substitute for systemic and sustained educational investment in Black communities and their schools. The tide may be turning in the public debate as well, as hinted in independent polling by the California Public Policy Institute that has shown a reduction in support for charter schools in Black communities. Ultimately, Black communities and the general public are craving solutions to the longstanding issues facing students who do not live in wealthy communities. There is a dire need to re-envision education reform as community-based and democratically controlled instead of focusing on private management and privatization as the best course of action (Horsford & Vasquez Heilig, 2014). In fact, Linda Darling-Hammond has made the case that the gold standard for positive impact on education involves systemic investments that are being implemented by the countries with the most successful educational systems in the world. These include but are not limited to: implementing resource equalization mechanisms among public school districts and public schools; requiring all schools to have certified teachers and principals; and a strategic national focus on higher education-based teacher training (Darling-Hammond et al., 2005).

I have summarized and considered the most common arguments in the public discourse by proponents and opponents of charter schools. The research, data, and media reports presented in this article demonstrate the problematic ways in which school choice and charter schools have, in fact, often intensified, rather than ameliorated, historical problems already present in U.S. schools. It is clear that the equity claims made by choice and charter advocates are often specious and thoroughly unsubstantiated. Ultimately, we must reconsider the deleterious impact of ongoing school choice experimentation and ideology on Black children. We also must come to terms with that fact that we are grinding towards a universal private management and privatization paradigm for the funding and control of U.S. education.

REFERENCES

Blume, H. (2015, September 21). Backers want half of LAUSD students in charter schools in eight years, report says. *Los Angeles Times*. https://www.latimes.com/local/lanow/la-me-ln-broad-draft-charter-expansion-plan-20150921-story.html

Brewer, J., Vasquez Heilig, J., Gunderson, M., & Brown, J. (2018). Chi-Town educator and community-based activism: Confronting a legacy of education privatization in the nation's Windy City. *Thresholds in Education, 41*(3), 138–153.

Brown, E. (2013). D.C. charter schools expel students at far higher rates than traditional public schools. *Washington Post*. https://www.washingtonpost.com/local/education/dc-charter-schools-expel-students-at-far-higher-rates-than-traditional-public-schools/2013/01/05/e155e4bc-44a9-11e2-8061-253bccfc7532_story.html?utm_term=.9ee2f2ccca6f

Burris, C. (2019). *Asleep at the wheel: How the Federal charter schools program recklessly takes taxpayers and students for a ride*. The Network for Public Education.

Center for Media and Democracy (2016). Federal Government Continues to Feed Charter School Beast Despite Auditor's Warning. PR Watch, October 10, 2016. https://www.prwatch.org/news/2016/10/13158/federal-government-continues-feed-charter-school-beast-despite-auditors-warning

Chicago Public Schools. (2014). *CPS suspension and expulsions reduction plan and data highlights*. https://www.cpsboe.org/content/documents/student_suspension_and_expulsion_reduction_plan.pdf

Cole, H., & Vasquez Heilig, J. (2011). Developing a school-based youth court: A potential alternative to the school to prison pipeline. *Journal of Law and Education, 4*(2), 1–17.

CREDO (2015). Urban Charter School Study. http://urbancharters.stanford.edu/index.php

Darling-Hammond, L., Holtzman, D. J., Gatlin, S. J., & Vasquez Heilig, J. (2005). Does teacher preparation matter? Evidence about teacher certification, Teach for America, and teacher effectiveness. *Education Policy Analysis Archives, 13*(42). Retrieved from http://epaa.asu.edu/epaa/v13n42/

Du Bois, W. E. B. (1953). Negroes and the Crisis of Capitalism in the U.S. Reprinted in Monthly Review (2003). https://monthlyreview.org/2003/04/01/negroes-and-the-crisis-of-capitalism-in-the-united-states/

EdBuild. (2019). *Fractured: The accelerating breakdown of America's school districts*. Author. https://edbuild.org/content/fractured/fractured-full-report.pdf

Frankenberg, E., Siegel-Hawley, G., & Wang, J. (2010). *Choice without equity: Charter school segregation and the need for Civil Rights standards*. The

Civil Rights Project/Proyecto Derechos Civiles at UCLA. https://files.eric.ed.gov/fulltext/ED509773.pdf

Horsford, S., & Vasquez Heilig, J. (2014). Community-based education reform in urban contexts: Implications for leadership, policy, and accountability, *Urban Education, 49*(8), 1–4. doi: 10.1177/0042085914557647

Journey for Justice Alliance. (2014). Death by a thousand cuts: Racism, school closures, and public school sabotage. https://docplayer.net/379700-Journey-for-justice-alliance.html

Losen, D. J., Keith, M. A., Hodson, C. L., & Martinez, T. E. (2016). *Charter schools, civil rights and school discipline: A comprehensive review*. Civil Rights Project/Proyecto Derechos Civiles at UCLA. https://www.civilrightsproject.ucla.edu/resources/projects/center-for-civil-rights-remedies/school-to-prison-folder/federal-reports/charter-schools-civil-rights-and-school-discipline-a-comprehensive-review/losen-et-al-charter-school-discipline-review-2016.pdf

National Association for the Advancement of Colored People. (2017). NAACP Task Force on Quality Education Hearing Report. Author. Retrieved from https://www.naacp.org/wp-content/uploads/2017/07/Task_ForceReport_final2.pdf

Orfield, G.; Ee, J.; Coughlan, R. (2017). *New Jersey's segregated schools: Trends and paths forward*. Civil Rights Project/Proyecto Derechos Civiles at UCLA.

Portales, J. & Vasquez Heilig, J. (2014). Understanding how universal vouchers have impacted urban school districts' enrollment in Chile. *Education Policy Analysis Archives, 22*(72). http://epaa.asu.edu/ojs/article/view/1427/1314

Portales, J., & Vasquez Heilig, J. (2015). Understanding universal vouchers and urban public schools in Santiago de Chile: Educational administrators' responses to choice. *Multidisciplinary Journal of Educational Research, 5*(2), 194–237.

Ravitch, D. (2013, November 13). When Albert Shanker turned against charters. https://dianeravitch.net/2013/11/28/when-albert-shanker-turned-cool-towards-charters/

Scott, J. (2011). Market-driven education reform and the racial politics of advocacy. *Peabody Journal of Education, 86*(5), 580–599.

Scott, J. (2018). The problem we all still live with: Neo-Plessyism, and school choice policies in the post-Obama era. In I. C. Rotberg & J. L. Glazer, Eds., *Choosing charters: Better schools or more segregation?* Teachers College Press.

Vasquez Heilig, J. (2013). Reframing the refrain: Choice as a civil rights issue. *Texas Education Review, 1*(1), 83–94.

Vasquez Heilig, J. (2015). *Should Louisiana and the Recovery School District receive accolades for being last and nearly last?* The Network for Public Education.

Vasquez Heilig. J., Brewer, J., & Adamson, F. (2019). The politics of market-based school choice research: A comingling of ideology, methods and funding, In M. Berends, A. Primus, & M. Springer (Eds.), *Handbook of Research on School Choice* (2nd ed., pp. 335–350). Routledge.

Vasquez Heilig, J., Brewer, T. J., & White, T. (2018). What instead?: Reframing the debate about charter schools, Teach For America, and testing. In R. Ahlquist, P. Gorski and T. Montano (Eds.), *Assault on kids and teachers: Countering privatization, deficit ideologies and standardization of U.S. schools* (pp. 201–217). Peter Lang.

Vasquez Heilig, J., Brewer, T. J., & Williams, Y. (2019). Choice without inclusion?: Comparing the intensity of racial segregation in charters and public schools at the local, state and national levels. *Educational Sciences*, 9(3), 205. https://doi.org/10.3390/educsci9030205

Vasquez Heilig, J., & Clark, B. (2018). New insights and directions: Considering the impact of charter school attributes on communities of color. *Journal of Transformative Leadership and Policy Studies*, 7(1), 3–9.

Vasquez Heilig, J., Holme, J., LeClair, A. V., Redd, L., & Ward, D. (2016). Separate and unequal?: The problematic segregation of special populations in charter schools relative to traditional public schools. *Stanford Law & Policy Review*, 27(2), 251–293.

Vasquez Heilig, J., Nelson, S., & Kronzer, M. (2018). Does the African American need separate charter schools? *Law & Inequality: A Journal of Theory and Practice*, 36(2), 247–267.

Vasquez Heilig, J., Williams, A., McNeil, L., & Lee, C. (2011). Is choice a panacea? An analysis of black secondary student attrition from KIPP, other private charters and urban districts. *Berkeley Review of Education*, 2(2), 153–178.

The Scandalous History of Schools That Receive Public Financing, But Do Not Accept the Public's Right of Oversight

David C. Berliner

There is repeated evidence of scandal in businesses, in religious groups, in the military, and in city, state and federal government, as well as among our own families and neighbors. So, it should not be surprising that scandals also occur within our nations' public schools. About 91,000 American public (non-charter) schools operate in about 13,000 school districts, each with a school board that collectively employs around 3.2 million teachers (plus huge numbers of custodians, food servers, bus drivers, nurses, gardeners, maintenance and computer staff, etc.), who together serve over 50 million students.

In a system of this size, of course scandals happen. Students, teachers and staff, and school and district administrators are all occasionally discovered to be cheating on tests, stealing public money, having inappropriate sexual relations, breaking state or federal educational law, and in other ways scandalizing their school community. But are the numbers and kinds of unseemly and often illegal incidents occurring in our genuine public schools of the same magnitude as those that occur in charter schools or schools receiving public dollars in the form of vouchers?

Because charter and voucher schools receive public funding, their proponents often refer to these schools as "public schools." But the public has no meaningful say in their management, so I do not regard these schools as genuine public schools. Genuine public schools, for example, almost always demonstrate extremely high compliance with local, state, and federal regulations. Many of their activities and policies are subject to oversight by state and local authorities, and by their elected school boards. Their curriculum, their monitoring of attendance and handling of disciplinary suspensions and expulsions, their special education policies and practices, their approaches to ensuring nondiscriminatory racial and gender policies and practices, and their spending of public dollars are all subject to oversight by representatives of local, state, and federal government agencies. In addition, oversight of genuine public schools is provided by active parent–teacher groups and public news media, each of whom are allowed access to school, budget, and administrative records, with little interference from school administrators. But none of this is likely to be true for charter or private voucher-receiving schools, though they are recipients of public money. What happens when there is no fiscal and program oversight of schools that take the public's money but reject public review?

In fact, what happens is often scandalous! I will amply demonstrate this in what follows. The research and critiques I cite here are merely a fraction of the scholarly and journalistic work supporting my claims. What I ask the reader to keep in mind are two questions. First, is the scandal or illegal act I describe more likely to occur in publicly regulated public schools, or in schools that take the public's money but create their own rules, regulations, and fiscal policies, with little to no public oversight and little regard for either the public good or for the consequences of their actions? Second, how much longer should America's taxpayers allow such scandalous behavior to continue?

I start my reportage about the surfeit of scandals among charter and voucher schools that receive public money but have no public oversight with recent news reports from my own state of Arizona. As I was writing this essay, the former principal of Discovery Creemos Academy charter school in Goodyear, AZ, was sentenced to nearly four years in prison for fraud. He was also ordered to pay more than $2.5 million in restitution for fraud ("Ex-Arizona Charter School Principal Sentenced," 2020). Among other problems, this school didn't have enough students to generate the money the staff desired. So, they made some up: 453 fake students, to be exact!

When two other leaders of this school were brought to court for fraud it was learned that they had no previous experience running a school (Harris, 2020). In fact, neither one had a college degree, and *before they ran this unregulated charter school, operating on public money, they had provided janitorial services to the school!* Scandalous? I think so! But it is what frequently happens when there is no oversight of the credentials of school staff and of the large amounts of money provided by states to charter or voucher schools. In fact, to see how remarkably common these scandals are among charter and voucher-receiving schools throughout the country, see the "Charter school scandals of the day" at the EdHive website (https://www.edhivemn.com/cssotd.php). It provides day-to-day and state-by-state reporting of scandal after scandal in these ersatz "public" schools.

Arizona, like many states, has few mechanisms to check if the money it gives out for charter and voucher schools is being used sensibly. At least one report (O'Dell & Sanchez, 2017) suggests widespread abuse of the state money given to parents for use as school vouchers to support their children's education. Some parents simply pocketed the money. Some bought things that were "educational" in order to have the receipts for reporting purposes, returned those purchases, and then they pocketed the money. To the horror of some legislators, it seems likely that in one case funds were used to pay for an abortion! Fiscal and program audits of charter and voucher programs in Arizona are almost nonexistent.

An investigative report on Arizona's roughly 540 charter schools, and the school chains to which some belong, was completed by the American Civil Liberties Union (ACLUAZ, 2017). The charter schools were all asked for information about curriculum, enrollment, and school policies. Seventy-two of these publicly supported charter schools refused to answer those questions, violating Arizona state laws about public records. Can you imagine if 13% of Arizona's *genuine* public schools told their state departments of education, or any inquisitive state legislator, to go fly a kite? Yet all these violators of state law got away with it. Scandalous? I think so!

The ACLU also found that Arizona's charter schools discriminate against special education students, which is against the law. For example, AmeriSchools Academy (in Phoenix, Tucson, and Yuma) blatantly and illegally noted that "Special Education placements are limited to a capacity of ten (10) students for each school site. Students in excess of this number are to be wait listed." The Rising School (in Tucson) blatantly and illegally noted that its special education program "is currently full, per guidelines set by the Arizona Department of Education. Thus, any student with an IEP will be put on our waiting list" (p. 6). There was, however, a problem with this charter school's statement, namely, that the Arizona Department of Education had no such guidelines. The school lied.

Imagine your local public school saying, "We already have enough of these kinds of students, so please take your child elsewhere!" Is this appropriate behavior for schools that owe their existence entirely to public money? Or are such actions scandalous?

At least 19 of Arizona's charter schools surveyed by the ACLU also tried to discourage or prevent low academic performers, or students with some previous discipline problems, from registering in their school. For example, students at the Southern Arizona Community Academy, in Tucson, were told upon entrance that they would be on probation for their first two weeks and would be checked every week thereafter. They were told that they would be removed from the school if the staff believed they were falling behind. I am quite sure that *public* school teachers, on the days that they struggle most with difficult-to-teach students, might want to support a school policy just like that. But they do not do so! Public school teachers know they labor in the public's schools, and their job is to work as hard as they can to make each student—even the most difficult one—a productive citizen.

The Leading Edge Academy (in Gilbert and Queen Creek) is another among many charter schools that says they "may elect not to admit students who have been or are currently under disciplinary action . . . (at) another school." Put a little differently, this charter school says "Sorry, although we take the public's money, we openly discriminate against hard to teach students."

These publicly supported charter schools are not subtle about it, acting more like private schools that can, and do, often segregate not only on the basis of special needs, academic proficiency, and behavior, but also by race and religion. Most readers will remember that it was once scandalous, as well as against federal law, when many Southern communities ran segregated schools with public money. Eventually, the majority of our nation recognized that such schools were not in America's best interest, and thus they were declared illegal. But equivalent illegal and immoral activities happen every day in publicly supported charter and voucher schools. For example, here are the criteria for entrance to the Fayetteville Christian School (FCS) in North Carolina, a recipient, in a recent school year, of $495,966 of *public* money in the form of vouchers, and scheduled to receive even larger amounts of public money in the future (before the pandemic, the plan was that appropriations for voucher schools in the state would rise from about $65 million a year in 2019–20 to over $144 million a year in 2027). Public monies now support schools with entrance requirements similar to these:

> The student and at least one parent with whom the student resides must be in agreement with the FCS Statement of Faith and have received Jesus Christ as their Savior. In addition, the parent and student must regularly fellowship in a local church. Accordingly, FCS will not admit families that belong to or express faith in religions that deny the absolute Deity/Trinity of Jesus Christ as the one and only Savior and path to salvation. . . . FCS will not admit families that engage in behaviors that Scripture defines as deviate and sin [illicit drug use, sexual promiscuity, homosexuality (LGBT), etc.].
>
> Once admitted, if the student or parent/guardian with whom the student resides becomes involved in lifestyles contradictory to Biblical beliefs, we may choose to dis-enroll the student/family from the school. (Fayetteville Christian School, n.d.).

So, despite receipt of the public's money, The Fayetteville Christian School is not open to the public. This school says, up front and clearly, that it doesn't want and will not accept Jews, Muslims, Hindus, and many others. Should public money be used in this way? And should schools supported by the public also allow students to be expelled for their parents' alleged sins? Admission and dismissal policies based on religion and lifestyle, in a school receiving about a half million dollars of *public* funds per year, strikes me as scandalous.

Furthermore, the Children's Law Clinic (2017; 2020), associated with Duke Law School, noted some things about North Carolina's voucher schools that frighten me. These schools do not need accreditation or state approval to operate and need not follow any state-defined or required curriculum. There are no required qualifications for teachers at voucher schools, students at voucher-accepting schools are not required to take any state-administered tests, and there are no requirements for the number of hours per day, or days of schooling per year, these schools must provide. And "They may . . . discriminate on the basis of religion, disability, sex, sexual orientation, gender identity, or any other characteristic" they choose (Children's Law Clinic, 2020, p. 38).

Scandalous? I do not know how any American citizen can think otherwise, though North Carolinians seem oblivious to the issues that their laws and rules raise in a democracy.

Another issue related to school access is that public schools, which America's charter schools claim to be, are supposed to be free for the families and children they serve. Isn't that why they are supported with public funds from the states and districts in which they are located? Arizona State law even states that charter schools *cannot* require parental donations, and cannot require involvement in school activities as a condition of admission. As in many states, the Arizona Constitution guarantees students the right to a *free* public education, and charter schools, when it is convenient, do claim to be public schools.

Nevertheless, the American Civil Liberties Union of Arizona (2017) apparently found a number of violations of state law. For example, they found that the Great Hearts schools (in the Phoenix metropolitan area) asks each family to contribute $1,500 per student, per year, to help cover gaps created by the "inadequacy of public funding." At the Scottsdale Country Day School parents are encouraged to donate anywhere from $200 to $2,000 to the school per year. Apparently, and also in violation of state law, the Mission Montessori Academy of Scottsdale asked parents to volunteer 15 hours every year per child enrolled or make a contribution of $150 to the school in lieu of volunteer hours. The Montessori Day Public School chain noted that "All parents are expected to contribute 40 hours of volunteer time per family, per year." The Freedom Academy in Phoenix and Scottsdale required a nonrefundable $300 "Extracurricular Arts Fee," due at enrollment. The San Tan Charter School in Gilbert, AZ, required parents to provide a credit card the school can keep on file to pay several fees, including a $250 technology rental fee for grades 9–12. These appear to be great ways to illegally keep some families from enrolling in these supposedly public schools. Scandalous? I think so.

It's no different in California. For just one example of many, the American Civil Liberties Union of Southern California (2016) informs us that Paragon Collegiate Academy (PCA), in Yuba County, asks its parents to sign a pledge that they will provide "20 or more hours of annual volunteer service with PCA." A buyout option is also available: "The fee is $15.00 per hour for each hour that parents are unable to volunteer" (p. 2). The Southern

California ACLU report asserts convincingly that about 20% of all California charters schools have illegally put in place exclusionary practices to avoid enrolling some students, sometimes because they find the students' parents objectionable. Both the Arizona and Southern California ACLU reports note that oversight in each state is quite lax.

In entrepreneurial/capitalistic America we allow privately supported private schools to charge whatever they want, and they can require of parents whatever they choose. But do we want our publicly supported schools to force the parents they serve to pay for school services, or be required to "volunteer" for school duties? That seems both un-American and scandalous to me! And it seems, as well, that these are bad faith policies, given the promises charters have made to the public, and the role charters claim they want to play in our nation. Of course, I find it even more outrageous that State Charter School Boards in most states, public entities with oversight of the public's money and of the well-being of the K–12 students in their state, care not a whit about these issues.

Moving to other scandalous events, I note that charters and voucher-supported schools compete for the students who now attend our nation's genuine public schools. One way they compete is to show how well they perform on achievement tests and how large a percentage of their students enroll in college. While often proud of their achievement test scores and college acceptance rates, boasting about these data in recruitment materials, they almost always accomplish this feat by culling (Berliner, 2020a). These schools cull the children they don't want, as they would cull the cattle or sheep they didn't want in their herds.

For example, Ursula Casanova (2012) wrote in *The Washington Post* about the Basis Charter School of Scottsdale, named that year as the top high school in Arizona. But the year it was so honored, Casanova found student enrollments from the 5th to the 8th grade to be 152, 138, 110, and 94. High school enrollments in grades 9 to 11 were 42, 30, and 23. Finally, the 12th grade graduating class had 8 students! With no shame whatsoever the Basis school was able to claim they graduated 100% of their seniors and that all were accepted at college! Scandalous? I think so! A similar repugnant pattern was found in the Basis school of Tucson, part of the same chain of charter schools. In the year Casanova reported her findings, the school started with 127 students in the 5th grade. But they had only 100 students in 8th grade, 69 in the 9th grade, 45 in 10th grade, and 27 in 11th grade. At the end of 12th grade they had only 24 seniors left to graduate. The graduating class was only 35% of the 9th-grade cohort, and they were less than 20% of the 5th-grade cohort.

Culling sheep or cattle may be sensible. But culling American youth as charter and voucher schools do—marking so many students as "problem children," or as "not fitting in," or as "unacceptable," or having "parents or guardians who are unacceptable"—seems scandalous to me.

Arizona is certainly not unique. Culling is common practice in charter schools throughout the nation. In the 2014 edition of the federal government's Common Core of Data it was noted that the Boston public school system graduated 85% of its grade 9 students from high school. But the City on A Hill Charter School graduated 46% of its grade 9 class; while the Boston Preparatory Academy, Boston Collegiate Charter, and Academy of the Pacific Rim Charter each graduated about 60% of their 9th grade class (NCES CCD). The same culling occurred in Philadelphia's Boys Latin Charter, as analyzed by Jersey Jazzman (2017). Boys Latin proudly boasted that 98% of its students were accepted into college. But in the years 2011–2015 the school graduated about 60% of its 9th grade class, culling approximately 40% of its student body, and thus allowing the school to make the claim that 98% of its senior students are accepted to college. What we see all across the United States is that the culling of children is endemic in charter schools. What do the students and their parents think about, and what are their relationships like, after a student has been culled: forced out/thrown out/dismissed? Surely families are strained by such practices. On the other hand, our public schools regularly try their best to work with difficult-to-teach children and youth, and their families. Public schools ordinarily have counselors and nurses to help a child who is having academic or behavioral difficulties get on the road to productive citizenry. In contrast, our charter and voucher schools simply dump difficult-to-teach students onto their parents, and back into the publics' schools.

This Darwinian approach, to push the weakest students out of school, to cull the herd, should not be tolerated in a democracy, and therefore should be absolutely inappropriate behavior for a school receiving public money. It may be hard to accept, but Darwinism really is the philosophy adhered to by some of the highest rated charter schools in Arizona. A respondent to a blog post by my colleague Gene Glass, where he too criticized the culling and creaming practices of charters, stated the following: "Basis schools does not engage in any form of thinning across any grade. Students do drop out because they are not fit to thrive in the difficult curriculum" (Anonymous, 2015).

Let's think about what "not fit to thrive" might look like as a guiding philosophy for our genuine public schools. We could do away with special education, bilingual education, counseling and guidance, transportation, free and reduced breakfasts and lunches, school nurses, etc. The students that need these services will find some way to survive, or they'll drop out. The Darwinian approach to schooling is not merely undemocratic—I think of it as evil, as well! If it were up to me, I wouldn't give another public dollar to any charter or voucher school that culls its students, or that cream-skims the pool of candidates that apply to their school.

"Skimming the cream" is how many charter and private schools have found a way to cut down on culling to improve their herds. They simply discriminate in who they let into their schools in the first place. For example, Potterton (2013) wrote in *Teachers College Record* about four highly rated charter schools in Arizona, the two Basis schools reported on above and two other schools from the Great Hearts Academy chain, which runs more than 20 schools in the Phoenix area. In the year of her study, she found that the average rate for free and reduced lunch in Arizona schools was 35%. But the average rate for free and reduced lunch in these four charter schools was not near to that. In fact, it was 0%, 0%, 0%, 0%! Highly selective admissions were clearly a major reason for such low rates of enrollment by poor children in these publicly supported schools. That same year the state average of English Language Learners in Arizona's public schools was 7.5%. What percent of English language learners were in these four high achieving charter schools? They had enrollments of 0%, 0%, 0%, 0%. Similar statistics were found for special education students at these schools. Compared to state averages, hardly any special education students were enrolled in these high achieving, publicly supported charter schools. What charter and voucher-receiving schools have learned is that cream-skimming during admissions lets them cull less and advertise more their high standards and their high performance on state assessments. The illegality of these actions seems to be tolerated by many states.

Related to illegal selective admissions is an Arizona state law that forbids Arizona's charter schools from requiring students or their parents to complete pre-enrollment activities, such as essays or interviews, or to take school tours. Nor can charter schools use students' performance on interviews or essays, or the student's decision not to complete requested pre-enrollment activities, to determine which students to accept. Nevertheless, the Arizona ACLU (2017) found that at the Flagstaff Arts and Leadership Academy students must write a one-page essay as part of their enrollment application. As part of the enrollment process at the Satori Charter School in Tucson, parents and students must meet with a school administrator. These are patently illegal ways to find out about, *and then keep out*, potentially undesirable students and families.

America once had employment signs in windows that shamelessly read "No Irish Need Apply," and we had mortgage documents that prevented Jews or Asians or Mexican Americans from buying property in many cities. And it was not long ago that many banks would not provide mortgages to Black Americans, in part, because federal mortgage insurance was denied to Black citizens of this country (Rothstein, 2017). But despite our embarrassing history, we are allowing some Arizona charters and voucher schools—*all of which receive public money*—to do it again. They are putting up invisible signs, but signs that are seen, nonetheless. These signs, invisible as they sometimes may be, can still be seen quite clearly to say: "Poor children need not apply," "Immigrants who speak their native language need not apply," and "Do not enter if you are in need of special education."

"If you are gay, go away!" Is it scandalous for publicly supported schools to so openly discriminate this way? I think so!

Voucher receiving private schools have even more autonomy than do the charter schools. So, it is no surprise that they have even bigger scandals. For example, *The Seattle Times* (Williams, 2004) reported on the Milwaukee voucher program, the nation's oldest and largest voucher program. They noted that "One school that received millions of dollars was founded by a convicted rapist. Another school reportedly entertained kids with Monopoly while cashing $330,000 in tuition checks for hundreds of no-show students. . . . At the Mandella Academy for Science and Math, school officials admitted signing up more than 200 students who never showed and then cashing $330,000 in state-issued tuition checks, which the principal used to buy, among other things, Mercedes-Benzes for himself and the assistant principal . . . . Mandella's principal [did] not have a teacher's license and was not required to submit any information about the school's philosophy or curriculum before receiving upward of $1 million in voucher funding." Scandalous? I think so!

But all these scandals are not unusual. In fact, they are quite common. Unlike genuine public schools, the voucher schools typically have little or no oversight because of the outrageous belief that a free market in schooling will be honestly run, a point easily disputed, below. If there is no oversight of great sums of public money, human greed stands a good chance of taking over the management of voucher schools. Thus, the Public School Forum of North Carolina (2018) reported that the ex-headmaster at Trinity Christian School in Rutherfordton "was indicted by a grand jury on 137 counts of embezzlement and obtaining property by false pretenses while serving in her official capacity at the school." The Forum quoted the local newspaper, the *Daily Courier*, as reporting that the former headmaster "faces 69 counts of embezzling money from a charitable or educational institution and 68 counts of obtaining property by false pretenses for the theft or misappropriation of over $134,973.82 of Trinity school's funds."

There is another Trinity Christian School in Fayetteville. I discussed this one earlier, describing how it refuses to take certain kinds of students, though receiving huge amounts of public money. Here we note that it is as corrupt as the Rutherfordton Christian school, with perhaps even bigger and better crooks. Their athletic director, also a teacher at that school, "pleaded guilty of embezzlement of employee state tax withholdings over an eight-year period while serving as payroll manager for the school" (Public School Forum of North Carolina, 2018). But it must not have been too scandalous to folks in Fayetteville since this admitted and convicted criminal "entered into a plea deal struck with the state that allowed him to serve three months in prison, pay a $45,000 fine and be placed under supervised probation for five years" (Public School Forum, 2018). Following his plea deal, this convicted crook continued to work and coach at Trinity Christian (the school, it turns out, was run by his father!). In fact, he served his jail sentence on the weekends as part of a work release option. Leniency to this convicted criminal seems related to the fact that the school is home to one of the state's top high school basketball programs and you just cannot jail a convicted criminal if they are the coach of a competitive athletic team.

Voucher schools are scandal-ridden not only because of theft, common as that is; they may also teach some things most of our nation regard as strange, or simply not true. There is ordinarily as little oversight of their curriculum as there is of their admission policies and their finances. Thus, in many schools supported with the public's money, children learn some things that many Americans regard as unacceptable. Examples of such content is found, especially, in the voucher schools strongly promoted in Louisiana by then governor, and once presidential hopeful, Bobby Jindal. The curriculum in the voucher schools Jindal and his colleagues supported frequently came from one of two sources: Bob Jones University Press (associated with the scandal-ridden university), or from Abeka, a publisher of Christian books. Between them, these publishers teach our youth some amazing things, as described by Pan (2012):

- *Slave masters were nice guys:* "A few slave holders were undeniably cruel. Examples of slaves beaten to death were not common, neither were they unknown. The majority of slave holders treated their slaves well."—*United States History for Christian Schools*, 2nd ed., Bob Jones University Press, 1991
- *The KKK was A-OK:* "[The Ku Klux] Klan in some areas of the country tried to be a means of reform, fighting the decline in morality and using the symbol of the cross. Klan targets were bootleggers, wife-beaters, and immoral movies. In some communities it achieved a certain respectability as it worked with politicians."—*United States History for Christian Schools*, 3rd ed., Bob Jones University Press, 2001
- *Abstract algebra is too complicated:* "Unlike the 'modern math' theorists, who believe that mathematics is a creation of man and thus arbitrary and relative, A Beka Book teaches that the laws of mathematics are a creation of God and thus absolute . . . A Beka Book provides attractive, legible, and workable traditional mathematics texts *that are not burdened with modern theories such as set theory.*"—*ABeka.com*
- *Gay people "have no more claims to special rights than child molesters or rapists."*—*Teacher's Resource Guide to Current Events for Christian Schools*, 1998–1999, Bob Jones University Press, 1998
- "Global environmentalists have said and written enough to leave no doubt that their goal is to destroy the prosperous economies of

the world's richest nations."—*Economics: Work and Prosperity in Christian Perspective*, 2nd ed., A Beka Book, 1999.

In *Salon*, Bruce Wilson (2012), citing a critic, Jonny Scaramanga, who reviewed materials by Accelerated Christian Education (another source for curricular materials) as well as Bob Jones and Abeka, lists some other claims made in these materials, all purchased with public money for the children of Louisiana and other states:

- Only 10% of Africans can read or write, because Christian mission schools have been shut down by communists.
- God used the "Trail of Tears" to bring many Indians to Christ.
- It cannot be shown scientifically that man-made pollutants will one day drastically reduce the depth of the atmosphere's ozone layer.
- God has provided certain "checks and balances" in creation to prevent many of the global upsets that have been predicted by environmentalists.
- The Great Depression was exaggerated by propagandists, including John Steinbeck, to advance a socialist agenda.
- Unions have always been plagued by socialists and anarchists who use laborers to destroy the free-enterprise system that hardworking Americans have created.

Jindal's "school choice" plan was designed to change perceptions of Louisiana's horrible racist past and promote the contemporary ideas of both the far right and the religious right. Of course, he and others have the right to do that, even though many Americans find such behavior unseemly, if not detestable. But do they have the right to promote their ideas with public money? I find that to be the issue. When that is actually the case, I find such actions scandalous.

Unlike public schools, we see that voucher schools typically have little or no oversight because of the outrageous belief that a free market in schooling will be competently and honestly run. I think only a fool would believe that! Perhaps there is an expectation that schools would be as competently and honestly run as GM's Chevrolet's Corvair division? That iconic American corporation literally killed people because of an engineering defect they knew about, and denied, until Ralph Nader forced them to admit it. And they learned nothing from that experience, because, a few years later, GM had an ignition key scandal. This also was a problem they knew about and could have fixed for about 90 cents per car. But instead, they covered up their problem, a decision that killed at least 124 people. Or, more recently, we can cite the case of one of our nations' great corporations, Boeing. They covered up defects that resulted in the crashes of two 737MAX aircraft, and the loss of 346 lives. Why? Boeing wanted income quickly, and to do that, they subverted the FAA's inspection system, releasing planes for service with a flawed steering system. So many other scandals come to mind: Wells Fargo Bank opening phony customer accounts; Deutsche Bank laundering criminals' money; Enron cooking their books and destroying our nation's economy; Volkswagen running phony emission tests. As I stated at the start of this essay, scandals are ubiquitous—in families and corporations, and of course among voucher schools and charter schools. It is not hard to develop a rule based on so many horrible examples. It was succinctly stated by President Ronald Reagan: "Trust, but verify." Trust alone will not work for auto manufacturers, airline manufacturers, or banks. And over the last 30 or so years, we have found out that trust will not work for charter or voucher schools, either.

In genuine public schools there is always oversight of public money. Scandals still occur, of course, but much, much less frequently. Furthermore, genuine public schools don't often close down, and even more rarely would they do so in the middle of a semester. But that is not true of charter and voucher schools. Many of the entrepreneurs who run these schools do not regard their students as precious youth that are needed by our nation to enhance our economy and perpetuate our democracy. They are, instead, each and every student, a profit center. And if the profit isn't there, the business must be shut. That is why these schools are frequently run more like small neighborhood restaurants than they are like public entities. And why Burris and Pfleger (2020) found that within the first three years, 18% of charter schools closed their doors, many of those closing within the first year. By the end of five years, 25% of charters had closed. By the 10-year mark, 40% of charter schools were out of business and about half of all charter schools had closed by their 15th year. Hundreds of thousands of students and their families had to deal with such turmoil because of their faith in market-driven education.

Voucher schools have a similar problem. For example, Wisconsin Public Radio (Quirmbach, 2014) reported that a number of voucher-receiving schools in Milwaukee had to close and one of them did so suddenly, just before Christmas, sending 66 students and their families scrambling for new placements. This might have been a Christmas blessing, because state test results found that only one student at this wonderful voucher school could read or do math proficiently in the year before the shutdown! And, in the unregulated free market in educational institutions that now characterizes the USA, the couple who ran the Milwaukee school opened another in Florida (Richards, 2014). Apparently, there are few if any checks of voucher school owners for credentials, experience, competency, legal status, and the like. That's what the free market is all about, and it always works—except when it does not.

It should be clear by now that I don't like voucher or charter schools. They take public money, and those funds usually come out of the budgets of genuine public schools that are trying to serve their whole community. Those public schools are almost always underfunded. Yet voucher or charter schools frequently pay founders and leaders of such schools—and their relatives—enormous salaries. It has often also been the case that charters and voucher schools buy their furniture, texts, and even custodial services from profit-making companies owned by the charter or voucher school owners. There is big money to be made in supplying a "non-profit" school with the services and equipment they need from a "for-profit" company that is owned by the schools' operators. Furthermore, charter and voucher schools are rarely unionized and so we see that many of these schools pay teachers poorly and demand of them more hours per week than would any genuine public school.

Furthermore, too many of these voucher and charter schools are not socializing students for democracy. I have personally been in some schools where the rules for children seemed not to be very different from those that were in place in Mr. Gradgrind's school, described in Dickens's *Hard Times*, published in 1854. The difference is that Gradgrind wanted "facts—nothing but facts," while today's obedience- and discipline-oriented schools want "scores—nothing but scores."

In addition to my many criticisms above, is this one: The predominance of research has shown that the academic performance of students with similar social class backgrounds actually is better in our nations' genuine public schools than in the voucher schools of Washington, D.C., Indiana, Louisiana, New Zealand, Sweden, and Chile (cf. Berliner, 2020b; Carnoy, 2017; Lubienski & Lubienski, 2013). There is some agreement now that the academic advantage often seen in charter, voucher, and elite private schools, is frequently due to selective admission and retention policies, e.g., cream-skimming and culling. It is not likely to be due to better instruction. In fairness, the respected scholar Douglas Harris (2020) would disagree with this analysis and argues cogently for what competition with public schools can do for all schools. He uses the New Orleans experience as the basis for his praise for an entirely non-public system.

But Tom Ultican (2020), a thoughtful and passionate defender of public schooling, has a reminder to Americans about the origins of the charter and voucher movement in our nation,

> Birthed in the bowels of the 1950s segregationist south, school choice has never been about improving education. It is about white supremacy, profiting off taxpayers, cutting taxes, selling market-based solutions and financing religion. School choice ideology has a long dark history of dealing significant harm to public education.
>
> Milton Friedman first recommended school vouchers in a 1955 essay. In 2006, he was asked by a conservative group of legislators what he envisioned back then. PRWatch [published by the Center for Media and Democracy]

reports that he said, "*It had nothing whatsoever to do with helping 'indigent' children; no, he explained to thunderous applause, vouchers were all about 'abolishing the public school system.'*" [Emphasis in original]

We should not allow this to happen! I say that not as a stubborn and blind defender of Horace Mann's development of what many of us regard to be a great American institution, now almost 200 years old. I say it because there are 10 excellent reasons to defend America's *public systems of schooling*, even with all their warts. Following Steven Singer (2017, whom I paraphrase and quote extensively, below) we find that:

1. Public Schools Attract Better Qualified Teachers. This happens because Public Schools usually have better hours, are better paying, have better benefits, better job protection, and more stability.

[handwritten margin note: not always true]

2. Public Schools Have Greater Community Responsibilities and Community Relations. They frequently are at the heart of the communities they serve, doing so much more than just teaching the communities' children. They may support continuing education courses for adults, especially in immigrant communities. They often sponsor extracurricular activities, such as sporting events and academic clubs. They may provide admission to their swimming pools, tennis courts, and baseball fields. And they may also invite in the local community for school events, such as concerts, plays, and seminars.

3. Public Schools Are Not Strangers to Educational Choice. It is not at all uncommon for public school districts to also offer choices to students and their families. Large urban districts, in particular, often have magnet or theme schools. Larger schools offer a wide variety of classes and curriculum, giving students choices of foreign languages, a vo-tech curriculum, or one in the arts and humanities. Public schools frequently provide access to independent studies, advanced placement, and college credit courses, as well. These too are choices. In addition, students can often take advantage of a plethora of services that can personalize their academic experience to meet their individual needs, as, for example, through special and gifted education. With adequate funding, which few public schools actually have, *all* public school districts could offer all the choice that young people and their parents want. No separate, unregulated, unsupervised, scandal-ridden alternative systems of schooling need to be developed. It appears to me that too many supporters of alternative systems of schooling are hopelessly antigovernment and in rapture with privatization.

4. Public Schools Have Greater Diversity. As Dewey noted decades ago, schooling is life itself—it is not separate from life. Thus, students learn a lot more than reading, writing and arithmetic in the schools they attend. In public schools they are more likely to learn how to deal with different kinds of people. They learn to share this world with other humans from various racial, ethnic, religious, and sexual backgrounds. It is quite possible that the more diverse the environment our youth grow up in, the better adjusted they are likely to be when they enter the adult world. There is a stronger likelihood that they will be less racist, sexist, and prejudiced than those attending schools with homogenous student bodies—regularly found in charter, voucher, private, and religious schools.

Alan Peshkin (1986) wrote about a private fundamentalist Baptist school, as homogenous a Midwest school as could be found. He spent 18 months on this brilliant ethnography and concluded that such schools could not see the paradox at the heart of their educational institution. They had the freedom in our democracy to believe in what they want and to teach what they want. But what they clearly taught in this homogenous school environment was intolerance to religious plurality. Religious and racial tolerance is far more likely to be learned in America's public schools.

5. Public Schools Are More Fiscally Responsible. As made clear in preceding sections of this essay, public school expenditures are manifestly public! Genuine public schools spend public money more wisely than charter and voucher schools, in part, because their records are an open book, as should be the books of any organization receiving the public's money. In the rare instances where public school employees break the law and try to embezzle funds, they are much more likely to be caught because fiscal records are available for all to see.

6. Public Schools Are More Reliable. As was made clear, above, when you send your child to a charter or voucher school you never really know if it's going to be there tomorrow. On the other hand, if there is one thing you can be reasonably sure of, it's that your neighborhood public school is quite likely to be there tomorrow. Public schools are bedrock. If a public school does close, it's almost always after considerable public comment and a protracted political process. As far as I know, no one has ever shown up to find their local public school suddenly chained shut. That is clearly *not* the case with charter and voucher schools.

7. Public Schools Have Greater Commitment to Students. As made clear above, charter and voucher schools don't have to accept your child. Public schools do, and they have a commitment to educate every child in the districts they are a part of, including homeless children and those who are seriously disabled. Typically, it is only under extreme circumstances that public school personnel actually expel a young person.[1] On the other hand, we know that there are numerous public school scandals about *who* is expelled and *why*, frequently leading to the exposure of systemic bias and racism among teachers and school leaders. But that is the point: It's not that public schools don't sometimes do awful things, it's that the actions of the public schools become public! Charter and voucher-receiving schools can keep their prejudices hidden and intact, and use public money to further their undemocratic policies. Unlike their brethren in charter, voucher, and independent private schools, public school teachers and administrators much more frequently have enduring faith that they can help almost all youngsters to succeed.

8. You Own Your Public Schools. With private, voucher, or charter schools, you are paying for a business to provide services. Genuine public schools belong to you—thus, if you want to exert your authority, you usually can do so.

Public schools are run by your friends, neighbors and coworkers; your school board members live in your neighborhood. The school PTAs and PTOs and advisory councils all are run by local folks. But charter and voucher schools are most often run by appointed boards of directors; frequently they are not local, and they certainly are not beholden to you, but to the owners and investors in the school. You may never get access to these owners and investors.

9. Public Schools Provide More Amenities. Public schools accept donations and sometimes teachers ask for help, but if parents can't (or won't) send in pencils or tissues, the school provides them *gratis*. When the district does not provide what is needed, teachers often make up the difference from their own pockets. On average this is about $600 per teacher per year, but this year, in the year of a pandemic, it appears that it will be even more!

Moreover, special education and gifted programs are often first rate at public schools. The public schools also often provide school buses, which are rarely provided by charter or voucher schools, and generally, there are fewer demands on parents' time for instructional support.

10. Public Schools Match or Outperform Privatized Schools. It seems implausible, particularly for those paying handsomely for private schooling, but a large and convincing amount of evidence, collected worldwide, suggests that the frequent advantage of charter, voucher, and independent private schools on standardized achievement tests is because of who attends those schools, not because their curriculum and instruction are superior.

Certainly, some charter, voucher, and independent, high-tuition schools do outperform genuine public schools. But when that does happen, it is more likely to be because of the social class characteristics of the children and families who are enrolled in those high-performing schools than because the public schools to which they are compared are not as good. Social class is quite highly correlated with standardized test scores. Who attends a public, charter, voucher, or independent private school often is the greatest influence on the scores achieved by students taking standardized tests (cf. Glass & Berliner, 2020). Thus, test scores alone, independent of other information, are never recommended as a way to judge the quality of any school.

I want to end this essay by giving my thanks to Horace Mann. I am a product of a stable and loving working-class family, and that surely matters; but I am also a product of many years of *public* schooling, influenced by Horace's fervency. I attended a *public* neighborhood elementary school and middle school, and then a *public* regional high school, in a highly urbanized environment. My bachelors and masters' degrees in psychology were both obtained at *public* universities. My doctorate was obtained at one of the most prestigious private universities in America. When starting my doctoral studies, I discovered that among my entering cohort I was the best prepared to thrive in that intellectually rich environment. For nurturing my skills, and accepting my countless foibles, I also want to thank my many *public* school teachers—from kindergarten to my masters' degree—for support that provided me such a rich and productive life.

NOTE

1. In 2013–14, only 0.2% of public school students were expelled (NCES, 2019).

REFERENCES

American Civil Liberties Union of Southern California (2016). *Unequal access: How some California charter schools illegally restrict enrollment.* https://www.aclu-socal.org/sites/default/files/field_documents/report-unequal-access-080116.pdf

American Civil Liberties Union of Arizona (2017). *Schools choosing students: How Arizona charter schools engage in illegal and exclusionary student enrollment practices and how it should be fixed.* https://www.acluaz.org/sites/default/files/field_documents/schools_choosing_students_web_new_logo.pdf

Anonymous (2015). Reply, Anonymous, May 15, 2015. Education in Two worlds. https://ed2worlds.blogspot.com/2014/05/a-parent-encounters-basis-schools-inc.html

Berliner, D. C. (2020a, April 13). Culling, creaming, skimming, thinning: Things we do to herds and school children. *Diane Ravitch's Blog.* https://dianeravitch.net/2020/04/13/david-berliner-how-successful-charter-schools-cull-and-skim-students-they-dont-want/

Berliner, D. C. (2020b). *Using the social and behavioral sciences to challenge the political roots of educational policy.* Paper presented at the meetings of the American Psychological Association, at a symposium titled: The Relevance of Educational Psychology to Education Policy: Past Lessons to Inform the Future. https://www.youtube.com/watch?v=oJ4X6hAWP-g

Burris, C., & Pfleger, R. (2020). *Broken promises: An analysis of charter school closures from 1999–2017*. Network for Public Education. https://networkforpubliceducation.org/wp-content/uploads/2020/08/Broken-Promises-PDF.pdf

Carnoy, M. (2017). *School vouchers are not a proven strategy for improving student achievement*. Economic Policy Institute. https://www.epi.org/publication/school-vouchers-are-not-a-proven-strategy-for-improving-student-achievement/

Casanova, U. (2012, April 13). The newest problem with graduation rates. *Washington Post, The Answer Sheet* [blog]. https://www.washingtonpost.com/blogs/answer-sheet/post/the-newest-problem-with-graduation-rates/2012/04/12/gIQAwsH2DT_blog.html

Children's Law Clinic. (2017, March). *School vouchers in North Carolina: The first three years*. Children's Law Clinic, Duke Law School. https://law.duke.edu/childedlaw/docs/School_Vouchers_NC.pdf

Children's Law Clinic. (2020, May). *School vouchers in North Carolina: 2014–2020*. Children's Law Clinic, Duke Law School. https://law.duke.edu/childedlaw/School_Vouchers_in_North_Carolina-2014-2020_(5-13-20).pdf

EdHive. (n.d.) *Charter school scandals of the day*. https://www.edhivemn.com/cssotd.php

Ex-Arizona charter school principal sentenced in fraud case. (2020, September 14). *USNews & World Report*. https://www.usnews.com/news/best-states/arizona/articles/2020-09-14/ex-arizona-charter-school-principal-sentenced-in-fraud-case

Fayetteville Christian School. (n.d.). *Admissions*. https://www.fayettevillechristian.com/copy-of-criteria-1

Glass, G. V, & Berliner, D. C. (2020, August 14). Why bother testing in 2021? *Diane Ravitch's Blog*. https://dianeravitch.net/2020/08/14/david-berliner-and-gene-glass-why-bother-testing-in-2021/

Harris, C. (2020, September 23). Second charter school executive sentenced in $2.5M enrollment scheme. Arizona Republic/AZ Central. Retrieved September 23, 2020 from: https://www.azcentral.com/story/news/local/southwest-valley-education/2020/09/23/discovery-creemos-academy-charter-school-executive-jail-enrollment-fraud/5858729002/

Harris, D. N. (2020). *Charter school city*. University of Chicago Press.

Jersey Jazzman (2017). When "Miracle" charter schools shed students. https://nepc.colorado.edu/blog/when-miracle

Lubienski, C. A., & Lubienski, S. T. (2013). *The public school advantage: Why public schools outperform private schools*. University of Chicago Press.

NCES (2019). National Center for Education Statistics. Indicator 15: Retention, Suspension, and Expulsion. https://nces.ed.gov/programs/raceindicators/indicator_rda.asp

NCES CCD. National Center for Education Statistics Common Core of Data: America's Public Schools. https://nces.ed.gov/ccd/ccddata.asp

O'Dell, R. & Sanchez, Y. W. (2017, June 22). Oversight of Arizona ESA school-voucher program 'almost a sham.' *Arizona Republic/Arizona Central*. https://www.azcentral.com/story/news/local/arizona-education/2017/06/22/oversight-arizona-esa-school-voucher-program-almost-sham/407961001/

Pan, D. (2012, August 7). 14 wacky "facts" kids will learn in Louisiana's voucher schools. *Mother Jones*. https://www.motherjones.com/kevin-drum/2012/08/photos-evangelical-curricula-louisiana-tax-dollars/

Peshkin, A. (1986). *God's choice: The total world of a fundamentalist Christian school.* University of Chicago Press.

Potterton, A. U. (2013, November 1). A citizen's response to the president's charter school education proclamation: With a profile of two "highly performing" charter school organizations in Arizona. *Teachers College Record.* https://www.tcrecord.org/Content.asp?ContentId=17309

Public School Forum of North Carolina (2018, June 27). Another embezzlement scandal rocks private voucher school. https://www.ncforum.org/another-embezzlement-scandal-rocks-private-voucher-school/

Quirmbach, C. (2014, January 15). *Tax-funded voucher school in Milwaukee closes abruptly.* Wisconsin Public Radio. https://www.wpr.org/tax-funded-voucher-school-milwaukee-closes-abruptly

Richards, E. (2014). Leaders of closed Milwaukee voucher school are now in Florida. *Milwaukee Journal Sentinel.* https://archive.jsonline.com/news/education/leaders-of-closed-milwaukee-voucher-school-are-now-in-florida-b99185323z1-240384541.html

Rothstein, R. (2017). *The color of law: A forgotten history of how our government segregated Americans.* Liveright/Norton Publishers.

Singer, S. (2017, October 4). Top 10 reasons public schools are the BEST choice for children, parents and communities. *HuffPost.* https://www.huffpost.com/entry/top-10-reasons-public-schools-are-the-best-choice-for_b_59d541cae4b0666ad-0c3ca48

Ultican, T. (2020). School choice is a harmful fraud. *Tultican.* https://tultican.com/2020/09/07/school-choice-is-a-harmful-fraud/

Williams, J. (2004, April 6). Scandals rock Milwaukee's school-voucher program. *The Seattle Times.* https://archive.seattletimes.com/archive/?date=20040406&slug=vouchers06

Wilson, B. (2012, June 19). Shocking Christian school textbooks. *Salon Magazine.* https://www.salon.com/2012/06/19/shocking_christian_school_textbooks_salpart/

This photo, by Jacob Riis—the antipoverty crusader and journalist who drew attention to horrific conditions in New York's slums—shows studious-looking boys packed into crowded rows at the Lower East Side Essex Street Market School. The year was 1887. Heat was via a coal stove.

Source: https://commons.wikimedia.org/wiki/Category:Jacob_Riis#/media/
File:Classroom_-_Jacob_A._Riis.jpg

Can Public Common Schooling Save the Republic?

D.C. Phillips

In the United States of America at the end of the second decade of the new millennium there are signs that the nation's great experiment in implementing liberal democracy is under potentially fatal threat.

In this essay[1] I make the case that there may be no escape from the resulting dilemma facing American liberal democracy and the public education that plays an important role within it.

Before turning to the nature of this dilemma and how it plays out in public schooling, I need to establish some background. I should make clear that in the discussion that follows I do not claim to have provided comprehensive coverage of all the relevant factors.

THE CURRENT THREAT TO AMERICAN DEMOCRACY

Recent events have made it clear that many elected leaders pay only lip service to the principles and values that underlie the American form of democratic government. These individuals make a show of espousing these values and principles, but evidently feel free to contravene them or rationalize them away when they judge it to be advantageous.

The United States now faces a constitutional crisis. Gerrymandering and widespread voter-suppression undermine the principle of universal suffrage and "one person, one vote." Campaign financing practices have ensured that big money plays an unfettered role in shaping election outcomes. Prior to the November 2020 presidential elections, agencies of the Federal government—such as the Department of Justice, the FBI, and the State Department—instead of working for the general public good show signs that they might have become agencies that serve the personal interests of the Chief Executive (demonstrating blatant disregard for the nation's Constitution). Furthermore, the incumbent of the office of the Presidency has profited personally from some of the actions he has taken while in office, actions that again display disdain for the Constitution. Steps have been taken to weaken the ability of Congress to oversee the Executive Branch, an ability that is legally mandated. Lying to the press and to the public and obstruction of justice have become regular features of political life, and have curtailed public access to the information necessary for them to participate actively as well-informed citizens. And worst of all, many of those who have been elected to public office have turned a blind eye to the corrupt practices that surround them—they seem not to be concerned with the preservation of democracy that they swore an oath to defend.

Where in the Constitution has it been established that in Presidential elections, it is allowable to jettison commitment to honesty, fair dealing, the principle of one person one vote? Where does it state that leaders of a democracy are allowed to lie and break the law?

So, the question arises: What allowed this situation to happen, and how is education involved?[2]

THE COMPLEX ROLE OF EDUCATION IN A COMPLEX DISEASE

What has led a significant number of our elected representatives in Congress—and for that matter many ordinary citizens—to jettison their adherence to the fundamental principles of democracy when it is expedient to do so? Education (or rather mis-education) has had a role to play here![3]

John Dewey recognized this perennial problem. His diagnosis was that political leaders might possess knowledge about democracy, but may be lacking in the know-how to be able to act appropriately in crisis situations. He wrote, in his *Problems of Men* (1946), that "Politicians are able to talk glibly and write elegantly and argue forcibly, but when it comes to the crises and necessities of action, they are not competent" (p. 55). Dewey's point was that they have *information* or *knowledge* about democracy and its working but, because they have not acquired this in the context of action, they lack *understanding*. Furthermore, whether or not politicians and citizens understand the principles of democracy, they often lack *commitment* to them. The fact is that understanding is neither a necessary nor a sufficient condition for the attainment of commitment.

It is worth noting that commitment to society's fundamental principles has been addressed in the classical anthropological literature. Durkheim wrote of the importance of a society's basic categorical concepts upon which others were built. These had a "compulsive" nature and were so fundamental that they had to be powerfully sustained—by means (he thought) of ritual. (See the discussion in Gellner, 1973, Chapter 2.) This, essentially, is my position; my case is as follows.

1. Schools are not the only sites where education takes place. Families, churches and other religious institutions, libraries, and the media all play a role in shaping the habits, values, and intellectual and social predispositions of each individual. Foundations of commitment or lack of it are laid down at these sites. The results of these influences differ from person to person, and are unpredictable. It is unreasonable to claim that the combination of these out-of-school factors never induce commitment to democratic principles and values on the part of any youngsters. But it also is unreasonable to doubt that for many other youngsters these influences help produce a conflicting mass of beliefs and commitments (for these factors themselves often point in different directions) or—even worse—that they lead to no deep commitments being held at all! There is no mechanism operating in democratic societies, no so-called "invisible hand" that ensures all of the out-of-school factors are exerting their influence in compatible or mutually-reinforcing directions. And most families do not exert such control over these influences. The result of all this is that any influence common schooling has in moving students in a socially-desirable democratic direction might be countered by out-of-school forces that tend to move them in different (and possibly undemocratic) directions.

2. Not all schools are public common schools. A variety of types leads to a variety of purposes or functions. Some of these other schools produce commitment as well as (or in place of) understanding—but the issue is, commitment to what?

There are many youngsters who are home schooled because their parents find aspects of public schooling deficient, usually in the domains of religious or sociopolitical beliefs and values. Schools affiliated with religious denominations aim to produce believers or to strengthen the commitment of those who already believe. There are schools like the English "Greater Public Schools" (such as Eton and Rugby) and U.S. military academies such as the Citadel that for centuries have catered to the offspring of the leaders of society, including the landed classes and industrial plutocrats; these expensive and elite institutions have fostered the commitment of at least some of their students to a classist (if not caste-ist), racist, and sexist view of society wherein they themselves are fitted by breeding to be the natural leaders of society. The fact that it took generations of struggle to achieve universal suffrage demonstrates the strength of the commitment that past leaders had to the nondemocratic values and principles that were foundations of the status quo and that their elite schooling played a role in promulgating. This attitude—the resistance to extending the franchise to classes of society that, according to one's upbringing, were intellectually and/or morally inferior—is understandable although not excusable. Under these circumstances it was one's duty to govern. Assuredly this attitude has not completely died.

The aforementioned factors severely limit what the common school can do to spread commitment to democratic principles among the populace. Even if all graduates from public common schools display enduring commitment, they almost certainly will be countered by numbers of graduates from nonpublic schools and from home schooling who adhere to different values or who have no significant value allegiances at all.

3. A further complexity arises when attempting to assess the impact of formal schooling (of any type) on the core beliefs acquired by individual students. This is due to the fact that schools have at least two curriculums that operate in parallel. The first of these is the explicit curriculum—the one consisting of the subjects taught, the teaching methods adopted, and the available extracurricular activities. The second curriculum is sometimes referred to as the "hidden curriculum," and it embraces those things that are taught informally. This hidden domain contains content and biases conveyed by the attitude and practices of the teachers, by the type of student conduct that is rewarded or punished, and even by the very offerings and non-offerings of the explicit curriculum itself. The value placed on specific types of social hierarchy, the advocating of a specific take on gender roles, attitudes about the academic ability and leadership potential of different genders and members of different social classes and ethnicities can all be part of the hidden curriculum.

The existence of the two curriculums poses difficulty for the argument that schooling is ineffective in producing commitment—for while in some cases the explicit curriculum no doubt fails to produce this deep commitment (to democratic values, for instance), the lessons imparted by the hidden curriculum might tell a different story. But if the latter did inculcate commitment, the question once again is: Commitment to what?

4. The common school has a considerable prehistory. Cubberley (1933) provides an account of "our educational evolution" which begins with this statement:

> Free state schools, as we know them today, are a relatively recent creation. As with the older European countries from which our early settlers came, schools with us arose generally as children of the Church. From instruments of religion they have gradually changed into institutions to promote the welfare of the State. (p. 1)

In the early days of U.S. schooling, then, imbuing students with religious doctrines was the paramount function, and making students literate was in the service of enabling them to read the Bible, which was thought to be the key to preserving the status quo and suppressing lawlessness. This schooling, which paid little or no heed to developing the independent rational and moral faculties of the students, would now be identified as socialization or perhaps indoctrination. Since that time abhorrence of the use of teaching techniques that indoctrinate has been steadily growing. And there are good reasons for this: Indoctrination treats its victims as objects and not as independent rational and moral agents whose development should be respected and fostered, rather than being manipulated to serve outside ends. By the end of the 20th century philosophers of education had joined the discussion, attacking indoctrination (see Snook, 1972). Interest, and hostility, has continued in the present day; and there is little doubt that if a teacher is called an indoctrinator, no compliment is being paid. Callan and Arena have put the matter clearly:

> When charges of indoctrination are made, the imputation of moral wrongdoing has to do with a systematic distortion of some kind in the teacher's presentation of subject matter—a distortion that elicits, or could reasonably be expected to elicit, a corresponding distortion in the way students understand the subject matter. Furthermore, the distortion is not, at least in paradigm cases, to be explained by the intellectual laziness or indifference that often explains merely ineffective teaching, *but by an ill-considered or overzealous concern to inculcate particular beliefs or values.* (Callan & Arena, 2009, p. 105, italics added)

History has favored abandoning indoctrination, and instead has taken seriously the fact that when we provide schooling we are engaged in educating our students. This is an open-ended process, the end point of which cannot be predicted. And this brings us face to face with our dilemma: In avoiding indoctrination we are respecting the rational autonomy of our students, but we run the danger of losing the strongly held and enduring commitments that indoctrination can instill (see Siegel, 1988).

5. The discussion now must turn to what is often considered to be one of the jewels of the U.S. education system, the common school. This undoubtedly has many of the virtues pointed out by activists and reformers such as Horace Mann, but it also has at least one structural feature that, in crucial areas, at best works in favor of instruction to produce understanding but does not permit the use of methods that directly produce wholehearted commitment. And this contributes to the democratic "constitutional crisis" outlined at the outset.

The core principle of common schooling is that children of all backgrounds—of different religions, ethnicities, cultures, races, genders and sexual identities, intellectual abilities, with or without physical or mental disabilities, and from different socioeconomic groups and families with differing political and ideological orientations—should be educated *together* and not in separate classes, schools, or educational systems. I will concentrate on the particular consequence of this that in the long run has turned out to be deleterious.

My argument has several prongs.

A. For more than a century it has been an important underlying principle that schools in a democracy should educate, not indoctrinate, for if they were to do the latter they would be guilty of moral wrongdoing. Thus it now is usual to insist that the procedures used in educating must equip learners to keep on learning in the future, and have the flexibility to be able to make decisions about what to learn and how deeply to pursue this learning in any given sub-branch of (as Dewey sometimes put it) "the funded wisdom of the race." Education must be conducted by appealing to the student's rational faculties, and it stands in contrast to indoctrination wherein the freedom—the autonomy—of the student is not respected and he or she is treated as an object suitable for manipulation.

But there is another reason supporting the principle that schools should not indoctrinate. Earlier, I described the chief virtue of common schools in a pluralistic democracy is that they are pluralistic. The ideal is that students with different ethnicities, cultures, sexual orientations, genders, abilities, religions, cultures, political persuasions, and interest will learn together—and crucially will learn from (and about) each other. However, a consequence of this diversity is that it makes indoctrination very difficult to carry out in practice. In many cases the indoctrinator would be taking sides—to which, rightly, there would be resistance. For example, it would be difficult for the common school to inculcate a Protestant Christian worldview when the institution harbors not only Protestants but also Catholics, atheists, Muslims, Jews, and Hindus. Could the common school aim to indoctrinate the belief that abortion is a sin (or alternatively that it is a woman's right to choose) when many students come from backgrounds where this view is not held? And can the common school instill belief in the theory of evolution when many cultures and religions in the community being served by the school do not regard it as valid?

It seems that the common school must educate, but must avoid indoctrinating. It can teach *about* controversial or diverse issues, but students are free to hold their individual beliefs—and crucially, their believing should not have been *inculcated* (Macintyre, 1964).

Unfortunately, this standard position, that advocates understanding but is chary of producing belief and commitment, is the Achilles' heel of common schooling. As a result, schools cannot help circumvent the crisis of democracy discussed at the outset.

B. We have arrived at the second prong of my case. Dewey wrote admiringly of Horace Mann and his ideal of the common school. However, he added this warning:

Only as the schools provide an understanding of the movement and direction of social forces and an understanding of social needs and of the resources that may be used to satisfy them, will they meet the challenge of democracy. (1946, p. 48)

Dewey proceeds by focusing on the key term in this passage, "understanding," which marks the deepest (and in Dewey's view the most important) level of contact with the subject matter being learned. The first and most superficial level is what I personally call "acquaintance with" but which Dewey identifies as the level at which the subject matter is treated merely as "information." Dewey favors the level wherein students attain "knowledge" of the subject being studied, but he eschews the use of this term because so often "knowledge" is used as a synonym for the more superficial "information." So instead he opts for the term "understanding" which, crucially, comes when one *acts* using (or acquiring) knowledge:

there is no guarantee in any amount of "knowledge about things" that understanding—the spring of intelligent action—will follow from it . . . . I do not mean that we can have understanding without knowledge, without information . . . . Understanding, by its very nature, is related to action. (p. 49)

To illustrate his point, Dewey uses the example of the early years following the introduction of Civics into the curriculum of the common school:

When the subject was first introduced, I think there was a good deal of evidence of faith in the truly miraculous and magical power of information. If the students would only learn their federal and state Constitutions, the names and duties of all the officers and all the rest of the anatomy of the government, they would be prepared to be good citizens. (p. 51)

But from Dewey's perspective, to actually *become* good citizens the students would need to have the understanding that comes from actually *acting* upon the knowledge acquired of Civics. And for Dewey, the function of Civics education is to *produce* democratic citizens—that is, to form appropriate pro-democracy dispositions in the students. And according to Dewey this could only happen when they were able to act upon the knowledge they were acquiring.

Dewey comes close to my point of view. He is sensitive to the fact that the future citizens of our democracy must acquire, during their schooling, the appropriate attitudes and beliefs (the Durkheimian categorial concepts) of our democracy. He also seems to have been aware that his position was skirting close to indoctrination, for it would be problematic to go further and hold that schools should aim for students to *commit* to democracy or whatever else was being taught. (The supporter of teaching for understanding who at the same time skirts away from instilling commitment could point out that there is never a question on the final examination in Civics courses asking, "Have you become a devotee of democracy?" Certainly it is not the aim of other courses in the curriculum to produce devotees.)

In making his case, Dewey asserted the following:

> Education must have a tendency, if it is education, to form attitudes. The tendency to form attitudes which will express themselves in intelligent social action is something very different from indoctrination. (1946, pp. 55–56)

Dewey argues that there is a difference between shaping a student's attitudes educationally and inculcating these by means of indoctrinatory techniques. Although he does not make the difference between these two perfectly clear, the passage is worth quoting in full:

> There is an intermediary between aimless education and the education of inculcation and indoctrination. The alternative is the kind of education that connects the materials and methods by which knowledge is acquired with a sense of how things are done and of how they might be done; not by impregnating the individual with some final philosophy, whether it comes from Karl Marx or from Mussolini or Hitler or anybody else, but by enabling him to so understand existing conditions that an attitude of intelligent action will follow from social understanding. (p. 56)

So, Dewey's case amounts to this: Students need to acquire democratic attitudes and values, but these must not be implanted by indoctrination. However, the requisite attitudes and values will be acquired by students when they achieve the deep knowledge that constitutes understanding— which will happen when they are immersed in situations in which they need to *act* intelligently to achieve a satisfactory resolution.

The philosopher of education Gert Biesta has developed a similar view. He discusses "education for democracy" and "education through democracy," but focuses his attention on the nature of the democratic individual. He appeals here to Hannah Arendt, who shifts our attention from the attributes of individuals to the quality of human interaction. He describes her position in these terms:

> Individuals might have democratic knowledge, skills and dispositions, but it is only in action—which means action that is taken up by others in unpredictable and uncontrollable ways—that the individual can *be* a democratic subject. (Biesta, 2006, p. 135)

Later Biesta elaborates:

The question is, in other words, whether children and students can actually *be* democratic persons in the school. What we need to ask, therefore, is whether schools can be places where children and students can act—that is, where they can bring their beginnings into a world of plurality and difference in such a way that their beginnings do not obstruct the opportunities for others. (Biesta, 2006, p. 138)

Dewey and Biesta are right in holding that students must acquire (or develop) certain values and attitudes, and the commitment to these should be enduring. But this is close but no cigar! In my analysis Dewey and Biesta make at least two mistakes: First, in supposing that this strong commitment can be achieved without resorting to indoctrination, and second, in failing to see that acting (whether in a classroom setting, or in a participatory environment in the school or in the community) is neither a necessary nor a sufficient condition for producing commitment. They also do not acknowledge the messiness produced by the fact that there are out-of-school influences on students, there are many types of school each trying to promulgate their own favored sets of values, and there are hidden curriculums offered by schools (even by common schools). It is anyone's guess where this disorderly array of often conflicting influences may lead.

Putting Biesta to one side, it is far from obvious that the mechanism Dewey proposes (the acting upon one's knowledge and the subsequent acquisition of understanding), or for that matter the similar one postulated by Arendt, *will* produce widespread deep adherence to democratic principles and values. It is an empirical issue as to whether the mechanism being advocated is strong enough to be successful. However, Dewey offers no evidence to counter the view that it is too weak and open-ended—some students may be able to relate their knowledge to action the way Dewey advocated, and thereby gain understanding, but nevertheless fail to become believers or adherents. But for society to survive the challenges that it faces, virtually all citizens need to buy into its fundamental principles. And here is where Plato enters the scene.

But first it may be instructive to consider an example that runs counter to Dewey's belief that understanding will lead to commitment or belief, namely the case of learning the theory of evolution. These days it is not possible to progress very far in any biologically based discipline, such as medicine, physical anthropology, genetics, geology, or many others, without drawing upon insights and methods linked with the modern theory of evolution. But it is possible to achieve understanding of evolutionary theory as a guide without accepting the theory as true. A considerable number of evolution deniers function this way while holding that the theory is fiction. It does not follow that using one's knowledge in conjunction with one's actions necessarily results in unswerving acceptance or commitment or belief. (See the discussion in Laats and Siegel, 2016.)

To return to the main theme: Maybe the liberal democratic supporters of the education delivered by common schools—an education that respects the autonomy of the learner—have gone too far in rejecting direct education for commitment. Perhaps we should reconsider implementing a strong mechanism, like indoctrination or the rituals discussed by Durkheim, to facilitate enduring commitment to the principles and values of democracy. And this is why we face a dilemma: We have a deep-seated belief in *educating* students, which involves respecting their rational autonomy; however, in the context of imparting fundamental values, normal educational processes might be ineffective because they do not aim to produce *commitment* to this underlying foundation.

Indoctrination is the unpalatable alternative. Recognizing that this is the path taken over two thousand years ago in Plato's *Republic* might possibly mitigate distress over this proposed solution.

C. In Western thought, Plato's *Republic* was an early—if not the earliest—masterpiece that thoughtfully discussed the role played by education not only in preparing those citizens destined to move into leadership roles, but also in preparing citizens in all classes to live fruitful and fulfilling lives in a stable society. In drawing on Plato to throw light on our present crisis of democracy, it is not being argued that he was a democrat;[4] but he had important insight into the requirements of social stability, and how to promulgate it.

In Plato's work, the same education was open to all citizens—children from all classes, and all genders, had equal access. Everyone progressed through the required regimen, only quitting to take up their trades or professional occupations when they had reached the maximum level that was accessible to them, given their natural physical and mental endowments. Built into this scheme was the assumption that the further one could go in this educational regimen, the better, for at its climax one would be able to perceive the ultimate reality, the keystone, as it were, of all existence: the "form of the Good." This insight prepared one to join the ranks of the Guardians, the selfless and enlightened rulers of the republic. One 20th-century educationist, Robert Hutchins, summarized Plato's point this way: "The best education for the best is the best education for all." Only a few could make it through to become Guardians, but all would profit from moving as far as possible along this educational path. The ensuing society would be perfectly just, as all citizens would be doing work and cast into roles for which they were perfectly suited.

As a result of this regimen, there were three broad classes in the republic: The ruling class, called the Guardians (made up of those who, after rigorous education, had insight into the "form of the Good"); the Auxiliaries (essentially civil servants, the military, and other professionals); and general citizens who had left the educational ladder relatively early (farmers, shopkeepers and others in commercial fields). Two further things are worthy of note. Although they were the republic's rulers, the lifestyle of the Guardians was quite spartan and devoid of luxury, and while most children would be expected to have endowments that fitted them to belong to the same class as their parents, occasionally one would be born whose native endowments were different, and this child would be educated to the appropriate level and would end up in a different class.

It was here that Plato was prescient, and had insight that is pertinent for our time. He realized that something was needed to hold this society together, something that would make all citizens accepting of their place in it, and that would ensure that its classes would function smoothly and cooperatively—that would, as he said, "serve to increase their [i.e. all citizens] loyalty to the state and to each other." And furthermore, as the structure of the republic was based upon the Guardians' grasp of the unchanging ultimate reality—the form of the Good—the republic itself would be unchanging, which reinforced the need for some mechanism that would underwrite social cohesion and stability. And so Plato hit upon the idea of promulgating what in modern (or postmodern) terms might be called a justificatory metanarrative, or a foundation myth, but that he called a "magnificent myth" and even a "fairy story" (all quotations are from Plato, 1956, pp. 158–161). In effect, what he had in mind to promulgate—for commitment—was equivalent to an account of the principles and values that underlie our democratic republic, one that is presented in civics classes, which Dewey realized was needed to be accepted as underpinning our society. In present-day USA, there is no universal commitment to these principles and values.

In the *Republic* Plato's protagonist, Socrates, is depicted as putting it as follows:

> Now I wonder if we could contrive one of those convenient stories . . . some magnificent myth that would in itself carry conviction to our whole community, including, if possible, the Guardians themselves?

Socrates tells the story he has devised about the origin of the republic, stating that in the distant past it had been ordained that each individual would be born with one of three metals in his or her makeup—gold, silver, or iron (or bronze); and it was this metal that would determine the class to which the individual would belong. The dialogue continues:

> "That is the story. Do you think there is any way of making them believe it?"
> "Not in the first generation," he said, "but you might succeed with the second and later generations."
> "Even so it should serve to increase their loyalty to the state and to each other."

Plato realized the republic he envisioned must be erected upon some founding principles that were *believed* by everyone—that had what Durkheim called a "compulsive" quality. They should be objects of universal commitment. He goes further than Dewey and opts for a strong mechanism of indoctrination. For only unwavering acceptance of the society's foundation could ensure that there would be social stability, and that actions and policies would be pursued for principled reasons and not for crass expediency.

The principles and values that constitute the foundation of our democracy are taught in schools as information, or sometimes even as objects of knowledge and understanding—but because we believe in education and not indoctrination, we do not teach to produce *conviction* or *full-blooded belief*. And this is a contributing reason why some of our fellow citizens feel free to jettison parts of this foundation when it is expedient to do so.

It seems that we face a terrible dilemma: On one hand, we can abandon our commitment to educate, and actually seek to bypass the autonomy of our students by attempting to ensure that all educational institutions use indoctrinatory methods and resort to rituals to sustain the compulsive nature of society's founding or categorical principles; or on the other hand we can remain on the educational high road and suffer the consequence that from time to time our political leaders—because of lack of total commitment—will sell out to the highest bidder.

Let us pray we have the wisdom to choose correctly.

POSTSCRIPT: BUT . . .

Unfortunately, this cannot be the end of the story. For even if individuals have unwavering allegiance to the foundational principles of democracy, the fundamental categorical principles do not, by themselves, determine what course of action should be followed in a real-world situation. There is a gap between theory and practice—the general or abstract principles (the "theory") need to be linked to the specifics of the particular field of practice by means of so-called auxiliary or linking premises, and different links will result in different (even opposing) courses of action being brought under the ambit of the same fundamental premise. So, in effect, two individuals who hold the same democratic principles may be led to advocate drastically different courses of action about a specific problematic situation because they link these principles to the specific situation in different ways. As a result, one or other of these individuals may *appear* to have abandoned allegiance to democratic core principles, when in fact he or she adheres to them but holds one or more different linking or auxiliary premises.

Consider an example. Several individuals might be committed to the core principle of "one citizen, one vote," and nevertheless hold different positions with respect to voting policy. One might hold that a citizen is any person over eighteen years of age who was born in the country under consideration; another might hold that a citizen is any adult over eighteen who is legally resident in the country; while a third might define a citizen in terms of ownership of property worth at least a certain amount or the attainment of a certain level of education; and a fourth thinks of citizenship as being a category that does not apply to women or to members of racial minority groups. Thus, despite their advocacy of different voting policies—differences that give rise to the appearance that several of these individuals must have sold out on their commitment to a basic principle of democracy—all four actually must be credited with endorsing the principle of "one citizen, one vote." It is an unavoidable fact that to give traction to this categorical principle (to link it to practice) one also must have a view of what it takes to be a citizen.

And this brings into focus another dilemma. Perhaps a member of Congress who appears to have abandoned commitment to the principles of democracy in favor of expediency has not sold out at all, but has accepted one or more different linking or auxiliary premises which has resulted in him or her arriving at a seemingly aberrant conclusion. How are we to tell—and what can we do to remediate?

Who ever said that life was meant to be easy?

NOTES

1. The 2020 presidential election resulted in the election of Joe Biden. However, the issues the author explores related to the threat to one person one vote, the adherence to fundamental principles of democracy by some elected representatives in Congress, and the role of (mis)education are still very much at play at the time this essay is being of published.

2. I thank Johannes Bellmann, Eric Bredo, and Valerie Phillips for valuable formative input.

3. By focusing on the role of education I do not wish to downplay the role of other factors such as the need for members of Congress to face re-election every two years (which is a force that favors expedience over principle).

4. For an interesting discussion see T. L. Thorson's edited volume *Plato: Totalitarian or Democrat?* (1963).

REFERENCES

Biesta, G. (2006). *Beyond learning: Democratic education for a human future*. Paradigm Publishers.

Callan, E., & Arena, D. (2009). Indoctrination. In H. Siegel (Ed.), *The Oxford handbook of philosophy of education* (pp. 104–121). Oxford University Press.

Cubberley, E. (1933). *An introduction to the study of education*. Houghton Mifflin.

Dewey, J. (1946). *Problems of men*. Philosophical Library.

Gellner, E. (1973). *Cause and meaning in the social sciences*. Routledge & Kegan Paul

Laats, A., & Siegel, H. (2016). *Teaching evolution in a creation* nation. University of Chicago Press.

Macintyre, A. (1964). "Is understanding religion compatible with believing?" In
    J. Hick (Ed.), *Faith and the philosophers* (pp. 115–133). Palgrave Macmillan.
Plato. (1956). *The republic* (H. P. Lee, Trans.). Penguin Books.
Siegel, H. (1988). *Educating reason.* Routledge.
Snook, I. (1972). *Indoctrination and education.* Routledge.
Thorson, T. L. (Ed.) (1963). *Plato: Totalitarian or democrat?* Prentice-Hall.

Public Schools and Acting Against the Threats to Democracy

Michael W. Apple

We are being constantly told that so much that is wrong with this society can be laid at the feet of our public education system and the people who labor under such difficult conditions in it. While much of this criticism is over-stated, it is still the case that across the political spectrum, large numbers of people recognize that there is a crisis in education. They agree that something must be done to make it more responsive and more effective. Of course, a key set of questions is: Responsive to what and to whom? Effective at what? And whose voices will be heard in asking and answering these questions? These are among the most crucial questions one can ask about education today.

Let us be honest. The educational crisis is real—especially for the poor and oppressed. But, as usual, dominant groups have used such "crisis talk" to shift the discussion onto their own terrain. Those of us who lived through the years of No Child Left Behind and similar movements to "reform" pub-lic schools and the damaging effects of these policies on education hoped there would be a major shift in educational policies. The threat of privat-ization would no longer hang over schools. A large portion of the school curriculum would no longer be simply made up of low-level facts to be mas-tered for seemingly mindless tests, especially but not only for economically poor and minoritized students. Teachers would no longer have to spend weeks doing little but test preparation with their students. Children of color would no longer be so over-represented in special education classes, shunted there as an excuse for not dealing with the realities of racism in the larger society. Public schools would finally get the resources they needed to try to compensate for the loss of jobs, ever-increasing impoverishment, lack of health care, massive rates of incarceration, and loss of hope in the commu-nities that they served. A richer and more vital vision of education would replace the eviscerated vision of education that now reigns supreme.

Ah yes, all would change. And even if all did not change, we would see very different approaches to education than those that had dominated in the previous years. Some things have changed. But much still remains the same.

This situation has been aided by an epistemological fog that enables powerful groups to make these conditions less visible to all too many people, and hence allow them not to act in significant ways to challenge the basic realities that produce these inequalities. In essence, a politics of *not knowing* has existed, since to know is to be called upon to act. However, such not knowing is much harder to accomplish now. The inequalities that are now being produced by the economic, employment, housing, policing, and health structures and resources that dominate the United States and other societies are becoming ever more visible, as are the underlying dynamics that cause them. The police shootings of men and women of color, the disappearances of indigenous women, the exploitative and disrespectful conditions of paid (and unpaid) work, and so much more can no longer be hidden from view.

The COVID-19 crisis that enveloped our country in 2020 and its unequal and often tragic effects has made it even harder to hide this reality behind nice-sounding rhetoric. What is happening in schools plays a crucial role here. This has certainly not gone unnoticed in the critical discussions by educators, communities, parents, and students. Taking the often disastrous race- and class-differentiating effects of the pandemic seriously is, of course, absolutely essential. Unfortunately, among the less discussed long-term effects is that what is happening in schooling as a response to these realities can paradoxically reproduce the ideological underpinnings that make these inequalities seem legitimate.

Let me say more about this. Most schools are part of the public sphere. Their task is not only to teach (and, when necessary, challenge) "official" content and its goals and values, but just as importantly to embody the norms of a larger social community that (more than rhetorically) is truly respectful of diversity, is based on fully critical and participatory citizenship, and that interrupts gender, class, and race inequalities. This list has thankfully been extended by the movements throughout society for thicker forms of redistribution, recognition, and representation.

Unfortunately, these slow but still significant recognitions and the democratic gains that come from them are seen by powerful neoliberal and conservative populist groups as dangerous, as attacks on "traditional values," as giving benefits that are "undeserved," as favoring "takers" not "makers," and as denying "democracy." With the possible normalization and acceptance of the movement of education from the public to the private sphere, and under current realities of the COVID-19 crisis in movements from the school to the home, we may lose many of these more critically democratic goals. With the growth of public racisms, of hate crimes, of anti-Muslim beliefs and policies in the West, of antisemitism, of anti-immigrant policies, of homophobic and patriarchal sentiments, we should be very cautious of normalizing forms of education that may not be committed to thicker forms of democracy (Verma & Apple, 2021; see also Miner, 2020).

In understanding the implications of effects that accompany such changes, we need to distinguish between two forms of democracy: "thin" and "thick." Thin democracy is the practice of defining democracy as simply choice on a market. It limits democracy to individual consumption practices. Social justice will take care of itself. In essence, the private sphere "eats" the public sphere. Thick democracy, sometimes also called participatory or deliberative democracy, is based on a set of practices associated with full participation in the institutions that affect our lives. Collective social welfare and the elimination of inequalities that deny "human flourishing" are its aims. Social justice does not "take care of itself." It must be worked on in all of our institutions, including schools.

The contraction of the public sphere is even more dangerous now that the COVID-19 crisis and the move to online education are being used as an excuse to defund public education and to shift large amounts of funding to private schools. When the proposals to use public funds to support homeschooling are added to this, the threat to a strong public school system becomes even more real.

I mention home schooling here because it is one of the fastest growing educational "reforms" in the country right now, with millions of children not attending public or private schools. One of the effects of the current (often necessary) turn to distance education aimed at the home by many school systems is to make home schooling seem even more legitimate. Online academies and commercial publishers are already aggressively entering what promises to be a lucrative market. But it is not simply opening up the educational sector even more to commodification and profit (see Au & Ferrare, 2015, and Burch, in press) that is a problem. A very large portion of home schoolers are doing so for quite conservative social and religious reasons. The vision of the home school as a "gated community" that supposedly protects people's children from the culture and bodies of "the Other" is also a direct challenge to the building of a truly inclusive "we" (Apple, 2006) that is ideally one of the fundamental principles of public schools.

These worrisome things do not stand alone. They have been accompanied by a deep disrespect for the labor of public employees and an attack on our very sense of the role of public institutions in supporting the conditions for the common good. The political Right has engaged in the creation of a new commonsense that emphasizes that public is necessarily bad and private is necessarily good (Mayer, 2016; McLean, 2017). The effect of these trends has been to make it ever more difficult to maintain an education that is committed to social justice.

All of this is truly damaging. And it makes it even more imperative that two specific questions be placed at the forefront of educational policy and practice. First, what can be done now and in the future to defend public schooling? Second, just as important, is an issue that sits side by side with this: What can be done to make public schools more critically democratic?

LEARNING FROM THE RIGHT?

Dealing honestly with these questions is even harder in an age when the usual rules of governance have been trampled by Trump and Trumpism, when rightist populism is growing nationally and internationally, and when well-funded conservative groups are able to spend huge amounts of money in quite manipulative ways on local, regional, and national issues that enhance their own interests (Mayer, 2016; McLean, 2017). There is almost a perverse sense of enjoyment, of "Can you believe this!", in each outrageous tweet, each demeaning comment, each move toward much more destructive environmental, health, housing, and educational policies. It is too easy to shift our attention to what is a strange combination of the comical and the diabolical. Yet all of this is happening at one and the same time, so that not only are national policies in all these areas being radically transformed, but so too are our close-to-home institutions and relations (Apple et al., 2018).

As I have shown in *Educating the "Right" Way* (Apple, 2006), the Right has been engaged in a large-scale social-pedagogic project in support-ing radical neoliberal and neoconservative agendas. They do this not only with large amounts of money and a great deal of media savvy, but also with feet on the ground. In addition, in the United States and other nations, they also engage in the writing and disseminating of model conservative legislation that is sent to state legislatures and governors throughout the nation, and coordinate political efforts to get these laws approved (see, e.g., Anderson & Montoro Donchik, 2016; Underwood & Mead, 2012). Just as importantly, they run educational programs and legislative "camps" that equip current and future legislators and youth with the kinds of media and legislative skills to ensure that they can shift the balance of arguments in their direction. For those of us who are deeply committed to a more respon-sive public school ideal, we have much to learn from the Right in this regard (Apple, 2006; 2013).

Let me say more about this as well. We can learn a good deal from the Right about how one engages in the long-term building of movements—with our own legislative training, "camps" for young activists, model legislation that is ready to go, and by working with youth, teachers, and community members on developing and spreading tools such as participatory action research (Winn & Souto-Manning, 2017) that can be used to interrupt the epistemological fog so depended upon by dominant groups. We too can and must build critical media skills and groups, and so much more—all in sup-port of a robust and long-term agenda that supports critically democratic public schooling.

Yet, just as we need to learn from what the Right has been doing for many years, we also have much to learn from the creative and dedicat-ed strategies of progressive alliances, media work, and movement-building being developed now by the participants in a multitude of groups inside and outside of education. These have been successful in building alliances and in creating cultural and educational possibilities that are transformative (see, e.g., Baldridge, 2019; Ferman, 2017; Jenkins et al., 2020; Verma & Apple, 2021). But this also requires that we actively teach each other about what works and what doesn't—and that we are *willing* to be taught. This also requires that we do a much better job of making widely visible the schools and programs that document the realities of fully participatory public schools that make a real difference in the lives of students and communities. This is what I call acting as "critical secretaries" of powerful educational policies and practices in *Can Education Change Society?* (Apple 2013; for an earlier example of this, see Apple and Beane, 2007).

Part of our learning will come from being less rhetorical and more strategic. We should be asking certain questions. What *specifically* did the educators, social movements, community activists, youth, and progressive workers in these more critically democratic public educational sites do to build real critically democratic institutions and practices? How did they work across their differences? How did they defend the gains that had been made? How are they acting now? What specific strategies were employed? What compromises had to be made? (See, e.g., Apple et al., 2018; Ferman, 2017). Answering these questions could provide crucial lessons for all of us. Thus, ongoing, long-term, politically engaged work on such things is more important than ever.

If you will forgive the military metaphors, in essence what I have been advocating is a term I've discussed elsewhere, what Antonio Gramsci (1971) called "a war of position." This is a set of critically engaged social and educational actions in which *everything* counts. Critically democratic action in education, in health care, in community lives, in paid and unpaid workplaces, in the family—all of these count. Actions against dominant relations involving gender and sexuality, race, class, ability, age, environmental degradation all count. The task is to then work hard to *connect* these actions to each other and to build alliances across our differences so that the "we" is broader and more mutually supportive (Apple et al., 2018). In Nancy Fraser's words, the politics of recognition and of representation count as well as a politics of redistribution (Fraser, 1997; 2013).

This is not new. In fact, it is exactly what the Right has been doing for decades. The Right clearly recognizes the importance of winning at multiple levels and along multiple dynamics and then connecting those victories to each other. They think the conflicts over curriculum, teaching, assessment, indeed over the very nature of schooling, are crucial to the kind of society we live in and the values that dominate that society. We need to take all of this just as seriously. At the same time, it is important to remember that while criticism of their attacks on public schools is necessary, it is definitely not sufficient.

THINKING LONG-TERM

Of course, educators are not puppets. Large numbers of educators continue to work hard to build and defend public schools and more democratic
policies and practices. And they continue to have many victories in this.
After all, why would the Right be so angry at us if there had not been victories? But this also points to other important lessons to be learned. One of
them that stands out is that victories can be temporary. Cementing them
in place requires that the long-term mobilizations and hard practical work
that brought them about must not stop. Rightist attacks, fiscal crises, overly
managerial initiatives, privatizing and marketizing pressures—all of these
will not cease on the day that we declare "we won" in this school, in this
curriculum conflict, in this electoral campaign, in this fiscal battle, in this
policy arena. Exactly the opposite is usually the case. The Right *learns* from
each of its campaigns. It widens its discourse to take account of what did
and did not succeed, and so that more groups find "answers" under its
umbrella of leadership. They are always in it for the long term. Their use
of the COVID-19 crisis to withdraw support from public schools and to
provide even more funding and ideological support for private and religious
schooling and for home schooling demonstrates what this means in our lives
right now.

Conservative forces have not rested. At the same time, they have constantly attempted to limit the sphere of progressive reforms, to make them
more rhetorical than embodied in real schools and communities, and to make
them "safer" in ways that don't truly challenge the status quo. Yet these
thick democratic policies and practices have still lasted in many public spaces
because of the ongoing dedicated labor of teachers, community members,
and social movements. This is an ongoing dynamic, one that never ceases.

Of course, we need to celebrate the gains that we make in defending
and rebuilding more responsive public institutions. Joy is an emotion that
needs to be cherished. But at the same time, we cannot rest. The hard work
of defending the gains that so many educators are making continues.

HOPE AS A RESOURCE

Let me conclude with saying something about hope as a resource. Given the
ongoing attacks on public institutions, should we be pessimistic? The great
democratic cultural analyst and activist Raymond Williams reminds us that
creating and defending a fully participatory democracy requires providing
the conditions that make it possible for all people to actually fully participate (Williams, 1989). There is much to do and many places where it needs
to be done. There is growing recognition that truly radical changes in our

structures, policies, and commonsense are essential. The task seems so big. This can be disheartening, and even paralyzing. But we must start somewhere. As I have argued at much greater length in *Can Education Change Society?* (2013) and *The Struggle for Democracy in Education* (2018), we need to resist the all-too-widespread assumption that education is epiphenomenal, that it can only change after "society" is transformed. Truly public educational institutions and the people who work in them are key parts of society. Struggles in these educational spaces are essential parts of larger efforts to maintain thick forms of democracy that refuse to reduce everything of importance to the "unattached individualism" of private choice on a market (Apple, 2013). Chantal Mouffe makes a key point when she states that "Now we first need to restore democracy, so we can then radicalize it" (quoted in Judas, 2016). The act of restoring socially committed democracy is where we can start in education. Defending and rebuilding a public education that is committed to a robust sense of social justice, and to ensuring that it is truly responsive to all of us, is essential to this task.

As I have said earlier, this will not be easy. Yet despite what we know about this and about the tensions and contradictions that are visible, educators here and throughout the world do continue the struggle for thick democracy inside and outside of the institutions of education that seem so very important to the project of social empowerment to us and to so many millions of people in the world (see Wright, 2010).

My own position can perhaps be characterized as optimism with no illusions whatsoever. Thus, we can be and frequently are disappointed in the results of the labors of building an emancipatory politics in and through education. But we must actively refuse to be disillusioned. Let me again draw upon Raymond Williams. As he says, "We must speak for hope, as long as it doesn't mean suppressing the danger" (Williams 1989, p. 322). As he goes on to say,

> It is only in a shared belief and insistence that there are practical alternatives that the balance of forces and chances begins to alter. Once the inevitabilities are challenged, we can begin gathering our resources for a journey of hope. If there are no easy answers there are still available discoverable hard answers, and it is these that we can now learn to make and share. This has been, from the beginning, the sense and impulse of the long revolution. (Williams, 1983, pp. 268–269)

The struggle for democracy in education is a key part of challenging the inevitabilities. But hope is only one element. It needs to be joined with something that is getting a good deal of attention in education today, grit, with consistent and ongoing dedicated labor to change the material and ideological conditions we face. Educators and public schools have important roles to play in such challenges. Let us continue our commitment to them.

REFERENCES

Anderson, G. L. & Donchik, L. M. (2016). Privatizing schooling and policy making: The American Legislative Exchange Council and new political and discursive strategies of education governance. *Educational Policy, 30*(2), 322–364.

Apple, M. W. (2006). *Educating the 'right' way: Markets, standards, God, and inequality* (2nd ed.). Routledge.

Apple, M. W. (2013). *Can education change society?* Routledge.

Apple, M. W. & Beane, J. A. (Eds.) (2007). *Democratic schools: Lessons in powerful education* (2nd ed.). Heinemann.

Apple, M. W., Gandin, L. A., Liu, S., Meschulam, A., & Schirmer, E. (2018). *The struggle for democracy in education: Lessons from social realities.* Routledge.

Au, W. & Ferrare, J. (Eds.). (2015). *Mapping corporate educational reform: Power and policy networks in the neoliberal state.* Routledge.

Baldridge, B. (2019). *Reclaiming community: Race and the uncertain future of youth work.* Stanford University Press.

Burch, P. (in press). *Hidden markets: The new education privatization* (2nd ed.). Routledge.

Ferman, B. (Ed.) (2017). *The fight for America's schools: Grassroots organizing in education.* Harvard Education Press.

Fraser, N. (1997). *Justice interruptus.* Routledge.

Fraser, N. (2013). *Fortunes of feminism: From state-managed capitalism to neoliberal crisis.* Verso Books.

Gramsci, A. (2017). *Selections from the Prison Notebooks.* International Books.

Jenkins, H., Peters-Lasaro, G., & Shresthova, S. (Eds.) (2020). *Popular culture and the civic imagination: Case studies of creative social change.* New York University Press.

Judas, J. (2016, June). Rethinking populism. *Dissent.* www.dissentmagazine.org/article/rethinking-populism-laclau-mouffe-podermos

Mayer, J. (2016). *Dark money: The hidden history of the billionaires behind the rise of the radical Right.* Doubleday.

McLean, N. (2017). *Democracy in chains: The deep history of the radical Right's stealth plan for America.* Viking.

Miner, B. (2020, August 17). School vouchers, Black Lives Matter and democrcy. *Wisconsin Examiner.* https://wisconsinexaminer.com//2020/08/17/school-vouchers-black-lives-matter-and-democracy/?utm_source=Wisconsin+Examiner+utm=-76065231da-EMAIL-CAMPAIGN-2019_07_2

Underwood, J. & Mead, J. F. (2012). A smart ALEC threatens public education. *Phi Delta Kappan, 93*(6), 51–55.

Verma, R. & Apple, M. W. (Eds.) (2021). *Disrupting hate in education: Teacher activists, democracy, and pedagogies of interruption.* Routledge.

Williams, R. (1989). *Resources of hope.* Verso.

Winn, M. T., & Souto-Manning, M. (2017). *Review of research in education: Disrupting inequality through education research.* Sage.

Wright, E. O. (2010). *Envisioning real utopias.* Verso.

A New Deal for Public Schools

William Ayers

Historically, pandemics have forced humans to break with the past and imagine their world anew. This one is no different. It is a portal, a gateway between our world and the next. We can choose to walk through it, dragging the carcasses of our prejudice and hatred, our avarice, our databanks and dead ideas, our dead rivers and smoky skies behind us. Or we can walk through lightly, with little luggage, ready to imagine another world. And ready to fight for it.

—Arundhati Roy, 2020

Before the 2020 pandemic and the public murder of George Floyd by police, our society was embroiled in a cascading range of crises: mass incarceration, permanent war, an apartheid-type school system, an increasingly militarized police force acting as an occupying power in many communities, a widening health gap and unequal access to quality medical care, massive homelessness and widespread hunger, accelerating income inequality, a tax system that rewards the wealthy and punishes the poor, enormous student debt, a humanitarian emergency on the southern border, an imminent capitalist-created environmental collapse—and more, each crisis inflamed and often defined by the brutal legacy of white supremacy and anti-Black racism that characterizes racial capitalism and every aspect of American life.

The urgent desire to "return to normal" is an impulse, then, to return to what amounts to a state of emergency for poor and oppressed people, masses of Black and Indigenous peoples, and people in countries under the military boot of invasion and occupation. It includes a return to a domineering and barren ideology that weaponizes the concept of individualism while it destroys any gesture toward collective well-being and community progress; it attempts to undermine any enterprise that is shared or gives off the mildest scent of socialism: the U.S. Postal Service! Amtrak! Public education! National parks and federal land! The orthodox in this camp work overtime to convince citizens of a set of anemic and self-defeating propositions marketed as freedom: public safety equals "own a gun," for example, and public health means "don't get sick"—in fact, this dogma racially colors and codes the word "public" itself: public housing, public welfare, public hospital.

The pandemic illuminates some dark places, making it difficult to return to the taken-for-granted of 2019. A "return to normal" in public schooling means accepting enforced racial segregation and class separation in schools rather than organizing and mobilizing to dismantle them. Reflecting on the 2020 6th Circuit Court finding affirming a Constitutional right to a foundational level of literacy, Bob Moses, the legendary organizer and leader of the Student Nonviolent Coordinating Committee, said, "What it took to successfully wage a struggle for African American voting rights should remind us that this is no small matter and that the 6th Circuit Court decision offers us a foothold in the ground for today's activists to establish organizing efforts to demolish the nation's educational caste systems" (Moses, 2020). This is a time for resisting, reimagining, rebuilding—and then organizing, organizing, organizing.

Everything the powerful claimed was impossible is suddenly realistic. Medicare for All was impossibly expensive—$3 trillion dollars over ten years! With the pandemic, $5 trillion over a few months was suddenly available to bail out predatory banks and profit-making corporations (including airlines, luxury hotels, and cruise lines). From now on, when the powerful chorus starts up in response to a common good proposal—"It's unaffordable!"—point to the trillion dollar tax cuts for the rich passed by Congress, or the trillion dollar bailouts always available to Wall Street.

What other myths had taken on the aura of common sense? How can we challenge and reimagine public education?

The banksters and educational profiteers claimed we needed increasing numbers of high-stakes, standardized tests as the only way to know if schools were any good, and whether kids were learning. That's a lie worth exposing.

In early 2020 California could suddenly allow the unthinkable: Teacher candidates who had graduated from teacher education programs could enter classrooms and the profession without completing the controversial but formerly-mandated Education Teacher Performance Assessment (EdTPA) portfolios, which were ineffective, expensive, and widely unpopular; the College Board postponed the SAT and made the Advanced Placement exams an open-book test taken at home; and 1,160 four-year colleges and universities, including Harvard, Stanford, and the University of California, announced that SAT and ACT scores were optional for admission in 2020. Many planned to extend that policy indefinitely. Returning to inequitable policies would be social insanity.

In the best of times, the use of high stakes standardized tests had been problematic—exacerbating existing racial, social, and educational inequities by doling out rewards largely to the privileged; distorting the work of teachers by placing undue emphasis on a limited set of skills; and devaluing the most humane aspects of schooling. Further, the ranking of schools by test scores placed unwarranted pressure on teachers to "teach to the test" rather than to the child, and it perpetuated the elitist idea that good public schools are for some—disproportionally white and wealthy—but not for all. And, of course, testing is massively expensive, money better used to create smaller classes, expand arts programs, and staff every school with nurses and counselors.

The myth or the racket is further illuminated by applying "Goodhart's Law," named after the British economist Charles Goodhart: *A performance metric is only useful as a performance metric as long as it isn't used as a performance metric.* If you want to build a "good high school," say, and you announce up front that 100% college attendance is the indicator of whether you've achieved that goal, people will work frantically and single-mindedly toward that designated target, and it might even be achieved, but to the detriment of the larger goal. One hundred percent of its graduates could indeed go to college because every effort was bent in that direction, but proponents glossed over an anemic curriculum, autocratic and rote teaching, a massive pushout rate, a sketchy list of what counts as "college," and astronomical college failure. The target had become the goal, and the school itself (the larger universe) continued to be an educational wasteland.

Albert Einstein famously noted that not everything that can be counted counts, and not everything that counts can be counted. Think, for example, about love, joy, justice, solidarity, curiosity, beauty, kindness, compassion, commitment, peace, effort, interest, engagement, awareness, connectedness, happiness, self-awareness, sense of humor, relevance, honesty, self-confidence, respect for others, and keep counting. Let's not return to the testing fraud.

A "return to normal" would also reinstate the tenets of "educational reform" that have dominated the debates and discussions for decades and restore a landscape already littered with ruin. The three most destructive pillars of the united school "reform" agenda are these: turning over common assets and public spaces to private managers; dismantling and opposing any independent, collective voice of teachers; and reducing education to a narrow testing regime that claims to recognize an educated person through a simple metric—a single score on a high-stakes, standardized test. While there's no substantive proof that any of this improves schooling for children, it chugs along unfazed, fact-free and faith-based at its core, resting firmly on ideology and opportunism rather than evidence.

Those three pillars are nested in a seductive but inaccurate and mythological metaphor: Education is a commodity like any other—a car or a refrigerator—that can be bought and sold in the capitalist marketplace. The schoolhouse is a business run by a CEO, with teachers as workers and students as the raw material on an assembly line while information is incrementally stuffed into their heads. We can do better.

Titans of school-reform-as-a-market-driven-commodity have worked relentlessly to promote the product metaphor, and, when all else fails, spread massive amounts of cash to promote their particular brand of school change as common sense. It may have begun in earnest with President Reagan. Then Bill Clinton embraced the Reagan revolution wholeheartedly; and Clinton begat Bush who begat Obama and on to Trump—each one more backward on educational policy than the last. Trump and his Secretary of Education, Betsy DeVos, a relentless champion of channeling public money into religious and elite private schools and an open enemy of public education, were high-powered amnesia-producing machines. It's hard to remember the dreadful policies of President Obama and his Secretary of Education, Arne Duncan—endorsed in their efforts by Newt Gingrich, Paul Ryan, and a host of reactionary politicians and pundits— when DeVos is in our faces with her draconian schemes—but we must, because if we don't remember, a "return to normal" will be a recurring catastrophe.

While this corporate-sponsored "reform" agenda has gained almost unanimous support from the wealthiest foundations, leaders of the two establishment political parties, liberal as well as conservative mainstream media, banks and hedge funds and law firms, and while it has wielded the big megaphone and deployed bottomless pots of money, it has failed to win support from parents, students, or teachers, and failed, most tellingly, to make a moral argument for why destroying public education would be a good thing.

Let's move forward guided by an unshakable first principle: *Public education is a human right and a basic community responsibility.* Any campaign to improve education must maintain its balance and focus by asserting that first principle early and often—*public education is a human right*—and rejecting anything implying that schooling is an entitlement for the children of the privileged and wealthy few.

In the United States, Massachusetts passed the first compulsory school law in 1852, and New York followed a year later. By 1918 all American children were required to attend at least elementary school. Today all 50 state constitutions contain a provision for a public school system, and public schooling is legally guaranteed for all.

Article 26 of the Universal Declaration of Human Rights is clear:

1. Everyone has the right to education. Education shall be free, at least in the elementary and fundamental stages. Elementary education shall be compulsory. Technical and professional education shall be made generally available and higher education shall be equally accessible to all on the basis of merit.
2. Education shall be directed to the full development of the human personality and to the strengthening of respect for human rights and fundamental freedoms. It shall promote understanding,

tolerance and friendship among all nations, racial or religious groups, and shall further the activities of the United Nations for the maintenance of peace.
3. Parents have a prior right to choose the kind of education that shall be given to their children.

Every child has the right to a free, high-quality public education. A decent, generously staffed school facility must be in easy reach for every family. This is easy to envision: What the most privileged parents have for their public school children right now—small class sizes, fully trained and well compensated teachers, physics and chemistry labs, sports teams, physical education, and athletic fields and gymnasiums, after-school and summer programs, generous arts programs that include music, theater, and fine arts—is the baseline for what we want for all children.

The curriculum must be forward-looking, recognizing the dignity of each person, and strengthening tolerance, understanding, peace and friendship among all people, and respect for fundamental freedoms and human rights. Schools must be geared toward the full development of the human mind and the human personality, and that includes encouraging intellectual freedom and the ongoing consideration of fundamental questions: Who are we? Where do we come from? What does this time require of us now? Where do we want to go?

In a free society education must focus on the *production*—not of things, but—*of free people* capable of developing minds of their own even as they recognize the importance of learning to live with others. It's based, then, on a common faith in the incalculable value of every human being, constructed on the principle that the fullest development of all is the condition for the full development of each, and, conversely, that the fullest development of each is the condition for the full development of all. Further, while schooling in every totalitarian society on earth foregrounds obedience and conformity, education in a democracy must consciously emphasize initiative, courage, creativity, self-confidence, mutuality, respect for self and others—the arts of liberty.

Schools don't exist outside of history or culture: they are, rather, at the heart of each. Schools serve societies; societies shape schools. Schools, then, are both mirror and window—they tell us who we are and who we want to become, and they show us what we value and what we ignore, what is precious and what is venal. Authoritarian societies are served by authoritarian schools, just as free schools are necessary to support free societies.

Given the harsh, unresolved history of white supremacy in the U.S., and the adaptable and slippery nature of racial capitalism, it's no surprise that the descendants of enslaved workers, African-ancestored youth, the children of Indigenous people and the laboring classes and immigrants from formerly colonized nations, often experience schooling as oppressive and colonizing rather than liberating. This must change. The public schools must become primary sites of resistance, vigorously combatting institutional racism, racial discrimination, segregation, and oppression.

A New Deal for Public Education must be shaped from the grassroots—fire from below. Imagine popular assemblies sponsored by community organizations, unions, and faith-based groups, mobilized by organizers, educators, activists, student, parents, and community members in order to demand the schools we need and the schools we deserve.

Imagine beginning with a focus on first questions: In your dream of dreams, what should a good school look like in a free and democratic society? What do schools need to do in order to fulfill the needs of free people with minds of their own? What could schools be, and what should they become, as fundamental pillars of a free society? Dare the schools build a freer and more just social order?

TEN(tative) POINTS (for discussion)

1. Education is a basic human right and a fundamental freedom—it cannot be reduced to a product to be sold at the marketplace. We demand generous, full, and equitable funding for public schools, and not another penny of public money used to privatize public education. What would schools look like if organized within a human rights framework?

2. Education is freedom. We demand an end to racism and White supremacy in both policy and curriculum, the termination of zero tolerance policies and the police presence in our schools, and the elimination of the school-to-prison pipeline. What could our schools do if combatting white supremacy guided our curriculum and teaching?

3. Education for free people stands firmly on two legs: enlightenment and liberation. We demand curriculum and teaching that allows young people to imagine and construct the kind of economy and society that they can thrive in, and that foregrounds, not obedience and conformity, but rather the arts of liberty—respect for oneself and others, initiative and courage, imagination and curiosity, problem posing and problem solving, mutual aid and solidarity—which are essential to a free people. How could we transform the school environment to embrace liberation as goal?

4. Education must allow each person to reach the fullest measure of their promise and potential. We demand an end to the massively expensive, high stakes standardized testing regime and its obsession with sorting "winners" from "losers," which serves only to exacerbate existing racial, social, and educational inequities. What are sensible

and productive alternative approaches to assessment that are close to classrooms and that center learning and growth rather than ranking?

5. Education, like life, begins in wonder, and so does art—learning to construct and create, to question and to experiment, to imagine and interrogate. This is the sturdiest foundation upon which to build an education of purpose for a free people. We demand a full arts program in every school. How can the arts revolutionize other aspects of curriculum and teaching?

6. Education is embedded in community, and schools belong to and must serve the needs of those communities. We demand safe and secure high quality public schools—community schools and after-school programs for all children, universal child-centered early childhood programs, nurses and counselors onsite, and free universal school meals—without regard to wealth or location. What are the implications and design challenges for a school fully engaged with its community?

7. Education builds on relationships, and sustainable relationships are difficult to achieve in large, impersonal factory-type schools. We demand smaller class size, and smaller schools. How can we immediately move toward smaller learning communities even if situated in larger buildings?

8. Education depends on thoughtful, caring people in every classroom performing the essential work of teaching, and good schools build on the collective wisdom of teachers and staff in conversation with one another. We demand a standard starting salary for teachers of no less than $80,000 annually, and expanded collective bargaining rights. How can we recruit a wide range of community folks to work in schools, and how can teachers and parents and community members support one another in "common good" efforts?

9. Education recognizes that each person is the one-of-one—sacred, unique, and immeasurably valuable—and, at the same time, that we are each one part of the whole human family. We demand a curriculum that affirms both our individuality and our collectivity, that acknowledges the ongoing human struggle to achieve equality and justice, and that ensures generous funding for special education and the Individuals with Disabilities Education Act (IDEA). How might a generous embrace of our differently abled peers and colleagues create a healthier and more productive learning environment for all?

10. Education recognizes that everything that counts can't be counted, and that everything that's counted doesn't necessarily count. We demand schools that recognize children and youth as three-dimensional beings and not a collection of deficits and defects, and that acknowledge explicitly—and make count—the value of justice, beauty, kindness, compassion, commitment, curiosity, peace, effort, interest, engagement,

awareness, connectedness, happiness, humor, relevance, honesty, self-confidence, and more. How can we create spaces that are marked by joy, justice, and love?

We want schools that prepare free people to participate fully in a free society. We want schools that young people don't have to recover from. We want schools that act as the hopeful launchpads for the dreams of youth.

REFERENCES

Moses, B. (2020). The 6th Circuit Court and the Constitutional Right to a Foundational Level of Literacy. https://www.crmvet.org/comm/moses20.htm

Roy, A. (2020). The pandemic is a portal. *Financial* Times. https://www.ft.com/content/10d8f5e8-74eb-11ea-95fe-fcd274e920ca

About the Editors and Contributors

David C. Berliner is Regents' Professor of Education, Emeritus, at Arizona State University. He has also taught at the Universities of Arizona and Massachusetts, at Teachers College and Stanford University, and at universities in Canada, Australia, the Netherlands, Denmark, Spain, and Switzerland. He is a member of the National Academy of Education, the International Academy of Education, and was a past president of both the American Educational Research Association (AERA) and the Division of Educational Psychology of the American Psychological Association (APA). He has won numerous awards for his work on behalf of the education profession, and authored or coauthored over 400 articles, chapters, and books. Among his best-known works are *The Manufactured Crisis*, coauthored with B. J. Biddle, and *50 Myths and Lies that Threaten America's Public Schools*, coauthored with Gene V Glass. He has interests in the study of teaching, teacher education, and educational policy.

Carl Hermanns is a clinical associate professor at the Mary Lou Fulton Teachers College at Arizona State University. He designs and teaches courses in leadership, organizational change, critical issues in education, and the history of the American education system for the college's MEd in Educational Leadership. He also serves as the ASU Faculty in Residence with the Roosevelt School District. Prior to joining ASU, he served as a teacher, principal, and assistant superintendent in California and Oregon public schools. He received his Ed.D. in Administration, Planning, and Social Policy (Urban Superintendents Program) from Harvard University. His research interests include K–12 district and school leadership, language development for English language learners, democracy and education, and issues pertaining to equitable educational opportunity and student success. In addition, Dr. Hermanns also spent a number of years as a professional musician. He has an undergraduate degree in music education from Temple University, a master's degree in symphonic and opera conducting from Carnegie-Mellon University, and prior to returning to education in 1997, spent 15 years as a conductor in the symphonic, commercial, and Broadway arenas.

Michael W. Apple is the John Bascom Professor Emeritus of Curriculum and Instruction and Educational Policy Studies at the University of Wisconsin–Madison. A former elementary and secondary school teacher and past president of a teacher's union, he has worked with educational systems, governments, universities, unions, and activist and dissident groups throughout the world to democratize educational research, policy, and practice.

William Ayers, formerly Distinguished Professor of Education at the University of Illinois at Chicago (UIC), has written extensively about social justice, democracy, and teaching as an essentially intellectual, ethical, and political enterprise. His books include *About Becoming a Teacher* and *To Teach: The Journey, in Comics*.

Martin Brooks is executive director of the Tri-State Consortium. Previously, he was superintendent of schools on Long Island for 16 years. He also was a school principal, guidance counselor and teacher. He earned his doctoral degree in educational administration at Teachers College, Columbia University, and has served on numerous boards, presented at national and international conferences, and written extensively about education. He is coauthor of *Schools Reimagined: Unifying the Science of Learning With the Art of Teaching* (2021).

Jacqueline Grennon Brooks is professor emerita in the Department of Teaching, Literacy & Leadership at Hofstra University. She has studied how people learn through her work as a teacher, researcher, professor, and co-founder of a children's museum. She consults nationally and internationally on topics of design thinking and challenge-based instruction and their roles in students' development of reasoning and agency. She has served as the founding director of science teaching laboratories and clinical practice settings and is the author of multiple publications on constructivist pedagogy, with a focus on STEM education.

Carol Corbett Burris is executive director of the Network for Public Education. She served previously as principal of South Side High School in the Rockville Centre School District in New York. Prior to that, she was a teacher at both the middle and high school level. She received her doctorate from Teachers College, Columbia University, and her dissertation, which studied her district's detracking reform in math, received the 2003 National Association of Secondary School Principals Middle Level Dissertation of the Year Award. In 2010, she was named Educator of the Year by the School Administrators Association of New York State, and in 2013, she was named New York State High School Principal of the Year. Her articles have appeared in *Educational Leadership, Kappan, American Educational Research Journal, Teachers College Record, Theory Into Practice, School Administrator, American School Board Journal* and *Education Week*.

Prudence L. Carter is Sarah and Joseph Jr. Dowling Professor of Sociology at Brown University and president-elect of the American Sociological Association. Carter's expertise ranges from issues of youth identity and race, class, and gender, urban poverty, social and cultural inequality, and the sociology of education. Specifically, she examines academic and mobility disparities shaped by the effects of race, ethnicity, class, and gender.

Edward B. (Ted) Fiske, a former education editor of the *New York Times,* is a journalist who has written widely on school reform issues in the United States and other countries for UNESCO, the World Bank, and other international organizations. He is the author of numerous books on college admissions and education policy. Along with Helen F. Ladd, his wife, he has coauthored books on school reform in New Zealand and South Africa as well as papers on education policy in the Netherlands and the U.K. Fiske and Ladd live in Chapel Hill, NC.

Peter Greene (Curmudgeon) was a classroom English teacher for 39 years, most of them in the same rural northwest Pennsylvania high school from which he graduated. He has been blogging for almost a decade at Curmudgucation, and also writes about education for *The Progressive* and *Forbes.com.* He plays trombone in a 165-year-old town band and lives next to the river with his wife (an elementary education teaching goddess) and their twin sons.

James Harvey has served as executive director of the National Superintendents Roundtable since 2007, following a decade in a similar position with the Danforth Forum for the American School Superintendent. Harvey, a native of Ireland, is the author or coauthor of dozens of articles and five books on education and education policy. Earlier, he served in the Carter administration as an education lobbyist and on the staff of the Committee on Education and Labor of the U.S. House of Representatives.

Julian Vasquez Heilig is the dean and a professor of Educational Policy Studies and Evaluation at the University of Kentucky College of Education. He has held a variety of research and practitioner positions in organizations from Boston to Beijing. These experiences have provided formative professional perspectives to bridge research, theory, and practice. He blogs at Cloaking Inequity, consistently rated one of the top 50 education websites in the world by Teach100. Follow him on Twitter: @ProfessorJVH.

Jack Jennings for 27 years was the foremost expert for the U.S. Congress in the field of education. For 17 years he was the founder/president/CEO for the Center on Education Policy, a highly regarded Washington-based nonpartisan, nonprofit education research organization. Currently, Jack devotes his efforts to writing.

David F. Labaree is Lee L. Jacks Professor, Emeritus, at the Stanford University Graduate School of Education. His research focuses on the historical sociology of American schooling, including topics such as the evolution of high schools, the growth of consumerism, the origins and nature of education schools, and the role of schools in promoting access and advantage more than subject-matter learning. He was president of the History of Education Society and member of the executive board of the American Educational Research Association. He is now blogging at https://davidlabaree. com/.

Helen F. Ladd is the Susan B. King Professor Emerita of Public Policy Studies and Economics at Duke University. Her research focuses on topics in education policy including school accountability, parental choice and market-based reforms, school finance, and teacher labor markets. With colleagues at Duke, she has explored the relationship between teacher credentials and student test scores, the extent of school segregation, and the effects of early childhood initiatives. She is a past president of the Association for Public Policy Analysis and Management and is a member of the National Academy of Education.

Gloria Ladson-Billings is professor emerita and former Kellner Family Distinguished Chair in Urban Education at the University of Wisconsin–Madison. Her scholarly work focuses on successful teachers of African American students, commonly known as Culturally Relevant Pedagogy, critical race theory applications to education, and incorporating youth culture or hip hop in pedagogy. She is a member of the National Academy of Education, an American Educational Research Association Fellow, a Fellow of the American Academy of Arts & Sciences, and a Fellow of the Hagler Institute of Texas A&M University.

Carol D. Lee is professor emerita of Education in the School of Education and Social Policy and in African American Studies at Northwestern University in Evanston, Illinois. She received her PhD from the University of Chicago. She is president-elect of the National Academy of Education. She is a past president of the American Educational Research Association (AERA), AERA's past representative to the World Educational Research Association, past vice-president of Division G (Social Contexts of Education) of the American Educational Research Association, past president of the National Conference on Research in Language and Literacy, and past cochair of the Research Assembly of the National Council of Teachers of English. She is a member of the National Academy of Education in the United States and the American Academy of Arts and Sciences, a fellow of the American Educational Research Association, a fellow of the National Conference on Research in Language and Literacy, and a former fellow at the Center for

Advanced Studies in the Behavioral Sciences. Her research addresses cultural supports for learning that include a broad ecological focus, with attention to language and literacy and African American youth. Her career spans a 50-year history, including work as an English Language Arts teacher at the high school and community college levels, a primary grade teacher, and a university professor. She is a founder of four African-centered schools that span a 48-year history, including three charter schools under the umbrella of the Betty Shabazz International Charter Schools where she serves as chair of the Board of Directors.

Martin Lipton is a former public high school teacher and has had a parallel career as education writer and consultant, including serving as Communications Analyst at UCLA's Institute for Democracy, Education, and Access. Among his publications is *Learning Power: Organizing for Education and Justice*, with Jeannie Oakes and John Rogers. Lipton is also the recipient of the American Educational Research Association's Outstanding Book Award.

William J. Mathis is a senior policy advisor and the former managing director of the National Education Policy Center at the University of Colorado–Boulder. He earlier served as superintendent of schools for the Rutland Northeast Supervisory Union in Brandon, Vermont. He is a corecipient of the Horace Mann League's national Outstanding Public Educator award and was a National Superintendent of the Year finalist and a Vermont Superintendent of the Year. He previously served as vice-chair of the Vermont State Board of Education. He has published or presented research on finance, assessment, accountability, standards, cost effectiveness, education reform, history, and Constitutional issues. He also serves on various editorial boards and frequently publishes commentaries on educational policy issues.

Deborah Meier has been working in public education as a teacher, principal, writer, and advocate since the early 1960s, and ranks among the most acclaimed leaders of the school reform movement in the U.S. She started her work as an early childhood teacher in Chicago after graduating from the University of Chicago. In New York City, in 1974, Meier became the founder and director of the alternative Central Park East school, which embraced progressive ideals in the tradition of John Dewey in an effort to provide better education for children in East Harlem, within the New York City public school system. She is also a founder of the Mission Hill School in Boston and a MacArthur Award winner. Her work as a principal and scholar has earned her honorary degrees from a number of institutions, including Harvard University and Teachers College.

H. Richard Milner IV (also known as Rich) is Cornelius Vanderbilt Chair of Education and Professor of Education in the Department of Teaching and

Learning at Peabody College of Vanderbilt University. His research, teaching and policy interests concern urban education, teacher education, African American literature, and the social context of education. Professor Milner's research examines practices and policies that support teacher effectiveness in urban schools. He is an elected member of the National Academy of Education, and both a Fellow and recent president of the American Educational Research Association. Professor Milner's work has appeared in numerous journals, and he has published seven books. He can be reached at rich.milner@vanderbilt.edu.

A member of the National Academy of Education, **Sonia Nieto** is professor emerita of Language, Literacy, and Culture, College of Education, University of Massachusetts–Amherst. Her teaching has spanned early elementary through doctoral education and her research has focused on multicultural education, teacher education, literacy, and the education of students of culturally and linguistically diverse backgrounds, with a special emphasis on Latin@ students. She is the author of dozens of journal articles and book chapters and has written or edited 13 books, including a book coauthored with her daughter Alicia López, *Teaching, a Life's Work: A Mother–Daughter Dialogue*. She is the founding editor of the Visions of Practice series. Dr. Nieto has received dozens of awards for her scholarly work, teaching, activism, and advocacy, including 9 honorary doctorates and, most recently, the 2021 Governor's Award in the Humanities from Mass Humanities, the state affiliated of the National Endowment for the Humanities.

Jeannie Oakes is Presidential Professor Emerita in Educational Equity at UCLA's Graduate School of Education and Information Studies, Senior Policy Fellow at the Learning Policy Institute, and former Director of Educational Opportunity and Scholarship at the Ford Foundation. At UCLA, Oakes was the founding director of UCLA's Center X; the Institute for Democracy, Education, and Access; and the University of California's All Campus Consortium on Research for Diversity. Her more than 100 scholarly books and articles examine the impact of social policies on the educational opportunities and outcomes of low-income students of color. Oakes' many other awards include the Southern Christian Leadership Conference's Ralph David Abernathy Award for Public Service, the World Cultural Council's Jose Vasconcelos World Award in Education, and membership in the National Academy of Education.

D. C. (Denis) Phillips was born, educated, and began his professional life in Australia; he holds BSc, BEd, MEd, and PhD from the University of Melbourne. After teaching in high schools and at Monash University, he moved to Stanford University in 1974, where for a period he served as Associate Dean and later as Interim Dean of the School of Education, and where he is currently Professor Emeritus of Education and Philosophy. He is a philosopher of education and of social science, and has taught courses and published widely on the philosophers of science Karl Popper, Thomas Kuhn, and Imre Lakatos; on philosophical issues in educational research and in program evaluation; on John Dewey and William James; and on social and psychological constructivism. For several years at Stanford, he directed the Evaluation Training Program.

Jeanne M. Powers is a professor in the Mary Lou Fulton Teachers College, at Arizona State University. Dr. Powers received her PhD in sociology from the University of California–San Diego. Her research agenda is oriented around issues of equity and access in education policy. Recent projects focus on school segregation, school choice, and the implementation of complex education reforms. She has published in the *Review of Research in Education, American Educational Research Journal, Educational Policy, American Journal of Education, Equity and Excellence in Education,* and *Law and Social Inquiry.* Dr. Powers was the editor of *Review of Research in Education* (2018, 2020), and is a fellow of the National Education Policy Center.

Diane Ravitch is a historian of education who was a member of the faculty at Teachers College, Columbia University, and New York University. She served as Assistant Secretary of Education in the first Bush administration and was appointed by the Clinton administration to the National Assessment Governing Board. In her many best-selling books she draws on over 40 years of research and experience, to critique today's most popular ideas for restructuring schools, including privatization, standardized testing, punitive accountability, and the feckless multiplication of charter schools. She is one of the nations' strongest defenders of public education, and the teachers who work in the public schools.

Mike Rose was a professor in the UCLA School of Education and Information Studies. He taught in a wide range of educational settings, from elementary school to adult literacy and job training programs, and for many years administered tutorial centers and writing programs at the college level. He was a member of the National Academy of Education and the recipient of a Guggenheim Fellowship, the Grawemeyer Award in Education, and awards from the Spencer Foundation, the National Council of Teachers of English, the Modern Language Association, and the American Educational Research Association.

Peter Smagorinsky is Distinguished Research Professor in the Department of Language and Literacy Education at the University of Georgia, emeritus, and Distinguished Visiting Scholar at the Universidad de Guadalajara, Jalisco, Mexico. Recent awards include the 2020 Horace Mann League

Outstanding Public Educator Award, 2018 International Federation for the Teaching of English Award, and 2018 Distinguished Scholar recognition by the National Conference on Research in Language and Literacy. His research and teaching take a sociocultural approach to issues of literacy education, literacy teacher education, and related social concerns.

Joshua P. Starr has been the Chief Executive Officer of PDK International since July 2015. Since then, PDK has relocated its headquarters to Arlington, VA, and celebrated more than 50 years of the PDK Poll and 100 years of *Kappan* Magazine. Under Dr. Starr, PDK has launched Educators Rising, the first national CTE program that puts high school students on the path to becoming teachers. He is the author of numerous essays, book chapters and op-eds and writes a monthly column, "On Leadership," for *Kappan*. Prior to joining PDK, Dr. Starr was superintendent of schools in Montgomery County Public Schools in Maryland and superintendent of schools in Stamford, Connecticut. As a superintendent, Dr. Starr led systemwide transformation efforts grounded in equity, excellence and engagement. Dr. Starr began his career teaching special education in Brooklyn. He became a central office leader in school districts in the New York metropolitan area, including the New York City Department of Education. Dr. Starr has a bachelor's degree in English and History from the University of Wisconsin, a master's degree in special education from Brooklyn College, and a doctorate in education from the Harvard University Graduate School of Education. Dr. Starr and his wife have three children who have gone through public schools.

Mark Weber is the Special Analyst for Education Policy at the New Jersey Policy Perspective and a lecturer at Rutgers University's Graduate School of Education. Weber is also a music educator in Warren Township, NJ; in 2020, he was named a New Jersey Exemplary Educator for his work. In addition to many articles for peer reviewed journals and book chapters, Weber has authored policy briefs for the National Education Policy Center, the Education Law Center, the Fordham Foundation, the Shanker Institute, and others. He is the data analyst for the School Finance Indicators Database, which provides comprehensive, national school finance data and analysis. Weber's blog on education policy, Jersey Jazzman, is read nationally, and his writings on education policy and teaching have appeared in *The Washington Post*, *Education Week*, and the *PBS News Hour*, among other outlets. Weber's research work concentrates on school choice, school finance, teacher quality, and arts education.

Kevin Welner is a professor of education policy at the University of Colorado–Boulder School of Education and (by courtesy) at the School of Law. He's also the director of the National Education Policy Center, housed at CU–Boulder, which works to build bridges between the research world and the broader public. Welner has authored or edited more than a dozen books and more than 100 articles and book chapters. Professor Welner is a Senior Research Fellow at the Learning Policy Institute and an AERA Fellow. He's been given the AERA's Outstanding Public Communication of Education Research Award, Early Career Award, and Palmer O. Johnson Award. The Horace Mann League gave Welner its Outstanding Public Educator Award in 2018. He received his BA in Biological Sciences from UCSB and his JD and PhD from UCLA.

Ken Zeichner is a proud graduate of Philadelphia Public Schools, a former public school teacher and a teacher educator in the U.S. Teacher Corps. After 34 years at the University of Wisconsin–Madison as a professor in teacher education, he moved to the University of Washington, where he is currently the Boeing Professor of Teacher Education Emeritus. Ken's scholarship has focused on teacher education.

Index